The Reform of the Bolivian State

The Reform of the Bolivian State

Domestic Politics in the Context of Globalization

Andreas Tsolakis

FIRSTFORUMPRESS
A DIVISION OF LYNNE RIENNER PUBLISHERS, INC. • BOULDER & LONDON

Published in the United States of America in 2011 by
FirstForumPress
A division of Lynne Rienner Publishers, Inc.
1800 30th Street, Boulder, Colorado 80301
www.firstforumpress.com

and in the United Kingdom by
FirstForumPress
A division of Lynne Rienner Publishers, Inc.
3 Henrietta Street, Covent Garden, London WC2E 8LU

Library of Congress Cataloging-in-Publication Data
Tsolakis, Andreas, 1980–
The reform of the Bolivian state: domestic politics in the context of globalization / by Andreas Tsolakis.
Includes bibliographical references and index.
ISBN 978-1-935049-27-2 (hc: alk. paper)
1. Bolivia—Politics and government—1982–2006. 2. Bolivia—Politics and government—2006– 3. Bolivia—Economic conditions—1982–
4. Bolivia—Social conditions—1982– 5. Globalization—Bolivia. I. Title.
JL2831.T86 2011
320.984—dc22 2010040132

British Cataloguing in Publication Data
A Cataloguing in Publication record for this book
is available from the British Library.

Printed and bound in the United States of America

The paper used in this publication meets the requirements of the American National Standard for Permanence of Paper for Printed Library Materials Z39.48-1992.

5 4 3 2 1

Contents

Tables and Figures

Tables

Figures

Acknowledgments

This book would not have been possible without the continued support and trust of my parents, of Isabel and of my brothers and my friends. I am grateful to them for bringing me happiness and conviction when I needed them most.

I also want to thank the Politics and International Studies Department and the Institute of Advanced Study at the University of Warwick for their institutional and financial support.

Finally, I want to express my thanks to Iván Mollinedo, who fuelled my passion for Bolivia and helped me with the logistics of my research in La Paz, as well as to the people who gave me access to relevant material and who agreed to give their time for interviews. I am particularly grateful to Guido Riveros, Teresa Ossío and the staff at the Library of Congress and the library of the UDAPE for offering me their assistance at crucial moments of my fieldwork.

* * *

À mes parents

Abbreviations and Acronyms

ADN	*Acción Democrática Nacionalista* (Nationalist Democratic Action)
ALBA	*Alternativa Boliviariana Para los Pueblos de Nuestra America* (Bolivarian Alternative for the Peoples of Our America)
ANMM	*Asociación Nacional de Mineria Mediana* (National Association of Medium-sized Mining)
ASOBAN	*Asociación de Banqueros de Bolivia* (Bolivian Bankers' Association)
BCB	*Banco Central de Bolivia* (Central Bank of Bolivia)
CAINCO	*Cámara de Industria y Comercio de Santa Cruz* (Chamber of Industry and Commerce of Santa Cruz)
CAN	*Comunidad Andina de Naciones* (Community of Andean Nations)
CAO	*Cámara Agropecuaria del Oriente* (Chamber of Agriculture of the East)
CCPSC	*Comité Civico Pro-Santa Cruz* (Pro–Santa Cruz Civic Committee)
CEAL	*Consejo Empresario de América Latina* (Business Council of Latin America)
CEPAL	*Comisión Económica para América Latina y el Caribe* (Economic Commission for Latin America and the Caribbean)
CEPB	*Confederación de Empresarios Privados de Bolivia* (Confederation of Private Entrepreneurs of Bolivia)
CIDOB	*Confederación de Pueblos Indígenas de Bolivia* (Confederation of Indigenous Peoples of Bolivia)
CNE	*Corte Nacional Electoral* (National Electoral Court)
COB	*Central Obrera Boliviana* (Bolivian Worker Central/Confederation)
COHA	Council on Hemispheric Affairs
COMIBOL	*Corporación Minera de Bolivia* (Bolivian Mining Corporation)
CONAMAQ	*Consejo Nacional de Ayllus y Markas del Qullasusyu* (Kollasuyo Ayllu and Marka National Council)

CONDEPA	*Conciencia de Patria – Movimiento Patriótico* (Conscience of Fatherland – Patriotic Movement)
CSUTCB	Confederación Sindical Única de Trabajadores Campesinos de Bolivia (Unique Confederation of Rural Workers of Bolivia)
DAC	Development Assistance Committee
DC	Development Committee
DEA	Drug Enforcement Agency
DPC	*Delegación Presidencial Para la Revisión y Mejora de la Capitalización* (Presidential Delegation for the Revision and Improvement of Capitalisation)
DS	*Decreto Supremo* (Supreme Decree)
ENAF	*Empresa Nacional de Fundición* (National Smeltering Enterprise)
ENDE	*Empresa Nacional de Electricidad* (National Electricity Enterprise)
ENFE	*Empresa Nacional de Ferrocarriles* (National Railroad Enterprise)
ESAF	Enhanced Structural Adjustment Facility
ESF	Emergency Social Fund
EU	European Union
FDI	Foreign Direct Investment
FSB	*Falange Socialista Boliviana* (Bolivian Socialist Falange)
FSTMB	*Federación Sindical de Trabajadores Mineros de Bolivia* (Union Federation of Mining Workers of Bolivia)
FUN	*Frente de Unidad Nacional* (National Unity Front)
GES	*Grupo Especial de Seguridad* (Special Security Group)
GDP	Gross Domestic Product
HIPC	Heavily Indebted Poor Country Initiative
IBRD	International Bank for Reconstruction and Development
IDB	Inter-American Development Bank
IFC	International Finance Corporation
IFHR	International Federation for Human Rights
IMF	International Monetary Fund
IPE	International Political Economy
IU	*Izquierda Unida* (United Left)
LAB	Lloyd Aereo Boliviano
MDIs	Multilateral Development Institutions
MAS	*Movimiento Al Socialismo* (Movement Towards Socialism)

MBL	*Movimiento Bolivia Libre* (Free Bolivia Movement)
MIGA	Multilateral Investment Guarantee Agency
MIR	*Movimiento de Izquierda Revolucionaria* (Revolutionary Left Movement)
MNR	*Movimiento Nacionalista Revolucionario* (Revolutionary Nationalist Movement)
MNRH	*Movimiento Nacionalista Revolucionario Histórico* (Historic Revolutionary Nationalist Movement)
MNRI	*Movimiento Nacionalista Revolucionario de Izquierda* (Left Revolutionary Nationalist Movement)
MRTK	*Movimiento Revolucionario Tupac Katari* (Revolutionary Tupac Katari Movement)
MITKA	*Movimiento Indio Tupac Katari* (Indian Tupac Katari Movement)
MSM	*Movimiento Sin Miedo* (Movement Without Fear)
NEP	New Economic Policy
NFR	*Nueva Fuerza Republicana* (New Republican Force)
ODA	Official Development Assistance
OECD	Organisation for Economic Cooperation and Development
PCB	*Partido Comunista de Bolivia* (Communist Party of Bolivia)
PDC	*Partido Demócrata Cristiano* (Christian Democratic Party)
PODEMOS	*Poder Democrático y Social* (Social and Democratic Power)
POR	*Partido Obrero Revolucionario* (Revolutionary Workers' Party)
PSD	Private Sector Development
PFP	Policy Framework Paper
RDC	Regional Development Corporation
SAFCO	*Administración y Control Gubernamental* (Administration and Government Control)
SAP	Structural Adjustment Programme
SBEF	*Superintendencia de Bancos y Entidades Financieras de Bolivia* (Superintendency of Banks and Financial Entities of Bolivia)
SIDA	Swedish International Development Agency
SIREFI	*Sistema de Regulación Financiera* (System of Financial Regulation)
SIRESE	*Sistema de Regulación Sectorial* (System of Sector Regulation)
THM	Transnational Historical Materialism

WB	World Bank
WBG	World Bank Group
UCS	*Unión Cívica Solidaridad* (Civic Solidarity Union)
UDAPE	*Unidad de Análisis de Políticas Económicas y Sociales* (Unit for the Analysis of Economic and Social Policies)
UDP	*Unión Democrática y Popular* (Democratic and Popular Union)
UJC	*Unión Juvenil Cruceñista* (Cruceñista Youth Union).
UN	*Unidad Nacional* (National Unity)
UNDP	United Nations Development Programme
US	United States of America
USAID	United States Agency for International Development
YPFB	*Yacimientos Petrolíferos Fiscales de Bolivia* (Fiscal Hydrocarbon Deposits of Bolivia)

1
Bolivia's Political Trajectory Since 1985

Bolivia was part and parcel of the global debt crisis of the early 1980s, which plunged the country into an uncontrollable hyperinflationary and fiscal crisis (Morales and Sachs 1990). In November 1984, total outstanding debt had reached US$4.1 billion (110 percent of a declining Gross Domestic Product [GDP]), including a $3.2 billion public sector debt; the Siles government declared a moratorium on debt servicing before calling elections half a year later. By then, inflation had reached 23,500 percent in annualised terms.[1] Virtually bankrupt, the Paz Estenssoro government elected in August 1985 reversed the long-standing state capitalist model of development by vowing to stimulate privatised accumulation and maintain monetary stability. Its economic team, constituted by leaders of the Bolivian business confederation, the *Confederación de Empresarios Privados de Bolivia* (CEPB) and monetarist economists, elaborated a radical stabilisation plan behind closed doors (Supreme Decree 21060, dubbed New Economic Policy [NEP]), before resuming cooperative relations with Multilateral Development Institutions (MDIs), thereby re-engaging with private and public creditors, and renewing the Bolivian state's commitment to debt servicing (Dunkerley 1990; Conaghan 1990; Conaghan and Malloy 1995; Climenhage 1999).

The election of Victor Paz Estenssoro to the presidency and his enactment of the *Decreto Supremo* (DS) 21060 two days after his investiture signalled the commencement of a dual transformation of profound magnitude for Bolivia: economic liberalisation and political democratisation. These two developmental cycles had finally been synchronised. The long crises of authoritarian management and of state capitalism had engendered the first peaceful government turnover through transparent elections and an unprecedented opportunity for liberal restructuring. The 1985 general election and the implementation of DS 21060 simultaneously opened new horizons for sustainable capital accumulation, liberal hegemony and democratic development. A new era of radical social and state restructuring had apparently emerged with a bang.

By 2005, the optimism that had characterised specialist circles in the late 1980s, 1990s and even early 2000s regarding economic stabilisation, Private Sector Development (PSD) and democratic transition/consolidation/viability, had manifestly waned (Crabtree and Whitehead 2008).[2] Subaltern violence had become *monnaie courante*, lack of business confidence was prompting capital flight, corruption and nepotism in the state were flourishing, and indianist discourses advocating a clash of Andean and Western civilizations and the creation of a sovereign indigenous republic in the historic territory of *Kollasuyu* were undermining the multi-ethnic/national democracy hailed a decade earlier.[3] Sustained restructuring efforts had evidently failed to transform Bolivia into a hub of social progress, and Evo Morales, achieving the feat of congealing nationalist and indigenist 'currents of opinions' (Gramsci 1971) in the *Movimiento Al Socialismo* (MAS) and his person (Dunkerley 2007), was elected to the Bolivian presidency in a climate of intense social conflict and disorder.[4]

The landslide election of Morales in December 2005 constituted a milestone in the landlocked country's historical development. It signalled the conclusion of a long crisis that had defined, for a quarter of a century, the liberalisation of the Bolivian state. The outright majority enjoyed by the political party MAS in general elections is an unprecedented occurrence since the emergence of a liberal democratisation process in 1978. It endowed Evo Morales, the first elected Latin American President explicitly identifying himself as indigenous, with an exceptional legitimacy and significant political space for the drastic reorganisation of Bolivian society. It also symbolised a popular disenchantment with, if not acute bitterness towards the policies implemented by successive Bolivian governments since the hyperinflationary crisis that hit the country in 1985 (see table 1.1). Morales was elected with promises to deconstruct the entire political and economic edifice painfully erected since 1985, by refounding Bolivia through the re-nationalisation of its strategic jewels (gas, mining, telecommunications), by sponsoring the election of a Constituent Assembly,[5] by ridding the Bolivian state of its corrupt and inefficient comprador lackeys, by promoting traditional coca production and by redistributing Bolivia's social surplus to its subalterns. Morales promised a dual decolonisation of Bolivia, by challenging external neo-colonialism generated by bilateral and multilateral development agencies (instruments of 'the Empire'), and by ending the internal colonialism perpetuated by *criollo* elites (white, of Spanish descent) through the defence of indigenous sovereignties (Crabtree 2005; Dunkerley 2007; Do Alto and Stefanoni 2008; Webber 2008).[6]

Table 1.1: Bolivian Governments, 1985-2005

Year	President	Coalition
1985-89	Victor Paz Estenssoro (MNR)	*Pacto por la Democracia* (Congressional - with ADN)
1989-93	Jaime Paz Zamora (MIR)	*Acuerdo Patriótico* (MIR-ADN)
1993-97	Gonzalo Sánchez de Lozada (MNR)	*Pacto por la Gobernabilidad* (MNR-MRTKL-MBL-UCS) *Pacto por el Cambio* (MNR-MRTKL - MBL)
1997-2001	Hugo Banzer Suárez (ADN)	*Megacoalición: Compromiso por Bolivia* (ADN-MIR-NFR-PDC-CONDEPA-UCS)
2001-02	Jorge Quiroga Ramirez (ADN)	*Megacoalición* (ADN-MIR-CONDEPA-UCS)
2002-03	Gonzalo Sánchez de Lozada (MNR)	*Plan Bolivia Para Un Acuerdo de Responsabilidad Nacional* (MNR-MBL-MIR-UCS)
2003-05	Carlos Mesa Gisbert (no party affiliation)	Transitional government – technocrats/intellectuals
2005	Eduardo Rodríguez Veltzé (no party affiliation)	Transitional government
2005-	Juan Evo Morales Ayma (MAS)	MAS incorporates prominent members of smaller parties (MSM-CONDEPA-PCB) and social movements

Source: Presidencia de Bolivia

Following the string of anti-neoliberal landslides in Latin American Presidential elections in 2005 and 2006, the mood was euphoric among commentators defending labour and indigenous rights. Protracted resistance had ruptured neoliberal globalisation and Latin America was entering an unprecedented era of alternative development. The conditions surrounding the investiture of Morales generated a honeymoon period lasting about a year, during which the MAS was vigorously supported by organised labour, rural indigenous communities, marginalised urban movements but also sizable fractions of *mestizo* professionals, managers and intellectuals (Stefanoni and Do Alto 2008; Webber 2008). The exotic shape of socialism's new vanguard also attracted a battalion of young left-leaning researchers and journalists to Bolivia, while a number of organic intellectuals of the transnational bloc, who had collaborated with previous governments as well as the World Bank (WB) and other MDIs were, perhaps opportunistically, jumping on the Morales bandwagon (Gray 2007). Galvanised by the MAS leadership's anti-capitalist discourse, sympathetic analysts explained Evo Morales's investiture as heralding a revolutionary change of the Bolivian state-society complex;[7] while socialists were actively criticising its un-revolutionary credentials.[8] The latter emphasised the reformist tendencies of Evo Morales, pointing to his electoral strategy as signalling a conservation of the existing liberal state form. The former hailed the MAS as constituting something new, something more than a political party: an inclusive, grassroots organisation unifying a wide variety of historically oppressed urban and rural social forces, which successfully sidelined the racist alternative on its flank (the indigenist *Movimiento Indigena Pachacuti* [MIP] led by Felipe Quispe). Indeed, in the run-up to the 2005 general elections, the MAS effectively co-opted the leadership of a wide array of communist (*Partido Comunista de Bolivia* [PCB]) and social democratic (*Movimiento Sin Miedo*) parties, well-established socialist and nationalist militants as well as indigenist intellectuals and leaders of labour organisations.

Conservative observers, overshadowed by these radical debates, were left with no alternative but to trace the causes of the demise of restructuring efforts, to emphasise how external conditions (elimination of its entire debt stock with MDIs; high and rising prices for its main export commodities [gas, minerals and soy]) were facilitating the work of a fiscally irresponsible government that, however, was dangerously re-politicising economic management (see *Fundación Milenio* 2008; Gamarra 2007; Morales 2008). They appropriately began to challenge idealisers of the indigenous by questioning their occultation of internal relations of domination (primarily class and gender, but also race) (Lavaud 2007), to reassert the ideal of *mestizaje* (Toranzo 2008) and to re-articulate regionalist discourses (Roca 2008).

What went wrong, then? How and why did restructuring efforts unravel? Why did political democracy fail to be consolidated,[9] and indeed proved unviable (Whitehead 2002a)? Problem-solving scholarship has tended to lay the blame on domestic factors.[10] These factors include bureaucratic inefficiency, corruption, presidentialism and the weakness of the legislative branch of the state,[11] military and trade union embroilment of legitimate policymaking,[12] the exaggerated multiplicity, weakness and traditional structure of political parties (i.e. reliant on one-man caudillo dominance and patron-client relationships), a breeding ground for patrimonialism,[13] a generalised lack of education (i.e. indigenous ignorance) and unskilled human resources,[14] inducing undemocratic subaltern worldviews;[15] and the cultural discrepancies between bureaucratised and stagnant highland and modern, dynamic and democratically-oriented lowland regions.[16]

The Critical side of the academic spectrum has, in turn, been imbued with dependency and world-system theory critiques of the market and imperialism (Frank 1975, 1978; Wallerstein 1989[1974]). Critical researchers have conventionally incriminated the International Monetary Fund (IMF), the WB, the United States Agency for International Development (USAID) and the Drug Enforcement Agency (DEA) for imposing neoliberal restructuring onto Bolivia and for coercing coca farmers (*cocaleros*) and indigenous people into abandoning their ancestral ways of life, with the collusion of corrupt and racist *criollo* (white) elites.[17] They have attributed neoliberal reforms, in a logic of inquiry characterised by Cartesian dualism, either to structural necessity (chiefly determined by the law of polarisation between core and periphery through the control of terms of trade by the former and ever-unstable market price of agricultural and extractive commodities) or to autonomous agency (actors such as the United States superpower or the IMF and WB) (Lora 1995, Garcia 2001, 2005, Fernández 2003).

The present study returns to historical materialist principles by contending that these failures were, above all, the product of protracted class and intra-elite struggles, beyond and *within* the state. I reassert the need to adopt a holistic, historical and dialectical approach to restructuring in Bolivia from 1985 to 2005 by interpreting and explaining it as elemental to global transformations since the 1970s, which influenced the trajectory of Bolivia's development. I have decided to focus on the restructuring of the Bolivian state. I base this focus upon the principle that states are relations embedded in broader relations, which reflect but also *constitute* these relations, a principle to which I arrived by analysing empirical evidence on restructuring. I will return to this point subsequently, because it is important if one is to systematise research located in *praxis*. I argue here that the dialectical process of state transformation unfolding from 1985 can only be explained by analysing the contradictory social forces constituting the state, and in turn by positing that an understanding of the historical developmental paths of society can only be achieved by explaining state polity. This, however, cannot be analysed merely through the prism of the nation-state, because the internal relationship between state and social forces is constituted by and constitutive of transnational and interstate relations (Gill 1993; Van der Pijl 1998; Overbeek 2000; Van Apeldoorn 2004).

More specifically, the research analyses whether, how and why processes of state transformations that are commonly dissociated or ignored in the academic literature (i.e., liberal democratisation, internationalisation and depoliticisation) have, in reality, been internally related and mutually supportive in Bolivia since 1985. Whilst the story of democratisation or, to be more accurate, the emergence, consolidation and recent unravelling of Bolivian polyarchy from 1985 to 2005 has been told and retold *ad nauseam*,[18] processes of depoliticisation and internationalisation have on the whole been overlooked. This scholarly gap needs to be bridged if a more nuanced and sophisticated analysis of the Bolivian state is to be made, and if an understanding of contemporary reforms is to be achieved adequately. This study therefore offers an in-depth analysis of the internationalisation, depoliticisation and liberalisation of the state. I demonstrate that these processes have not only taken place but were correlated. The internationalisation of the Bolivian state was not superimposed upon an endogenous process of political and economic liberalisation by external forces; rather, by consolidating a transnationalised elite fraction in Bolivia and the depoliticisation of economic management, the internationalisation of the state sustained polyarchy after the hyperinflationary crisis of 1985. The engagement of MDIs and private banks by a nucleus of competitive and denationalised Bolivian elites in 1985 and in turn their unconditional integration into an expanding transnational historic bloc of elite social forces drove the internationalisation of the Bolivian state. Internationalisation, in turn, consolidated the structural power of the transnational bloc in Bolivia by concurrently depoliticising central government agencies and promoting polyarchy. Polyarchy was an attempt to legitimise elite domination and the restructuring of society and state through a procedural conception of democracy.

The focus of this study is, hence, on the dialectical relationship between the formation of transnational elites, social – in particular state – restructuring and domestic resistance to restructuring between 1985 and 2005. This dialectic helps to explain the constraints under which the transnational bloc acted to liberalise the Bolivian social space. Liberalisation is interpreted as an attempt, by an enlightened transnational fraction of Bolivian elites, to generate development in Bolivia by grafting polyarchy, neoliberal hegemony and the business perspective onto a corrupt, nepotistic, and statist social organism, with the active support of MDIs. Transnational elites were nonetheless part of and dependent on clientelistic social networks for the implementation of liberal reforms, which helps to explain their failure to generate neoliberal hegemony and legitimise the high social costs of Bolivia's deepening integration into the world market.[19] The re-composition of labour and indigenist forces in the late 1990s, manifested in the intensification of street violence (Water Wars, Febrero Negro, Gas Wars) and the eventual election of Evo Morales in 2005, expressed the gradual unravelling of restructuring efforts in Bolivia.

This study builds on the results of close to five years of research, including several months of field work undertaken between May and September 2003, and May and September 2007 in La Paz, Bolivia, and is based on both primary and secondary sources (Burnham et al. 2004). As primary sources, I relied on classified and publicly available WB, IMF, Development Committee (DC) and Development Assistance Committee (DAC) documents on the reforms of the Bolivian state in the period under study, as well as twenty-four interviews with Bolivian government ministers, business leaders and high-level civil servants. A significant proportion of these interviewees held multiple positions, as businessmen, public officials (in government and MDIs) or academics over two decades of radical social and state restructuring. Many of them have now distanced, or been forced to distance themselves from policymaking, but remain informed observers of recent processes of change currently pursuing private business or consulting activities. The information that they agreed to provide to me was triangulated through documentary analysis and other interviews (Richards 1996; Lilleker 2003; Burnham et al. 2004). The reliability of the empirical evidence used to reflect on the validity of my hypothesis should therefore secure an adequate measurement (in a qualitative sense) of the concepts employed here (Adcock and Collier 2001).

Before explaining in more detail the research questions, hypothesis and theoretical perspective underpinning the research and structure of this book, it is necessary to engage critically with the existing academic literature on liberal democratisation, and on the relationship between MDIs and successive Bolivian governments.

Democratisation and Polyarchy

Problem solving scholarship (Cox 1981: 88) has extensively analysed the institutional and legal reforms accompanying liberal democratisation in Bolivia since 1978 – expressed in concepts of democratic transition, governability (*gobernabilidad*),[20] modernisation,[21] consolidation,[22] viability,[23] and of a seemingly accomplished, consensual multiethnic democracy.[24] Until the early 2000s, when the contradictions of liberalisation had become too manifest to be brushed aside, a generalised optimism and positive appraisal of institutional change had characterised specialist academic circles. It was broadly accepted that 'Despite a history of political instability and a tumultuous transition process, Bolivia, since 1985, offers an example of a relatively stable political and economic post-transition environment' (Domingo 1993: 1; Domingo 2001), and demonstrated 'that neo-liberal economic reforms can be harmonised with political democratization' (Whitehead 1997: 71).

Institutional reforms in Bolivia after 1985 have been measured according to minimalist, procedural conceptualisations of democracy, understood as *polyarchy*, the most sophisticated exponent of which arguably remains Robert Dahl (1971). Democracy has been measured in terms of *representation* and *participation* (universal suffrage and equality of rights in voting), and *competition* (freedom of association and contestation, resulting in multi-partism and – through elections – in the possible turnover of government representatives and legislators). Thus O'Donnell and Schmitter (1986: 8) suggested that 'there is likely to exist a "procedural minimum" which contemporary actors would agree upon as necessary elements of a political democracy. Secret balloting, universal adult suffrage, regular elections, partisan competition, associational recognition and access, and executive accountability'.

Scholarship focusing on democratisation in Bolivia has been overwhelmingly informed by *problématiques* restricted by a closed system of meaning and norms (Howarth 2000; Gramsci 1971; Cox 1981, 1987; Gill 1993, 2003). Problem-solving appraisals and prescriptions are in line with hegemonic developmental discourses informed by Parsonian evolutionism (Parsons 1977). Democracy in a liberal representative form (based on heuristic measurements of the rule of law, of the existence of representative institutions of governance, of a cold and rational bureaucratic apparatus, of a balance of power between the executive, legislative and judicial organs of the state, and last but not least, of the necessary retreat of the state from the naturalised invisible hand of the market) hence becomes the institutional device necessary to solve the combined challenges of growth, poverty reduction and *stability*.[25]

The focus of problem-solving scholarship has consequently been the central role of political parties in democracy-building, their internal stability and sustainability, the nature of electoral law and the problem of Proportional Representation (Domingo 1993), consensus- and coalition-building between dominant parties (O'Donnell and Schmitter 1986; O'Donnell 1992; Valenzuela 1992), the learning-process whereby a technocratic group – ideally business leaders – converge towards a pragmatic approach to economic management (Conaghan 1992; Climenhage 1999); and the extent to which political parties have demonstrated good will regarding the peaceful resolution of conflicts, the endorsement of constitutional rules of the game, and the elimination of fraud and corruption.[26] The prescriptions logically deriving from this multi-causality are simple: better governance including stronger, legitimate and fiscally viable state institutions, ever more representative, consensual, decentralised and inclusive democracy (if possible multi-ethnic), but also financial transparency and the development of a knowledge-based economy.[27] Political analysts readily acknowledge the limitations of minimalist definitions – in particular the potential contradictions between economic restructuring and political democratisation – but for various reasons (including political predispositions and convenience) take them as a starting-point for the purpose of empirical measurement.[28] Some have gone as far as *advocating* that 'democratic consolidation ... be linked ... to a minimalist, not maximalist, conception of democracy' because, after all, 'even long established democracies rarely have all the attributes that can ideally be associated with such regimes' (Valenzuela 1992: 60; O'Donnell 1992).[29] These approaches may appropriately be criticised for ascribing autonomy to 'state life', i.e. for their 'statolatry', to use Gramsci's terminology (Gramsci 1971: 268).

In methodological terms, problem-solving studies of Bolivia's political system explicitly or implicitly rely on Weberian pluralism or structural-functionalism (Durkheim 1982; Weber 1991), which are informed by a positivistic epistemology.[30] Structural variability in Weberian pluralism alludes to the inexistence of an underlying historical structure and to the absolute autonomy of the factors (economy, society, the state) constituting a specific social order; it therefore justifies the historical contingency of empirical evidence. As pointed out by Burnham (1991) this approach systematically lapses in empiricism (begging the question why a particular fact has been given more importance than another in a specific historical setting) and in methodological atomism – the simple starting-point is individual world views and motivated behaviour, which has systematically failed to pierce surface market relations. In Weberian pluralism, the historically specific value, commodity, money, and capital forms of production are consciously or unwittingly presented as natural and hence trans-historical social laws: thus the essence of these forms (i.e. the particular manner in which propertied classes historically control the production process to extract surplus, itself the foundation of their social power and supremacy), is occulted (Burnham 1995: 97).[31]

In order to evade statolatry, the state cannot be understood independently from broader social struggles: it simultaneously is shaped by and shapes them. Indeed, Cammack (1991: 541) eloquently problematised the 'persistent emphasis on institutions and political choice ... vacuous in the absence of any means of conceptualising the structure of constraints upon them, and hence their limits; in particular they undertake no sustained consideration of the links between class interests of elites and patterns of institutional initiatives and political choices'.

Critiques of minimalist definitions of Bolivian democracy abound in specialist circles.[32] These critiques are often, and not surprisingly, rooted in the historical materialist tradition. Antonio Gramsci had exposed in the 1930s the classical liberal ideal-type form of state-society relations construed as laissez-faire (the nightwatchman state above/beside self-regulating capital) as a legally and ideologically buttressed form of governance subjecting labour to capital: 'one cannot speak of the power of the state but only of the camouflaging of power' (Gramsci 1995:217). William Robinson (1996) effectively reinterpreted the meaning of *polyarchy* by integrating it into a neo-Gramscian analysis of transnational elite domination in Latin America within the structural constraints of global capital. He defined polyarchy as the liberal democratic form of social organisation, 'in which a small group actually rules and mass participation in decision-making is confined to leadership choice in elections carefully managed by competing elites' (Robinson 1996:49).[33]

This is the meaning given in this study to liberal democratisation. However, Robinson's (2002: 215) instrumentalist conceptualisation of the state is rejected here.[34] On their side, Critical analyses of neoliberalism in Bolivian scholarship have systematically adopted an instrumentalist approach to the state, pitting for instance organised labour and indigenous movements *against the state*.[35] The state thus becomes reified as a unitary coercive apparatus used by *criollo* (white, of European descent) elites to dominate labour and exclude indigenous movements.[36] By implication its executive, legislative and judiciary institutions, at all levels (especially at the level of government), become devoid of internal rivalries and antagonisms. As will be elaborated subsequently, the present analysis embeds Robinson's definition of polyarchy within a relational approach to the state.

Deepening Democracy: Decentralisation, Popular Participation and Multiethnic Representation

An institutional process interpreted in the literature as integral to the consolidation or viability of polyarchy is the 'audacious' administrative and fiscal decentralisation of the state in the mid-1990s (Grindle 1999; Van Cott 2000; Gray 2001; Faguet 2002, 2003). Decentralisation was among the central measures implemented by the Sánchez de Lozada government (1993-1997), and resulted in the territorial reorganisation of the state into 311 municipalities (including the creation of 187 new municipalities), mandated the assignment of 20 percent of tax revenues to local governments (including autonomous indigenous communities, dubbed *Organizaciones Territoriales de Base* [OTB]), and organised local democracy through the establishment of electoral rules for local government (Grindle 1999; Gray 2001). Decentralisation has been one of the most debated themes in the academic literature, in part because it relates directly to issues of democratisation (more specifically, the territorial expansion and intensification of democratic governance, elemental to democratic consolidation or viability), the redistribution of state resources (from cities to countryside, from wealthier to poorer municipalities), and the relationship between the state and indigenous nations.

The majority of commentators have tended not to question decentralisation *per se*: it has been hailed as a largely commendable and progressive institutional innovation by virtue of its satisfaction of indigenous demands for organisational autonomy while integrating indigenous nations into a viable multi-ethnic democracy (Grindle 1999; Van Cott 1994; Gray 2001; Klein 2003). Some contended that the *imposition* of new consensual and democratic procedures addressing the demands of indigenous movements would potentially herald a 'friendly liquidation of the past' (Van Cott 2000). Debates have therefore been restricted to the adequacy of its implementation and the extent to which it achieved its intended objectives (Gray 2001; Faguet 2003). Yet what were the objectives of an administration whose leaders had implemented the DS 21060, actively sought to depoliticise economic management and concentrated decision-making power in the Bolivian Central Bank (BCB) and economic Ministries, privatised state-owned corporations, promoted micro-credit in rural areas in order to spatially expand market relations, attempted to render the labour market more flexible, and turned a blind eye to (if only for its political survival) patronage and corruption in the state (see chapters 3, 4 and 5)?

Problem-solving research has generally been impervious to the concurrence of government policies – and interpreted decentralisation as a largely autonomous policy response to excessive centralisation, lack of democratic practice, corruption and patronage. The *intent* of agents devising and managing decentralisation reforms remain largely unquestioned: 'deliberate acts by beneficiaries of political power to divest themselves of some of that power are "puzzling phenomena"' (Grindle 1999: 2). Did President Gonzalo Sánchez de Lozada (1993-1997), interviewed by Grindle (1999), really take the audacious decision to reduce his government's hold on the institutions of the state by 'redistributing power downward' and 'opening political competition to new voices, new interests and new demands' (via local representation) (Grindle 1999: 2)?[37] For aforementioned commentators, Sánchez de Lozada and his Popular Participation team genuinely aimed to 'democratize access to political and economic power' (Gray 2001: 63) by satisfying the demands (organisational autonomy) of indigenous peoples, and by increasing transparency and administrative efficiency for social and welfare investment (by divesting responsibility for a welfare and productive oriented-infrastructure to municipalities). Popular Participation aimed to enhance the legitimacy of representative democracy by 'appeas(ing) divergent interests and maintain political stability' (Grindle 1999: 3).

Indeed, the emergence of organised indigenous movements (more specifically peasant union and political party offshoots of the 1970s *Katarista* movement) has been seen, in both Critical and problem-solving academia, as a major force for administrative decentralisation and the creation of an institutional space for participation and new forms of representation.[38] The increasing political clout of indigenous organisation has been problematic for the urban-based COB, because its phoenix-style rise occurred concurrently to the collapse of mining production and of the social and organisational base of labour movements. Indigenous nationalists and urban-based socialists have tended to offer, despite transient historical alliances, contradictory policy programmes, and were historically torn apart by the Military-Peasant Pact (1960s and early 1970s) (see chapter 2).

The intensification of indigenous resistance against agro-business encroachment in the early 1980s – which intersected with resistance to ecological degradation in the tropical rainforest in Bolivia, Brazil, Ecuador, Peru and central America – has been bolstered by an international climate combining environmentalism and a renewed idealisation of Rousseau's noble savage in the European and US left-wing (see Van Cott et al. 1994). Furthermore, media-friendly indigenous marches and the increasing efficiency of nationalist Quechua, Aymara and Guarani organisations in the early and late 1990s against neoliberal globalisation, for the defence of the autonomy of the *ayllu* and communal ownership and production, for the promotion of traditional coca-production and of indigenous languages, for the improvement of welfare services in rural areas and for the reduction of poverty have been regarded as legitimate and unquestionable requests. Much emphasis has been placed on the increasing influence of indigenous movements on policymaking, expressed in part by the incorporation of indigenous discourses and their more palatable demands (all of them excluding, notably, redistribution of privately-owned fallow land to *ayllus*) in the programmes of dominant political parties until 2005. These processes informed the notion that Bolivia is and should be a pluri-ethnic and multicultural nation, and that administrative decentralisation and educational reform (incorporating bilingual education) are the main policy instruments to secure this ideal (Gustafson 2002).

The key issues informing problem-solving research on decentralisation have therefore been the degree of indigenous representation through the Law of Popular Participation, i.e. to what extent political power has been diffused to indigenous peoples and generated more meaningful forms of citizenship; whether and to what extent it has increased the state's institutional density and hence facilitated a rapprochement between the state and the people, especially in rural areas; whether and how far decentralisation has improved administrative accountability and the satisfaction of basic needs; and whether it has undermined or upheld the power of local elites or oligarchies. Commentator have offered positive (Van Cott 1994, 2000; Centellas 2000; Faguet 2002, 2003; Ardaya and Thevoz 2001; McNeish 2002) or negative (Hiskey and Seligson 2003; Altman and Lalander 2003; Kohl 2003) answers to these questions.[39] The power diffusion generated by decentralisation has been seen as a central reason for the 'bold' alliance between indigenist leaders and the neoliberal political party MNR in the 1993 elections (Albó 1994; Van Cott 2000).

In contrast to aforementioned appraisals of decentralisation, Gustafson (2002) and Kohl (2003, 2006) offer more critical understandings of its purpose and implementation. In their compelling analyses of the law of Popular Participation (1994), they rebuke complacent interpretations of decentralisation by arguing that decentralisation and the inclusion of a multi-ethnic and pluri-cultural definition of the Bolivian nation, rather than concretely including previously excluded indigenous populations, constitute:

'contradictory shifts of political languages institutions that seek to reorder and legitimate changing expressions of social difference, citizen identity, and hierarchical forms of participation. These new tactics of governance represent a transformative renewal of discourses and institutions through which elites seek to insulate centralized power (spatially, conceptually and institutionally) from various forms of "indigenous" and other "popular" forms of political engagement. Certainly laudable for a reformist sensibility, interculturalist reforms do not, however, pursue robust versions of indigenous rights or overhaul structures of economic inequality' (Gustafson 2002: 270).

Gustafson rightly emphasised the MNR's lip service to the notion of interethnic equality rather than active legal and administrative struggles for a meaningful transformation of hierarchical relations of domination. Nevertheless, his approach is ethnographic – and tendentiously state-centric – rather than defined by a holistic approach to social relations. He overlooks intra-elite conflicts, transnational elite formation, struggles within the institutions of the state as well as the contradictions between Marxist discourses and indigenous nationalism, and rather focuses specifically on the contradictory relationships between the MNR government and indigenous movements, – in particular their two principal institutional crystallisations, i.e. the *Confederación Sindical Única de Trabajadores Campesinos de Bolivia* (CSUTCB), dominant in the *Altiplano* (highlands) and representing Aymara and Quechua nations, and the *Confederación de Pueblos Indígenas de Bolivia* (CIDOB), representing lowland nations such as the Chiriguano and Guarani.

More importantly, the analysis of depoliticisation cannot be restricted to decentralisation. Other crucial elements included the very implementation of the DS 21060 in the wake of hyperinflation in 1985; the granting of legal autonomy to the BCB, and civil service reform. Furthermore, the present research offers another dimension to Gustafson's analysis of the insulation of central organs of the state: the process of depoliticisation is, I argue here, internally related to polyarchy and state internationalisation. Each process unfolded as part of, and were reciprocal with, others processes – generating new political opportunities but also constraints that are increasingly apparent under the Morales administration. As demonstrated effectively by Gustafson, the process of depoliticisation has not achieved the strategic objectives of Goni's government by effectively opening the Pandora's Box of indigenous nationalism.

Kohl's (2003) analysis, on its side, is undermined by a definition of neoliberalism as an economic system based on market-based growth, rather than an ideological underpinning of underlying relations of domination and production. I will return to Kohl's work in the coming section. Like Gustafson, his research is tendentiously state-centric, and does not relate processes of decentralisation and internationalisation.

The Transition to a Neoliberal Economy and the Relationship Between MDIs and the Bolivian State

The story of the implementation of neoliberal reforms in Bolivia has already been told many times.[40] The policymaking process in Bolivia, a model partner in development of the WB and the IMF since 1985,[41] is widely perceived to have formed part of a global convergence pattern informed by the so-called Washington Consensus through the implementation, over fifteen years (1985-2000), of first-generation and second-generation reforms by successive Bolivian governments (Williamson 1990; Biersteker 1995: 174; Climenhage 1999).[42] First-generation reforms, implemented by President Paz Estenssoro's government between 1985 and 1989, involved stabilisation and structural adjustment.[43] These reforms focused on fiscal and monetary stabilisation, essentially through 1) a shift from fiscal to monetarist instruments of economic management, and restraints on public spending; 2) the reduction of tariff and non-tariff barriers to trade and investment; 3) an increase in the flexibility of the labour market (eliminating the preceding government's indexation of wages to inflation; freezing the wages of state employees, and facilitating the hiring and firing of workers in both private and public companies); 4) changes in state practices which affected the balance of payments, such as the simplification of tax regulations (including the introduction of an indirect tax on consumption) and the improvement of tax collection; the decentralisation (transfer to Regional Development Corporations [RDCs])[44] of loss-making corporations, and their decapitalisation (reduction of investment by the Treasury); and 5) the elimination of imbalances between the national price system and global market prices. The elimination of imbalances involved the removal of subsidies to businesses, the elimination of price distortions – aligning commodity prices, in particular energy and food prices, with global market prices. It was assumed by MDIs that first-generation reforms would encourage private investment.

These policies perpetuated, if not accentuated, the social costs caused by the debt and monetary crisis, as they antagonised the hitherto protected, domestically-oriented manufacturing fraction of capital, and deflated real wages and the purchasing power of labour (WB 1989b,

1989c, 1991c). Although arguments for the privatisation of accumulation were increasingly influential in the late 1970s and early 1980s, and numerous governments were beginning to withdraw the state from the production process, MDIs and governments in the 1980s focused primarily on restructuring or liquidating loss-making state-owned corporations rather than strictly conditioning financial assistance on privatisation – in part a realisation of the further social and political destabilisation that privatisation would generate (WB 1989b, 1992a, 1998a).

So-called second-generation reforms, negotiated by MDIs and the Paz Zamora administration from 1989, and executed under the presidency of Gonzalo Sánchez de Lozada from 1993,[45] are conventionally understood as involving the privatisation of state-owned corporations and welfare services, and the substitution of targeted safety nets benefiting only the poorest sectors of society for universal health and pension welfare, along with administrative and fiscal decentralisation (Climenhage 1999; Kohl and Farthing 2005). However, these attributes do not convey the comprehensiveness of second-generation reforms, which are centred essentially on PSD. PSD was formalised as a blueprint of MDIs in 1989, but several of its central elements had already been adopted prior to its formalisation (DAC 1989; IBRD 1993; Miller-Adams 1999). The WB and IMF regarded PSD as a continuation of measures implemented in the mid-1980s. The IBRD thus argued in 1993 that:

'relative price reform and macroeconomic stabilization are not sufficient conditions for restoring (or launching) efficient private sector growth. The World Bank Group's (WBG) strategy for supporting PSD reflects a move toward a "second generation" of efforts which integrate institutional changes with policy reforms. The approach aims to help countries overcome legal and institutional obstacles affecting the business environment and relax constraints to firms at the day-to-day operating level' (IBRD 1993: i, 2).

Improving the day-to-day environment in which private businesses operate required a dynamic, reflexive and holistic approach in order to understand the dynamics of capital accumulation. It required understanding that 'The business environment is shaped by a complex interaction of formal policies and laws, informal practices, institutions and infrastructure' (IBRD 1993: 4); it required 'learn(ing) from successful country experiences in implementing PSD reforms', and 'forg(ing) linkages between the various local institutions critical to PSD' (IBRD 1993: iii; 16).

The second generation of reforms thus focused on conditioning private capital accumulation. This involved supporting Foreign Direct Investment (FDI), supporting capitalist class formation (primitive accumulation), and supporting existing domestic businesses in the periphery, through state institutions but also the non-profit private sector. It focused on coordination between MDIs – information sharing, common development projects, and a global centralisation of decision-making and strategies for accumulation; collaboration between the staff of MDIs and national governments, expressed in extensive physical presence of the former and a hands-on approach to development. Most importantly perhaps, it focused on collaboration between dynamic business and technocratic elites (public-private partnerships) (DAC 1989).

However, despite regular mentions in the literature of external leverage or influence on domestic reforms, the institutional connections between the Bolivian state and MDIs has only been superficially addressed until now. Surprisingly few researchers have taken the pains to undertake an in-depth analysis of this relationship (Climenhage 1999; Fernández 2003; Kohl and Farthing 2005). Existing studies, overwhelmingly based on interviews (Climenhage 1999) and secondary and tertiary material (Kohl and Farthing 2005, 2009), have either resulted in contentions that the WB and the IMF, remaining at a distance, reactively offered encouragement and financial support for government reform initiatives (Climenhage 1999), or more often, that MDIs, monolithic entities at the behest of American and British economists and imperialist interests, and utterly devoid of internal contradictions (Kohl and Farthing 2009: 62-63), imposed neoliberal reforms onto Bolivian society. The latter contentions systematically lapse into a structuralist critique of neocolonialism, focusing in particular on US dominance (Kohl and Farthing 2005; Fernández 2003).[46] Allusions to global governance institutions are made to emphasise US and European imperialism in Bolivia and the rest of Latin America (García et al. 2000, 2002; Fernández 2003; Webber 2008),[47] without considering the theoretical implications of transnational production and organisational networks for North-South, inter-state but also intra-elite relations (Van der Pijl 1998; Overbeek 2004; Robinson 2005). Furthermore, institutional coordination via technical assistance on the one hand, and civil service reform on the other as processes integral to internationalisation have all too often been neglected in existing scholarship on Bolivia.

On their side, Robert Cox's (1981, 1987) original propositions and their reformulation by William Robinson (2002, 2005) have rarely been employed in empirical research. Exceptions include the work of Andrew Baker (1999) and Stuart Shields (2004) with reference to, respectively, the British and Polish states. Baker's (1999: 80) contention that 'the concept of the "internationalization of the state" suffers from a lack of empirical grounding' remains painfully true to this day. The central purpose of this manuscript is therefore to ground the concept of internationalisation in empirical evidence, by engaging critically with Cox's original understanding of the term, weaving theoretical and empirical elements of research into one reflexive whole. Such praxis may help to produce an alternative, generalisable conceptualisation of internationalisation, threreby allowing the operationalisation of empirical research in other national contexts. By breaking new empirical ground through the documentary analysis of primary evidence – internal documents of the WB and IMF – this book seeks to achieve a more nuanced understanding of restructuring in Bolivia than existing scholarship, by evading platitudes regarding neoliberal restructuring or neoliberal globalisation.

The World Bank, the IMF and the Bolivian State

Scholarly explanations of the relationship between MDIs and Bolivian governments after 1985 have diverged into two polar extremes: either MDIs imposed neoliberal reforms onto Bolivian society or they distantly supported government reform initiatives. Fernández (2003) argues the former, but his argument is problematic: few concepts are defined and measured adequately (for instance 'transnational capitalists'), his analysis of the WBG, the IMF and the Bolivian state is typically instrumentalist, and the empirical evidence used to justify his contention is all too often anecdotal. MDIs are considered as tools of colonial powers (led by the US) acting in concert to impose restructuring on developing countries by attaching neoliberal policy conditions on multilateral loans for the extraction of wealth from Bolivia, which perpetuates, if not increases poverty for the majority (see also Chossudovsky 1998: 33). Fernández presents Bolivia's managerial elite as a group of comprador lackeys who subserviently implemented the emerging Washington dogma. His argument is typically Latin Americanist in exuding a profound structuralist nationalism, imbued (however implicitly) by work of Raúl Prebisch and of the United Nations' Economic Commission for Latin America (CEPAL) in the 1950s. It idealises both state capitalism – state-ownership of strategic means of production, Import Substitution Strategies defined by protectionism, price controls and subsidies for nascent industries – and locates squarely the causes of Bolivia's underdevelopment in imperialism and neo-colonialism (for an effective, class-analysis critique of structuralism, see Pastor 1987). It offers a relatively myopic and superficial historical analysis, which conveniently overlooks the profound contradictions of state capitalism that led to the hyperinflationary crisis of 1985. The validation of his hypothesis – i.e. the IMF and WB are institutional instruments of Western neo-colonialism, and by extension, so is the debt-ridden Bolivian state – is thus *a priori* undermined by inadequate conceptualisations and historical contextualisation.

Alvaro García Linera and the *Comuna* collective neglected – perhaps as a political strategy – to distinguish between the various elite forces that were constituting and reconstituting the state through internal struggles and class domination, by lumping them all into a neoliberal 'political class' that ruled through a procedural democracy 'empty of content', and whose governments 'followed the blueprint pre-established by international financial organisms, following to the letter the instructions of sale of previously nationalised enterprises' (García and Gutiérrez 2002: 11, 15; author's translation). Alvaro García (2000, 2001, 2002, 2006, 2007), Luis Tapia (2002b) and Raúl Prada (2002) have adeptly conceptualised and analysed the decomposition and re-composition of labour and indigenist movements since the 1980s. They have, however, grossly simplified elite formations and the relationship between governments and MDIs – systematically lapsing, like Fernández (2003) in a structuralist critique of neo-colonialism mediated by MDIs in Bolivia.

In contrast, Climenhage's (1999) analysis of transnational networks and the emergence of a neoliberal epistemic community in Bolivia offers a compelling theoretical model, founded on Haas's (1992) notion of 'epistemic community', and employs it reliably in her empirical study of transnational forces. It identifies transnationalised elements of the Bolivian business and policymaking elite and analyses effectively *how* they internalised the neoliberal approach to economic management through a learning process in think tanks (UDAPE, *Fundación Milenio*), workshops (*Foros Económicos*) and transnational policy and educational networks. It offers an inspiring reflection on the potential emergence of a Harvard school and Harvard boys who devised economic policy in Bolivia (paralleling Chile's Chicago boys) (see also Conaghan 1990). It appropriately rejects the relevance of a Harvard school, emphasising that Jeffrey Sachs's role as an advisor of the Bolivian government for orthodox macro-economic stabilisation in 1985-90 and Bolivia's debt buyback programme in 1988 was certainly influential, but that it has been vastly exaggerated in the literature (see for example Kohl and Farthing 2005). Sachs was only one organic intellectual among others within a transnational elite social movement: collective action by monetarist economists in key governmental and private policy advice institutions was far more meaningful in creatively implementing neoliberal reforms adapted to Bolivian conditions. Nevertheless, her overreliance on interviews with WB and IMF staff has led her to argue inappropriately that the initiative for restructuring always lay in Bolivian governments; the IMF and WB merely offered post-factum, reactive fiscal and ideological support to Bolivian elements of the transnational epistemic community, rather than systematic, policy-related dialogue and collaboration. Reliance on secondary, rather than primary WB and IMF documents precluded any in-depth analysis of the institutional articulation of MDIs with central government agencies, which is at the core of the internationalisation of the Bolivian state.[48]

The documentary analysis of primary evidence (written sources intended solely for internal distribution) (Burnham et al. 2004), however difficult access may be, is essential to achieve an appropriate understanding of the social contradictions underlying restructuring in Bolivia. Research on the restructuring of peripheral states have either been misled by their over-reliance on interviews (in the Bolivian case, Climenhage 1999; Van Cott 2000; Grindle 2000; Bauer and Bowen 1997) or by the restrictions and distortions generated by the reliance on secondary material (Kohl and Farthing 2005; Petras and Veltmeyer 2005).[49] The present research analyses both secondary (publicly available) and primary (recently declassified) documents by the DAC, the DC, the WB and IMF as well as semi-structured and unstructured interviews. These primary sources help to explain the global centralisation of authority and decision-making since the 1970s and the strategic shifts informing MDIs' development agenda since the early 1980s. Inferential treatment of the evidence can be achieved because these documents allude to a global strategic blueprint for capital sustainability in first- and second-generation reforms, centred initially on stabilisation and structural adjustment, and subsequently on PSD. Issues of generalisation and contextualisation (respectively valued by quantitative and qualitative researchers) are jointly resolved here by analysing both multilateral policy documents informing the *global* implementation of structural reforms and declassified IMF and WB documents on restructuring in the Bolivian case (King, Keohane and Verba 1994; Adcock and Collier 2001; Brady and Collier 2004).

The evidence indicates the emergence of new patterns of multilateral coordination since the early 1980s, including 1) the enhancement of ideological cohesion and institutional coordination between national and multilateral technocrats, as national development strategies and programmes began to be devised jointly by governments, the WB, the IMF and the UNDP to facilitate aid coordination, which became the responsibility of the recipient government (DAC 2006: 23); 2) increasing coordination and division of labour between MDIs, originally between the IMF and the WB, and extended through the mediation of the DAC to the UNDP, regional development banks such as the Inter-American Development Bank (IDB) and bilateral development agencies; 3) a consciously *holistic* and reflexive approach to problem-solving, within the structural constraints of global accumulation and capital expansion (including primitive accumulation); and 4) a profound awareness of subaltern resistance to the conditions required (flexible labour market, removal of barriers to trade and investment, fiscal and monetary stability) for capital accumulation and PSD (see DAC 1989; IBRD 1993, DC 1996).

WB-IMF coordination was formalised in 1966 in a memorandum on Fund-Bank collaboration (IMF/WB 2001: 19),[50] consolidated at the strategic decision-making level by the establishment of the DC in 1974, upgraded by the introduction of the Policy Framework Paper (PFP) in 1987,[51] and reconfigured by the signing of a 1989 Concordat on aid coordination between the two institutions.[52] In the early 1980s, 'as the two institutions moved to overlapping fields of economic activity, collaboration intensified and produced positive results. However, at times collaboration between the two institutions ran into problems, prompting further periodic reviews of existing practices... When the Bank began making structural adjustment loans (SALs) for medium-term balance of payments financing in 1980, it had to reconcile that activity with the Fund's "primary responsibility" for the balance of payments' (IMF/WB 2001: 18-19).

The crystallisation of a coordinated approach to restructuring in the 1980s between the two institutions, supported empirically by the Bolivian case (see chapter 4), contradicts Joseph Stiglitz's (2002) contention that the WB and the IMF engineered diametrically opposed approaches to development in the 1990s, and that the IMF's 'other approach' founded on 'a curious blend of ideology and bad economics, dogma that sometimes seemed to be thinly veiling special interests', undermined the WB's balanced perspective (Stiglitz 2002: xiii). Indeed, the donor community must not be conceptualised as a bloc or unit devoid of internal contradictions, as disputes regularly arise in relation to overlapping responsibilities and parallel development projects (Taylor 2005; see also chapter 4).[53] Nevertheless, MDIs' overall strategic approach to development, crystallised in PSD reforms and buttressed by the authority of the DC and DAC, indicates ideological convergence and the consolidation of a transnational historic bloc, in part through the activities of MDIs. Efforts by the DC and DAC since the mid-1980s to generate a harmonious and efficient coordination of development activities culminated in the 2005 Paris Declaration on Aid Effectiveness (DAC 2005; 2006).

Kohl and Farthing (2005), on their side, have taken a middle ground by referring to 'collaborative practice' between MDI staff and Bolivian administrations. Nevertheless, they do not attempt to decipher the actual institutional interconnections between MDIs and the Bolivian national state, preferring to present reified 'international governance agencies and financial institutions' as having 'imposed in large part' a 'neoliberal hegemonic regime' upon Bolivia 'in collusion with national elites' (Kohl and Farthing 2005: 7).[54] They eschew an in-depth analysis of the process of integration into a globally-oriented institutional complex, focusing more specifically on an analysis of an externally imposed neoliberal globalisation and neoliberal hegemony. Despite the use of enlightening empirical evidence and an excellent concluding chapter, Kohl and Farthing's analysis is founded on blurry conceptual foundations and (primarily) tertiary sources.[55] So many inconsistent meanings are given to the two central concepts of the book, *neoliberalism* and *hegemony*, that meaning is effectively obscured and lost. Kohl and Farthing equates neoliberalism indiscriminately to a 'global system that privileges the market' (2005: 2), to a 'regime' (2005: 7), to a 'project' (2005: 8), or a set of 'policies that subordinate the broader public interest by privileging the private sector while minimizing the role of government in production' (2005: 2; 12). The concept of hegemony, on its side, is applied equally to 'a regime' (2005: 7) or a 'state' (2005: 7) or indeed to a 'set of ideological assumptions' (2005: 15). By referring to nebulous notions of 'neoliberal system' and 'neoliberal globalization', Kohl and Farthing provide the image of an independent ideational variable associated indiscriminately with the state, the market, and an overbearing US hegemon.

Neoliberalism is thus reduced in both Fernández's (2003) and Kohl and Farthing's (2005: 2-3; 2009) texts to shadowy and arbitrary 'manifestations of US imperialism' and 'transnational conditionality',[56] while the complex institutional relationships between Bolivia's 'national elites' and MDIs is simplified to the extreme through the un-problematised use of the term 'collusion'. A more careful historical analysis of multilateral economic management by the IMF undertaken by such researchers as Fred Block (1977a) and Manuel Pastor (1987) point adequately to monetarism (supply-side management, often associated with free trade and conceptually related to neoliberalism) and Keynesianism (demand management, conventionally interfaced by trade protectionism) as the two principal ideological forces around which capitalist historic blocs have concretely coalesced and struggled for capital hegemony.[57] These two heuristic projects, rarely implemented in their pure form but combined with more emphasis placed either on supply or demand, have sought to resolve the fiscal, monetary and trade policy issues that define the organisation of an inherently unstable global capital accumulation process (Van der Pijl 1984).

Broader Limitations in the Academic Literature on Bolivia

Analyses of Bolivia's political economy have been suffused with concepts of democracy, globalisation and neoliberalism. Yet these analyses have generally suffered from interrelated shortcomings, which need to be redressed: Smithian logic, state-centrism, state-market and domestic-foreign dichotomies.

Globalisation As Smithian Magic?

Globalisation has been on the lips of many International Relations theorists since the collapse of the Soviet Union, used and abused to the point of lapsing in an 'empty circularity' whereby 'the *explanandum* – globalisation as the developing outcome of some historical process – is progressively transformed into the *explanans*: it is globalisation which now explains the changing character of the modern world – and even generates "retrospective discoveries" about past epochs in which it must be presumed not to have existed' (Rosenberg 2001: 2-3). Globalisation is consequently interpreted as the unprecedented world-wide extension of an impersonal force (an independent transnational economic variable, or relatively autonomous infra-structure) undermining the capacity of national states to manage their hitherto autonomous, well-protected social economies (Cox 1987; Gill 2003; Robinson 2005).

In order to uncover the underlying mechanisms veiled by Smithian liberalism, one must historicise the emergence and globalisation of capitalist relations of production, the commodification of labour (i.e. turning workers into inputs for production) through a process of primitive accumulation,[58] the spatial expansion of capital through over-accumulative tendencies and imperialism, and the historical tension between transnational and inter-state relations.[59] I can only briefly address the latter issue here: in historical materialism, the transnational is not analysed as a new phenomenon; rather it is seen as old as, and as dialectically inter-related with international relations since the dawn of civilization (van Apeldoorn 2004: 144-145). On their side, the complete circuits of capital (articulating industrial, financial and commercial circuits) were constituted transnationally as a structure essentially distinct from and contradictory to international relations and their territorial logic.[60] The a-spatial and expansionary development of capital since the eighteenth century from its transnational 'Lockean' heartland (defined by a form of social regulation based on the rule of law and the protection of private property, and in which political power has tended to operate consensually rather than through direct coercion) has gradually accentuated the historical contradiction between transnational and international relations.[61]

From that perspective globalisation accompanied the birth of capital, and capital determines the global essence of contemporary society. Van der Pijl (1998: 38) suggests that the expansion of capital 'into uncharted territory' has occurred both in temporal and spatial, concentric phases, causing the contemporary perpetuation of processes of primitive accumulation. The rhythmic, non-linear expansion and intensification of capitalist relations of production has equally generated variegated forms of primitive commodified labour, semi-proletarianised peasants, vagrants hired on a temporary basis into workhouses, employed in small family enterprises (putting-out systems), or suffering the dissolution of artisan guilds and forced to work in new factories.

Beyond primitive accumulation, the maturation of capitalist relations of production through industrialisation has deepened commodification processes by generalising the wage relation (Hobsbawm 1995). Under industrial circuits of capital, market exchange of commodities veil the subordination of the labour process to capital self-valorisation, or value expansion. From this perspective, the state prior to the 1970s was unable to achieve autonomy from transnational capital circuits just as it is unable to manage capital circuits now. Therefore, the transformations occurring since the early 1970s have not constituted a new transnational structure of capital, but are rather defined by new social contradictions caused by the emergence of a dominant, transnationally organised elite bloc, which struggled to restructure economic, ideological and institutional relations through its appropriation of revolutionary technological developments (chiefly in transport and information technologies).

Dependency and Underdevelopment

Processes of capital globalisation and transnational elite formation, if seen in this light, problematise dependency and world-system theories, which have conditioned analyses of the post-colonial state and of its weakness or strength.[62] World-system theorists define capital as the appropriation, by metropolitan states, of the surplus of the entire world economy through a 'system of hierarchical economic organisation Centre/Periphery/Semi-Periphery, recognisable ... since the first agrarian/colonial capitalism' (Espasandín and Iglesias 2007: 44). These chains of dependency and hence domination are founded on a conception of capital as a world market of exchange, i.e. as circulation of commodities.[63] The attempt to unveil the magic of the world market is immediately veiled by reducing capital relations to commercial circuits: relations of production have been turned into relations of exchange between core and peripheral states (Rupert 1995, Robinson 1996). The circulationist definition also implies that the mercantile and chiefly agrarian economic structure of sixteenth century Europe and Americas was essentially capitalist. This loose definition could (and has) lapse(d) into an understanding of slave, feudal or hacienda structures of production as capitalist. I will rather follow in the historical materialist tradition by arguing that capital emerged as a complete structure of production in England during the eighteenth century, where the imposition of land rents onto peasants triggered early forms of (primitive) accumulation and the development of an urban-based, industrial circuit of capital as the central axis of capitalist social relations.[64]

The world-system/dependency models also over-emphasises the causal relationship between the underdevelopment of peripheral social complexes and the circulation and exchange of commodities within a capitalist world market, which has been empirically contradicted by rising capitalist formations (East Asian Tigers, India, Russia and Brazil). Besides, it unwittingly reproduces the ontological (and thus analytical) primacy of the infrastructure, or forces of production ('the methods and means of appropriating and transforming nature, including tools, technology, work organisation'), which implicitly veil the underlying class content of worldwide production relations (Roseberry 1989: 17). From that perspective, the essential problem of constructed peripheral nations and of the states protecting them is the unfair trade regime that defines their relations with the capitalist metropolis. Consequently, the only viable and justifiable political course of action for them to take is national emancipation either through 'delinking', or through state capitalism involving import-substitution strategies (Amin 1990; Antezana 1983; Fernández 2003).

State-Centrism and Neoliberalism as Tools of the US Government

The empty circularity of globalisation theory has all too often been resolved by understanding globalisation as world-wide Americanisation – i.e. the global imposition, by US administrations and US-based multinational corporations, of (neoliberal) capitalism and epiphenomenally, of American culture.[65] Within this global metaphor, prevalent in world-system and dependency theory but also in Gramscian thought,[66] one national hegemonic state, or the metropolis as a whole dominates the world system by suppressing the development of the periphery through imbalanced commodity trading. From that perspective, global governance institutions are perceived as instruments of metropolitan elites (see Cammack 2003 for a Marxist critique). While understanding globalisation as *explanans* reproduces Adam Smith's understanding of market forces as an invisible hand enjoying magical qualities that cannot be comprehended (Van der Pijl 1998), perceiving neoliberalism as a tool of the US is fundamentally state-centric.

State-centrism generates a duality between structure and agency by ascribing a unilateral, agency-driven power to nations or states, pitting national elite blocs against each other, and/or metropolitan against peripheral formations. This in turn causes a neglect of the constitution of structure by agency, and hence their dialectical, internal relationship.[67] State-centrism is directly related to globalisation theory, which perceives transnational market forces as undermining the sovereignty of the state. It thus persists in implicitly or explicitly perpetuating the problematic assumption in mainstream International Relations and International Political Economy (IPE), of a zero-sum relationship between market and state.[68] It also is a fertile breeding ground for national starting-points.

National and Local Starting-Points: Creating Internal-External Dichotomies

Scholarship on Bolivia has been predominantly informed by a national epistemological and ontological starting-point.[69] The research core here is the peculiar national or local essence of social relations, which may or may not be influenced by external constraints (capital, changing world prices, globalisation, neoliberalism). On the one hand, the fact that a majority of the Bolivian population appears 'still deeply enmeshed in an ancient autochthonous culture' (Dunkerley 1984: xiii), has favoured an anthropological focus upon rural, pre-capitalist forms of social organisation and their articulation with the capitalist mode of production, rather than holistic historical analyses of its political economy; a problem identified by anthropologists themselves in the late 1980s.[70] This issue has prompted anthropologists to broaden their methodological horizons towards urban-rural linkages (Assies 2003), as well as regional or national spaces.[71] Yet they continue to see the national as a valid object of study in and of itself. On the other hand, Realist and Pluralist theories of International Relations and Political Science have predisposed researchers to assign an a priori, absolute primacy to the national unit, even if seen as part of an anarchic international system (Waltz 1990-1). Bolivia, with its peculiar indigenous makeup and relative geographical isolation is all too often wrapped with eternal qualities reminiscent of Niebuhr's (1932: 83) assertion that the nation is 'the most absolute of all human associations'.

However, studies of the relationship between MDIs and the Bolivian state, have adopted top-down, and external-internal perspectives on the establishment of a neoliberal market. Influenced as they continue to be by structuralism, they have systematically lapsed into nationalist critiques of neo-colonialism. They have thus focused in particular on the unchallenged dominance of the US superpower in international relations through veto rights in the IMF and its bilateral leverage on Latin American governments to lower existing barriers to trade and investments.[72]

This tendency has been evident in much classical Marxist, including Gramscian scholarship.[73] Neo-Gramscian approaches' most important departure from Gramsci is their revival of Marx's (2003: 386-7) holistic starting-point (world-wide social relations), which posits that the social whole is greater than the sum of its parts. They have accordingly focused their inquiry on *global* relations of production, rather than the internal/domestic political struggles and hegemonies defining national formations.[74] In doing so, they have consciously opened up Gramscian thought by breaking away from its contention that domestic hegemonies and domestic economic relations between social forces should be the prior, essential level of analysis, from which external interactions between national state-society complexes unfold. In other words, the Bolivian or Aymara nation is not an ontology – it does not exist as an entity defined by essential and exclusive attributes – and is not worthy of study in and of itself but always as constitutive of global social relations.

States vs. Markets

State-centrism, globalisation theory, statolatry and national starting-points are correlated to the states-vs.-markets dichotomy (Strange 1995; Krasner 199). Statolatric analyses of democratisation have, for example, systematically sought to rigidify the state, the market and society into absolute, autonomous structures or factors (Holloway 1995a). National starting-points inevitably perceive the world market – or indeed globalisation – as an external and somehow overbearing force. It is important to problematise the distinction between market-based (pre-1952 and post-1985) and state-led (1952-1985) development as ontologically distinct in the literature on Bolivia. This has contemporary political relevance, as the Morales administration is seeking to revive state capitalism through the renationalisation of corporations privatised in the 1990s.

Critical research has effectively undermined problem-solving attempts at reducing economic relations to technical specificities – ideologically framed in a way that persistently naturalises liberal democracy (the political sphere) and the world market of commodity exchange (the economic realm), concurrently veiling the worldwide, underlying structure of capital accumulation defining the contemporary social world.[75] Nevertheless it persists in assuming a zero-sum relationship between state and market. In the specialist literature on Bolivia, either growth is market-based (a neoliberal system/economy) or effected via the state (state-based economies, state capitalism, state socialism) and these two forms of growth are defined by distinct, mutually exclusive, if not contradictory logics.[76] Kohl and Farthing (2005), as already pointed out, refer to notions of market-led neoliberal system and neoliberal globalization. Climenhage begins her work with these words: 'In the last two decades, nations all over the world have been undergoing transitions to neoliberal, market-based economies' (Climenhage 1999: 1). Lesley Gill (2000) borrows Susan Strange's (1996) conceptual framework to describe the implementation of Bolivia's neoliberal reforms as a militarised 'retreat of the state'.[77] Herbert Klein (2003), Fernando Mayorga (1991), and Pilar Domingo (1993), on their side, refer to the occurrence of a 'structural revolution' in 1985, just as sympathetic analysts with a privileged access to the MAS leadership have explained Evo Morales's investiture as heralding a 'revolutionary' change of Bolivian society and economy (Stefanoni and Do Alto 2006).[78] One should be reminded of Malloy's (1991: 54) wise suggestion: 'What was new in Bolivia was not the neoliberal program of the New Economic Policy but the political creativity that backed it up'.

A Historical Materialist Alternative: The State As Contradictory Organisation of Subjection

The alternative suggested here seeks to transcend external-internal and state-market dichotomies, statolatry and economic determinism by focusing on patterns of collaboration between the staff of MDIs and a transnational elite fraction in Bolivia, incorporated into an expanding transnational bloc as equal partners in development in the struggle for the restructuring of social relations, including of the state, since 1985. Transnational elite networks are seen here as transcending bilateral relations between Bolivia and the United States of America (US), which have all too often been rigidified in Critical scholarship.

This study contends that private-public and market-state dichotomies obscure meaning and restrict our understanding of what constitutes growth by applying a circular and fetishised logic to its conceptualisation:[79] growth becomes a process defined merely by the exchange of commodities abstracted from the very labour relations that defines their specific value (Bonefeld 2000), an abstract distancing permitted by the reification of market and state (turning internally related economic and institutional processes into mutually exclusive entities). It has been pointed out before (Cliff 1955; Picciotto 1978) that state-owned corporations integrated into the world market do not essentially evade the logic of surplus appropriation and the containment of labour power; labour remains employed by state managers in order to generate surplus value. Resistance to elites *within* the state is an expression of the fact that capital accumulation, via private or state ownership always constitutes exploitative labour relations.[80]

Theoretical Underpinning

The alternative offered here is a historical materialist approach grounded in substantive (historically-constituted) dialectical logic. Historical materialist research is grounded in reflexive *praxis*, in the fused unities of dialectics and history, of abstract and concrete thought (theory and practice), and of subject and object. Each unity presupposes and is the result of the other. The philosophy of praxis obliges the theorist to constantly confront and adapt concepts abstracted in prior knowledge constructions to changing historical conditions, and if necessary replace them with more valid, *practical*, ones. Hence the ever-incomplete nature of scholarship and the ever-open nature of concepts.[81] These perspectives induce a readier emphasis on the historical specificity, subjectivity and therefore partiality of any social theory. Yet far from being relativist, they abstractly-concretely develop, using substantive dialectical logic, a synthetic ontology: social relations of production, in other words antagonistic class relations (Marx 2003: 'The Gundrisse'; Overbeek 2000; Van der Pijl 2002). Dialectics is located both in concrete history and in the intellectual process (logic grounded in praxis) itself.[82]

Substantive dialectical logic helps us to overcome superficial distinctions between state and market by understanding growth as capital accumulation. Accumulation only exists as capital-in-movement, which is a movement of exchange-value. Value can only be generated through labour; hence capital accumulation can only exist via the appropriation of labour surplus, which in effect constitutes exploitation.[83] The social reality, the ontological premise and result of dialectical thinking, is therefore the *class struggle*: the contradictory labour (or production) process is the essential contradiction-in-movement, the underlying social relation which defines and constitutes the totality of apparently distinct forms (Overbeek 2000; Bonefeld 1991: 99-100). Class antagonisms, manifested in the power struggles arising from the ownership of the means of production and the distribution of wealth, are the dynamic core of imagined social constructions and as such drive social history. The class struggle as movement entails constant change both of social reality and of the forms expressed in and through that reality; hence the unpredictability of struggle itself and the rejection of any dogmatic historical determinism; and hence the ever-incomplete nature of scholarship and the ever-open nature of concepts (Gill 2003; Burnham 2001).

The ontological *concept* as an abstract, synthetic totality is analytically prior to its apparent manifestations.[84] To interpret the ontological concept as a social whole greater than the sum of its parts helps to unveil the invisible essence that lies underneath the sensory surface of the social world, and to identify recurring historical patterns as structures (Bonefeld et al. 1991, 1992; Archer et al. 1998; Van Apeldoorn 2004). To consider the concept of class struggle as essential, synthetic starting-point is not a purely logical (metaphysical) exercise, but is also, and concurrently, the result of historical analysis: capitalism is seen as a historically specific and transitory social structure defined on the one hand by the separation of labour from the means of production and its corollary, the commodification of labour, and on the other by 'a particular social form of production within which the production of useful goods is subordinated to the expansion of surplus value' (Burnham 2000: 16). The class struggle in capitalist form emerges out of a plethora of historical evidence of the expropriation, by emerging capital, of the means of production (land, tools, technology) hitherto in the hands of labourers. Capital exploits and dominates labour by extracting surplus-value on a daily basis, thereby generating resistance and inducing the constant intervention of the state to sustain the reproduction of the total circuits of capital. Capital as self-valorising value exists only through the appropriation of labour because labour is the substance of value.[85]

Class struggles are not economic struggles separate from cultural or ideological relations. They are underlying *social* antagonisms expressed in complementary economic, ideological and institutional forms. Social structures take plural local, national and regional forms (yet these levels of analysis cannot be distinguished because each is constitutive of the others): economies, ideologies (including religions) and institutions are necessarily varied expressions of historical relations of production (Apeldoorn 2004: 144). Such an approach precludes any determinism, economic or otherwise, because social change is not predetermined by class relations but has historically been generated also by struggle (expressed in domestic and foreign wars, in imperialistic relations) between contending elite forces (Overbeek and Pijl 1993).

The holistic approach used here entails placing the liberalisation of the Bolivian state within the context of the latest phase of capital globalisation that emerged in the early 1970s. Liberalisation is understood here as social restructuring, involving struggles to adjust the Bolivian space to global market prices and privatise accumulation; to achieve the hegemony of capital via the diffusion of neoliberalism; and to secure the viability of polyarchy.[86] The central attribute of this phase has been the increasing predominance of what Stephen Gill (2003) termed a transnational historic bloc of elite social forces, incorporating fractions of capital, technocrats, and organic intellectuals.

Generating the Research's Hypothesis

Debates between critical and problem-solving scholars on the causes of underdevelopment; on the limitations of a democratic structure informed by various pacts and coalitions between the three dominant political parties in the 1985-2003 period (the *Movimiento Nacionalista Revolucionario* [MNR], the *Acción Democrática Nacionalista* [ADN], and the *Movimiento de Izquierda Revolucionaria* [MIR]); on the morality, modernising inevitability or efficiency of so-called neoliberal restructuring generate important empirical and philosophical issues, which continue to inform contemporary appraisals of nationalisation and land redistribution implemented by the current Morales administration.

Normative questions relating to the nature or desirability of a democratic polity, to the appropriate form of such democratic polity must certainly not be brushed aside and should be tackled with the ingenuity of conceptual openness. It is, however, not the purpose of the present study to enter normative debates, but rather to identify and analyse thoroughly research areas that have been overlooked or glimpsed at.

In light of the limitations of Weberian pluralism and of instrumentalist conceptions of the state, I began my research by asking myself: how did the Bolivian state transform itself to sustain the general interest of capital in the period under study? In other words, how did the state achieve its function: the (re)production of capital through labour exploitation? This functionalist hypothesis challenged existing Critical research on the Bolivian state and on its relationship with MDIs since 1985, which have systematically lapsed into critiques of neo-colonialism and instrumentalist understandings of the state. I subsequently encountered evidence that threw a reflexive light on the validity of the hypothesis itself and forced a change in the questions I had to ask myself. The questions driving this investigation consequently became: did the Bolivian state act as a whole, as a bloc, to sustain capital reproduction? Is it ever unitary? Does it always know what it is supposed to do? Is it an 'it' or several 'it's? What are the forces that constitute the state and how do their struggles unfold? How did the relationship between Bolivia's central government and multilateral development agencies in the period under study affect, and was affected by what is conventionally seen as domestic struggles? Evidence from Bolivia meant that I had to reconsider my understanding of the state.

The concept of the state is elusive and subject to endless debate and controversy. However, despite its centrality to the unnecessarily fragmented disciplines of political science, International Relations and IPE, and probably because of its ambiguous and contested nature, its conceptualisation has often been obscured or neglected in empirical analyses of the political (Burnham 1994b). The result of under-labourer analyses of the state has been a set of assumptions regarding the role or functions of the state and its relation to the market, which undoubtedly informed my initial hypothesis (Bonefeld and Psychopedis 1991; Gunn 1992). This fixation all too often results in a consideration of the state as a unitary institution under the overarching leadership of its executive agencies, hence tending towards a conflation of state and government.[87]

The State as Contradictory Organisation of Subjection

I approached the research on the Bolivian state with a view to generate theoretical propositions that can be coherently integrated into a historical materialist approach. The concept of the state has been a major preoccupation of so-called political Marxist, German Marxist, Open Marxist and neo-Gramscian theorists since the late 1970s,[88] who attempted to transcend the two conventional historical materialist approaches to the state elaborated respectively by Ralph Miliband (1968) and Nikos Poulantzas (1978 [1968]): instrumentalism and structural-functionalism. Yet, Open Marxist and neo-Gramscian scholars have persisted in reproducing the Miliband-Poulantzas debates of the 1970s on the state:[89] in a variety of forms, they either conceptualise the state as an instrument of the ruling class (Morton 2000; Robinson 2002, 2005) or as a relatively autonomous structure that functionally reproduces capital.[90]

The basic instrumentalist approach to the state defines it as an expression of the interest of the ruling-class, used (like a tool) to sustain its structural domination over labour: 'an instrument has no will of its own and is thus capable of action only as the extension of the will of some actor. To understand the state as an instrument of the capitalist class is to say that state action originates in the conscious and purposive efforts of capitalists as a class' (Finegold and Skocpol 1995: 176). Instrumentalism has been criticised from various perspectives. It offers an image of capitalist forces as an economic bloc capable of consciously ruling through the institutions of the state; tainting the theory with agency-centeredness and voluntarism (Hay 1999). It also fails to identify fractures and power struggles within dominant social forces (Van der Pijl 1984), and overlooks the substantive distinctions between strictly technocratic (employees of the state) and business forces (private owners of the means of production) which generates contradictions in their approaches to social reproduction and accumulation strategies (Block 1977b).

The cruder version of structural-functionalism, on its side and in direct contrast to instrumentalism, views the state as possessing or being attributed a set of functions (such as the defence of private property, the reproduction of labour, the provision of infrastructure), which sustain the long-term interest of capital (Poulantzas 1975, 1978 [1968]; Holloway and Picciotto 1978). It has been criticised for subduing conscious agency to the causal pre-eminence of the structure, creating an artificially mechanistic metaphor for the internal dialectic between production relations and the cold, rational, state class managing them

(Hay 1999). Poulantzas emphasised the relatively autonomous existence and self-reproduction of an institutional/political structure sustaining the general interest of capital through its functional achievement of accumulation. Relative autonomy generated two essential problems: structural-functionalism and factorial analysis. As pointed out by Burnham (1994b: 2), the basic flaw of functionalist approaches is that they 'define the state by its consequences': the state is a bearer of social functions such as the maintenance of order and the reproduction of capital, and 'knows best' what these functions are. Hence there is no space for struggle within the institutions of the capitalist state, since the logic of accumulation and class domination always structures state behaviour and role. However, the disjuncture between autonomous infra- and superstructures has been appropriately disputed by Marxists for its covert association with a Weberian pluralistic methodology (Burnham 1991; Holloway 1995). Economic (infra-) and political (super-) structures were studied by Poulantzas as autonomous factors obeying distinct logics of inquiry ('autonomous and specific objects of science'), exemplified by the usage of different conceptual frameworks for each structure – the economic level would be explained by concepts such as value, surplus value, accumulation and indeed capital while the political level would be analysed using alternative concepts such as hegemony or power bloc (Holloway and Picciotto 1978; Picciotto 1990).[91]

Poulantzas and Miliband did move away, in their later work, from this structure-agency dichotomy by making significant concessions to each other's arguments. Poulantzas began seeing the state in more relational terms, while Miliband began emphasising the relative autonomy of the state from ruling-class interests (Miliband 1977; Poulantzas 1978). Indeed, Poulantzas's conceptualisation of the state as a 'condensation', in its institutional midst, 'of the relationship of forces between classes and class fractions' is a perfect starting-point for relational approaches to the state (Poulantzas 1978: 132). Nevertheless Poulantzas and Miliband ultimately failed to move debates on the state far beyond early structuralist and instrumentalist positions (Hay 1999: 164-168). The central problem of neo-Gramscian theories of the state is that they have remained fixed in these early propositions.[92]

The present research is firmly grounded in the neo-Gramscian movement, applying reflexively concepts of transnational bloc, hegemony, internationalisation, global governance and polyarchy. Neo-Gramscian research has, in my view, been at the cutting-edge of historical materialist scholarship, seeking to understand and explain emerging social phenomena that, neo-Gramscians would argue, do not fit readily in conventional Marxist categories. My analysis of the Bolivian case espouses neo-Gramscian attempt to rescue historical materialism from its naturalistic, deterministic and monistic tendencies by weaving ideological struggles into an analysis of transnational relations, global elite formation, and the emergence of supranational regulatory forms, but it also seeks to evade their instrumentalist and structural-functionalist iterations.

There have been sophisticated and creative attempts to transcend the caricatured theoretical dichotomy between relative autonomy and instrumentalism, most notably by Fred Block (1977b), by Poulantzas in his later work (1978) and by Bob Jessop (1990, 2007). Although the present conceptualisation of the state draws significantly on the work of Bob Jessop (1990; 2007) and especially Poulantzas (1978), it emphasises that Poulantzas, in his later work, did not resolve the tension between his earlier structural-functionalism and his tentative relational approach (Bruff 2008). Jessop's strategic-relational theory of the state, on its side, mistakenly rejects class relations as integral to the state.[93] Crucially, they remained ethereal, i.e. ungrounded, and exceedingly difficult to ground in history. I aim here to evade Poulantzas's and Jessop's respective structural functionalist overhang and neglect of class, and to define the concept of the state through empirical evidence.

I suggest that an appropriate way of opening up historical materialist theories of the state involves grounding the state in relations of production. As already pointed out, relations of production are relations of domination in the sense that capital exists only through the extraction of surplus value from labour (i.e. exploitation), while free labour resists exploitation (Burnham 1994; Overbeek 2004). These relations are coercively organised by the institutions of the state. However, these institutions are relations themselves. Hence the state is a complex set of social relations embedded within broader relations (as suggested by Bieler and Morton [2003]): it reproduces and coercively expresses the power relations between the social forces constituting it and that it necessarily organises; hence it is the organisational and coercive constitution of domination itself. The state is thus seen as a fluid, *contradictory organisation of subjection*:[94] a necessary coercive and regulatory expression of relations of domination – which are the premise and result of production relations.

In principle, all relations of domination exist through and as organised subjection. As such, whenever relations of domination have historically arisen, they have been organised by a distinct institution, or set of institutions attempting to legitimise these relations and to monopolise authority and the means of coercion: in other words, a state.

Societies defined by domination are state societies. The state is internally related and conceptually indispensable to the underlying reality of structural domination: rather than conceptualised as social form (Bonefeld 1991; Burnham 1995, 2002; Holloway 1995), the state must therefore be seen as *social content*: it is not a level of abstraction below the substantive, dialectical abstraction of class relations, but constitutes and is constituted by this abstraction. The state is always presupposed in production relations, always a specific apparatus of coercive and regulatory institutions, of which the government, the legislative apparatus and the judiciary system in capitalist form are a part but not the whole (Burnham 1994: 5). This approach allows the clear delimitation of the institutions constituting the state, hence avoiding the shortcomings of the Gramscian 'integral state', which unwittingly allows any institution in civil society – the information media, the Church, trade unions – to be considered part of the state if they sustain the legitimacy of existing class relations (Burnham 1994: 2).

This approach however rejects the tendency in Marxism to conceptualise the state as a unitary entity.[95] To paraphrase Holloway's 'capital is class struggle', form-as-relation is form-as-struggle; hence organised subjection must be reflexively examined, as pointed out briefly but obscured subsequently by Holloway (1995a). The fact that the state most often acts in the interest of capitalist forces (and appears not only to provide social stability but also to be stable itself) is indeed a reflection of the structural (economic, ideological, institutional) power of these forces, but does not negate the reality of institutions as loci of antagonism and instability. Social organisation is always contested, always a movement of struggle, in which the power of a social force is expressed in its ever-unstable control of (or influence on) state institutions as well as civil society organisations. Hence the contradictory, unstable and fluid existence of its historical forms.

As a contradictory relation, the state is constantly torn, as is society, by social antagonisms: hence state policy is never perfectly implemented in the interest of the dominant class, is always an expression of struggle (however silent, invisible and apparently non-violent). Hence, the state is constantly subject to dissolution by social forces outside and within it. Given that the state is a site of struggle, it may be temporarily dominated by fractions of capital (in particular, transnationalised capital fractions) or indeed by dominant fractions of labour.[96] This proposition is not inconsistent with Jessop's (1990; 2007) strategic-relational approach, but places far greater emphasis on class struggles within the state: the state is always an expression of broader production relations and of the organisational capacities of social forces. State legislation itself reflects institutional struggles: the constitution of the state by organised labour induces political struggles generating legal compromise limiting the capital accumulation process and precluding absolute subjugation by dominant social forces. The state necessarily expresses the social (economic, ideological, organisational, coercive) power of elite forces (whether national or transnational) and of organised labour at a particular moment of its history, but also redirects and transforms these power relations: in capitalism, it is therefore not functionally related to the capital accumulation process and neither is it relatively autonomous from the production relations that constitute it.

Fluid, conflict-ridden production relations are reproduced in all state institutions – whether formally (clearly defined positions and functions) or informally (influence and tacit authority of certain social agents in an organisation). Fiscal policies, such as the reduction or increase of public spending (on services, investment and wages), and of direct and indirect taxes (on businesses and/or labour in the formal economy), reflect multiple contradictions and demands within the state, between the state and MDIs, and between the state and civil society. Government initiatives are never implemented in a political vacuum but are responses to external and domestic constraints. Historical analyses of class-relevant social forces and social struggles must therefore always address *how* the state is materialised by and shapes the material existence of these forces. The trajectory of class and intra-elite struggles is internally related to and exists through the state. As a terrain of intra-elite and class struggles, the state never fully manages to manage the antagonistic content of capital accumulation.

This approach places far more emphasis on struggles between dominant and subjugated social forces within the state than existing scholarship. The question then is, how do we delineate these social forces (Gramsci's currents of opinions)? How can we systematically identify and measure them, in a qualitative sense? Delineation – with a view to always understand forces as *movements* and *processes* in order to avoid reification – is indispensable in order to operationalise research (Cox 1996; Gill 2003; Robinson 2005; Bieler and Morton 2001). Once the synthetic reality of class relations has been established, the movements or forces (the two terms are used interchangeably here) that shape its contours must be concurrently conceptualised and analysed empirically. This is the fundamental precondition of any analysis of the national state, because it links generalising principles (worldwide labour relations) to contextual (local, national, or regional) specificities. The notion of movement provides a metaphor for apparent social forms as fluid, socially constructed, and undergoing constant changes. It also problematises the positivistic undertones of Marxism, which understands the class struggle not merely as essential social reality but all too often as directly observable also in the forms taken by the confrontation of capital and labour, perceived as a conflict between two rigid class blocs (Bieler and Morton 2003).

Yet using the terms force and movement interchangeably forces an engagement with the social movements literature, which in turn induces a clarification of the concepts under focus: what characterises a social movement/force? What are its attributes? What unites, or distinguishes it from more precisely defined (yet equally contentious) concepts such as class? The social movements literature conventionally confines movements (and civil society by implication) to subalternity and resistance (Tarrow 1998; Eckstein 2001; Tilly 2004).[97] Sidney Tarrow (1998: 3-4) thus defines a social movement as 'collective challenges by people with common purposes and solidarity in sustained interactions with elites, opponents and authorities'. He explicitly distinguishes social movements from political parties and interest groups. Tilly (2004: 3), on his side, understands social movements as vehicles for 'ordinary' people's participation in the public sphere (in reactive form, through public displays of resistance to specific policies, and in proactive form through specific demands). These public displays are manifested in various ways (a 'repertoire' of political action – including public meetings, solemn processions, rallies and demonstrations, campaigns, special-purpose associations and coalitions, vigils, petition drives, statements to the media, and pamphleteering campaigns).

These definitions beg the questions: resistance to what and whom, in the first place? Are owners of capital and dominant social forces (i.e. elites) to be considered as something that exists beyond the realm of social movements and hence of resistance – what do we make of struggles between elite forces, conspicuous in native elite resistance to colonialism and to restructuring, for instance? To reduce the notion of movement to subalternity implicitly confines administrative and business elites to a condition of permanence and stability. More importantly perhaps, conventional approaches to social movements beg the same question as Weberian pluralism: how do we distinguish between relevant and irrelevant movements? In other words, how can we operationalise the investigation of social movements/forces by avoiding a focus on transient or meaningless issues? Ontological pluralism forces an arbitrary choice of objects of study (social movements), but it also potentially negates the primacy of class relevant social forces in politics. A study underpinned by the substantive abstraction of class must distinguish between relevant and irrelevant movements in this chaotic multitude, in part because social analysis cannot rely on an aggregation of any one of these movements but rather on the social relations of production as a totality.

Studies of the rise of social movements in Latin America (Eckstein 2001) are problematic because the questions raised above are brushed aside to analyse any civil society conflict with, or resistance to the state (see Espasandín and Iglesias 2007 on Bolivia). Social movements in the literature are necessarily outside of and dominated by the state (García et al. 2001; Gutiérrez et al. 2002). Social elites, in contrast, *are* the government or, in other words, they instrumentalise the state. This involves a regression from the advances made in the theorisation of the state by implying the autonomous and static existence of state *and* elites. Yet substantive dialectics demonstrates that elite forces exist precisely by virtue of their exploitation of labour power (Burnham 2001).

For our research purpose, a broader and more comprehensive understanding of social movement is suggested here: social movements are *forces* in the sense that they are involved in politics, in power struggles to impose or defend collectively constructed interests and identities. They may or may not act within the confines of class discourses, and may or may not coalesce and find an organisational expression. Yet, for the purpose of measurement, the present study relates social *forces* coalesced in social *organisations*, and focuses on class-relevant organisations. The issue of conceptualisation and its adequate measurement is central to this definition, and affects every abstraction, from 'democracy' and 'democratisation' (O'Donnell 1992; Mainwaring 1992) to 'internationalisation'. After all, collective action is effective only as organised action and the notion of social forces has little meaning if it cannot be measured in one way or another (Adcock and Collier 2001). Identifying social organisations helps to identify forms of collective action and helps the empirical measurement of a social movement's attributes.[98] However, social organisations must also be *relevant* to a historical materialist ontology: this entails a focus on organisations that act within the framework of class struggle by consciously seeking to control or to dominate state institutions, or even to eliminate the state, in order to maintain a particular order or generate a new one (Tapia 2002b: 32-34). Social forces must be related to class because the relation between classes is the underlying mechanism defining the specific forms through which social forces emerge, are reproduced and eventually disappear. The state is constituted by and in turn shapes class-relevant social organisations. I will therefore focus my analysis on formal organisations driven by the explicit aim to sustain the capitalist structure, to change it, or to isolate social spaces from it – such as political parties, business organisations and trade unions.[99] The unstable and ever-shifting balance between labour and capital, is expressed through complex organisational manifestations, some formally attempting to control the executive and legislative agencies of the national state (political parties), others attempting to influence state policymaking informally, through economic and ideological pressure (lobbies, business associations, research institutes, trade unions, worker councils).

The following chapters empirically ground these propositions by analysing state reform in Bolivia since 1985. Chapter 2 will place these reforms in the historical context of the 1952 National Revolution, the first wave of state internationalisation from 1956 onwards, and the subsequent consolidation and unravelling of state capitalism.

I am aware that Open Marxist and neo-Gramscian approaches have preoccupied themselves essentially with theorising metropolitan capitalist rather than neo-colonial or post-colonial states – although Morton (2000) and Robinson (1996) did focus their analysis on Latin American elites and states, offering broadly instrumentalist interpretations. Yet the approach offered here, while taking into account the fact that the concrete forms taken by creditor and debtor, by pre-colonial and post-colonial, by metropolitan and peripheral states are not, and cannot be, the same, seeing the state as a strategic terrain of struggle opens up the possibility of studying the state in its multiple concrete historical and spatial forms by adapting conceptual attributes to empirical specificities, yet without necessarily discarding the concept itself (Collier and Mahon 1994).

The Bolivian case is thus used to reflect on the concept of the state and to show that understanding and empirically analysing the state in explicitly relational terms, as contradictory organisation of subjection, may enrich and consolidate historical materialist perspectives and political theory in general. However, beyond its reflection on how to best theorise the Bolivian state, the study seeks to answer this set of inter-related questions: are internationalisation, depoliticisation and liberal democratisation (polyarchy) valid explanatory concepts for the post-1985 transformations of the Bolivian state? Are these processes of institutional change correlated at all? If so, how and why has the Bolivian state been undergoing these changes? What is the relationship between domestic institutional transformations and broader processes of social change? How are we to understand capital globalisation, what social formations have constituted the latest era of capital globalisation, and how have they articulated their social interest and power? How have intra-elite and class struggles transformed and been shaped by the reform of the Bolivian state since 1985? In other words, how have transnational elite forces restructured the state, and how have domestically-oriented elite and labour forces reacted to and distorted, in turn, state restructuring?

The hypothesis underpinning the present study is that following the global debt crisis of the early 1980s, a transnational capitalist elite bloc expanded to incorporate a small elite faction in Bolivia. This bloc has attempted to liberalise the Bolivian state since the hyperinflationary crisis of 1985. I further hypothesise that the Bolivian state concurrently underwent mutually reinforcing processes of internationalisation, liberalisation, and depoliticisation of its polity from 1985 onwards. The transnational bloc struggled to entrench the hegemony of capital by grafting polyarchy and a business perspective onto the Bolivian social organism. Nevertheless, restructuring efforts were distorted and undermined by protracted resistance by domestically-oriented elites on the one hand (manufacturers, sugarcane owners and family-owned banks, professional politicians, including leaders of minor coalition partners in government, high-level civil servants and managers of state-owned enterprises); and subaltern social forces on the other (miners, teachers, civil servants and employees of state-owned enterprises, coca farmers [*cocaleros*], smallholding farmers and the urban unemployed and underemployed). Failure to achieve neoliberal hegemony regularly compelled the transnational bloc to reveal the coercive underpinning of capital domination. I will elaborate these propositions below.

The conceptual tools generated by neo-Gramscian and Open Marxist scholarship concurrently help to explain holistically the three-dimensional transformations of the Bolivian state.[100] Similar analyses of the processes under focus, or similar concepts are, as emphasised in the review of the literature, not altogether absent in mainstream and Critical research. The conceptual framework, research questions and hypothesis have driven my analysis of state transformations in Bolivia since 1985. Yet the elaboration of the concepts and questions themselves did not occur immaculately: it necessarily derived from evidence uncovered and analysed by other scholars adopting other theoretical perspectives. The very same legislation, government policies and discursive constructs can be interpreted in multiple ways (Cox 1983, 2002; Howarth 2000). However, these processes have been underpinned by an inadequate theory of the state (Zavaleta 1987; Tapia 2002a, Gutiérrez and García 2002; García 2006; Fernández 2003; Kohl and Farthing 2005), studied from theoretically implicit perspectives, or analysed separately

(Gustafson 2002, Dunkerley 1990, 2007 [1998]; Conaghan and Malloy 1995; Malloy 1991; Malloy and Gamarra 1988; Gamarra 1996).

Contribution and Limitations of Present Study

In light of the theoretical limitations of historical materialist approaches to the state, the provision of an empirically-based theoretical alternative constitutes not just a valid intellectual exercise but also becomes a political necessity. The present research therefore seeks to make a contribution to knowledge in political science, both theoretically and empirically. Its theoretical originality lies in its attempt at opening up historical materialist conceptualisations of the Bolivian state: the latter has in my view been inadequately theorised – whether by separating it ontologically from the market (i.e. statolatry) or by viewing it as a mere instrument of the ruling class. However, it is empirically original because certain historical processes affecting the Bolivian state, in particular transnational elite formation and the internationalisation of the state, have been neglected or obscured in the existing literature. The empirical grounding of the concept of a transnational historic bloc of elite social forces remains thin, especially in the Latin American context. This book offers an in-depth analysis of transnational elite formation in the Bolivian case. It deciphers the anatomy of capital in Bolivia and challenges fractionalism as theorised by the Amsterdam school of transnational historical materialism. It identifies key Bolivian agents of the transnational bloc and analyses *how* the transnational bloc expanded from its transatlantic heartland to restructure economic, ideological and institutional relations in the Bolivian space. The transnational bloc is not analysed as external to capitalist formations in Bolivia but rather as domestically rooted.

As emphasised previously, only two scholars (Baker 1999; Shields 2004) have attempted a critical reflection on Coxian concepts of state internationalisation or transnationalisation through in-depth empirical analysis. The logical and historical compatibility of the concepts of internationalisation, depoliticisation and polyarchy has not yet been established in relation to the Bolivian case; and a reflexive application of these concepts to the Bolivian case has not yet been attempted. The present study, based on primary documents, offers a more nuanced analysis of collaborative practice between transnational social forces through internationalisation than existing Critical studies (Fernández 2003; Kohl and Farthing 2005, 2009): institutional *coordination* via technical assistance on the one hand, and civil service reform on the other are analysed as processes integral to internationalisation. They unfortunately have all too often been neglected in existing scholarship on Bolivia.

However, Open Marxist and neo-Gramscian approaches have preoccupied themselves essentially with theorising metropolitan capitalist rather than neo-colonial or post-colonial states – except for Morton (2000) and Robinson (1996). The present historical materialist study aims to shift our object of study towards a state that offers lessons for Latin America and the developing world in general. Investigating the institutional transformations engendered by Bolivia's deepening integration into the world market helps to understand broader processes and issues derived from globalisation.

The period under study (1985-2009) is a valid subject of scholarly focus (as already identified in both problem-solving and critical analyses to restructuring) because it spans almost two decades of intensive and extensive economic, ideological and institutional reforms and resistance. The year 1985 was a watershed for Bolivia because it was a period of crisis-as-rupture that effectively marked the formal collapse of its pre-existing relations of production and domination (see chapter 2). Following eighteen years defined by liberalisation efforts, another national watershed occurred in 2003: the unravelling of restructuring under worldwide market constraints and systematic resistance by labour was accelerated through widespread upheavals met with heavy military repression, which eventually caused the demise of the Gonzalo Sánchez de Lozada administration and the *in extremis* escape of the President and his key ministers to Washington DC and Miami (García 2005; Hylton and Thomson 2007). The re-composition of labour in the late 1990s and its increasingly successful struggles against restructuring have involved a gradual retraction of some of the most unpalatable elements of liberalisation since 2000, and opened new opportunities and challenges for labour movements, especially under the Morales government (2005-2009).

The concept of *social crisis* at the core of historical materialist approaches (expressed in economic instability, the de-legitimisation of dominant discourses and state crises – i.e. fiscal and monetary imbalances), can arguably be validated more effectively by undertaking empirical analyses of the global periphery rather than more effectively ordered metropolitan social formations. Indeed, the contradictory mechanism (structural domination and resistance to it) underlying apparent forms, understood through substantive dialectical logic rather than through positive observation or hermeneutic analysis (Marx 2003; Bonefeld et al. 1991, 1992; Van der Pijl 2002), is more clearly manifest in the global periphery: domination takes rawer forms, while the relatively and, I would argue, increasingly developed class consciousness of Bolivia's oppressed social strata renders a historical analysis of the Bolivian state all the more useful if the aim of Critical research is to identify historical points of rupture in national (dis)order and to analyse the processes generating structural transformation (Cox 1981, 1983). Class struggle must not be reduced to the structural determination of all relations by a pure form of capitalism: to argue that all the problems of Bolivia are 'caused' by capitalism simplifies to the point of distortion its crisis-prone historical development (Marx 2003; Lora 1978; Zavaleta 1987). Class struggle is defined by, and in turn defines pre-existing relations of production, which are often located in the *longue durée* of world society and of its localised forms of domination (Braudel 1980; Cox 1996, 2002). Hence a constant process of primitive accumulation and its dialectical destruction of, and reconfiguration by, pre-existing production relations defines the *refracted* and *dialectical* globalisation of capital (Van der Pijl 2002; Bonefeld 2000).

For reasons of space and in order to retain a specific research focus, the study must unfortunately overlook some social relationships, constructed identities and interests that would ideally constitute a more accomplished and reflexive research agenda. I will have to disengage from controversies regarding complex issues of identity formation, production and territory, which invariably revolve around the dialectic between class, race and gender (Arnold and Spedding 2007).[101] What is it that constitutes the uniqueness of the Bolivian nation,[102] of indigenous formations and,[103] indeed, of the *Cambas* of the lowland region of Santa Cruz?[104] The issue of social constitution, prone to reification and to spurious analyses of the clash of Andean and Western civilizations (Huntington 2002[1996]; Mamani 2007), problematises the historical process of *mestizaje*.[105] It also underpins contemporary attempts to generate hegemonic discourses aiming at the articulation of new societal projects or refoundations in a period of crisis and disorder (Whitehead 2008).

The Bolivian case certainly forces a reflexive analysis of the ontological result and precondition of dialectical thinking: the class struggle. At the same time, empirical analyses of race and gender relations in Bolivia have generally been informed by a Weberian pluralist methodology. The necessary integration of race and gender relations into substantive dialectical logic requires a substantial reworking of historical materialism's synthetic abstraction, the result of which is constituted by but cannot be reduced to class relations. Rather than considering domination as an epiphenomenon of class, a more accomplished research project would see domination as both precondition and result of production relations. This negates in no way the achievements of historical materialism, but would help to overcome its scholarly limitations – which spring essentially from the consideration of class as the essence of historical order and change, and may consequently induce economic determinism. I am therefore aware of the present study's core shortcoming: its conscious silencing of gender and race relations as constitutive of and constituted by the state. Yet I do not regard it as inherently flawed, but incomplete and in need of further theoretical analysis and empirical study.

Book Structure

The concepts internationalisation, depoliticisation and polyarchy have been generated through two closely related but distinct strands of historical materialism: neo-Gramscian and Open Marxist perspectives (Bieler et al. 2006). I do not find any incoherence between these concepts, and indeed, Burnham's (2000) approach to depoliticisation, bears some resemblance to the concept of new constitutionalism coined by Stephen Gill (2000, 2003), which explains the legal mechanisms used by transnational capital to lock-in neoliberal policies. Through depoliticisation, state managers seek to detach themselves from the capital-labour dialectic by improving rationally the efficiency of state regulation. They strive to 'place the political character of decision-making at one remove' via the use of new 'governing strategies ... involving a shift from discretion to rules in economic policy, a reassertion of the boundaries separating "legitimate" political, economic and industrial activity and a fragmentation/devolution of decision-making in numerous arenas' (Burnham 2000: 10).

The research suggests accordingly that an approach conciliating *compatible* elements of these theoretical currents be adopted in the analysis of the post-1985 transformations of the Bolivian state. It is crucial at this point to emphasise that the present contribution integrates *specific* arguments made by scholars whose theoretical approaches are mutually inconsistent. This may induce accusations of eclecticism. Nevertheless, the point made here is that precisely because every approach (including my own) is incomplete and limited, it is valid to integrate *compatible* arguments into a specific, coherent whole. This allows me, in turn, to develop a distinctive argument in relation to the analysis of the Bolivian state.

The following chapter offers a contextualisation of Bolivia's post-1985 state reforms by focusing on the development of the state since the

National Revolution of 1952. In order to be consistent with Braudel's (1980) concept of *longue durée*, and to adequately identify continuity within structural and formal changes, a historical analysis of the rigidified Bolivian social space must start with Quechua and Aymara social structures, but also that of the Spanish Empire within the international European system, prior to their violent encounter and synthesis.[106] Nevertheless, there is no space to undertake such a macro-historical analysis of social change. All that can be attempted is a brief exposition of the *longue durée* of social relations in Bolivia, and of conjunctural conditions leading to the 1952 revolution. This is followed by a broad analysis of the early years of the revolution, the 1956 restructuring accompanying a first wave of state internationalisation, the post-1964 attempts at privatised accumulation under authoritarian regimes, and the long social crisis of 1978 to 1985.

The third, fourth and fifth chapters offer a reflexive analysis of interrelated processes of transnational elite formation and state transformations articulated in the research hypothesis. Chapter 3 focuses on the historical formation and expansion of a bloc of transnational elite forces beyond its Lockean transatlantic heartland (Van der Pijl 1998). It expounds briefly global economic, ideological and institutional restructuring since the early 1970s, including the crystallisation of a global strategy for restructuring in global MDIs since the profound debt crisis of the early 1980s. It then focuses on the anatomy of capital in Bolivia and the emergence of a small nucleus of transnationalised capitalist modernisers in the 1970s. Empirical evidence on portfolio diversification in Bolivia challenges the notion that divisions between industrial, commercial and banking capital are necessarily translated into contradictory interests and political strategies between business fractions (Poulantzas 1975; Van der Pijl 1984, 1998; Van Apeldoorn 2001; 2004; Overbeek 2004). It then analyses the process of transnational bloc expansion into Bolivia. This process unfolded primarily through official channels of development assistance, but also through the creation of new business organisational networks, International Finance Corporation (IFC) investments, and FDI in the mining, hydrocarbons, banking, and telecommunications sectors.

Chapter 4 builds on the preceding analysis of transnational bloc formation and of the first wave of internationalisation by analysing the second wave of the internationalisation of the Bolivian state since 1985. It uses the Bolivian case to reflect on the validity of Cox's original concept and Robinson's reformulation. I define internationalisation broadly, as the integration of the state into a consolidating global governance complex through elite collaboration and institutional coordination. Internationalisation alludes to the fact that supranational constraints upon national policymaking have become so severe that the national state may perhaps be perceived as a contradictory administrative component of MDIs. Yet paradoxically, supranational constraints are (inter)nationally constituted and are not simply caused by multilateral institutions but, at least in the case of Bolivia, were often generated by government policy decisions following the 1985 hyperinflationary crisis. Most often, decisions were negotiated and agreed upon through cooperative mechanisms. National policy decisions thus absorbed supranational constraints, adapted them to Bolivian conditions and used the authority of MDIs to implement accumulation strategies in the face of systematic resistance in the state (including in government) and in the street. The internationalisation of the state configured a systematic attempt, by transnational elite forces, to depoliticise economic management by shielding the Ministry of Finance, the BCB and regulatory agencies (SBEF, SIRESE) from attempts, by domestically-oriented elites and labour, to instrumentalise them.

I have refrained from focusing on the ways in which the US-sponsored war on drugs affected the internationalisation of the Bolivian state. It cannot be denied that internationalisation was affected by the existence of narco-trafficking capitalist forces, by the continued (if rescinding) financial dependence of the Bolivian state on USAID credits and preferential trade agreements with the US contingent on the DEA's repressive management of coca and cocaine circuits. However, I am focusing here primarily on the relationship between successive governments, the WB and the IMF, because we can witness a clear division of labour between these MDIs and USAID, and a geographical confinement of the latter's activities to the coca-producing Chapare region. The WB (1998b; 1999), when assessing how multilateral efforts to sustain restructuring were to be effected into the twenty-first century, explicitly left Banzer's 'Plan Dignidad' (which referred to a policy of 'coca zero') to be a domain of activities of USAID and, to a lesser extent, the European Commission. However, it is undeniable that the military repression of cocaleros with USAID technical, financial and military assistance fuelled the projection of the MAS's organisational power beyond the department of Cochabamba and its subsequent electoral success at the national level (see chapters 5 and 6). US intervention has also defined the trajectory of the Morales government by actively supporting an elite opposition movement on the defensive since the widespread rebellions of 2003.

Internationalisation precedes other institutional transformations (not in time but logically) in the sense that it legally locks-in liberal principles such as the protection of private property and the generalisation of privatised forms of capital accumulation. It generates a virtuous process of capital globalisation by bolstering liberal hegemony and transnational capital centralisation through institutional integration: by deepening the institutional presence of a transnational bloc of experts and technocrats unified by liberal concepts of control (Overbeek 2004), internationalisation enhanced the technical know-how and legal conditions facilitating the attraction of FDI, joint ventures and organisational synergies; economic integration thereby generated (however loose and embryonic) new transnational interconnections and attracted denationalised elite fractions into the transnational bloc. Transnational elite linkages in turn socially consolidated the integration of national state agencies into the global governance complex through supranational legal covenants and accords underpinned by hegemonic, cosmopolitan liberal norms. Therefore, internationalisation generated new and increasingly powerful constraints on national policymaking. These supranational 'legal padlocks' (*BBC News* 2006b), have effectively neutralised the revolutionary changes desired by prominent members of the current Morales government. The logical precedence of an institutional process that has been broadly ignored in the literature warrants greater empirical detail than polyarchy in the present study.

For reasons of space and despite their relevance, the present study does not analyse relations between labour and elite movements, Non-Governmental Organisations (NGOs) and bilateral aid agencies in Bolivia but focuses primarily on the WB, the IMF, and in the second and sixth chapters, on USAID. Analysing the integration of Bolivia into regional organisations such as the Andean Pact and Mercosur – as well as the particularly unpopular US pressure for the creation of a hemispheric Free Trade Area (*Area de Libre Comercio de las Americas*) is also beyond the scope of this study. The focus on the articulation between national state agencies, macro-regional and global organisations, civil NGOs and bilateral aid agencies should be the subject of further research.

Chapter 5 analyses the liberal democratisation of the state, defined by the concept of polyarchy. *Polyarchy* is the 'liberal democratic' regulatory model, 'in which a small group actually rules and mass participation in decision-making is confined to leadership choice in elections carefully managed by competing elites' (Robinson 1996: 49). The concept was first coined by Robert Dahl (1971) and incorporated by Robinson (1996) in his neo-Gramscian analysis of US democracy promotion in Latin America. It purposely sustains the apparent separation of political and economic relations under a hegemonic liberal democratic form, thereby maintaining elite fractions organised in political parties in control of the national state apparatus.

The consolidation or viability of polyarchy has, not surprisingly, been the institutional transformation most widely investigated in specialist circles. Indeed, such national changes are easily linkable to a Ricardian approach to political economy in which the international system is an aggregate of essentially autonomous national economies (and hence institutions). Going beyond and overcoming the confines of national institutions (via the concept of internationalisation) constitutes a more tentative and dangerous path to tread. This research, however, explicitly links democratisation processes to global institutional change: it was an integral element of internationalisation and depoliticisation strategies. Polyarchy was sustained essentially through electoral legislation, coalition building and ideological convergence between the three dominant parties of the era under study. Yet polyarchy did not achieve its legitimising function. Organised violence – or the threat of violence – remained the primary means of generating order. However, the social costs of restructuring efforts – on domestically-oriented elites as well as labour, *within and beyond* the state – and the gradual reorganisation of the latter, conditioned an intensification of social struggles in the late 1990s. The disjuncture between the emergent liberal state form and the socio-economic content defining the Bolivian population generated explosive social contradictions, and opened new 'revolutionary horizons' for labour movements in the early twenty-first century (Hylton and Thomson 2007).

Chapter 6 analyses how the Morales government closed these revolutionary horizons over four eventful years of struggle. The Morales administration has certainly opened new historical possibilities for the Bolivian state by organising a Constituent Assembly, promoting land reform and re-nationalising corporations in the hydrocarbons, mining and telecommunications sectors (Dunkerley 2007; Hylton and Thomson 2007; Do Alto and Stefanoni 2008; Webber 2008). The Morales-sponsored reforms have generated vigorous and sometimes violent resistance by Bolivian elites, both within and beyond the state, spearheaded by business organisations, regional Civic Committees, and conservative political parties (Eaton 2007). Bastions of the opposition in the state – the senate, the prefectures, municipalities – have hindered and redirected social change (Do Alto and Stefanoni 2008). How have broader social struggles transformed the Bolivian state in the past three years, and how has the penetration of government agencies by indigenist, nationalist and socialist forces represented by or allied with the MAS affected the institutional balance of social forces in Bolivia?

How has, in turn, the MAS leadership been transformed by its newfound capacity to organise subjection in Bolivia? Contemporary state transformations validate a conceptualisation of the state as a contradictory organisation of subjection, and internationalisation, depoliticisation and polyarchy have been entrenched despite (or perhaps because of) the Morales administration.

These domestic developments – traversed by transnational elite collaboration with domestic forces to oppose MAS-sponsored reforms – should be placed within worldwide and macro-regional processes of social and institutional change. The election of Evo Morales in 2005 formed part of a hemispheric rejection of neoliberalism and US imperialism. It has therefore significantly changed relationships between the Bolivian state, the US, and MDIs. How have the US government, the multilateral donor community and transnational capital reacted to Morales's investiture and his reform project? How has, in turn, the Morales government managed its relationship with transnational elite forces? How have alternative macro-regionalist projects such as the *Alternativa Boliviariana Para los Pueblos de Nuestra America* (ALBA) transformed Bolivia's foreign relations? Has the internationalisation of the Bolivian state been entrenched, and if so, how are emerging multilateral lines of conflict transforming its form?[107]

The Bolivian electorate ratified the new Constitution by referendum on the 25th of January 2009, and Evo Morales was re-elected with an astounding 64.22 percent of the vote in the December 2009 general elections (*Corte Nacional Electoral* [CNE] 2009). To use the Gramscian terminology imbuing the language of Vice-President García Linera, the ratification of the new Constitution closed a cycle of both war 'of position' and 'of movement'.[108] The firm control of both congressional houses by the MAS following the 2009 elections, buttressed by the indubitable popularity of Morales on the one hand and by unprecedented capital accumulation on the other, has temporarily stabilised the Bolivian space and crystallised a (transient) hegemonic order organised by the MAS.

I will refrain from the attractive, yet self-defeating temptation to predict future events – for instance, how the institutional changes mandated by the Constitution will affect production relations, in particular in rural areas of the *Oriente*; how the intensifying regionalisation of commerce and growing Chinese and Indian demand for Bolivia's commodities (including lithium for the car industry) are changing the geo-economics of Bolivia's production relations; whether Evo Morales will be re-elected, and how the worldwide economic crisis will affect, in the longer term, the nationalisation project of Morales and the government's relationship with MDIs. Prediction is a particularly redundant exercise in a social space defined by recurrent political crisis, instability and erratic historical directions. One can only discern past directions as a way to understand present forms. I will conclude, however, that in view of the fact that the Morales government has not erased capitalist social forms, and that the Bolivian space remains integrated into worldwide market relations, incessant elite resistance and class struggles, including within state institutions will most likely continue to imperil the Morales government.

Notes

[1] 'Crisis' was an expression of democratisation pressures, capital flight and military coups – compounded by declining terms of trade and the drying up of external financing. By mid-1985, public sector debt accounted for 78 percent of total debt ($3.2 billion; 93 percent of GDP), including $650 million for the nine major state-owned companies, and $115 million for state-owned banks. The state capitalist model of development (whereby 70 percent of GDP was generated by state corporations) was collapsing under the weight of its contradictions. Over five consecutive years, GDP had declined by 16 percent, GDP per capita by 27 percent, unemployment had increased from 10 percent to 18 percent, and tax revenues had declined from 9 to 3 percent of GDP. Real wages had already begun to plummet (32 percent between 1978 and 1982); thus, following its election in 1982 and in an attempt to satisfy labour demands, President Siles Zuazo's government intensified the balance of payments crisis by increasing state employment (from 201,000 in 1981 to 245,000 in 1985), by offering bonuses to state employees and by indexing wages to inflation. The latter policy proved unmanageable with the acceleration of inflationary pressures (IMF 1986a: 16, 18, 78; WB 1986: 5).

[2] Salient examples of the vast literature on democratic transition/consolidation/viability include Mayorga (1988, 1999); Lavaud (1990, 1991); Morales and Sachs (1990); Mayorga et al. (1991); Mansilla (1994); Campero Prudencio et al. (1999); Grindle (1999); Van Cott (2000); Crabtree, Whitehead et al. (2002); Klein (2003); Grindle, Domingo et al. (2003).

[3] See Huntington (2002 [1996]); Gustafson (2002); Kohl (2003); Mamani (2005, 2007). The Kollasuyu refers to the Andean territories controlled by the Aymara nations before being conquered by the Inca Empire in the early sixteenth century. It is now incorporated in Northern Chile, Argentina, Peru and Bolivia.

[4] For adequate descriptions of political conflicts between the downfall of the Sánchez de Lozada government in October 2003 and the general elections called in urgency in 2005, see Kohl and Farthing (2005); Crabtree (2005) Hylton and Thomson (2007); Petras and Veltmeyer (2006); Do Alto and Stefanoni (2006, 2008). This period of rebellion (Skocpol 1979: 4) was characterised by the increasing assertiveness of subaltern social forces congealing around nationalist and indigenist discourses (road blockades and

marches on the Presidential *Palacio Quemado* in La Paz); the entrenchment of white elites in the Prefectures of the so-called *Media Luna* (lowland provinces) elected for the first time in Bolivian history in 2005, and in the lower and upper houses of Parliament; and the passivity of the Carlos Mesa government. This period of acute crisis witnessed a territorialisation of indigenist and white supremacist discourses. These conditions accentuated capital flight and unemployment, which was partially offset by rising (from 2004 onwards) world market prices for Bolivia's exports.

[5] The Bolivian electorate ratified the new Constitution by referendum on the 25th of January 2009, and new Presidential elections are to take place in December of this year (*Corte Nacional Electoral* [CNE] 2009).

[6] Elite is understood here as dominant social force, rather than ruling class *per se*. This opens the space to conceptualise transnational social formation while acknowledging that the elite does not necessarily 'rule', in the sense of 'managing' social relations (see Block 1977b; Pijl 1998; Hay 1999).

[7] See Stefanoni and Do Alto (2006); García (2006); Stefanoni (2005); Dunkerley (2007: 25-26); Williams (2008: 168).

[8] See Webber (2005; 2006; 2008); Petras (2006; 2008); Petras and Veltmeyer (2005); Spence and Shenkin (2006).

[9] See O'Donnell and Schmitter (1986); O'Donnell (1992); Valenzuela (1992); Mainwaring (1992).

[10] Theoretical and empirical analyses of state restructuring in Bolivia may be broadly categorised as 'traditional' ('mainstream' or 'problem-solving') and 'critical' (Horkheimer 1982; Cox 1981, 1983). Cox defines a problem-solving theory as one that 'takes the world as it finds it, with the prevailing social and power relationships and the institutions in which they are organised, as the given framework for action. The general aim of problem solving is to make these relationships and institutions work smoothly by dealing effectively with particular sources of trouble' (Cox 1981: 88). Cox's definition of problem-solving is congruent with Huntington's (1999) understanding of conservatism: 'classic conservatism is not directed to realizing a particular vision of the good society. It embodies instead a general attitude toward order and change, defending the former and constraining the latter. The goal of conservatism is to "preserve, protect and defend" existing social, economic and political culture and institutions. Conservatives, however, may well support modest changes in the existing order so as to maintain it against revolutionary change or collapse'. The purpose of problem-solving theories is to stabilise existing relations of domination by legitimising the established social order.

The purpose of Critical theories is accordingly to identify the particular interests and values that give birth to and orient a theory (Cox 1981: 88), and to explain crisis as open ended struggle, not only as peril or menace but as *opportunity* to alleviate or overcome relations of domination (Bonefeld and Psychopedis 1991). I place the present study firmly in the Critical theoretical movement.

[11] See Malloy and Gamarra (1988); Mayorga (1988); Mayorga et al. (1991); Gamarra (1994); Conaghan (1992); O'Donnell (1992); Crabtree, Whitehead et al. (2002).

[12] See O'Donnell (1992); Lavaud (1990, 1991); Grindle, Domingo et al. (2003).

[13] See Malloy and Gamarra (1987, 1988); Domingo (1993); Gamarra (1994, 1996); Campero et al. (1999); Klein (2003).

[14] See Morales and Sachs (1990). Jeffrey Sachs (1999: 24; author's translation), for example, contends that Latin America's dependency on natural resources as a 'symptom of more profound traits. To a significant measure, Latin America's dependence reflects its geography and natural riches. Yet it also reflects its principal failure: the insufficient development of its human resources, caused primarily by problems in education and democratisation'.

[15] See Mansilla (1994); Gamarra (1996); Lavaud (2007).

[16] See Roca (1980; 2008).

[17] Key proponents of this view include García et al. (2000, 2002); Patzi (2001); Fernández (2003); Kohl and Farthing (2005); Petras and Veltmeyer (2005); Mamani (2005, 2007); Webber (2008).

[18] See Mayorga (1991); Gamarra (1991, 1994, 1996, 2002); Morales (1994); O'Donnell (1992, 1993); Domingo (1993); Van Cott (2000); Crabtree, Whitehead et al. (2002), among numerous others.

[19] In contrast to realist understandings of 'hegemony' as dominance in inter-state relations, neo-Gramscian approaches define hegemony as the ideological power of ruling over subaltern classes within a given national social formation but also globally, which generates and sustains social cohesion and order (Gramsci 1971: 169-170; Van der Pijl 1998: 51).

[20] For discussions of democratic transition and gobernability, see Toranzo (1991); Mayorga (1991); Lazarte (1993); Malloy and Gamarra (1988).

[21] See for instance Mayorga (1988; 1999).

[22] Discussions of democratic consolidation are developed in Domingo (1993); Conaghan (1992); Gamarra (1996); Van Cott (2000).

[23] See Whitehead (2002a) on concepts of consolidation and viability in relation to democracy.

[24] See Klein (2003) and Grindle (1999).

[25] This argument has been made by Morales and Sachs (1990); Toranzo (1991); O'Donnell (1992); Valenzuela (1992); Morales (1994); Crabtree et al. (2002); Van Cott (2000).

[26] See Mayorga (1991, 1993); Domingo (1993); Grindle (1999); Whitehead (2002a); Toranzo (1999); Berthin (1999); Van Cott (2000).

[27] See Sachs (1990, 1999); Toranzo (1991); Mayorga (1991); Lavaud (1991); Faguet (2002, 2003); Klein (2003); Crabtree et al. (2002); Grindle (1999); Grindle, Domingo et al. (2003); Van Cott (2000).

[28] These limitations have been discussed before endorsing minimalist definitions by Domingo (1993); Gamarra (1994, 1996); Whitehead (2002a); Van Cott (2000); Grindle (1999). On issues of conceptualisation and measurement, see Adcock and Collier (2001); Brady and Collier (2004).

[29] Valenzuela (1992: 60) justifies his preference for minimalist definitions with the questionable teleological contention, well critiqued by Whitehead (2002), that: 'If such and other assorted ills can be found in democracies whose "consolidation" is not at issue, situations that have recently made the transit out of authoritarian rule should hardly be held to strict and comprehensive standards either. Otherwise no democratic regime is truly "consolidated" for the lack of an ingredient deemed essential, and it is impossible to assign a reasonable closure to the second transition process'.

[30] O'Donnell (1992: 18) explicitly sees the consolidation of a democratic 'regime' as one limited to 'political democracy (or polyarchy)', because 'the conquest of political democracy is worthwhile in its own right; and second, because the distinction between political democracy on the one hand and socioeconomic and cultural democratization on the other is precisely what allows us to explore the various relationships between the two'. Political, cultural and socio-economic spheres are therefore seen as ontologically distinct, driven by mutually exclusive internal mechanisms, which may or may not enter in 'various relationships'. However, O'Donnell is adamant that the consolidation of polyarchy in the 'political sphere' is a condition sufficient for a definition of society as 'democratic'. In other words, polyarchy iself is to be analysed as independent variable. This tendency to 'emphasise the autonomy of political factors', and to understand democracy/polyarchy as a 'product of political elites and arrangements' has accompanied the revival of institutionalism in Latin American Studies in the 1980s and 1990s (Mainwaring 1992: 326). Malloy and Gamarra (1987, 1988) Seligson (1987) and Mainwaring (1992: 327) helped to break the 'autonomy' of politics by striking a 'balance between socioeconomic and political factors'. Yet they continue to see these 'factors' as externally related, thereby keeping a veil on underlying social mechanisms that dialectics (Marx 2003; Bonefeld et al. 1991, 1992; Overbeek 2000) and the Critical Realism of Roy Baskhar (Archer 1998) have helped to reveal.

[31] These problems affect Critical theory. Burnham (1991) and Bonefeld (2000) have criticised effectively the pluralist tendencies of Coxian IPE, expressed in the relative autonomy of economic, ideological and institutional 'structures'. Cox contends that 'the method of historical structures is one of representing … *limited totalities*. The historical structure does not represent the whole world but rather a *particular sphere* of human activity in its historically located totality' (Cox 1996[1981]: 100; emphasis added). These heuristic structures enjoy no 'predetermined hierarchy of relationships', being essentially autonomous (Cox 1996: 100). However, Cox suggests that 'the question of which way the lines of force run is always a historical question to be answered by a study of the particular case' (Cox 1996: 98). The exaggerated focus of Coxian IPE on the ideological structure as an independent variable (as 'limited totality') has resulted in two interrelated logical problems: the negation of the dialectical logic through which the synthetic concept (the class struggle) is abstractly reached and, under the weight of a sophisticated base-superstructure metaphor (see Cox's definition of civilizations 2002), the unwitting suppression of history as 'contradiction-in-movement'.

[32] See for example García (2001, 2004); García et al. (2000, 2002); Assies and Salman (2003); Kohl and Farthing (2005); McNeish (2006); Hylton and Thomson (2007); Dunkerley (2007, 2007[1998]); Webber (2008).

[33] Democracy in its strictest sense refers to rule by the *demos (*the people), a horizontal form of policymaking involving every single member of society, equal in rights, power, and access to resources. Questions regarding the viability and desirability of this heuristic model of governance will be avoided here. I rather focus on why and how liberal democratisation developed and unravelled in the period under study.

[34] Instrumentalism, as will be elaborated subsequently, conceptualises the state as permeable, and immediately responsive to the interests of the ruling-class (Lenin (1965[1917]; Miliband 1969; Mandel 1975).

[35] An instrumentalist understanding of the state pervades the work of Lora (1977); Grebe (1983); Zavaleta (1983, 1987); Rivera (1983, 1984); García (2001, 2006); Gustafson (2002); Tapia (2002a, 2002b); Kohl (2003); Kohl and Farthing (2005); McNeish (2006); Hylton and Thomson (2007). This is the implicit underpinning of Gray's (2007, 2008) line of analysis of a 'weak state' facing a 'strong society', combined with the proposition that the Bolivian state is a 'state with holes'. He writes: 'the historical form taken by a "weak state/strong society" trajectory in Bolivia helps to explain a number of features that puzzle social and political analysts and policymakers' (Gray 2008: 109). He neglects to conceptualise either 'weakness' or 'strength', and indeed the 'state' and 'society', thereby resting his analysis of 'various forms of institutional pluralism that accommodate social pressures from above, and a society that takes on many features of de facto statehood from below' on rather shaky grounds. He implicitly conflates the state ('from above') with 'government', 'elite' and 'ruling-class', and quite explicitly did so at a seminar organised in Oxford University in June 2007, in which he asserted that Evo Morales and the *cocalero* association that he presides constitute a new 'elite'. Gray under-theorises the relationship between the state, capital and labour, and thereby misjudges where structural power lies by equating (claims to) authority with power. Crucially, his 2008 article fails to analyse the state as a social relation.

The UNPD-sponsored conceptualisation and empirical analysis of the Bolivian state is far more interesting, and departs from conventional definitions as the 'monopoly of the legitimate use of force' (UNDP 2007: 92), by viewing it 'as a labyrinth of unresolved tensions – struggles and divisions related to the colonial legacy, the property of national resources, regional diversity and the intercultural character of democracy' (UNDP 2007: 83). This fruitful beginning lapses in a view of the 'state with holes' that obscures relations of exploitation internal to the state.

[36] Exceptions include Dunkerley (1984, 1990, 2007), Malloy and Gamarra (1987) and Conaghan and Malloy (1995). It must be emphasised that contemporary institutional struggles under the Morales administration are rendering intra-state contradictions so apparent that they perhaps compel a reconsideration of classical conceptualisations of the state.

[37] Grindle (1999: XI) thus asks the question: 'why would politicians be experimenting with changes that would diminish their control over political resources?', which misconceives the essence of power by reducing it to the control of the central agencies of the national state. She accordingly answers: 'for the dilution of power' (Grindle 1999: 3).

[38] See Van Cott (1994, 2000); Albó (1994, 1999); Gray (2001); Patzi (1999); García (2001, 2002, 2006); Gustafson (2002); Kohl (2003); Kohl and Farthing (2005).

[39] Worries of some Bolivian commentators (Blanes 1991) that decentralisation may have resulted in greater wealth discrepancies between municipalities are alleviated by Faguet's (2002: 1) conclusions: 'In Bolivia, decentralization made government more responsive by re-directing public investment to areas of greatest need. Investment shifted from economic

production and infrastructure to social services and human capital formation, and resources were rebalanced in favour of poorer districts'. Klein (2003) buttresses this point by contending that these reforms have led to the 'creation of a multiethnic democracy'.

[40] Authoritative accounts, from various perspectives, include Crabtree (1987); Dunkerley (1990, 2007); Morales and Sachs (1990); Conaghan (1990); Malloy (1991); Conaghan and Malloy (1995); Gamarra (1994); Hollis Peirce et al. (1997); Klein (2003); Kohl and Farthing (2005).

[41] 'Bolivia is one of the best performing IDA portfolios' (WB 1998b: i).

[42] Williamson (1990) coined the term 'Washington consensus', referring to the policy measures that the institutions of the US state (both the 'political' and 'technocratic' Washington) agreed should constitute the framework of adjustment programs in the global periphery.

[43] Stabilisation refers to 'policies (generally relying on demand management) to achieve sustainable fiscal and balance of payments current account deficits and to reduce the rate of price inflation' (WB 1990a: 8). However, structural adjustment consists in the reform of institutions involved in micro-(taxes and tariffs) and macro-economic (fiscal policy) management (WB 1990a: 8).

Neoliberal restructuring involved ten key policy instruments, according to one of its key ideologues (Williamson 1990): fiscal discipline, necessitating the reduction of public expenditure, especially for welfare (which should focus on primary education and preventive medicine), and the scrapping of subsidies; tax reform that broadens the tax base and moderates marginal tax rates; the privatisation of unprofitable state-owned corporations and the deregulation of the domestic market are directly related to fiscal discipline and are assumed to increase industrial efficiency, while promoting competition and reducing corruption. With regards to monetary policy, interest rates should be positive but moderate (in order to encourage growth) and determined by the market; the exchange rate should also be market-determined, and sufficiently competitive for export-led growth. Trade policy should strive to eliminate any barrier to trade (if protectionism there is, it should only involve tariffs for infant and transitory industries and be ridden of import licensing), in order to facilitate FDI. To buttress all these measure, the state should establish clear property rights and secure private property.

[44] RDCs were established between 1967 and 1971 to decentralise investment projects. Financed with royalties from regional commodities such as oil, gas and minerals (or the Treasury for Beni and Pando), and authorised to seek external financing, RDCs were primarily used by the Banzer government to accelerate the development of Santa Cruz relative to the rest of the country (Barragán 2008). In the 1970s and 1980s, Santa Cruz's RDC thus administered a budget between 7 and 12 times greater than that of La Paz, the second RDC in terms of resources (Lavaud 1991: 202), inducing Roca (1980) to argue that 'the RDCs have institutionalised regionalist practices'.

[45] However, various elements of what is considered as second-generation reforms, such as privatisation and administrative decentralisation, were already being addressed by the economic teams of the ADN and MNR political parties, and debated with the WB and the IMF from 1985 onwards (WB 1986, 1989a, 1989b, 1989c).

[46] Nkrumah (1965), who with Che Guevara coined and theorised neo-colonialism, offered a valuable definition of the concept, which however illustrates its economic determinism, or base-superstructure underpinning: 'The essence of neo-colonialism is that the State which is subject to it is, in theory, independent and has all the outward trappings of international sovereignty. In reality its economic system and thus its political policy is directed from outside'.

[47] Imperialism is conventionally defined in two ways, which are not inconsistent but rather perceived to have historically sustained each other: 1) imperialism as an over-accumulative need by metropolitan capital to appropriate resources and labour on its periphery – through portfolio capital or, increasingly, FDI (Cox 1981 1987) – in order to expand the market for commodities produced in the metropolis and thereby alleviate structural crises of over-production; and 2) as political-military domination in international relations. See Kemp (1972); Clarke (2001); Halliday (2002); Sutcliffe (2002).

[48] In her defence, at the time of her research, the vast majority of relevant WB and IMF documents were classified and very difficult to access.

[49] This is particularly manifest in the work of Paul Cammack (2003, 2006), who presents the WB, IMF and OECD as institutions achieving relative autonomy and utterly devoid of internal tensions over accumulation strategies (Taylor 2005).

[50] The WB was assigned 'primary responsibility for the composition and appropriateness of development programs and project evaluation, including development priority', while the IMF dealt with exchange rates, adjustment of payments imbalances, and the evaluation of countries' stabilisation programmes (IMF/WB 2001: 18-19).

[51] The creation of the Structural Adjustment Facility in 1986 and of the Enhanced Structural Adjustment Facility in 1987 by the IMF 'required borrowers to negotiate medium-term structural reform programs with the IMF. While conditionality was similar in many respects to that of the EFF, these facilities called for a more formal coordination with the Bank than in the past and required explicit procedures to avoid cross-conditionality. The principal innovation was the introduction of the Policy Framework Paper (PFP), a document to be negotiated by the borrowing country with the staffs of both the Fund and the Bank and approved by the Executive Directors of both institutions' (IMF/WB 2001: 20).

[52] The 1989 Concordat reiterated the 1966 memorandum on WB-IMF collaboration and clarified their respective responsibilities. The IMF was to manage 'public sector spending and revenues, aggregate wage and price policies, money and credit, interest rates and the exchange rate', and the WB dealt with 'development strategies; sector project investments, structural adjustment programs; policies which deal with the efficient allocation of resources in both public and private sectors; priorities in government expenditures; reforms of administrative systems, production, trade and financial sectors; the restructuring of public sector enterprises and sector policies' (IMF/WB 2001: 20-21).

[53] For instance, the WB's creation of Structural Adjustment Loans (SALs) for medium-term fiscal support in 1980 encroached on the IMF's balance of payment turf and required reviews of collaborative practices. Tensions did arise

between the WB and IMF, as overemphasised by Stiglitz. 'While most disputes were resolved before they disrupted the provision of assistance to countries, the willingness of staff in the field to defer to each other in assessing countries' balance of payments or development requirements was not uniformly high' (IMF/WB 2001: 19-20).

[54] In their latest work, Kohl and Farthing (2009: 66) reiterate previous assertions that the fiscal dependence of the Bolivian state on IMF and WB assistance 'ensured an almost slavish following of the institutions' prescriptions in order to guarantee a steady flow of funds'.

[55] Despite useful empirical evidence, these authors' analysis of 'international influences' is based essentially on tertiary (and some secondary) sources.

[56] Potential and real contradictions between the US government and transnational elite forces are all too easily brushed aside in the analysis of Bolivian dependency. It is also notable that transnational corporations (TNCs), transnational elites and MDIs are presented as overbearing entities, external to domestic political relations.

[57] Influenced by the work of Friedrich von Hayek (1944) and Milton Friedman (1962), monetarism understands inflation as an imbalance between the supply and demand of money – the former being larger than the latter. By controlling the money supply, Central Banks regulate inflationary pressures, but also consumption and investment patterns.

[58] For sophisticated analyses of commodification and primitive accumulation, see Bonefeld (1991, 2000) and Van der Pijl (1998). Primitive accumulation refers to a process whereby labour power is turned into a commodity among other items required for the production and circulation of commodities on the world market. This process is interlinked with the emergence and increasing social power of a capitalist class.

[59] See Marx (2003); Holloway (1995); Van der Pijl (1998); Overbeek (2000, 2004); Van Apeldoorn (2004); Bonefeld (1991, 2000).

[60] See Harvey (2003); Lacher (2002, 2003); Lacher and Teschke (2007).

[61] On the transnational essence of the British (Lockean) heartland of capital, see Van der Pijl (1998).

[62] See Frank (1975; 1978); Wallerstein (1989[1974], 2000); Boswell and Chase-Dunn (2000). With reference to the Bolivian formation, see Vandycke (1987); Espasandín and Iglesias (2007); Gray (2008).

[63] Espasandín and Iglesias (2007: 43) brush aside rather swiftly Laclau's (1971) critique of the conflation, by Wallerstein and Frank, of *world market* (or world economy articulating various forms of labour relations, primarily through merchant capital) and *global capital* (founded on wage/free labour and industrial production). They justify their contention that 'one cannot force a definition of capitalism conditioned by the existence of wage labour' by referring to Wallerstein's (1989[1974]: 99-101) notion of agrarian capitalism: 'in the era of agrarian capitalism wage labour is only one form of recruitment among others' (Espasandín and Iglesias 2007: 44; author's translation). This induces them to reiterate Boswell and Chase-Dunn's (2000) three attributes of global production relations: capitalism, an inter-state system showing continuity as 'units of administrative ordering at least since 1648', and institutional mechanisms of surplus appropriation by the core. See Lacher (2002, 2003) and

Lacher and Teschke (2007) for convincing rebuttals of images of the (capitalist) world market *as* an inter-state system arising (out of what?) in 1648 with the Westphalia Treaty.

[64] See Marx (2003: 'Capital Vol.1'); Hobsbawm (1995); Meiksins Wood (1981, 2002a); Van der Pijl (1998).

[65] See Jameson (1998); Augelli and Murphy (1988). Constant diatribes against US supremacy and its imperial, worldwide infliction of neoliberal reforms and plunder of Latin America through FDI are endemic in publications such as *Le Monde Diplomatique* and pamphlets by ATTAC in France, *Open Democracy* in the UK, *The Nation* and *Znet* in the US. In critical academic approaches, this argument has been made by Petras and Veltmeyer (2002), Chomsky (2003), Amin (2004), Bellamy Foster (2006) and Wallerstein (2006), among numerous others.

[66] See the earlier work of Robinson (1996), Augelli and Murphy (1988).

[67] For critiques of the dichotomy between structure and agency, see Jessop (1990); Bonefeld and Psychopedis (1991); Bieler and Morton (2001, 2003).

[68] See Kohl and Farthing (2005); Climenhage (1999); Fernández (2003); Hirst and Thompson (1995); Strange (1996); Krasner (1999, 2001).

[69] See Lora (1977); Zavaleta (1983, 1987); Grebe (1983, 2002); García et al. (2000, 2001, 2004, 2005); Tapia (2002a).

[70] Salient examples include Orlove (1989); Orlove and Foley (1989); Foley and Lambert (1989); Parkerson (1989).

[71] See Assies and Salman (2003); Salman (2006, 2007); McNeish (2006).

[72] See the studies of Fernández (2003); Kohl and Farthing (2005); Webber (2008); De La Cueva (1983).

[73] A close reading of the *Prison Notebooks* arguably warrants an understanding of Gramsci's methodological starting-point as national, despite his emphasis on the need for an 'international perspective' (Gramsci 1971: 176-177; 240). Gramsci thereby conceptualises the international system as the sum of nation-state entities and their unrelated (or at best analogically posited) political processes. In contrast to this atomistic position, holism (inherent to the dialectical method) asserts that the social whole cannot be understood by the sum of its components but must originally be interpreted as a conceptual totality (Marx 2003, 'The Gundrisse': 386; Burnham 1994: 227).See for instance Gramsci's (1971) almost exclusive focus on Italian relations of production, Augelli and Murphy's (1988) focus on US imperialism in the Third World, and Robinson's (1996) analysis of US promotion of polyarchy in Latin America. Gill (1993) has rightly identified the limitations of Gramscian thought, reproduced in nationalistic Latin American scholarship. For a salient Bolivian example, see Zavaleta (1987).

[74] See Cox (1981, 1987); Gill (1993, 2003); Van der Pijl (1998); Van Apeldoorn (2004); Overbeek (2000, 2004).

[75] See for example Crabtree (1987); Dunkerley (1984, 1990); Conaghan and Malloy (1995); Kohl and Farthing (2005).

[76] For notable exceptions, which focus more specifically on business-state relations, see Malloy and Gamarra 1988; Conaghan 1990, Dunkerley 1990; Malloy 1991; Conaghan and Malloy 1995.

[77] Strange's (1996) approach has been rejected by historical materialist scholars because it misconceives state restructuring and the reconfiguration of

its regulatory capacities – which have tended to improve administrative efficiency and often augment its institutional density – as retreat or deregulation (Burnham 2000; Cerny 2005).

[78] Evo Morales himself has referred to the implementation of an 'agrarian revolution' and to his socialist goal of 'changing the structure of the state', in http://www.zmag.org/. Accessed 21 November 2007.

[79] They furthermore induce diatribes against neoliberalism leading to the reformist prescription that 'a reinvented state will be faced with the challenge of simultaneously maintaining legitimacy in the eyes of its citizens while also creating and maintaining the conditions for markets to operate' (Kohl and Farthing 2005: 5).

[80] Indeed, it has long been argued that what had been defined as Soviet state-socialism is essentially a capitalist endeavour by a bureaucratic class appropriating the product of labour (Cliff 1955, available at http://www.marxists.org/. Accessed 21 September 2007).

[81] See Gramsci (1971); Bonefeld et al. (1991); Gunn (1992); Burnham (2001, 2002); Overbeek (2000); Bieler and Morton (2003).

[82] Cox's (1981: 95) exemplary definition of dialectics is worth quoting: 'At the level of logic, it means a dialogue seeking truth through the exploration of contradictions. One aspect of this is the continual confrontation of concepts with the reality they are supposed to represent and their adjustment to this reality as it continually changes. Another aspect, which is part of the method of adjusting concepts, is the knowledge that each assertion concerning reality contains implicitly its opposite and that both assertion and opposite are not mutually exclusive but share some measure of the truth sought, a truth, moreover, that is always in motion, never to be encapsulated in some definitive form. At the level of real history, dialectic is the potential for alternative forms of development arising from the confrontation of opposed social forces in any concrete historical situation'.

[83] See Bieler and Morton (2003); Overbeek (2000); Van der Pijl (1998); Bonefeld et al. (1991); Marx (2003); Holloway (1995); Burnham (2001).

[84] Holism (inherent to the dialectical method), in contrast to positivistic atomism, posits that the social whole cannot be understood by the sum of its components but must originally be interpreted as a conceptual totality. Burnham writes: 'dialectical research starts with the whole and then proceeds inwards to the part, conceiving all parts as processes in relation of mutual dependence. Notions of externality and structure are replaced by the dialectical categories of process and internal relationship. [...] The dialectical method rejects the seemingly fragmented nature of society and instead seeks to trace out the inner connection between social phenomena, searching for the substantive abstraction which constitutes their social reality as complex, interconnected forms, different from, but united in, each other' (Burnham 1994a: 227). This epistemological principle is not followed by Marxist frameworks implicitly reproducing a positivist epistemology relating economic forces of production (infrastructure) and political superstructure as autonomous, externally interacting structures. For an early critique of structural Marxism, see Holloway and Picciotto (1978).

[85] The labour theory of value is central to NG theories, especially the THM variant. The conscious focus of NG scholarship on ideological relations and

transnational elite formation does not invalidate this appreciation (Bieler and Morton 2003: 481-482).

[86] The central tenets of neoliberalism are: fiscal and monetary stability, structural adjustment to global market pricing, monetarism and the privatisation of accumulation. Considering the systematic emphasis on 'state-, in particular 'government-building' in internal documents produced by neoliberal multilateral institutions (IBRD 1993: 12; DAC 1989: 31), understandings of neoliberalism as a 'retreat of the state' is rejected here (Strange 1996; Gill 2000).

[87] These tendencies are evident in critical approaches such as Open Marxism (Burnham 1994b; 2002; Bonefeld 1991, 2000; Holloway 1995), world-system and dependency theory (Wallerstein 1974, 2000; Frank 1969), and neo-Gramscian perspectives (Cox 1981, 1987; Robinson 2002, 2005; Rupert 1995).

[88] Neo-Gramscian approaches to International Political Economy (IPE) have been growing, since their emergence in the late 1970s on the fringes of Marxist academia, into a highly dynamic and reflexive intellectual movement. Under the impetus of Robert Cox, Kees van der Pijl, and later Stephen Gill, Henk Overbeek, Otto Holman, Mark Rupert, William Robinson, Andreas Bieler, Adam Morton and Bastiaan van Apeldoorn among others, Gramsci's heterodox Marxist categories (hegemony, historic bloc, *trasformismo*, passive revolution) have authoritatively informed empirical research on international relations, transnational processes and historical forms of world order.

The neo-Gramscian movement, founded on a purposive synthesis between naturalistic materialism and idealism (van der Pijl 2002), must not be considered as a homogenous bloc of intellectual labour, and is subject to internal controversy as well as significant criticisms from the Marxist movement as a whole (Morton 2001; Burnham 1991, 2000; Bonefeld 2000). However, a central trend may be identified with regards to the neo-Gramscian research agenda: its organisation around the study of the dynamic formation of strategic consciousness and ideological projects of ruling classes in international relations. These projects, when successfully achieving a hegemonic form, become the core 'motivation for action' of historically contingent constellations of social forces clustered into 'historic blocs', which sustain 'world order' (Cox 1981, 1987; Gill 2003; Van der Pijl 1984, 1998, 2002; Overbeek 2000, 2004).

Without oversimplifying, we can identify two broad variants of neo-Gramscian theory: the discrepancies between Coxian IPE (defended by Anglo-Saxon NG theorists such as Cox, Gill, Rupert and Robinson) and the 'Amsterdam School' of transnational historical materialism (THM), best expounded by Overbeek (2004) are significant: these include, for instance, Cox's integration of Weberian methodological and conceptual elements into his historical materialist model, leading to charges of eclecticism. Neo-Gramscian understandings of the state have similar roots (chiefly Marx, Gramsci, and Poulantzas) and hence build similar explanations of what the state is, how and why it has historically emerged and changed. Nonetheless, variations in prominent theorists' conceptualisation of the state and empirical application (and adaptation to empirical evidence) of the concept warrant a separate focus on the strengths and shortcomings of each understanding and explanation, although this chapter will point out the inter-connections between them

On their side, since the late 1980s, Open Marxist theorists have consciously furthered and ameliorated the theoretical paths traced by so-called political Marxism and especially German 'state derivation' approaches, which sprang in the late 1970s in reaction to structuralism. Andreas Bieler and Adam Morton (2003) expounded appropriately the three constitutive elements of Open Marxist critiques of political economy: firstly, a rejection of problem-solving dichotomies between society and state, and between politics and economics. Secondly, a reassertion of the class struggle as ontological presupposition and result of substantive dialectical logic, which entails a rejection of the crude base-superstructure metaphor immanent in classical Marxism. The third and most creative element of Open Marxist scholarship is its reformulation of Marxist state theory via an understanding of national states as multiple political manifestation of class relations of production in global(ising) capitalist form (Holloway 1995: 136). Major Open Marxist theorists include Simon Clarke (1988, 1991, 2001), Werner Bonefeld (1991, 2000), John Holloway (1978, 1995), and Peter Burnham (1994b, 1995, 2000, 2002).

Political Marxism is embodied in the work of Brenner (1977) and Meiksins Wood (1981). Prominent participants in the German debates include Gerstenberger (1978), Hirsch (1978) and Von Braunmuhl (1978).

[89] For a comprehensive analysis of the Poulantzas-Miliband debate, see Hay (1999).

[90] See Cox (1981, 1987); Van der Pijl (1998); Clarke (1988, 1991); Burnham (1994, 1995, 2002); Bonefeld (1991, 2000); Holloway (1995).

[91] Coxian IPE has reproduced this covert Weberian pluralism (Burnham, 1991). Gill, for instance, follows Gramsci's 'persuasive' contention that there is 'no necessary relationship between economic and political crises, or vice versa' (Gill 1993: 52).

[92] See Cox (1987); Morton (2000); Bieler and Morton (2003); Robinson (2005).

[93] Jessop (1985: 341) interpreted Poulantzas's (1978: 43) argument that although 'class division is not the exclusive terrain of the constitution of power...in class societies all power bears a class significance' as a 'residual penchant for essentialism and class reductionism'.

[94] This definition is embedded in the historical materialist tradition that finds its roots in the more open work of Marx. The definitions offered by theorists from sometimes incompatible approaches are surprisingly similar: thus Bonefeld (1991: 120) appropriates Marx's definition of the state as the 'concentrated and organised force of society'. Abrams (1988: 63) understands the state as 'politically organized subjection'. This definition is adopted by Burnham (1994b: 2), who sees the state 'as a set of distinct institutions, grounded within particular social relations, whose specific concern is with the organisation of domination (in the name of common interest), within a delimited territory'. Ironically, Burnham's Marxist definition of the state is highly congruent (despite his recurrent criticism of Weberian pluralism) with Weber's (1991: 82-83) own conceptualisation as a 'compulsory association which organises domination', and 'monopolises the legitimate use of physical force as a means of domination within a territory'. Jessop (1990: 341), on his side, re-interprets the work of Poulantzas by defining the state as a 'distinct ensemble of institutions and organizations whose socially accepted function is to define and

enforce collectively binding decisions on the members of a society in the name of their common interest or general will'. However, these authors do not envisage the state as a site of class struggle.

[95] See Tsolakis (2010) for an explanation of this contention.

[96] This is apparent in contemporary left-wing governments throughout Latin America (from former trade unionist Lula Da Silva's administration in Brazil, to Evo Morales's MAS in Bolivia).

[97] For a convincing critique of the social movements literature, see Cohen and Rai (2000).

[98] It is crucial at this point to clarify that potentially various movements constitute and thus may divide organisations: 'one' organisation does not equal 'one' movement – the institution is twisted by the social contradictions defining it and may or may not accommodate these contradictions. If it fails to do so, a scission occurs.

[99] It is not incidental that indigenist movements, miners and cocaleros only became meaningful historical forces in Bolivia from the moment that they took the organised form of trade unions and political parties (Zavaleta 1983; Rivera 1983; 2007).

[100] Neither Open Marxist nor neo-Gramscian theories have individually been applied to research on Bolivia, not to mention a historical approach attempting to incorporate, in a coherent manner, concepts generated through these two strands. One must acknowledge the creative use, by René Zavaleta in the 1980s and intellectuals of the collective *La Comuna* (Gutiérrez and García 2002, Tapia 2002, Prada 2002) in the late 1990s and early 2000s, of Gramscian categories such as hegemony and historic bloc to explain the recomposition of labour in a 'plebeian' form since the late 1980s (García et al. 2000, Tapia 2002). However, their national starting-point and quasi-exclusive focus on Bolivian social movements (pitted against the state) renders their work rather idiosyncratic and neglects to place Bolivian social relations within broader structural developments. The valid attempt by Espasandín and Iglesias (2007) to do just this, however, employs a world-system approach to explain Bolivia's bilateral relations with the US government, and Bolivia's dependent underdevelopment within worldwide commodity circulation, thereby overlooking transnational processes of elite formation and the concrete transformations of the state in Bolivia.

[101] Arnold and Spedding (2007: 161-164) problematise the contention, in indigenist ideologies, that 'in a "pure" indigenous culture, there would be absolute equity between women and men', which obscures and subsumes gender relations under an ethnicist discourse. This belief is reminiscent of the socialist ideologies that brought cohesion to the urban workers and miners' unions in the 1940s and 1950s. Arnold and Spedding appropriately compare politicised women in contemporary *ayllus*, farmers' unions or 'neighbourhood micro-governments' in El Alto (Mamani 2005, 2007) to the subalternity of women sections (the so-called "*barzolas*") in the MNR party of the early 1950s.

[102] For sophisticated discussions of the Bolivian nation, see Démélas (1980); Zavaleta (1983), Antezana (1983); Tapia (2002a).

[103] For reflections on indigenous movements and nations, see Lora (1977); Rivera (1983, 1987, 2007); Albó (1990, 1996; 1999; 2008); Toranzo (2008); Patzi (2000); Mamani (2007).

[104] See Roca (1980, 2008), Barragán (2008).

[105] The emergence, through miscegenation, of a 'crucial middle cultural and economic layer between the whites and the Indians [...] greatly modified the bipolarity' of early colonial society (Klein 1971: 30). For nuanced discussions of mestizaje in Bolivia, see Sanjinés (2004); Dunkerley (1984, 2007); Klein (1982, 2003).

[106] A perfectly holistic approach would offer an in-depth explanation of global processes of change generated by the emergence and increasing predominance of industrial capital as the social pivot of global capital accumulation since the eighteenth century, and then locate the creation of 'Bolivia' and its post-independence social development within global relations of domination. See Van der Pijl (1998) and Hobsbawm (1995) for comprehensive historical materialist analyses of long-term change.

[107] For reasons of space, I will not analyse how the intensifying regionalisation of commerce and growing Chinese demand for Bolivia's commodities (including lithium for the car industry) are changing the geo-economics of Bolivia's production relations.

[108] See the recent interview of Alvaro García, in which he exposes with remarkable clarity his interpretation of the recent cycles of elite 'wars of position' and 'movement' against the popular masses represented by the MAS. See: http://alternativabolivariana.org/. Accessed 9 September 2009. In Gramscian thought, the complexity of modern social relations requires the avoidance of a frontal assault (war of movement) against the bourgeoisie and the state by the working class (akin to trench warfare). Instead, systematic ideological struggle, cunning political leaderhip and if necessary guerrilla tactics, conceptualised as a war of position will undermine capital hegemony and thereby generate the conditions required to undertake a war of movement (Gramsci 1971: 108-111; 229-234).

2
The Impact of the National Revolution

This chapter contextualises the radical restructuring efforts undertaken by successive Bolivian governments since 1985. For reasons of space, I have to stringently restrict the depth of the present historical analysis in order to focus adequately on the dialectical process of transnational historic bloc formation and state reforms after 1985.

I have claimed that merging coherent neo-Gramscian and Open Marxist categories helps to theorise adequately the post-1985 process of social restructuring, and have hypothesised that it is possible to validate empirically a conceptualisation of the state as contradictory organisation of subjection by focusing on restructuring. Although the dialectical method predisposes me to apply reflexively a grand theory of elites, labour and the state to the *longue durée* of social relations in Bolivia, it is beyond the scope of this study to attempt such generalisation. I am also aware that empirical evidence relating to the historical dialectic between class, race and gender will prompt a substantial reworking of the categories used in this study.

Some excellent studies of Bolivia's political economy prior to 1985 have identified and rehearsed the historical themes underlying recent processes of social and state transformation. Themes central to the pre-1985 social development of the 'imagined' Bolivian 'community' (Anderson 1991) include the expansion of capital in Bolivia via the axis of silver and tin production in the eighteenth and nineteenth centuries (Klein 1982, 2003; Grebe 1983) and through processes of primitive accumulation in *haciendas* of the Cochabamba region in the 1870s and 1880s (Rodriguez 1980); rural resistance to *hacienda* and capital encroachment in the nineteenth and early twentieth centuries (Klein 1982; Langer 1989); the relationship between military and civilian elites and the formation of liberal and conservative political parties in the nineteenth and twentieth century (Klein 1969; Dunkerley 1984; Lora 1987); the role of post-Chaco War military socialist governments in setting the terrain on which entrenched anti-oligarchic struggles would develop and eventually succeed (Klein 1965; Dunkerley 1984); imperialism and neo-colonialism;[1] the articulation between capitalist, hacienda and Incaic relations of production since the colonial era, and the transformations of indigenous formations through invasion, resistance and miscegenation;[2] shifts in the organisation of production and trade, related to worldwide developmental cycles and the articulation of Liberal and Revolutionary Nationalist ideologies;[3] the defining role of the MNR party as an instrument of power, the patrimonial dynamics of state organisation after the National Revolution, and the attempt to generate the hegemony of capital through Revolutionary Nationalism;[4] the excessive dependence of the state on the mining (in particular tin exports) sector since the late nineteenth century, and on the state-owned COMIBOL from 1952 to 1987 (Crabtree 1987; Burke 1987; Jordán 1999); the emergence and organisation of a robust and destabilising labour movement articulating revolutionary discourses, and its antithesis in the form of military interventionism and anti-constitutional governments;[5] the re-composition of indigenous movements in the late 1960s and 1970s through the articulation of katarist and indianist discourses and the constitution of indigenist unions (CSUTCB) and political parties (MRTK, MITKA) competing and cooperating with the urban-based socialist vanguard, the mining union (FSTMB) and the trade union confederation (COB);[6] the emergence of a cohesive capitalist class articulating regionalist discourses in Santa Cruz from the 1950s onwards (Roca 1980; Grebe 1983; Gill 1987); and processes of state transformations in the twentieth century generated by intra-elite tensions, military-civil alliances, and labour co-optations.[7]

An in-depth historical analysis of the Bolivian state prior to 1985 is beyond the scope of this study. It is appropriate, however, to emphasise that the contemporary development of Bolivian social relations and state is inextricably connected with the *longue durée* of world-wide relations of domination (Braudel 1980). The complex economic, ideological and institutional origins of the post-1985 internationalisation and liberalisation of the state must concurrently be sought in the National Revolution of 1952, in the historically contingent developments of the 1930s and 1940s (post-global economic depression and post-Chaco War political struggles) but also in Incaic, colonial and post-independence history.[8] Arguably the essential dialectic underlying the social constitution of the Bolivian state since the colonial era is one between a dominant *criollo* bloc of forces co-opting urban *mestizos* (mixed-race) on the one hand, and subaltern indigenous nations on the other.[9] This dialectic is defined by an intersection of production and race relations which have been crystallised in the institutions of the state – effectively distorting the colourless cash nexus defining capital relations in conventional Marxist theory.[10] This assumption unfortunately has to remain implicit in my study of the Bolivian state.

This chapter thus offers an analysis of the processes leading to the post-1985 internationalisation and liberalisation of the state, focusing in particular on the articulation between Bolivian governments, the USAID and MDIs following the inflationary crisis of 1952-1956. It emphasises two central processes: firstly, the era spanning thirty-three years between the revolution of 1952 channelled by the MNR and the implementation of the DS 21060 by the same political party in 1985 was defined by the expansion of capital through state-led industrialisation and import substitution strategies (Morales and Sachs 1990; Morales 2008; Moore 1990). Successive governments used the surplus generated by state-owned enterprises to promote (through subsidies, guaranteed credit and joint ventures) the formation of a private mining, agro-business and financial capitalist bloc.[11] Secondly, that the state-capitalist approach to development implemented by the MNR was underpinned by the internationalisation of the Bolivian state. The first of two waves of internationalisation occurred through multilaterally-assisted restructuring under the aegis of the US government, and does indeed bear some resemblance to neo-colonialism (Whitehead 1969). However, Bolivian governments and the Bolivian social formation – as the Ovando and Torres administrations demonstrated in 1969-1971 – were not absolutely dependent on, and at the behest of, decision-making circles beyond the Bolivian space. The US State Department, after all, was not in a position to unilaterally force the absorption of the Bolivian space within its backyard, and required that at least a segment of Bolivia's population actively appeal for US assistance. As demonstrated by neo-Gramscian scholarship (Cox 1983; Gill 2003; Bieler and Morton 2001), agency is structured and thus acts within and through collectively-produced constraints, but structures themselves are constituted and transformed by collective agency. The structure of capital in Bolivia was, throughout the 1952-1985 period, and as in the rest of Latin America, under recurrent threat of being collectively overwhelmed despite efforts by MNR and military governments to contain labour power. What internationalisation under US leadership demonstrates is that the leadership of anti-communist developmental parties was vitally dependent on US technical and financial assistance to secure their control of the state and to pursue capital accumulation strategies (Whitehead 1969; Wilkie 1969).

The Longue Durée and the National Revolution of 1952

The analysis of Bolivia's historical development must be undertaken from a holistic perspective incorporating the *longue durée* of social relations (Braudel 1980): holism locates changes in pre-colonial, colonial and capitalist forms within a global structural hierarchy, emerging whenever new points of contact, conflict and exchange were made between communities, and whenever communities came to dialectically merge into one (van der Pijl 1998). Furthermore, one must analyse the dialectical development of (emergence of new, persistence and disappearance of old) social forces in the Bolivian space and their economic, ideological and institutional relations. These intertwined, observable processes are Bolivia's local and national expressions of global struggles in and against domination (Bonefeld 1991). They are separated only for analytical purposes, yet they have dialectical bearing on theory, constituting the historical-concrete element of research grounded in praxis.

The 1952 National Revolution constituted a historical moment of structural rupture and change, as the revolution legally undermined non-capitalist production relations and opened new spaces for the state to promote the expansion of capital (Zavaleta 1983, 1987; Grebe 1983; Rivera 1983, 2007). Social revolutions are always underpinned by a long underlying crisis accelerated by economic dislocation, ideological rupture and the resulting weakness and instability of the state (Skocpol 1979:4):

'Social revolutions are rapid, basic transformations of a society's state and class structures; and they are accompanied and in part carried through by class-based revolts from below. Social revolutions are set apart from other sorts of conflicts and transformative processes above all by the combination of two coincidences: the coincidence of societal structural change with class upheaval; and the coincidence of political with social transformation. In contrast, rebellions, even when successful, may involve the revolt of subordinate classes – but they do not eventuate in structural change'.

While crisis defines the recurrence and intensification of political upheavals, it does not determine the inevitability of a successful revolution. Historical contingency generates a tipping point towards revolution in conditions of crisis (Gramsci 1971), which indeed precludes any form of determinism (Malloy 1970). Dismal living conditions in the mines and on *haciendas* (an average life expectancy of 35 years, 27 in the mines) (Burke 1987; Eckstein 1983: 108), the organisation of labour, in particular miners, around Revolutionary

Nationalist ideologies, and the diffusion of the latter in the army rank and file (Lora 1977; Mayorga 1978; Dunkerley 1984), the worldwide depression and debacle of the Chaco War in the 1930s (Klein 1965), massive currency devaluations (from 30.14 to the dollar in 1938 to 176.11 in 1951) and a fifty-fold increase in the cost of living since 1932 (Dunkerley 1984: 5),[12] unproductive *haciendas* requiring the import of foodstuffs, worsening terms of trade for mineral exports in the 1930s and 1940s (in 1952 the quantity and value of tin exports – the core of fiscal resources – reached their lowest point since 1940) (Jordán 1999), resentment against the concentration of capital into three mining dynasties (the *Rosca*) perceived to collude with US, British and Chilean imperialism (Jordán 1999)[13] conditioned a revolutionary situation. In order for these conditions to develop into a rapid and violent structural transformation, contingent accelerators were required (Malloy 1970): fraudulent elections in 1951, an annual inflation rate of 65 percent and food scarcity in markets due to speculative activities, and the collapse of an MNR-military conspiracy on the other, which transformed a conventional coup d'état into a profound social revolution (Dunkerley 1984: 2; Burke 1987).[14]

The contemporary history of Bolivia remains overwhelmingly influenced by the National Revolution: for good or ill, its symbolic aura as the Bolivian nation's genuinely successful anti-imperialist struggle remains at the core of anti-liberal and anti-capitalist discourses among subaltern social movements (Antezana 1983; Kohl and Farthing 2005). A buoyant, progressive, and yet highly contradictory *co-gobierno* emerged out of the National Revolution, polarised by the two organisations constituting it: the MNR, rapidly dominated by developmentalist (i.e. anti-communist) forces, and the socialist-leaning national trade unions' confederation (the *Central Obrera Boliviana* [COB]) created in the wake of the revolution. The policies implemented initially by the *co-gobierno* (i.e. nationalisation of the mines, railroads and electrical plants, co-management in the mines, land redistribution, universal suffrage, dissolution of the army and the creation of worker and peasant militias) generated uncontrollable inflationary pressures.[15] Hyperinflation directly undermined the benefit increases imposed by trade union representatives – reducing miners' real wage by 60 percent between 1950 and 1955 (Burke 1987).[16]

The petit-bourgeois leadership of the MNR never intended to use universal suffrage as the foundation of a representative, liberal democracy (see chapter 5). Rather Hernán Siles Zuazo and Victor Paz Estenssoro intended to emulate the Mexican Revolution and its particular form of social organisation by establishing a hegemonic (in the Gramscian sense) one-party state under the solid grip of its government (i.e. the party leadership), legitimised by the pluralist facade of procedural elections and by a nationalistic discourse of *mestizaje* (see table 2.4).[17] Although staunchly opposed to socialism and any alliance with the Soviet bloc, it envisioned a model of capitalist development articulated around state ownership of *strategic* means of production, i.e. state capitalism: "The clear implication of this arrangement was that the costs of capital accumulation would have to fall mainly on those groups mobilized by the revolution, such as workers and peasants. Hence the trick would be, as in Mexico, to mobilize and control these sectors even as surplus capital was extracted from them" (Malloy and Gamarra 1987: 94). The challenge for Paz and Siles was to channel proliferating demands of subaltern social forces into a consensual form of social order founded on an emotional bond with, and individual subjection to, the nation and the entrepreneurial party leadership.

In contrast to their Mexican model, MNR leaders did not manage to tame and co-opt the COB by integrating it into the corporatist form of the state. In fact, by granting the COB a *fuero sindical* and co-government, they endowed it with quasi-sovereignty over labour and allowed the formation of a burgeoning socialist state within the state (Zavaleta 1987). The COB flourished in the early years of co-government beyond the reach of the MNR leadership, systematically undermining the smooth implementation of its state capitalist project by diffusing Trotskyist discourses. By 1955-6, the COB had come to perceive the MNR and the *state* itself as an instrument of Bolivia's new capitalist elites (Malloy and Gamarra 1987: 95).

The MNR systematically attempted – and arguably failed – to entrench the hegemony of capital by diffusing a Revolutionary Nationalist ideology promoting *mestizaje* and silencing hitherto openly racist discourses by *criollos* (Antezana 1983; Sanjinés 2004). What the MNR achieved, however, was the violent internalisation and rural expansion of capital in spite of attempts by organised labour to validate the Thesis of Pulacayo (Lora 1977; Dunkerley 1984; Zavaleta 1987; Domingo 1993; Klein 2003).[18] The revolution ruptured pre-capitalist social forms by legally constraining the erasure of quasi-feudal *hacienda* relations but also by undermining the remnants of the *ayllu* structure via the integration of *campesinos* in national life – leading to the parcellisation of land into so-called *minifundios* (Klein 1982, 2003; Rivera 1987; Mamani 2007).[19] On its side, the nationalisation of Bolivia's mines and consequent dissolution of the *Rosca* paradoxically cemented the capitalist form of the state by constraining it to engage massively in production for the world market.[20] The preponderant role of the state in capitalist production radically changed pre-existing social relations. As such the National Revolution constituted a milestone in the penetration of capital in Bolivia and the expansion of the regulatory capacities of the state. Thereafter pockets of non-capitalist relations persisted in the Altiplano and the tropical lowlands, as indigenous formations were co-opted by the MNR through newly-formed peasant unions and were systematically integrated into, and systematically internalised capitalist production relations (Lora 1977; Rivera 1983).21

The 1964 to 1978 era of repressive military orders was constitutive of a broader regional trend in Latin America of developmentalist/anti-communist and/or populist military *juntas* (Mitchell 1977; Eckstein 1983; Dunkerley 1984; see table 2.1).[22] The Barrientos (1964-1969) and Banzer (1971-1978) governments perpetuated state capitalism while channelling fiscal resources towards the development of a national bourgeoisie investing in the agro-business, extractive (the so-called *mineria mediana*) and banking sectors (Conaghan and Malloy 1995). With the technical assistance of USAID and MDIs – the IMF, IDB and CAF – the Barrientos and Banzer administrations also worked towards forming a professional managerial stratum (Foxley and Whitehead 1980).

The First Wave of State Internationalisation

The 1952 revolution occurred within the broader context of the Cold War between two expanding blocs struggling for the control of the so-called Third World, defined by capitalist globalisation under overarching dominance by US elites, and the Soviet challenge to this process via the Russia-dominated communist Internationale and Warsaw Pact. The Bolivian revolution occurred at a crucial moment in the international conflict between these blocs: the Cold War had reached its apex following the Communist victory in the Chinese civil war. In the context of the Korean War, the McCarthy witch-hunt of communists in the US, the imperialist repression of the progressive regimes of Mossadegh in Iran and Arbenz in Guatemala, the Bolivian revolution was perceived by US elites as a potential take-over by communists in the very heart of Latin America, threatening the already precarious order in America's backyard. The (failed) Soviet courting of the revolutionary administration through loans and economic contracts validated such worries (Dunkerley 1984).

Interestingly however, the reaction of the US administration to the National Revolution was remarkably subtle and effective, in stark contrast with its Manichean foreign policy in East Asia. The distinction

Table 2.1: Bolivian Governments, 1951-1985	
1951	M. Urriolagoitia (PURS)
1951-52	H. Ballivián (military)
1952-56	V. Paz Estenssoro (MNR)
1956-60	H. Siles Zuazo (MNR)
1960-64	V. Paz Estenssoro (MNR)
1964	V. Paz Estenssoro (MNR)
1964-69	R. Barrientos (military)
1969	L. Siles Salinas (PDC)
1969-70	A. Ovando (military)
1970-71	J.J. Torres (military)
1971-78	H. Banzer (military)
1978	J. Pereda (military)
1978-79	D. Padilla (military)
1979	W. Guevara (PRA/MNR)
1979	A. Natusch Busch (military)
1979-80	L. Gueiler (PRIN/MNR)
1980-81	L. García Meza (military)
1981	Military Junta
1981-82	C. Torrelio (military)
1982	G. Vildoso (military)
1982-85	H. Siles Zuazo (UDP/MNRI)

Source: Dunkerley (1998: 5)

made by the US State Department between Communists and the Marxist-based yet non-Communist MNR was indeed 'a rarity during John Foster Dulle's years as US Secretary of State' (Wilkie 1969: 8). It recognised the revolutionary government in mid-1953, renewed commercial agreements for tin, and expanded 'the small technical assistance project begun ... in 1942 ... into a mammoth assistance programme beginning in 1954' (Wilkie 1969: 9). The forerunners of USAID (established in 1961)[23] gave preference to grants until 1963, when a shift towards loans occurred under the Alliance for Progress. Interestingly, a relatively large proportion of US assistance (16 percent until 1961, 10 percent afterwards) was directed at non-economic activity (health, education, food relief). A significant proportion of this aid (31 percent up to 1961, 21 percent thereafter) was directed at fiscal support for the government, and was also channelled by the latter towards social programmes. This 'unproductive' aid was supplanted in the late 1950s and 1960s by large-scale programs for military (more than half of total financial aid) and technical-economic assistance – administrative reforms and training, designed to improve the efficiency of state polity on the one hand, and subsidies and credits to the private mining and nascent agro-industrial sectors in Santa Cruz on the other (Wilkie 1969: 9-14; Eckstein 1983; Grebe 1983; Barragán 2008).

Thus, instead of antagonising the new government, the US state used soft financial and institutional power to support capitalist forces in the MNR on the condition that they would ensure that no communist takeover – no attack on private property and market forces – would occur. This gave the US the opportunity 1) to channel, through aid and cadre immersion in the executive organs of the state, the course of the revolution, by maintaining it within the strict bounds of capital accumulation; 2) to divide and eventually provoke the implosion of the potentially revolutionary COB-MNR co-gobierno; and eventually 3) to take advantage of the monetary and fiscal crisis of the state requiring (being disciplined by world money) the restructuring of the whole Bolivian economic edifice four years later (see Malloy and Thorn 1971; Wilkie 1969; Moore 1990).

In the face of hyperinflation, capital flight and declining terms of trade for its primary export (tin), the developmentalist wing of the MNR,[24] led by Paz Estenssoro and Siles Zuazo, took the seemingly paradoxical initiative, for a nationalist movement, to appeal for foreign support in order to contain the radicalisation of labour and peasants and thereby secure its political survival (Eckstein 1983; Mitchell 1977; Whitehead 1969). This decision was based on the understanding, by Paz and Siles, that 'since 1954, the US had funded the Revolution' (Wilkie 1969: 8) – more than 25 percent of the state's budget depended on US grants – and that the continuation of US assistance had been made conditional upon controlling inflation with IMF financial and technical assistance (Whitehead 1969). The MNR leadership, after a bitter struggle with Juan Lechín (head of the COB and Minister of Mines and Petroleum), chose to request IMF financial and technical assistance in 1956, resulting in the implementation of a stringent stabilisation and austerity plan not dissimilar to the one implemented thirty years later, contingent on changing historical circumstances, by the same MNR (Whitehead 1969; Dunkerley 1984, 1990).[25] IMF-induced restructuring was bolstered by USAID grants, WB loans and credits,[26] and the 1960 so-called Triangular Plan (a $67 million assistance plan spanning ten years between 1961 and 1970 involving the Inter-American Development Bank, USAID and the German development agency) ostensibly for the restructuring and recapitalisation of COMIBOL (Burke 1987).[27] The wave of US government financial and technical assistance to the weak and internally divided MNR was inexpensive for the former, but vital for the latter, which was under constant threat of being engulfed by widespread social upheavals, revolutionary militias, and the COB in government and in COMIBOL, while being unable to rein in inflation and GDP contraction (Dunkerley 1984; Wilkie 1969).[28]

The elimination of the *Rosca* and *hacendado* elites therefore gave way to a state-capitalist order cemented by the post-1956 internationalisation of the state under US guidance. The social revolution set in motion by urban and rural labour forces was effectively contained and channelled by the MNR leadership into a process of capitalist development. The line dividing capitalist reform and socialist revolution (i.e. the protection of private property, the promotion of private capital, the prevention of collectivisation in the countryside, the elimination of co-management in the mines, and money discipline), was not crossed.

The carrot of US assistance offered from 1954 onwards as a palliative to the lack of private capital investment (effectively bringing the MNR leadership under US aegis), was supplemented by the IMF stick of structural adjustment (Whitehead 1969). The social gains of 1952 in terms of labour rights and wages, already hampered by hyperinflation, were thoroughly undermined by President Siles's effective implementation of the Eder program for monetary stabilisation: the latter involved the elimination of the floating exchange rate, the devaluation of the currency, the termination of price controls and food subsidies, the freezing of wages, the opening up of foreign trade through the reduction of export tariffs, the enforcing of an austere fiscal and monetary policy to balance the state's budget, and the diversification of production and import-substitution strategy. It however retained the state-ownership of extractive industries as the central engine of national growth and yet opened up all sectors of production – agriculture, construction, manufacturing, oil and mining itself – to private investment, including FDI (Whitehead 1969; Burke 1987).

Diversification projects involved shifting capital resources from COMIBOL towards the underdeveloped *Oriente* (lowlands) (Eckstein 1983). Agricultural diversification and import-substitution was relatively successful, as subsidised agro-business in Santa Cruz began to produce a whole new set of staple foods such as rice and sugar, but also cash crops such as cotton (Grebe 1983). By the mid-1960s Bolivia had become broadly self-sufficient and became a net exporter of foodstuffs, in stark contrast to the preceding decade (Moore 1990).[29] Indeed, the demise of the *hacendado* class and land redistribution were confined to the *Altiplano* (highlands) and valleys, as *Cruceño/Camba* landowners, identified as pivotal for the IMF and USAID strategies of capital expansion, benefitted from an amnesty by the MNR leadership. Land reform was not implemented in the *Oriente*; the MNR and successive governments distributed more than 30 million hectares of state-owned land to 'a very reduced number of individuals, consolidating the process of *neolatifundismo*' (Urioste 2001: 2).[30] Foreigners, including Brazilian investors, German Mennonites, and Japanese settlers were privileged recipients of these land grants, and spearheaded capitalist farming (Urioste 2001: 2-3; Gill 1987). Therefore, 'the *Cruceña* oligarchy survived the revolution through a state and US-sponsored Junker-type transition that transformed it into an agrarian, commercial and financial bourgeois class-caste' (Moore 1990: 37).[31]

John Jackson Eder would subsequently boast, and not without reason, that his scheme had 'set the revolution on a new course', modernising, centralising and expanding the regulatory and coercive apparatus of the Bolivian state, most notably by training managers, economists and accountants through technical assistance teams and coordinating economic Ministries and the BCB with the IMF, USAID, the IDB and later the WB (Whitehead 1969; Moore 1990: 34). At the same time, the donor community turned a blind eye to the promotion of corrupt and clientelistic party-state relations by the MNR leadership. The revolutionary accomplishments of the *co-gobierno* were effectively obliterated, as civil and military governments would thereafter systematically (yet never perfectly, being constrained by labour resistance in state-owned enterprises) administer the social internalisation of capital through the lifeline of US and multilateral aid.

Internationalisation and restructuring caused the effective implosion of the *co-gobierno* in 1957 and the disconnection of the MNR from the mass movement that had brought it to power: the MNR became increasingly undermined by internal conflicts between its socialist-leaning left-wing, linked to the COB, and its developmentalist right-wing supported by metropolitan governments, foreign and local capital as well as remnants of the military. The Siles government (1956-1960) dissolved urban worker militias and reinstated, with US financial support and training, the enfeebled and fragmented army in order to coerce organised labour and its vanguard, miners, into accepting wage freezes and mass redundancies (Dunkerley 1984; Burke 1987). Meanwhile, it courted the Quechua *campesino* leadership of the Cochabamba and valley areas (rather than the intractable *Aymaras* of the Altiplano, who also tended to form the bulk of miners) by using methods of patronage and manipulating their conservative tendencies: it effectively co-opted peasants into the party's corporatist organisation through the National Confederation of Farmers (*Confederación Nacional de Trabajadores Campesinos de Bolivia* [CNTCB]), estranged the 20,000 or so peasant unions from the FSTMB and the COB, and set up MNR-peasant militias which participated in military-led actions to suppress miner unrest and indigenous rebellions against agro-business encroachment in the *Oriente* (Eckstein 1983; Rivera 1983; Dunkerley 1984; Moore 1990). In 1964, the restructured army factions, led by Vice-President Barrientos, engineered a coup-d'état against the MNR leadership, and imposed a military dictatorship systematising the repression of miners and the subsidisation of private capital with COMIBOL resources.[32] The clientelistic relationship between MNR, army and peasantry was substituted by an unwritten Military-Peasant Pact, underpinned by food subsidies shielding peasants from the vagaries of market-determined food prices and the army's direct control of peasant unions (Rivera 1983: 136-137).

Consolidating State Capitalism: 1964-1978

The Barrientos administration reaped the rewards of the policies implemented by the MNR with an average yearly GDP growth of 6 percent after 1965. Accumulation was also boosted by stability in the countryside despite continuing *ayllu* resistance to agro-business encroachment in the valleys and lowlands (Rivera 1987; Gill 1987), the systematic repression of the COB and miners (with a ban on all trade union activities, 40 percent wage cuts and mass redundancies in COMIBOL – from 36,000 in 1956, to 27,000 in 1960, to 20,000 workers in 1970) and the provision of relatively stable conditions for FDI.[33] In contrast to Eder's comprehensive developmental strategy, Barrientos reduced state planning and production and focused on a limited set of priorities – the improvement of the national road network, the privatisation of accumulation in the mining sector, the support of import-substitution strategies for agro-business in Santa Cruz and the development of cattle ranches in the Beni region (Dunkerley 1984; Klein 2003; Moore 1990).

The accidental death of Barrientos in a helicopter crash in 1969 fortuitously broke the liberalisation movement (Dunkerley 1992), and triggered a buoyant two-year interlude of military socialist governments (Generals Alfredo Ovando and Juan José Torres). Ovando's coup d'état, led by nationalist elements of the officer corps, established a government promoting centralised planning and the emancipatory intervention of the state, and antagonised the US government and private capital by nationalising the Gulf Oil Corporation.[34] Ovando's program, however, was insufficiently revolutionary for General Torres, who took power a few months after Ovando's investiture with the support of remnants of the COB and FSTMB, and a cluster of socialist and radical officers. The Torres administration proposed measures extolled by Zavaleta (1987) and other Marxist theoreticians, which have arguably influenced – and been diluted by – the current Morales administration (the pursuit of Ovando's nationalisation efforts, but also the formation of a Constituent Popular Assembly led by trade unions to debate and vote the creation a new Constitution).

The state socialist ghost of 1952 hung above Torres' reforms, and elite fears of a red threat resurfaced along with the possible emergence of a worker-led Congress. These fears extended to large segments of the Armed Forces, which upheld the twin traditions of nationalism and anti-communism since the late 1930s. These worries galvanised the US government and investors, as well as the *criollo* bloc, to attack indirectly the new administration through a stringent reduction in bilateral and multilateral aid, capital flight and a sharp fall in private investment and savings. Nevertheless, GDP growth only decreased slightly (from 6-7 to 5 percent), while gross capital formation remained stable (around 14 percent of GDP). Not surprisingly, unlike the privatisation program of Barrientos, which had increased the proportion of private capital formation, public capital became clearly preponderant in 1970 (about two thirds of total investments), as Torres doubled state expenditures to offset dwindling foreign aid and private investment (Dunkerley 1984; Moore 1990).

The threat of structural revolution became unbearable for conservative military circles and capitalist forces. Hugo Banzer, a relatively obscure *Cruceño* colonel led a coup d'état against the Torres government in 1971, with the overt support of the US government and in alliance with business federation and a civilian-bourgeois *Frente Popular Nacionalista*, an anomalous coalition unifying arch-rival political parties, the Fascist *Falanje Socialista Boliviana* (FSB) and Paz Estenssoro's MNR (Klein 1982, Moore 1990; Domingo 1993). The coup d'état must be placed within the context of a geo-economic shift from the highlands to the lowlands in the late 1950s and 1960s (Roca 1980). Indeed, "the territorial base [Santa Cruz] which constitutes the platform from which the preparations for [Banzer's] coup were initiated consists in the area in which the greatest economic might was concentrated" (Grebe 1983: 101, author's translation). The successful appropriation of oil rents by the Santa Cruz departmental administration (from 1957) and the state's transfer of the surplus from mining and manufacturing activities in the *Altiplano* towards the infrastructural agro-processing development of Santa Cruz had generated a second axis of accumulation in the *Oriente*, transnationally constituted by Brazilian sub-imperialism in the region (Grebe 1983; Gill 1987; Urioste 2001).

The *Banzerato* (1971-1978) interrupted in 1974 by an *autogolpe* (self-inflicted coup)[35] embodied the contradictions underlying state capitalism: export revenues were used (inefficiently) to sustain the emergence and consolidation of three national capital fractions: productive (agro-business and extractive industries), financial (Bolivia's main private banks were established during the 1960s and 1970s in La Paz and Santa Cruz), and commercial. Capital dominated an *criollo* bloc incorporating a public managerial stratum, petit-bourgeois middle strata, and the armed forces, deciding collectively the allocation of social surplus (Mayorga 1978; Dunkerley 1984).

The Banzer government distanced itself from Barrientos's laissez-faire approach by promoting export-led development through the state-owned oil and mining sectors; state subsidisation of the *Mineria Mediana* of agro-business expansion and diversification in the Oriente; and last but not least, the provision of favourable conditions for FDI – including an ultra-liberal tax regime (low tariffs on trade, special investment zones) and the systematic repression of labour (Moore 1990). A terroristic state form emerged after 1974, as military leadership would actively participate in the elaboration and execution, with Chilean and Argentinean dictators Pinochet and Videla, of the Plan Condor for the covert repression of organised labour (primarily miners) under the auspices of the Central Intelligence Agency (CIA).[36]

The policies implemented by the Barrientos and Banzer administrations, and the vigorous reconstitution, consolidation and expansion of capitalist forces did not occur in a political vacuum: the 1960s and 1970s witnessed recurrent, bloody battles in Altiplano mines and in the valleys and lowlands, as organised miners and *ayllus* continued their struggles against increasing exploitation and agro-business encroachment – despite the alleviating consequences of the Military-Peasant Pact (Rivera 1987; Dunkerley 1984). State capitalism and state socialism, buttressed by the well-entrenched Revolutionary Nationalist ideology, remained popular counter-hegemonic discourses of repressed labour organisations. On their side indigenous religions and anti-capitalist forms of communal organisation perpetuated by *ayllus* remained attractive ideologies and mass movement for the destitute rural indigenous majority toiling in *minifundios* or in large white-owned landholdings as tenants or employees (Rivera 1983, 1987). However, the state was relatively successful in containing labouring forces, through the active repression of miners and urban workers, and the co-optation of peasants (Moore 1990).

The notion of 'patrimonial state' offered by Malloy and Gamarra (1988) to describe the pre-1978 organisation of social relations in Bolivia is helpful only to the extent that it stretches the ideal type elaborated by Max Weber (Collier and Mahon 1993). Weber (1991) defined the patrimonial state as 'domestic authority decentralized through assignment of land and sometimes of equipment to sons of the house or other dependents'. Banzer did not rule on the basis of a patriarchal 'manorial' system whereby he would, as absolute dictator, arbitrarily allocate resources to his family and clients. Banzer led, constituted and *depended on* a national historic bloc of elite (*criollo* and *mestizo* civilian and military) social forces controlling the central institutions of the state and organising coercively production relations. Rather than merely a core group of military and administrative personnel, public-private and civil-military collaboration constituted this bloc: white and *mestizo* businessmen, administrators and military officers, controlling the executive institutions of the state, were united in their containment of labour power by repressive means. This national bloc was vitally dependent on its integration into a US-led business internationale, which in turn was beginning to undergo transformations under the impulse of transnational elite forces in the 1970s (see chapter 3). The coercive elitism and racism of the Banzer administration explains the 'mutual mistrust built up over time between the private sector and important segments of the population' (WB 1985: ii).

The institutional makeup of the state sustained corrupt and inefficient capitalist networks, chiefly centred on army officers and the business confederation CEPB, which provided numerous economic Ministers to the Banzer administration, although the latter sometimes had to implement policies against the interest of sectoral business interests – in particular the *mineria mediana* (Conaghan and Malloy 1995). The national elite bloc was never perfectly harmonious, however, in part because of the persisting centrality of the state in production. The coercive organisation of subjection by the Banzer administration required a certain degree of consent-formation. The high degree of state intervention, price distortions and subsidies for state agencies and companies was partly caused by subaltern resistance (organised around peasant, manufacturing and mining unions) and claims on the surplus generated through a highly politicised accumulation process. Although privileged business clients of the RDCs and state-owned companies benefitted from state guarantees, contracts, and subsidies, the government actively competed with private businesses in most sectors of the economy. Dynamic capitalists in the mining, banking and commercial sectors, facing systematic subaltern antagonism, and sometimes facing competition by the state, had come to feel, by the late 1970s 'that participation in Bolivia's development process entails an unacceptable degree of risk, and has therefore continued, whenever possible, to accumulate assets abroad' (WB 1985: ii). The incapacity of the state to fix capital in its territory meant that a number of privileged capitalists benefitted from state support for short-term profitable activities, the surplus of which was rarely reinvested in Bolivia but rather exported towards more secure/stable social environments. Thus, 'in spite of an unprecedented degree of political stability in most of the 1970s, private entrepreneurs did not find investing in Bolivia an attractive proposition and new private flows failed to materialise ... Capital flight amounted to over 60% of the value of the debt accumulated during the years 1971/81. Government foreign borrowing for public investment thus, in effect, financed the accumulation of privately-owned assets abroad' (WB 1985: ii-iii; see table 2.2).

Table 2.2: Capital Flight During Banzerato and Democratic Transition Era

Year	Amount (US$ millions)	Percentage of GDP
1973	29.6	1.1
1974	57.8	
1975	30.1	0.9
1976	119.3	
1977	297	7.5
1978	163.8	
1979	48	
1980	248.8	6.4
1981	347.2	
1981-1983	318.6	2.6
Total	**1,660**	
Percentage of ODA (%)	65-72	

Source: Lavaud (1991: 249); author's calculations

Along with capital flight, accumulation in the 1970s was hindered by high inflation rates and debt servicing. The decision to devalue the national currency by 40 percent in October 1972 in order to boost exports was fundamental to the government's accumulation strategy.[37]

Nevertheless it caused escalating inflationary pressures, from 6.5 percent in 1972, to 31 percent the following year, and around 50 percent in subsequent years. Inflation hit the labouring forces hard, despite the granting of bonuses to workers in state-owned corporations and the administration during these years, which actually did not make up for the general augmentation of prices. While state employees were partially protected from the brunt of inflation, the rest of labour was not, and the government, facing an impending agricultural crisis, pushed for politically dangerous measures which accelerated a regional crisis of *Cruceña* agriculture and hurt Cochabambino and Altiplano peasants most acutely. The end of food price subsidies and the prohibition of market price rises for agricultural commodities, in the context of rising inflation, reduced peasant incomes to the point of triggering a large scale uprising in Cochabamba, which signalled the effective termination of the Military-Peasant pact established a decade earlier and resulted in the army's mass murder of peasants at Tolata, which consolidated an emerging *katarista* movement and triggered the founding of the *Movimiento Revolucionario Tupac Katari* (MRTK) and *Movimiento Indio Tupac Katari* (MITKA) (Rivera 1983, 1987).[38]

Despite the conventional image of the *Banzerato* as a boom era, Banzer's policy of attracting FDI through labour repression and a liberal tax regime attracted meagre returns: following an early boom between 1972 and 1975 (6 percent growth, slightly superior to preceding administrations), GDP growth would thereafter gradually slow down – to 4-5 percent. In fact, FDI was higher during the politically volatile 1952-1964 era and in the four years following the ousting of Banzer, than during the *Banzerato* (indeed during the entire 1965-1978 period) (Moore 1990). This was partly due to the global recession and stagflation in the metropolis (which hindered worldwide fixed investments while stimulating the recycling of petro-dollars through cheap credit on the Euromarket) (Pastor 1987; Kuczinsky 1988), which consolidated domestic dynamics such as patrimonialism, corruption and internal power struggles within the government (Malloy and Gamarra 1988); as well as the emergence of the indigenist guerrilla *Katarista* and *indianista* movements and underground resistance by the COB and socialist parties (*Partido Obrero Revolucionario* [POR], *Partido Comunista de Bolivia* [PCB], MIR). These conditions predictably affected business confidence. FDI stagnated at an average of $24 million *per annum* during the entire *Banzerato* despite significant investments in the mining and hydrocarbons sectors (De La Cueva 1983). In contrast to the late Paz and Barrientos administrations, which had managed to increase FDI as a proportion of total investments, after 1975 FDI was overcome by foreign aid as a source of capital and foreign exchange reserves. Foreign, in particular US aid, almost absent during the Ovando and Torres administration, increased sharply during the *Banzerato*, to cover 22 percent of the state budget deficit by 1974 and 30 percent two years later, indicating, if not demonstrating that 'the US was in fact subsidizing the regime and helping Banzer to hold on to power' (Moore 1990: 42).

The predicaments of COMIBOL inherited from the *Rosca* persisted in the 1970s and into the 1980s: investment in new technologies did not pick up for this depleting resource and productivity decreased during the 1970s, causing production to stagnate and actually decrease after 1977 while the value of tin exports was falling. COMIBOL suffered continuous losses despite export increases during the 1970s. In contrast, the privately-owned *Mineria Mediana*, accounting for 20 percent of national production and subsidised by the state, managed to achieve honourable rates of return over the same period (a 27 percent profit rate). Hydrocarbons extraction gradually replaced mining as the central axis of Bolivian accumulation, as the rising global value of oil and gas following the 1973 energy crisis was compounded by decreasing tin prices and the rapid exhaustion of the richest and most accessible mines in the late 1970s and early 1980s. The rise of these sectors further shifted the geopolitical balance of power towards the *Cruceña* agro-business, banking and extractive capital within the *criollo* elite bloc.

The 1970s were characterised by increasing borrowing throughout Latin America, a process which Bolivia's state did not fail to participate in. During the 1970s, the Banzer administration quadrupled its debt burden (from $480 million in 1970 to $1.941 billion in 1979) (Morales and Sachs 1990: 216-217), relying increasingly upon private commercial bank loans (defined by high interest rates and short-term reimbursement) rather than multilateral and bilateral aid, which gradually dried up due to waste and the stagnation in FDI and production. The proportion of foreign private debt servicing thus increased from 22.6 to 44 percent during the *Banzerato*, while the ratio of debt to GDP had reached 87 percent by 1978. The burgeoning debt crisis, symptomatic of the limitations of state capitalism and import-substitution strategies, created some political space for the IMF and WB to increase their participation in state policymaking. The reform of the state-led model of capital accumulation was facilitated by the perception that its liberating potential was a chimera: the relations of production consolidated since 1952 were beginning to unravel in 1977-1978 under high inflation, low wages (inducing high social volatility), stagnant production and low productivity, as well as corruption, aggravated by an increasingly unmanageable debt crisis. This situation was compounded by the fact that the US, facing stagflation, and for geopolitical reasons (the support of an anti-Communist barrier against the People's Republic of China), was restricting the opening of its consumption market to Asian products. US benevolence became restricted to those allied state-society complexes deemed crucial for the territorial logic of domination still prevalent in Cold War international relations (Lacher and Teschke 2007; Van der Pijl 1998; Overbeek 2004). As Latin America was considered to be firmly in America's backyard and out of the Soviet Union's reach, it bore the brunt of trade restrictions.

General Banzer and his government Ministers do not merely bear a high level of responsibility for the notoriously repressive form taken by relations of domination in the 1970s, but also for the 1978-1985 crisis manifested in a profound disruption of the Bolivian economy and the quasi-bankruptcy of the state. The unwavering support given by the US government to the Banzer administration (through systematic technical assistance by USAID), the WB and IMF (through continued credit lines), and transnational banks (through guaranteed and non-guaranteed loans to the state and, to a lesser extent, to private businesses) also entail that responsibility for the debt crisis lies beyond the boundaries of the Bolivian space – in the decision-making spheres of donor governments, MDIs, and transnational banks (CEPAL 1983; Pastor 1987; Dunkerley 1990).

The apparent social stability defining the Banzer administration, as well as the discovery of hydrocarbon fields in the Chaco area (bordering Santa Cruz and Tarija) in the context of high oil prices, stimulated the interest of both public financial institutions and transnational private banks; thus began a credit bonanza for the Banzer administration. Yet business confidence in the creditworthiness of the Bolivian state evaporated just as democratising forces were beginning to challenge the government, generating instability (i.e. disrupting capital circuits through higher labour demands and strikes) and causing an acceleration of capital flight. The interruption of the private credit bonanza, the upsurge of capital flight, and decreasing oil, gas and tin prices in 1978-9, which showed the limitations of its export potential, was 'leaving Bolivia without the substantial foreign inflows needed to help service its large external debts – debts which had in turn financed a capital stock which could not contribute to paying them' (WB 1985: iii).

The 1978-1985 Crisis

By 1978, inflationary pressures, declining terms of trade, dwindling growth, the burgeoning debt crisis and the reconstitution of subaltern movements primarily around trade unions (both rural and urban-based)[39] but also a grand coalition of socialist parties (the *Unidad Democrática y Popular* [UDP], led by Hernán Siles Zuazo) [40] had begun to erode the fragile stability achieved by the Banzer administration since 1971 (Zavaleta 1983, Rivera 1983, 1984). The amplification and increasing effectiveness of resistance – through strikes, sabotage and violent skirmishes in mines against the army, and the unprecedented rapprochement between Marxist and indigenist currents of opinion (Zavaleta 1983)[41] were a manifestation of the *criollo* bloc's slipping grip on institutional, ideological and economic power. In the context of dismal economic performance, grumbling among army chiefs and desertions of businessmen, the increasingly isolated caudillo and his direct entourage were forced to create a political party (ADN) and call general elections.

The 1978 to 1985 struggle for popular democracy was a historical period of intense social crisis.[42] The long crisis of democratisation in the transitory 1978 to 1985 era witnessed a succession of civilian and military governments, which attempted to manage more or less coercively unstable social relations. This institutional crisis occurred *sur fond de* debt crisis; worsening terms of trade for key commodities, which reduced foreign exchange needed for imports; an exclusion from private circuits of financial capital due to the government's lack of credit-worthiness; and the increasing salience of a double exchange rate system which generated a widening gap between official and black market rates. The latter affected the credibility of the Bolivian currency, fuelling speculation, capital flight, and further preventing imports for productive activities. Private investment declined from 7.3 to 3.7 percent of GDP, while FDI was reduced to a trickle (see table 2.3).

Progressive political parties clustered in the *Unidad Democrática Popular* [UDP]) had been victorious in the 1978 and 1980 general elections, and were invested two years later after a particularly bloody military interlude (Dunkerley 1982; see table 2.4).[43] The UDP government inherited the contradictions of state capitalism upon taking formal control of the state in 1982.

Table 2.3: Fixed Investment, as Percentage of GDP, 1970-1985										
	1970 (1)	1975 (1)	1978 (2)	1980	1981	1982 (2)	1983 (2)	1984	1985	1980-1985 avg growth rate (%)
GDP (US$ millions)	2,521	3,346	3,824	3,920	4,250	4,146	3,969	3,870	3,750	-1.9
FDI (US$ million)	-75.5	35.2	23	43.9	75.6	31	6.9	7	10	-12.7
Net official transfers (US$ millions)	-	-	-	46.8	26.3	28.8	66	66	59.8	-
Investment										
Private	6.4	10.9	6.7	7.3	4.5	5.6	3.3	3	3.7	-22.3
FDI	-3	1.1	0.6	1.1	1.9	0.8	0.2	0.2	0.2	-12.7
Public	8.1	7.5	13.4	7	9.4	7.4	8.4	8.9	3.5	-22.1
Total	**14.5**	**18.4**	**20.1**	**14.3**	**13.9**	**13**	**11.7**	**11.9**	**7.2**	**-22.2**

(1) Indicates capital flight during the populist military regime of General Juan José Torres, and higher private capital formation and business confidence in the years following the 1971 coup d'état by Colonel Hugo Banzer.

(2) Indicates private capital strikes (1978-1985) in the face of democratisation and economic mismanagement by military governments. Nonetheless, FDI increased in 1980 and 1981, bolstered by the apparent stability provided by the Garcia Meza junta.

Source: WB (1985; 1989c; 1991c; 1999c; 2005); Morales (1990; 1993, 1994).

MDIs and Crisis

In the face of widespread urban and rural resistance to attempts, by military officers, to annul the 1978 election results, conservative political parties agreed to elect in the lower congressional house a benign political figure, Lidia Gueiler (allied to Paz's MNRH and head of Parliament), as head of a transitory government in 1979 (Zavaleta 1983; Dunkerley 1984; Malloy and Gamarra 1988). The fragile government of Gueiler, facing a profound fiscal crisis due to deteriorating terms of trade, capital flight, a brewing debt crisis and an increasing imbalance between the national price system and the global market due to a rigid exchange rate and domestic price distortions, collaborated with the WB and IMF during the last months of 1979 to devise and implement a Structural Adjustment Programme (SAP) antagonising organised labour and civil servants in the public administration and state-owned corporations.

The package combined a large devaluation in real terms of the Bolivian peso – which brought it in line with the lack of credibility of the national currency – and a stringent reduction in public expenditures – which reduced the state's demand for imports, and thus demand for foreign currency, in line with a declining supply of foreign exchange (WB 1985: iii). Stripped of the popular support needed to maintain its authority and legitimacy, and incapable of harnessing the coercive power of the army, the civilian government organised new general elections, won again by the UDP coalition. Before Siles and Paz Zamora (leader of the MIR and vice-presidential candidate) could be sworn in, the Gueiler government was overthrown by reactionary military officers led by Luis García Meza and supported by an Argentinean army battalion in July 1980. Two years of profound crisis ensued, which witnessed three military coups, systematic repression of the COB and left-wing political parties, a complete disorganisation of the state, and a significant rise in narco-trafficking sanctioned, if not actively promoted by, the military leadership (see Dunkerley 1982, 1984 for an in-depth analysis of the 1978-1982 political crisis). The military governments, more intent on emptying the state coffers than to reorganise – however coercively – production relations, lacked any civilian support and managed to alienate all donors but USAID – which however restricted its financial and technical assistance to the narco-dictatorship.

Despite attempts by the WB to collaborate with the Meza government in the elaboration of a Structural Adjustment Programme (SAP), it became obvious to the staff in its November 1980 mission that

Table 2.4: Pre-Transition Election Results (% vote; major parties only)

	1951	1956	1960	1964	1966	1978	1979	1980
MNR	42.9	82.3	74.5	85.9		10.8	31.1	20.2
UDP						24.6	31.2	38.7
ADN-							12.9	16.8
PS-1							4.2	8.7
FSB	10.5	13.7	8		12.5			
MNRA			14.1		8.6			
ASD	32.1							
PL	5.2							
PIR	5.3							
FRB								
PDC						8.5		
Blank		1.5	1.2	5.7	5.8	1.8	3.2	11.2
Null		1.1	1.2	6.5	2.4	0.9	10	6.3
Population	3,019,031	3,250,000			3,748,000	4,850,000	5,253,623	5,570,109
Registered voters (1)	204,649	1,119,047			1,270,611	1,922,556	1,876,920	2,004,284
Votes cast	126,123	955,349			1,099,994	1,971,968	1,693,233	1,489,484
Abstention rate (%)	38.4	14.6			13.4	(+2.6)	9.8	25.9

(1) Indicates restriction of vote to those who could read and write in 1951 elections, disenfranchising the indigenous. Universal suffrage established with National Revolution (1952).

Source: Dunkerley (1998: 3-4)

the military junta was merely paying lip service to the restructuring plans and was attempting to obtain any form of credit for wasteful consumption needs. The Meza administration provides valid evidence for Collier and Gunning's (1999: 645) argument that recipient governments may sign agreements with the IMF and WB and begin implementing policy reforms in order to obtain financial assistance; but once the first tranche of credits and/or loans has been received policies are either no longer implemented or even reversed. This evidence points to the relatively limited leverage available to the IMF and WB in policy-related, conditioned assistance (see chapter 4). Hence the Bretton Woods institutions disengaged from Bolivia and took a wait and see attitude from November 1980 until August 1985. Still, technical assistance teams and missions continued to visit Bolivia and sought to advise the Siles administration for the implementation of SAPs in 1982 and 1984 (WB 1985; WB 1986).

The relationship between governments and MDIs proves to be dialectic, as will be made apparent in chapter 4, in the sense that the former require public capital to make up for a lack of private domestic capital formation, in order to undertake productive and infrastructural investments, to provide welfare services, and to sustain the conditions for private capital accumulation – including the attraction of FDI – for employment generation and the maintenance of social stability. It is however in the interest of MDIs' staff to pursue an engagement with peripheral governments, even free riders, not merely to perpetuate their own indispensability to global capital accumulation – but to ensure government commitment to capitalist production, to debt servicing, and in order to leave a window open for ideological persuasion and institutional coordination for restructuring in the global context of money discipline.

It is commonly argued that the disengagement of the WB and IMF from Bolivia after November 1980 was total and that under the left-wing coalition government of Siles, Bolivia remained almost completely isolated from capital circuits for almost five years (Climenhage 1999, Fernández 2003, Kohl 2005). This is inexact: Bolivia certainly remained integrated in the world market through commercial relations with its neighbours (gas exports to Argentina had become its principal source of foreign exchange by the late 1970s), while Bolivian governments continued to service its foreign debt until March 1984 (although arrears were mounting), and both civilian and military governments continued to receive bilateral financing, in particular USAID credit. MDIs only suspended cooperative activities with the narco-trafficking military juntas (1980-1981) when it had become obvious that credits were wasted on the consumption of luxury goods.

MDIs continued to undertake reviews of various economic sectors during the Siles administration (1982-1985). The latter, in turn, continued to negotiate possible Structural Adjustment Programmes (SAPs) – although ODA had been curtailed due to the government's lack of creditworthiness. Lines of communication and exchange of information persisted despite the apparent chaos affecting Bolivia. Despite the effective boycott of the Bolivian government by transnational banks since the beginning of the long crisis of democratisation (1978-1985), USAID actually increased economic and military aid from $19.7 million in 1982 to $78.1 million in 1984 (Dunkerley 1990: 19). Notwithstanding weariness, an IMF mission in 1982 resulted in a 1983 Compensatory Financing Facility (SDR17.9 million – less than a third of the amount lent by the IMF in the March 1980 Standby agreement). On their side, four WB missions to Bolivia in March and November 1980, March/April and November 1984 provided insights into ongoing political and economic tensions to the Paris Club, the Organisation for Economic Cooperation and Development (OECD) and the DC (WB 1985, foreword; IMF 1982).[44]

In stark contrast to the conservative press in Bolivia, which systematically (and continues to) blamed the ineptitude of the Siles administration and the obstructive actions of the COB for the 1985 hyperinflationary crisis, the WB and IMF demonstrated an awareness that the profound social crisis of the 1980-1985 period rather found its roots in the 1952 National Revolution driven by the post-1985 liberalisers, and had been accentuated by the dictatorial administration of General Banzer in the 1971 to 1978 period (WB 1985, 1986, 1987; IMF 1982, 1986). However, it is arguable that MDIs' clear reprobation of the economic policies implemented by the Siles government, and their decision not to inject sufficient capital to stabilise the Bolivian government's fiscal situation accentuated the Bolivia's hyperinflationary crisis.

Accentuating the Crisis: The Siles Administration

The Siles Zuazo presidency (1982 to 1985) was hailed as signalling a democratic revolution. There was, however, no honeymoon between the coalition government led by Siles on the one hand, and elite or subaltern forces on the other. The UDP inherited a formal economy in ruins as there had been no economic management to speak of during the preceding three years. The Siles administration however, was unable to manage confrontational labour relations, to reorganise the state, and to muster sufficient support in Congress for the implementation of any comprehensive policy package. It was confronting a Congress under the effective control of the opposition and systematic obstruction by the CEPB and the COB in the media, the streets and, through the Congressional opposition, within the institutions of the state itself. It was, furthermore, unable to escape its credit-unworthiness, as MDIs and transnational banks were unwilling to extend new loans to a credit-unworthy government that was furthermore taking 'inappropriate' economic decisions. The chaotic situation inherited by the UDP thus deteriorated further – undermining the legitimacy of the government and of its socialistic discourse.

Economic dislocation was in part caused by the government's incompetence and internal contradictions – the fact that each ministry was controlled by one of the coalition partners (MNRI, MIR, PDC) induced a lack of coherence in the executive agencies of the state; while a swelling of public employment from 15 to 20 percent of the economically active population occurred between 1982 and 1985 (to 245,000 state employees), as party leaders were, as is customary in Bolivia, redistributing secure jobs to their clients (WB 1989a; 2000c: 9). Like the nationalist military governments of Ovando and Torres in the 1969-1971 period, the Siles administration further expanded the scope of state activities by penetrating a hitherto privately-led sector: passenger and freight surface transportation (WB 1985: ii). This in part was a product of political pressure by the COB and Siles's coalition partners, but also stemmed from initiatives by the management of the constellation of uncoordinated state agencies, including state corporations generated since the 1950s (Dunkerley 1990).[45]

The government perpetuated the economic mismanagement that had characterised its predecessors and furthermore gave contradictory signals to organised labour: in contrast to the 1979 SAP, which, in the view of the WB (1985: iii) 'contained relatively well defined and comprehensive policies for stabilisation', the subsequent five stabilisation packages were ad hoc, inconsistent and served to accelerate Bolivia's inflationary and balance of payments crisis. The implementation of stabilisation packages between February 1982 and February 1985 – designed to generate a modicum of business confidence and a repatriation of capital through the implementation of policies designed to control inflation and freeze real wages – faced systematic opposition in the streets by the COB. These packages precluded trade union consent because of their confusing wage policy component. Labour was required to accept cutbacks in real wages without being given the opportunity to discern whether the reductions were permanent or consisted in a transitory measure that would eventually result in real wage increases in the longer term, whether they were a one-off policy decision or would lead to further cuts in the near future. This vagueness effectively intensified COB resistance to any stabilisation decree and further disrupted production.

Moreover, the stabilisation packages were inconsistent with the government's concessions to labour demands. The government's willingness to reward labour with bonuses and nominal wage increases in almost every instance of industrial conflict 'put a premium on labor action and may help to explain the steady increase in strikes and work stoppages over the last five years' (WB 1985: iii-iv). Furthermore, systematic strikes affected production and productivity, worsening the deficit of already loss-making public corporations, hence draining further the depleted Treasury. Even Central Bank staff undertook a six-months strike in 1983, disorganising completely the state's monetary policy (WB 1985).

Labour-friendly policies, however, were systematically frustrated by CEPB opposition to the 'crypto-communist' UDP, and by a conservative parliamentary bloc led by the MNRH and the ADN. This legislative bloc would later cement party leadership support for the 1985 *Pacto por la Democracia* accord between the ADN and MNR (see chapter 5). Siles increasingly ruled by decree, negotiating wage increases (usually in the context of general strikes) with the COB, in order to maintain the purchasing power of low income earners. The negotiated wage increases were implemented across all sectors, often in the form of bonus payments. The government introduced a minimum wage indexed to inflation (*escala móvil*) towards the end of its incumbency, which further drained the coffers of the Treasury and accelerated inflationary pressures (IMF 1986: 18).

The accumulation of debts, interest dues and arrears on debts had reached uncontrollable proportions by 1984 (despite the drying up of transnational private and multilateral public loans from 1980: the slowdown in new commitments limited the accumulation of debts). The Bolivian government was financing its debt by ordering, through the Finance Ministry, the BCB to print new money, and by contracting new short-term credit facilities from both state-owned and private domestic banks. This caused a further depreciation of the Bolivian peso on the black market – generating a growing gap between the overvalued official and informal exchange rates, which accentuated the volatility of the Bolivian market exchange rate, further reducing the credibility of the Bolivian currency and beginning to impact the import capacity of, and access to further credit by, both private capitalists and state-owned enterprises. Above all, it generated a balance of payment crisis of monumental proportions which further stimulated inflationary pressures. However, in the context of inflation, capital flight and generalised economic disorder, the drying up of loans and grants accentuated the debt crisis, since new loans could no longer be used to repay outstanding debts; thus foreign liabilities were increasing at a rate of 12 percent per year. By December 1984, the state's total external debt (including private and public, principal and interest liabilities, and the build-up of arrears) had swelled to $4.5 billion, an amount that surpassed Bolivia's GDP and equivalent to five times the value of its commodity exports. Debt service obligations was expected at the time to range between $600 and 700 million a year from 1985 onwards (about 16% of GDP), excluding arrears (WB 1985: v). The Bolivian state was virtually bankrupt by late 1984, and declared a moratorium on its debt obligations in March of that year (WB 1986).

At the same time, the Conservative opposition bloc of MNR and ADN congressmen regularly criticised the UDP government for antagonising the workers through real wage depreciations. The MNR-ADN parliamentary bloc, savouring the tensions internal to the UDP and the unmanageable demands of organised labour, and increasingly envisaging a collapse of the government, took every opportunity to sabotage UDP attempts to stabilise prices (Dunkerley 1990; Conaghan and Malloy 1995). The MNR leadership criticised the November 1982 deflationary package for 'not respond[ing] to popular interests but, rather, to the requirements of the IMF, it seeks to reduce the level of internal demand, and in order to do this uses as an instrument a pitiless reduction in the purchasing power of wages' (cited in Dunkerley 1990: 18). The 1983 stabilisation package, in turn, was immediately undermined by the MNR's passing of a bill (with ADN support in the upper house) increasing nominal wages by 100 percent (Dunkerley 1990: 18). As pointed out by Dunkerley (1990: 18), the

'inconsistency of (the UDP's) policies ... reflected divisions within the UDP, "dedollarisation" being essentially a MIR initiative, the "heterodoxy" of November 1983 to May 1985 being largely the product of independent technicians who tried to move towards the IMF but were forestalled tactically by the left, and the "final fling", a traditional populist gesture in which the small cliques around Siles, exasperated by rightist criticisms that it had pampered the workers, decided to do just that'.

Between 1980 and 1985, Bolivia's GDP declined by 10 percent and GDP per capita by 24 percent (from $940 in 1979 to $540 in 1985), while formal unemployment increased from 5.8 to 20 percent. Real wages decreased by 9 percent in 1981, 27 percent in 1982, and 2.5 percent in 1983 with the indexation of wages to inflation, which however fed the explosion of inflationary rates – inducing a decline of more than 60 percent over the 1980-1985 period (WB 1985, 1986, 1989c: 6).[46] The informal sector, stimulated by the coca-cocaine circuit established during the Banzerato in Cochabamba and Santa Cruz, mushroomed (Gill 1987; Doria 1986). Creeping capital flight during the *Banzerato* became overwhelming. The crisis affected primarily the urban population, because the confinement of large portions of the peasantry to the informal economy and to subsistence maintained them relatively unaffected by the generalised crisis (affecting wages and purchasing power in the formal economy) and prevented total social chaos (WB 1991b). The Siles administration, beleaguered by an unmanageable foreign debt (110 percent of GDP), the sudden collapse of its gas exports to Argentina (its main source of foreign currency), a hyperinflationary crisis (23,000 percent inflation rates in annualised terms by March 1985), government decomposition (accelerated by the strategic desertion of Vice President Jaime Paz Zamora in 1984), recurrent strikes in the public sector and marches throughout the country, called early elections in August 1985.

Conclusion

The 1952 National Revolution was a rare moment of structural transformation, which erased production relations centred on the *hacienda* and profoundly undermined the *ayllu* through the creation of *minifundios*. The attempt by the COB leadership and worker militias to validate the thesis of Pulacayo by transforming what it considered as a bourgeois-national transition into a full-fledged socialist revolution was effectively suppressed by the stabilisation programme implemented in 1956 by the MNR government. Subsequent military *juntas* further consolidated the state capitalist form established in 1952 through the internationalisation of the state. State capitalism, underpinned by USAID and MDIs' fiscal support and technical assistance, effectively subsidised and sheltered the development of private production, conditioning the emergence of national capitalist elites articulated around the agro-business, extractive (the so-called *mineria mediana*) and banking sectors.

As emphasised by Grebe (1983) and Gill (1987), although an incipient process of primitive accumulation centred on agribusiness was observable in Santa Cruz well before 1952, it is only after the National

Revolution that the expansion of capitalist production relations unfolded in the *Oriente* (lowlands) of Bolivia. The agrarian reform of 1953 was restricted to the Bolivian highlands and valleys, and the Bohan strategy for import-substitution and economic diversification was implemented by the MNR (1952-1964) and subsequent military administrations by generating a new axis of capital accumulation in Santa Cruz, thereby conditioning the transformation of an unproductive, landowning oligarchy into a cohesive and increasingly dominant capitalist bloc unifying finance and (agro-industrial) production (Grebe 1983: 100-103; Barragán 2008; see chapter 3).

Regional rivalries have therefore been accentuated since the 1950s by elite struggles for the appropriation of state resources and ODA, but also because class struggles, mediated by territorially distinct cycles of expansion, maturation and decline for vital exports (silver, tin, rubber, gas, oil) in the highlands and lowlands have taken distorted spatial forms (Roca 1980), to the extent that they 'seem to express themselves as regional conflicts' (Grebe 1983: 102).

The contradictions of state capitalism had become irresolvable by the mid-1970s: the re-composition of indigenist movements stripped the state of a vital source of subaltern support, and led indigenous people to vote massively for the UDP in the 1978, 1979 and 1980 elections; waste and corruption were rampant in the state, systematically undermining the functional maintenance of appropriate conditions for accumulation; low business confidence stimulated capital flight, and foreign credit was beginning to dry up just as state-owned corporations – the primary sources of foreign exchange reserves – began to build up losses in the face of declining world prices for tin and oil. Dwindling capital resources, compounded by increasing labour resistance and elite disengagement accentuated the state's fiscal deficit and inflationary pressures, sealing the fate of the *Banzerato*.

The alternation between elections, resulting in the formation of fragile coalition governments, and military coups defines the 1978 to 1982 era, which was concluded by the investiture of Hernán Siles as head of the UDP government in 1982. The Siles administration certainly mismanaged the crisis. Yet it was also prevented from managing it by systematic obstruction in Congress, by negative media campaigns financed by the CEPB, by the lack of support of MDIs, and by demands by the COB that were impossible to satisfy. Internal bickering and divisions in government resulting in inconsistent government policies, compounded by sabotage in the legislature and opposition in the streets, only served to deepen the crisis.

The deeply traumatic hyperinflationary crisis and the near bankruptcy of the state seriously shook the ideological appeal of state-led capital accumulation despite the continuing potency of nationalism among socialist parties and the COB, but also the middle strata of the national hierarchy, i.e. domestically-oriented businessmen, managers and professionals. It offered an unprecedented opportunity for burgeoning transnational business elites to change the balance of forces within the MNR and ADN and vie for control of the state. The trauma of hyperinflation conditioned the electoral victory of the MNR in 1985, and opened a political space for the initiation of radical stabilisation and structural adjustment reforms by transnational elite forces, and for the liberalisation and internationalisation of the state (see chapters 4, 5 and 6).

I hypothesise, however, that the second wave of internationalisation since 1985 was qualitatively different from the first one, because 1) it complemented the expansion of a transnational historic bloc of relative equals, and 2) was no longer at the behest of the US State Department. The relationship between transnational elites in distinct national settings was founded on production networks underpinning 'denationalised interests' (no longer dependent, for their survival, on state subsidies and commercial barriers); ideological coherence (centred on *worldwide* sustainable capital accumulation strategies); and unprecedented organisational capacity (through macro-regional and worldwide business organisations). The transnational bloc struggled for the consolidation of global governance, which facilitated the transcendence of national imperialisms through multilateral and supranational decision-making processes. A crucial measure of multilateral transcendence of national imperialism – or North-South relations is the increasing pre-eminence of MDIs as creditors of the Bolivian state (see figures 4.1 and 4.2). The movement towards global governance intensified coordination between MDIs, and between MDIs and the depoliticised government agencies in Bolivia (see chapters 4 and 5).

The post-1985 penetration of transnational capital, legally and institutionally consolidated by the IMF and WB has deepened the process of capital accumulation in Bolivia's space. Processes of internationalisation, liberal democratisation and depoliticisation displaced the locus of authority towards multilateral, supranational institutions, generating a double institutional movement: the sheltering of the executive and legislative organs of the national state and MDIs from labour struggles; while displacing the focus of subaltern movements on municipalities – and sustaining the illusion that ultimate authority rests with national institutions. The following chapters will analyse in detail these processes, beginning with the formation and expansion of a transnational historic bloc of forces in Bolivia, before focusing in more detail on the actual implementation of the NEP in chapter 4 and the dialectical relationship between the Bolivian state and multilateral organisations, conceptualising its deepening integration into a global governance complex as a second wave of internationalisation.

Notes

[1] See the studies of imperialism and neo-colonialism in Bolivia by Marsh (1928); Whitehead (1969); Dunkerley (1984); De La Cueva (1983); Burke (1987); Vandycke (1987). For an excellent problem-solving analysis of fiscal and monetary policy in Bolivia in the late 1950s and 1960s, and USAID fiscal support and technical assistance to the MNR government, see Wilkie (1969).

[2] See the analyses of Klein (1982, 1993, 2003); Rivera (1983, 1987); Albó (1990, 1996, 2008); Gill (1987); Hylton and Thomson (2007).

[3] See Mitchell (1977); Antezana (1983); Crabtree (1987); Morales and Sachs (1990); Moore (1990); Morales and Pacheco (1999). The resilience of Revolutionary Nationalism to this day is due to the heterogeneity of its meanings and the flexibility of its conceptual premises (Antezana 1983). Revolutionary Nationalism has been the ideological pivot of varied and sometimes contradictory societal projects, and has historically oscillated between structuralist discourses equating development, modernisation and capital accumulation on the one hand, and socialist ideologies on the other. It also, and more insidiously, justified elitist and white supremacist discourses (promoted by the political party *Falange Socialista Boliviana* and regional Civic Committees) (Antezana 1983). The capacity of domestically-oriented and labour forces to sustain the hegemony of Revolutionary Nationalism has been under threat since the fiscal and monetary crisis of the early 1980s, which laid bare the irresolvable contradictions of state capitalism and opened an ideological breach for discursive and programmatic alternatives, all of which undermine the notion of a 'sovereign' Bolivian state: indigenism, neoliberalism and regionalism.

[4] See Malloy (1970); Mitchell (1977); Malloy and Gamarra (1988); Moore (1990).

[5] On these polarising forces, see Lora (1977); Dunkerley (1984); Lavaud (1990, 1991); Calderón (1999); García (2007).

[6] On indigenous movements and their relationship with the COB, see Zavaleta (1983); Rivera (1983, 1987, 2007); Albó (1990; 1999; 2007); Calderón (1999); Mamani (2007); Hylton and Thomson (2007); Crabtree (2007).

[7] See Dunkerley (1982, 1984, 1990); Malloy and Gamarra (1987, 1988); Moore (1990); Conaghan and Malloy (1995).

[8] See, among others, Klein (1982, 2003); Rivera (1983, 2007); Dunkerley (1984, 2007); García (2006: 74).

[9] See Rivera (1983, 1987, 2007); Mamani (2007); Klein (2003); Dunkerley (1984).

[10] See Marx (2003); Burnham (2001); Bonefeld (2000). See Van der Pijl (1998) and Cox (2002) for an attempt to integrate racism in neo-Gramscian class analysis.

[11] Chapter 3 will offer more in-depth examination of capitalist bloc formation.

[12] Wilkie (1969: 4) offers a figure of 5,664 percent from 1931 to 1952.

[13] The *Rosca* (small kernel) refers to the three tin mine owning dynasties (Patiño, Hotschild, Aramayo) dominating Bolivian politics in the first half of the twentieth century (see Dunkerley 1984; Hylton and Thomson 2007). Bolivian historians, being heavily influenced by nationalist ideology, have argued that the *Rosca* directly controlled, in the form of a '*superestado*' (a 'super-state'), the national state apparatus and policy process during the post-1899 liberal era. As pointed out by Dunkerley however, 'it is much easier to assert the general existence of a tin oligarchy/*rosca mineral*/*superestado minero* than it is to demonstrate in detail how such an elite secured its interests and enforced its rule' (Dunkerley 2003:136). Considering that mining rents formed the bulk of the state's fiscal resources, and that mine-owners resisted taxation, conflicts over the appropriation and redistribution of mining rents were recurrent (Morales and Pacheco 1999: 157): 'In general, the attitude of the entrepreneurial *gremio* [the mine-owners' association, the ANMM created in 1939] was of dissent in the face of demands by the state, landowners and merchants who tried to appropriate mining rents, and of the middle-classes and workers who were looking for better living conditions' (Jordán 1999: 227; author's translation).

[14] There is no space here to elaborate the details of theses struggles, but it is in the analysis of the conflicting relationship between the *Rosca* (the tin industry), other *criollo* elite forces, middle strata constituted by *mestizos*, and indigenous formations that an adequate understanding of the specific state form emerging during the first half of the twentieth century can be achieved (see Dunkerley 1984, 2003; Klein 1971, 2002; Rivera 1987 for detailed discussions of pre-1952 social-political relations). These social-political relationships must be placed in the context of global relations of production, as Bolivia's national struggles developed in the non-hegemonic era of national imperialisms characterising the *entre deux guerres*, which constrained Bolivia's dependent capitalist development (Cox 1987).

[15] Some of these policies (land redistribution, co-management) were not initiatives of the MNR but government responses to pressure from below: for example, land redistribution served to contain the widespread uprisings and land expropriations that immediately ensued from the revolution (Malloy 1970; Eckstein 1983; Rivera 1983; Mitchell 1977; Dunkerley 1984). The agrarian reform implemented by the *co-gobierno* clearly succeeded in constraining the eradication of pre-capitalist relations, and undercut the power base (land) of the *hacendado* elite in the *Altiplano* by expropriating and redistributing more than 10 million acres of land, from 5,515 estates, to 126,000 families (Carter 1971). Nevertheless, it consciously evaded a socialist collectivisation of the rural economy: it divided land *ad infinitum*, into minuscule parcels worked by individual peasants and their nuclear families (*minifundios*). The 'landowning' *campesino* integrated to national life was stripped of its communal lifestyle; while parcellisation was not conducive to agricultural mechanisation and productivity increases.

[16] Inflation rates skyrocketed from 1952 and 1958, when the effects of the IMF stabilisation programme began to be felt. From 33 percent in 1951, annual inflation rose to 101 percent in 1953, 124 percent in 1954, and 179 percent in 1956. From 1958 to the 1967, inflation was effectively kept under control through strict wage controls, layoffs in COMIBOL, and averaged 7.5 percent per annum (Wilkie 1969: 4).

[17] The Revolutionary Nationalist discourse of *mestizaje* envisioned a poly-classist transformation of *señores* into bourgeois and democrats, and of *indios* into citizens, united by the sovereignty of the Bolivian state and the dynamism of its domestic market. *Indios* were to eventually disappear through miscegenation, the diffusion of Hispanic civilization, migration to cities and to the *Oriente*, and land reform, which would purge the vestiges of the *ayllus* through parcellisation and private ownership of the land. Indigenous languages would also disappear through state education, which was perceived as underpinning national homogenisation and equality of rights (Rivera 1983, 1987; Sanjinés 2004).

[18] The famous Thesis of Pulacayo drafted by leaders of the Trotskyite POR and adopted by the miner's union (*Federación Sindical de Trabajadores Mineros de Bolivia* – FSTMB) in 1946, was to become the revolutionary ideological and organisational blueprint of urban labour movements in their struggles against the oligarchy, the MNR conservative wing and military governments. It defended the view (seemingly validated subsequently by the national revolution of 1952, in which an armed proletariat and petite-bourgeoisie overtook the oligarchic state within three days of urban fighting) that the mining and manufacturing 'proletariat was characterised by the possession of sufficient force to realise its own objectives and those of other classes; which is to say that it had the capacity to combine in a revolutionary process, conditioned by the semi-colonial reality of the country, the historical tasks of the bourgeois revolution and the socialist revolution' (Mayorga 1978: 89; see also the application of the Leninist concept of 'duality of powers' to the 1952 revolution by Zavaleta 1987 [1977]).

[19] The pre-colonial Andean *ayllu* as a body was neither a space nor a village: it was a bloodline (Klein 1971: 26). All Aymaras (including *kuraka* members of the nobility) pertained to a kinship group or clan, organised as a corporate agrarian social structure defined by collective land ownership. Although attached to a specific urban centre, *ayllu* members were spread, as colonists, in often distant environments, coexisting with other formations (thus territorial controls overlapped, in contrast to European estates), and producing collectively for the *ayllu* itself (in contrast to the personalised production and dependence of European serfs), the surplus of which was appropriated by *kurakas* allied into historic blocs led by monarchs. The rule of *kurakas* was hegemonically transmitted by elders and religious leaders (monopolising moral-legal authority) to the clan as a whole, which collectively controlled the land toiled by individual members, and through which a rotating system of duties and obligations underpinned public works. Generally speaking however, the *ayllu*, due to infrastructural-technological limitations, practiced rotation farming and only produced a small surplus above subsistence levels that was extracted by the nobility (Klein 2003).

[20] Nationalisation did not essentially change the logic of capitalist exploitation; it merely changed its form: a greater proportion of social surplus was thus appropriated by the state – in effect turning private accumulation, through state restructuring of capital, into a form of state capitalism. As already argued in chapter 1, assertions that state-ownership and organisation of production through nationalisation constitute a qualitatively distinct form of production (potentially generating a transitional platform towards socialism) fallaciously assume that state and market are two separate and contradictory entities: in fact, both (re)produce the exploitative containment of labour power (Faundez and Picciotto 1978; Picciotto 1978).

Nationalised industries, the YPFB – created in 1936 with the expropriation of the Gulf Oil corporation – and the state mining COMIBOL remained integrated in the competitive world market as capitalist corporations and thus reinforced Bolivia's dependent development instead of providing the economic means for its national liberation. This failure to emancipate the nation was caused on the one hand by the fact that extractive industries employed an extremely small workforce, and therefore the need to transform holistically urban and rural sectors of production was not addressed by a focus on such a limited labour base; on the other, these industries are export-driven, and remain ever-tied to the value attributed to it by the world market. The value of mineral (and later of hydrocarbon) exports – on which the entire Bolivian capitalist economic edifice rested until the 1980s – thus remained vulnerable to the vagaries of the world market, stringently moderating the sovereignty that nationalisation professedly achieved.

[21] It is of fundamental importance to remind ourselves that primitive accumulation in indigenous territories was not always imposed from outside or above. Aymara and Quechua peasants eagerly integrated the capitalist economy once the land reform freed them of their condition of servitude: 'Another dimension of the agrarian reform was the generalisation of commercial circuits and the restructuring of the channels of marketing. The rupture of the hacienda commercial monopoly immediately provoked an acute dearth of foodstuffs, but soon enough new commercial networks were structured, which permitted the circulation of growing volumes of agrarian produce towards consumption centres. This commercial restructuring was also a spontaneous process in the hands of *campesinos* themselves who, through their unions, intervened in the organisation of hundreds of fairs and marketplaces, and of new villages, which radically modified the agrarian landscape of the country' (Rivera 1983: 132; author's translation).

[22] The Luis García Meza junta (1980-1981) was neither, involved as it was in emptying the state's coffers and openly engaging in narco-trafficking (Dunkerley 1990).

[23] These include the Economic Cooperation Administration (1948-1951), Mutual Security Agency (1951-1953), Foreign Operations Administration (1953-1955), International Cooperation Administration (1955-1961) and Development Loan Fund (1957-1961) (Wilkie 1969: 9).

[24] The latter sought recognition by the US administration through the implementation of the Bohan Plan. The latter had been devised by a US economic mission led by Mervin Bohan in the early 1940s. It recommended economic diversification, import substitution and monetary stabilisation

(contrasting starkly with Bolivia's previous export-driven economic organisation relying quasi-exclusively on the mining sector). It was refined by another US expert, George Jackson Eder, who advised the MNR government to entrench post-1956 stabilisation policies and state capitalism (state-led industrialisation) under the aegis of USAID, the IMF and WB (Whitehead 1969). Diversification and macro-economic stability have remained, to this day, at the core of MDIs' and successive governments' strategic approach to capitalist development in Bolivia. The latest crop of liberal organic intellectuals in Bolivia continues – in an uninspiring fashion – to regurgitate the now clichéd mantra that an economy founded on a *'base ancha'* ('wide base') is Bolivia's ticket to social development (Gray 2007).

[25] Between 1956 and 1983, the IMF signed thirteen Stand-by Arrangements and two Compensatory Financing Facilities (1956, 1957, 1959, 1961, 1962, 1963, 1964, 1965, 1966, 1967, 1969, 1973, 1978, 1980, 1983), for an aggregate amount of SDR 250.5 million (author's elaboration from Korsner et al. 1986: 193). MDIs – including the Bretton Woods 'sisters' –, the IDB and bilateral aid agencies, boycotted the 'military-socialist' Ovando and Torres administrations between 1969 and 1971, and resumed collaboration following a military coup by Conservative army factions led by Colonel Hugo Banzer, which was legitimised by a civilian elite bloc organisationally constituted by the business confederation (CEPB), the MNR and the Falange Socialista Boliviana (FSB).

[26] The WB was involved in Bolivia once the restructuring process was already well under way. It began to offer development credits to Bolivia in 1962, and actively collaborated, like USAID and the IDB, with capital-hungry anti-communist military juntas until November 1980 for infrastructural projects (WB 1985, 1986).

[27] By 1960, COMIBOL was decapitalised (i.e. declared bankrupt) due to mismanagement, wage demands by trade unions, propaganda campaigns by conservative media and foreign government pressures. Considering the fiscal dependence of the state on COMIBOL, it effectively brought the mono-exporting Bolivian economy on the verge of collapse. The Triangular Plan ostensibly sought, through technical and financial assistance for the restructuring of its management structure and recapitalisation, to revitalise COMIBOL as an engine of growth and of technological development. As argued convincingly by Burke (1987) however, the creditors' veiled objective, supported by military juntas after 1964, was a vicious attack on the legitimacy of organised labour involving systematic repression by the army of miners' strikes, large-scale layoffs, and wage freezes and cuts. The Triangular Plan also forced the denationalisation of the mining industry, through joint ventures between US corporations and COMIBOL in which US managers and technical advisers dominated the decision-making process, the privatisation of non-tin mining production (favouring the consolidation of the private *mineria mediana*), and the systematic transfer of fiscal resources generated by COMIBOL towards Santa Cruz for the creation of a second axis of accumulation centred on agro-business. Bolivia's subsequent debt crisis and virtual bankruptcy in the early 1980s are, according to Burke, directly correlated to the policies implemented through the Triangular Plan.

[28] The lifeline of USAID – followed by the IMF, the IDB, the WB but also Japanese and European bilateral development assistance – to the MNR and

military governments cannot be overlooked. From 1954 to 1966, the US State Department committed $457 million to the Bolivian government, of which 217.4 million took the form of USAID grants and, from 1959, $95.6 million in loans. The share of Bolivian government revenue contributed by USAID was simply indispensable during the unstable decade that followed the National Revolution (it gradually increased from 25 percent in 1954 to 32 percent in 1957, before declining to 25.5 percent in 1961, and plummeting to 4.1 percent in 1965). USAID contributions averaged 6.8 percent between 1957 and 1964 (10.5 percent in 1964), before plunging to 3.1 percent in 1965 (Wilkie 1969: 13, 48-49; Appendix A, B). Including other bilateral and multilateral sources, ODA averaged 8 percent of Bolivia's GDP until the unleashing of democratic pressures in 1978.

[29] The 1953 land reform had caused steep declines in the production of agricultural commodities, as those large landholdings that had been producing for urban markets were turned into low-productivity *minifundios*, based on subsistence farming or production for small rural markets. In order to shield the MNR government from having to manage mass urban starvation and potentially uncontrollable rebellions, between one third and one half of all USAID grant assistance to Bolivia in the mid-to-late 1950s consisted of surplus foodstuffs purchased by the US government to subsidise US farmers (Wilkie 1969: 13-14).

[30] This must be constrasted to the 20 million hectares of land that was distributed to 550,000 families in the Altiplano in 1953 (Urioste 2001: 2).

[31] Financial and technical assistance by the Bolivian government, the IDB and USAID (credit facilities, subsidies and advice for local investors, the construction and administration of private schools, roads and hospitals in Santa Cruz) were crucial vectors of the transformation of the pre-capitalist, agrarian *Oriente* into a buoyant elite bloc dominated by wealthy, well-organised *Camba* businessmen defending *bec et ongles* Hispanic traditions, Catholic values, and capitalism (Moore 1990). The reconstituted *criollo* bloc was a racially and class conscious elite: a class-caste 'for itself', to paraphrase Marx, which would thereafter struggle relentlessly for national dominance and hegemony.

The new axis of accumulation centred on the production and export of sugar, soy, cotton and meat was relatively unrelated to mining in the *Altiplano* due to the geographical disconnection between highlands and lowlands. This spatial segregation was alleviated by the construction of an integrationist/nationalising road linking Cochabamba and Santa Cruz in the early 1960s, which connected lowlands and highlands and supported infrastructurally a mass migration movement from the former to the latter to work underutilised land (Grebe 1983: 93).

Migratory movements of seasonal workers from the *Altiplano* to the *Oriente* turned indigenous peasants (whether members of *ayllus* or owning small plots of land following the agrarian reform of 1953 [*minifundios*]) into a rural proletariat, which eventually settled in Santa Cruz and induced a dramatic expansion of the department's population through capital accumulation (Grebe 1983: 102; Gill 1987).

[32] Despite its gradual dismantlement, the state-owned COMIBOL remained throughout the 1960s and 1970s the matrix of economic development, used for the subsidisation of private investment, including in mining (Burke 1987). It also was the organisation in which the national managerial strata would learn

their profession through internships before moving to the private sector and state institutions (Moore 1990). The faltering state-owned corporation became the backbone of private accumulation and private business dominance, and their integration, as subordinate members, into the US-led capitalist bloc (Gill 2003).

[33] For instance, the Barrientos government promoted FDI by offering concessions in the *Oriente* to the US Gulf Oil Company. Despite the lack of investment in new technology and exploration ventures, the *mineria mediana*, privately-owned 'middle-sized' mining companies (often taking the form of joint ventures between US and local capital) throve thanks to rising prices. Thus private capital overcame COMIBOL as the dominant sector and became the principal exporting sector and primary source of foreign exchange reserves (Moore 1990; Burke 1987).

[34] Ovando's military administration established a Planning Ministry, which elaborated a twenty-year programme of state capitalist development. This programme was not inconsistent with Paz Estenssoro's 1960 development plan: state-ownership of strategic (export-driven, extractive) sectors of production as the nucleus of growth, import substitution for selected sectors, economic diversification and industrialisation through mixed and state-owned companies. State oil revenues would be used to subsidise investment in different productive sectors and redistributed in the form of welfare programs. This blueprint would survive the demise of Ovando's military government and be pursued under the Banzer dictatorship (1971-1978).

[35] Thereafter Banzer ruled with the collaboration of the CEPB: prominent business leaders would fill the ministry portfolios of his government and high managerial positions in state corporations and institutions (Dunkerley 1984; Moore 1990; Conaghan and Malloy 1995).

[36] See National Security Archive, http://www.gwu.edu/~nsarchiv/. Accessed 24 May 2006.

[37] The income distribution pattern, already shifting towards increasing inequality in the late 1950s and 1960s, underwent further polarisation under the Banzer-CEPB administration: the proportion of GDP allocated to labour payments, hovering at 37 percent in the 1960s, dropped sharply in the early 1970s to reach 31 percent in 1974, while investment was still relatively robust. Nevertheless after 1975 the economic crisis further reduced that percentage (Moore 1990).

[38] A burgeoning indigenist movement, centred on the so-called Independent Bloc, had begun to rebel against the corrupt leadership of the CNTCB, and affiliated itself to the COB in the late 1960s. Under the leadership of Genaro Flores, Macabeo Chila and (later) Victor Hugo Cárdenas, the Independent Bloc fissured the Military-Campesino Pact by taking control of the regional directorates of La Paz and Oruro in 1969. The indigenist movement, articulated by a growing number of urban and rural organisations, formalised its existence through the Tiwanaku Manifesto (1973), began with these words: 'A people that oppresses another cannot be free. We, the quechua and aymara farmers, just as those of other autochthonous cultures of the country, say the same thing. We feel exploited economically and oppressed culturally and politically. In Bolivia, there has not been an integration of cultures but a superposition and domination, and we have remained in the lowest and most exploited stratum of that pyramid...We are foreigners in our own country' (cited in Rivera 1983: 142;

author's translation). Indigenous nationalism was therefore crystallised by combining critiques of exploitation and of racial domination. The Katarist movement, which took control of the CNTCB, was relatively flexible in its political strategy, affiliated itself to the COB, and advocated an alliance with the UDP in the 1978 elections. This position generated substantial divisions within the indigenist movement. In April 1978, at the National Congress of the CNTCB, these divisions led radical indigenous nationalists opposed to an alliance with leftist *q'aras* (whites and mestizos) to form the MITKA. Under the leadership of Constantino Lima, Luciano Tapia and others, the MITKA articulated an indianist ideology which advocated the creation of a sovereign Aymara republic (reviving the *Kollasuyu)* and an 'internationale' of indigenist organizations throughout Latin America (Rivera 1983). The MITKA systematically undermined the cohesion of farmers unions and of the labour movement as a whole in the 1980s and 1990s, and effectively subverted the COB's class-based discourse through a racist worldview idealising 'Andean civilization' (Mamani 2007). The national farmer's confederation (CSUTCB) created in 1979 by katarista leaders Flores and Cárdenas was gradually taken over by indianist forces, headed by Felipe Quispe from the mid-1980s onwards. The CSUTCB, in turn, took advantage of the decline of the miners' FSTMB from 1986-1987 to become one of the dominant forces within the COB. The indianist movement underpinned the formation of the *Movimiento Indigena Pachakuti* in 1999, again led by Felipe Quispe (Gustafson 2002; Rivera 2007).

[39] García Linera (2007: 129; author's translation) emphasises that 'the union was for workers, primarily miners and factory workers, and at least for 50 years (1940-1990), the organizational network of class identity and of the accumulation of the class experience, that is, of their mobilized existence as a class... other organisational forms, which competed to develop this role of historical condensation of the worker's identity, such as political parties, remained transient and superficial' (author's translation).

[40] The MNR split into two factions in the early 1970s, each led by the 'fathers' of the National Revolution, Hernán Siles Zuazo and Víctor Paz Estenssoro. The profound division was caused by the latter's collaboration with General Banzer between 1971 and 1974, before Banzer undertook a self-inflicted coup which formally sidelined the leadership of allied political parties – the MNR and the FSB – yet continued to rely on the support of the CEPB and prominent members of both MNR and FSB. Siles set up the MNR de *Izquierda* (MNRI), the dominant party in the UDP coalition, while Paz remained as the head of the MNR *Histórico* (MNRH). The UDP was constituted by the MNRI, led by Hernán Siles Zuazo, the MIR and the PCB (Malloy and Gamarra 1988).

[41] A military coup by General Natusch Busch in 1979 was brought down by an unprecedented alliance between emergent *katarista* organisations under the leadership of Genaro Flores and of Victor Hugo Cárdenas (the political party MRTKL and the recently established farmers' union, the CSUTCB) on the one hand and the urban-based and socialist trade union confederation (COB) and miners' union (FSTMB) led by the legendary Juan Lechín Oquendo on the other (Zavaleta 1983). On the variety of indigenist movements (primarily indianist and katarist), their emergence, respective discourses, strategies, internal conflicts, and relationships with the COB, FSTMB and *cocalero* unions, see the seminal work of Rivera (1983, 1984, 2007). For an apology of indianist

discourses reifying Western and Andean civilizations, and advocating the establishment of an Aymara state in the Andes, see Pablo Mamani (2007). García (2007: 131) points out that 'the "farmers' union", beyond its name, has little in common with the worker's union, as it designates a type of traditional association of families unified by obligations and rights around the familial-communal position of lands and local political responsibilities'.

[42] The 1978-1982 period witnessed three elections, a succession of ten Presidents (including two civilians), and eight coup d'états, and an experiment with representative democracy repressed by a radical anti-communist junta led by General Luis García Meza (1980-1981). The latter became notorious not only for its brutality but also for harbouring narco-trafficking 'entrepreneurs' (Dunkerley 1982: 1; 1990; Gill 1987; Hylton and Thomson 2007).

[43] On the twists and turns of the 1978-1982 period, see Malloy and Gamarra (1987, 1988), Dunkerley (1982, 1984, 1990). See also chapter 2.

[44] WB missions conventionally involve between 4 and 8 members of staff. However, there has been a tendency to increase exponentially the number of Bolivian technocrats, private consultants, embassy staff and other MDI staff involved in its reports since the mid-1990s, and to produce joint studies with the IDB, the European Commission and bilateral development agencies (WB 2004; 2005). This is a sign of intensifying coordination between MDIs, and between the latter and the economic cabinets of Bolivian governments.

[45] The state accounted for 65 percent of mineral output, 80 percent of hydrocarbons production, 70 percent of energy production, 55 percent of banking assets, and 70 percent of passenger air transport. Although 'lack of information makes it hard to quantify the government's share in manufacturing ... private participation in Bolivia's industry is one of the smallest in the non-socialist world'. Thus, the state had come to comprise some 520 agencies in 1975 (120 central, 350 regional and municipal government institutions, and 50 state-owned enterprises and financial institutions) (WB 1985: 3).

[46] Inflation, already high in 1979-1982 (between 25 and 45 percent), reached 296 percent in 1982, 328 percent in 1983, 2,177 percent in 1984 and 8,000 percent in 1985 (WB 1986).

3
Transnational Forces and Global Restructuring

The purpose of this chapter is to offer a contextual analysis of the worldwide transformative processes within which the internationalisation and liberalisation of the Bolivian state unfolded after 1985, by focusing on the agency of an expanding transnational historic bloc of elite social forces, incorporating fractions of capital, technocrats, and organic intellectuals, i.e. a loose and competitive, transnationally-integrated bloc of elite forces owning the means of production, managing production relations, and shaping the 'common sense' of global society (Overbeek and Van der Pijl 1993; Van der Pijl 1998; Gill 2003; Robinson 2005).

As emphasised in chapter 1, Critical researchers conventionally explain restructuring in Bolivia as outside-in imperialism facilitated by global governance institutions. They have inappropriately contended that the US government, through the IMF and WB, actively promoted a 'globalisation of poverty' (Chossudovsky 1998) since the 1980s; and that Bolivian elites, acting as comprador lackeys, were forced to allow, or worse, betrayed the sovereignty of Bolivia by sanctioning the plundering of its resources, causing underdevelopment and mass misery. This is historically inaccurate and induces the kind of flawed structuralist critiques of neo-colonialism underpinning the nationalisations of the 1950s, late 1960s and mid-2000s (Kohl and Farthing 2005; Fernández 2003; Petras and Veltmeyer 2002, 2005). Allusions to US and European imperialism fail to consider the theoretical implications of transnational production and organisational networks for North-South and inter-state relations (Van der Pijl 1998; Robinson 2005).[1] As pointed out by Cammack (2003: 39): 'It is anachronistic to see the WB and the IMF as acting in principle at the behest of the United States as the world's leading capitalist state, or even on behalf of a larger set of advanced capitalist states'.[2]

The holistic methodology of neo-Gramscian perspectives helps to overcome this anachronism, by placing post-1985 social restructuring in Bolivia within the context of the structural contradictions underlying the latest phase of capital globalisation. The central attribute of this phase, which emerged in the early 1970s, has been the increasing predominance and spatial expansion of a transnational historic bloc of elite social forces beyond its transatlantic heartland, which accelerated following the debt crisis of the early 1980s.[3] Global restructuring since the widespread social crisis of the late 1960s and early 1970s is best explained by focusing on the variegated struggles unfolding in national social spaces between a transnational capitalist elite bloc, labour and domestically-oriented elite forces (Van der Pijl 1984, 1998; Overbeek 2000; Cox 1996; Gill 2003).

The transnational bloc emerged in the 1960s through transatlantic capital concentration, and incorporated an inner circle of transatlantic business elites, segments of the policymaking and bureaucratic elite of the US and European states, and high-level managers in transnational corporations (TNC) and global governance institutions (Cox 1981; Van der Pijl 1984; Gill 2003; Robinson 2005). It has been the dominant collective agency in the global decomposition and frailty of organised labour, socialist and other subaltern movements since the 1970s. Emphasising the central role of transnational elites in the restructuring of the global political economy is not a superfluous academic exercise but provides the empirical means to identify key agents involved in change, to understand how (i.e. through which institutional, ideological and economic mechanisms) this involvement occurred, and to grasp where structural power lies locally, nationally, regionally and worldwide.

Global social restructuring was manifested in the transformation of the economy, hegemony and state, each of which constituted internally related social sites of intense political struggle. Restructuring is understood as a worldwide political struggle by an expanding transnational historic bloc of elite social forces to reconfigure the capital-labour relation in order to sustain global capital accumulation. Bolivia's hyperinflationary crisis (1984-1985) offered an opportunity for a small nucleus of Bolivian businessmen forming a unified transnational banking, mining and commercial fraction of Bolivian capital, to change the balance of forces within the three dominant political parties and vie for control of the state. This elite nucleus, integrated into the transnational bloc primarily through the internationalisation of the state (see chapter 4), struggled against domestically-oriented elites and organised labour, within and beyond the Bolivian state (see chapter 5), to restructure economic, ideological and institutional relations in the Bolivian space. These struggles involved the privatisation of accumulation, the attempt to build capital hegemony (i.e. to generate a consensual capitalist order) and the liberalisation of the state.

I trace the struggle for capital hegemony to qualitative changes in the strategic approach of MDIs to development: monetarism, fiscal austerity, administrative transparency, the privatisation of accumulation, public-private partnerships, the support and intensification of primitive accumulation in the periphery (business class formation via micro-credit and technical assistance) and systematic coordination between MDIs. This strategic shift involved a systematic physical presence of MDIs' staff and contracted private consulting firms for policy-related technical assistance (a hands-on approach to development) (see chapter 4). In Bolivia, capital hegemony entailed shifting hegemonic discourses away from the Revolutionary Nationalism that had legitimised state capitalism (state-led capitalist industrialisation) since the mid-1930s and towards a hybridised form of neo-liberalism adapted to Bolivian conditions.

This chapter structures the analysis of transnational bloc expansion into Bolivia as follows: the first section focuses on the historical formation and expansion of a bloc of transnational elite forces beyond its Lockean transatlantic heartland (Van der Pijl 1998). For reasons of space, the second section expounds briefly the global economic, ideological and institutional changes occurring since the early 1970s and the crystallisation of a global strategy for restructuring in global MDIs since the profound debt crisis of the early 1980s. The third section analyses the anatomy of capital in Bolivia and the emergence of a small nucleus of transnationalised capitalist modernisers in Bolivia in the 1970s, demonstrating that portfolio diversification entails a rejection of fractionalism. The fourth section bridges this chapter and the following one by analysing how the transnational bloc expanded in Bolivia. It argues that Bolivia's transnational elite fraction was integrated in the expanding bloc as equal partners in development. This process unfolded primarily through official channels of development assistance (see also chapter 4), but also through the creation of new business organisational networks, IFC investments, and FDI in the mining, banking, hydrocarbons and telecommunications sectors.

The Transnational Historic Bloc of Elite Social Forces

Van Apeldoorn (2001: 72), following Overbeek and Van der Pijl (1993), identifies 'two primary structural axes along which class fractions are concretely formed': firstly, the division between money and productive capital; secondly, the division between domestic (national) and transnational capital.[4] Concepts of fractions and forces leave theoretical space for elite formations and historic blocs that rely on interstate cooperation for transnational investment practices, and strive to build a global organisation of production relations (Van der Pijl 1984, 1998; Overbeek 2004; Cox 1987; Bieler and Morton 2003; Robinson 2005). The transnational bloc's worldview approximates the interest of global capital. Its formation is explained by the neo-Gramscian analysis of social classes as dynamic social formations. Class analysis cannot merely rely upon an analysis of the structural distribution of wealth within a given social order. It is the consciousness of appurtenance to a class that maintains cohesion within the class itself – hence the alienated decomposition of the working class engendered by capital hegemony. The constitution of a capitalist class as a conscious social force must therefore be analysed in the light of Gramsci's distinction between three levels/moments of consciousness: the economico-corporative, the class, and the hegemonic (Cox 1983). 'Under capitalist conditions, ruling-class formation is a highly dynamic process that runs through and unifies these three moments' (Holman and Van der Pijl 2003: 74). The fractional (economico-corporative) interest is, from this perspective, the most basic, generating mutual loyalties among its members due to common experience and orientation. In order to temporarily crystallise identities and interests beyond basic corporative communities, and to shape self-reflecting agency in social struggles, the role of organic intellectuals becomes essential (Gill 2003; Bieler and Morton 2003).

Formation and Expansion of the Transnational Historic Bloc

Transnational elite bloc formation involved a movement unifying these three levels of consciousness: Transnational capital concentration (Overbeek and Van der Pijl 1993), concurrent to and consolidated by the construction of an increasingly sticky complex of multilateral institutions and the apparent demise of Keynesianism in the early 1970s (Holloway 1995), thus stimulated the emergence of a dominant transatlantic social bloc incorporating US, European and later Japanese and peripheral capitalist elites. New processes of transnational capital concentration on a transatlantic scale were under way by the late 1960s, which transformed both elite worldviews and their organisation, and directly affected their relationship to the international system and its territorial logic of power (Poulantzas 1975; Van der Pijl 1984; Robinson 2005). Marx's prophetic suggestion that capitalist competition and class struggle, mediated by escalating investment costs for increasingly sophisticated products, would drive the process of (local, national and potentially transnational) capital concentration has been occurring and is accelerating (Marx 2003 – 'Capital Vol.1'; Van der Pijl 1998; Robinson 2005). Transnational concentration increased the mobility of capital but also blurred the national boundaries dividing firms and hence their national interests, undermining the conventional Marxist and world-system metaphor of a global market constituted by rival national state entities (Holloway 1995; Burnham 1995, 2002; Frank 1975; Wallerstein 2000). Transnational capital concentration is embodied in the emergence of transnational productive and investment corporations (TNCs), struggling against each other through the incorporation of firms in distinct sectors – often unifying, for risk sharing purposes, banking, productive and commercial circuits of accumulation into single corporations. TNCs have expanded through transnational mergers and acquisitions, strategic alliances, interlocking and interpenetrating capital stock ownership and board directorates, which constitute the economic expression of an increasingly coherent and organised transnational capitalist bloc (Robinson 2005).

Placing emphasis on transnational elite agency in global restructuring begs the questions: why and how did its struggle for global restructuring develop since the early 1970s? Restructuring is rooted in the highly unstable global social conditions of the late 1960s and early 1970s, manifested in widespread recessions and high inflation, the Mai 1968 student and black Civil Rights movements of the late 1960s, the increasing financial and ideological cost for US elites of the Vietnam war, the Chinese Cultural Revolution and the 1969 border war between the Soviet Union and China, the early 1970s wave of nationalisations of oil industries by OPEC member states, and the 1973 energy crisis triggered by Arab states' oil embargo against metropolitan complexes due to the latter's active support for Israel in the Six-Day and Yom Kippur wars of 1967 and 1973. As saliently pointed out by Wallerstein (2006: 82), these large-scale events were compounded by a multiplicity of short-lived rebellions by subaltern social forces throughout the globe, cutting across the Soviet and capitalist geopolitical blocs. Crisis-as-rupture (Wallerstein's perhaps inflated notion of 'world revolution') conditioned an enhanced awareness by elites integrated via transnational production networks of the need to restructure increasingly unviable Keynesian and Soviet forms of international social organisation (Holloway 1995b; Cox 1987; Robinson 2005).

The profound crisis affecting the capitalist metropolis in the late 1960s and early 1970s conditioned the restructuring of the Bretton Woods System, which bolstered the political ascendancy of finance: the partial deregulation of exchange rates liberated speculative money capital from international constraints, while technological revolutions and the emergence of financial offshore markets significantly enhanced its structural power vis-à-vis relatively immobile labour and other capital fractions (industry and commerce) (Overbeek and Pijl 1993; Cox 1981, 1987; Bieler and Morton 2001). However, William Robinson has added two valid caveats to this conventional neo-Gramscian argument: most TNCs are involved simultaneously in industry, finance and commerce; and money capital 'must land in production, which ... is increasingly impermanent and dispersed in mobile worldwide production sites exhibiting accelerated turnover (and hence decreased fixity) time' (Robinson 2005: 53).

Stephen Gill (2003) has termed the constellation of social forces that has stimulated global neoliberal restructuring since the 1970s the 'US-centred transnational historic bloc'. This inner circle of transatlantic business elites, segments of the policymaking and bureaucratic elite of the US and European states, and managers of transnational corporations (TNC) and multilateral institutions, gradually incorporated transnationalised elite fractions in East Asia and Chile in the mid-to-late 1970s (Jones 1998). The transatlantic bloc, however, expanded dramatically into the global periphery following the global debt crisis of the early 1980s (Kuczynski 1988; Pastor 1987). The notion of a bloc may appear overly homogenous and devoid of internal contradictions; it nonetheless refers here to a constellation of elite social forces loosely unified by their common struggle against other forces for the restructuring of global production relations. Key attributes of individuals integrating the transnational bloc include investment in transnationalised production networks, involvement in both national and multilateral policymaking and organic articulation of strategic projects derived from classical liberalism. These attributes involve the construction of interests and identities broader than the nation.[5] These attributes are of the family resemblance type, and the absence of one or more of them does not invalidate the appurtenance of individuals in the transnational bloc (Collier and Mahon 1993).

One should not conflate the meanings of transnational, a-spatial and de-territorialised: Robinson (2005: 39) mistakenly locates transnational forces beyond social spaces, 'increasingly less tied to territoriality or driven by national competition' (Robinson 2005: 39), as if 'production had become *extra-terrestrial* rather than *spread across numerous territories*' (Cammack 2007: 7; original emphasis). Likewise and as emphasised in chapter 1, transnational social formation must not be analysed as a new phenomenon; rather it has been dialectically related with international relations since the dawn of civilisation. The transnational is 'a phenomenon that extends across, and thereby links as well as transcends, different (territorial) levels' (Van Apeldoorn 2004: 142). Transnational social forces (Cox 1987) or transnational circuits of capital (Robinson 2005) therefore do not exist as a level beyond or outside the national level but within and through it, 'in several national contexts simultaneously' (Van Apeldoorn, 2004: 144-145). The consolidation of a transnational historic bloc of *capitalist* elite forces is rooted in the *longue durée* of world production relations (Braudel 1980), and its expansion beyond its Transatlantic heartland in the early 1980s defined a protracted struggle for the restructuring of production relations, simultaneously in various national contexts, as the literature on global convergence demonstrates convincingly (Cox 1987; Gill 2003). Domestic struggles for and against restructuring have thus been constituted by and constitute other domestic struggles.

Against Robinson's contention that the blossoming of a transnational sphere of accumulation and governance renders national relations of power superfluous it is argued here that national contexts remain relevant and that transnational formation is constituted by and *constitutes* domestic and international conflicts. In that sense transnational capital reproduces the asymmetries – i.e. combined and uneven accumulation – between its constitutive nodes (Morton 2007: 147-149).[6] Just as national nodes do not equalise capitalist development throughout their bounded territory, as the Bolivian case demonstrates so conspicuously (Grebe 1983; Rivera 1983, 1984), transnationalisation does not sustain the 'homoficence of capitalism' – its unitary diffusion across different regions (Morton 2007: 147). It rather equalises relations between transnationalised elite fractions, simultaneously in various national contexts, in their common struggle for global restructuring.

The concept of an *expanding* transnational bloc struggling for *global* accumulation and poverty-reduction also undermines dependency and world-system theories, which relegate peripheral elites to a role of comprador or junior partners consenting to the underdevelopment of their national spaces through unfair trade relations and their reduction to a role of primary commodity producers (Frank 1978; Wallerstein 1989[1974]). Documentary analysis suggests a process of expansion of the transnational elite bloc via the incorporation of small nuclei of competitive and transnationalised elite fractions (capitalists, technocrats and organic intellectuals) in the global periphery and increasingly treating them *as equal* competitors or managers in the world market, *equal* members of the bloc, concurrently struggling to restructure global relations of production and to sustain accumulation in *both* metropolis and periphery (IBRD 1993; DAC 1989; WB 1985, 1986, 1989, 1991, 1998, 2001; IMF 1986, 1998, 2007). This fluid and contradictory bloc, driven by competition in the global market, and hence subject to internal tensions and potential dissolution due to the vagaries of market prices and temporary reassertions of territorial logics of power (Harvey 2003), has struggled on two fronts: first and foremost against labour, but also against domestically-oriented capital and reluctant policymakers and technocrats, in the directorates of MDIs themselves. Documentary sources illustrate the persistence of a protracted ideological struggle between transnationalised technocrats who had a long-term perspective for the sustainability of global capital (stabilisation, structural adjustment and PSD) and mercantilist forces, which continued to support national price distortions, tariff and non-tariff barriers to trade, and guaranteed credits for private and state-owned national champions (IBRD 1993; DAC 1989). The Uruguay Round signalled a manifest victory for the former.[7]

The struggle for and against restructuring has unfolded in the global market (for profit and shares) and in production sites themselves (i.e. in the workplace), but also in the form of ideological debates between neoliberal and heterodox ideologies (nationalist/structuralist, Keynesian, socialist, populist). Struggles between monetarists and Keynesians, between advocates of free trade and of protectionism unfolded in numerous institutional loci, such as ruling political parties, multilateral institutions and national state institutions, as well as business associations (Robinson 2005). In Bolivia this politics of production, finance and trade affected the CEPB and the three political parties dominating state institutions in the period under study: the MNR, the ADN since the late 1970s, and the MIR from the late 1980s onwards.

Multilateral organisations have been vital in sustaining the formation of a transnational bloc: while perpetuating hierarchical relations between states, they also foster correspondence and the consolidation of a 'network of interest' (Stallings 1992) between their cosmopolitan staff.

Restructuring Revisited

Restructuring is understood here as an attempt to reconfigure the capital-labour relation in order to sustain global capital accumulation; in other words, it means a struggle to empower businesses by reforming economic, ideological and institutional relations in order to generate worldwide *sustainable growth*. Economic change involved the transnational concentration of capital and the emergence of more flexible forms of economic organisation (Harvey 1990; Overbeek and Van der Pijl 1993; Robinson 2005); ideological struggle was manifested in the substitution of monetarist/neo-classical liberal (neoliberal) hegemony for Keynesian and state capitalist ideologies (Cox 1987; Gill 2003; Overbeek and Van der Pijl 1993; Morales 2008: 218); and institutional restructuring binding these processes involved the consolidation of global governance institutions reproducing the contradictions of global society in their institutional midst by integrating the executive agencies of national states, a process conceptualised here as internationalisation (Cox 1981; 1987). Global governance in turn refers to a multilateral institutional complex organising worldwide production relations without relying on centralised government (Cox 1987, 1992). Global governance is an emergent form of hierarchically defined social organisation, which has not been imposed from above but has emerged out of the fundamental contradiction between the a-spatial, globally oriented capitalist space and the fragmented, territoralised form of the international system (Lacher and Teschke 2007). Chapter 4 explains in more detail the relationship between global governance institutions and state restructuring in Bolivia. The consolidation of the global governance institutions created during or directly after the Second World War, and built upon pre-existing, yet internationalising national organisations of subjection has been elemental to global struggles for and against the restructuring of capitalist forms in the latest era of globalisation. Global governance institutions reproduce within their midst the tensions of global society – including institutional struggles within and between national states. It must therefore be emphasised that global governance is a highly contradictory process and therefore cannot be assumed to inevitably achieve a final or complete form. Multilateral institutions are distinct from civil organisations such as lobbies, educational and research institutes; they have been built through inter-governmental collaboration; and most importantly, they enjoy supranational authority and have historically tended to 'privilege the investor as dominant political subject' (Gill 2000: 3).

The Global Debt Crisis and the Crystallisation of a Global Development Strategy

The global debt crisis of the early 1980s intensified the transnational bloc's struggle for global restructuring; it also enhanced its cohesion around a global strategic blueprint centred in the short-term on monetarism, free trade and structural adjustment (the elimination of price distortions and subsidies), and later crystallised around the notion of PSD (DAC 1989; IBRD 1993; DC 1996). The PSD strategy, implemented since 1989 by national governments in collaboration with MDIs, including the WBG,[8] the IMF, regional development banks and the United Nations Development Programme (UNDP), has systematically emphasised the privatisation of accumulation, state- (in particular government-) building through depoliticisation strategies (Conaghan and Malloy 1995; Burnham 2000), fiscal and monetary stability, and capitalist class formation – a process of primitive accumulation – in the periphery (Van der Pijl 1998: 38). It has also focused on stimulating collaborative practice between MDIs, between MDIs and national governments, and between dynamic business and technocratic elites (public-private partnerships) (IBRD 1993; DC 1996). This strategy has driven the expansion of the transnational elite bloc from its Transatlantic, Lockean heartland (Van der Pijl 1998), and has effectively conditioned global accumulation.

The process of multilateral coordination involved a gradual centralisation of decision-making in the DC (through the WBG and the IMF), which has come to constitute the pivotal multilateral institution for global policy elaboration and strategic programming. The establishment of the DC in 1974 formalised the symbiotic strategic approach to global capital accumulation of the board of governors of the IMF and the WB, who are typically grounded nationally – being constituted by Finance Ministers and Central Bank governors.[9] The establishment of the DC also facilitated the articulation of these two large multilateral bureaucracies in their respective approaches to SAPs since the late 1970s, if not since the wartime creation of the General Agreement on Tariff and Trade (GATT).[10] In contrast to transnational elite organisations (business organisations such as the European Roundtable of Industrialists, the Bilderberg group and Trilateral Commission, among numerous others) (Gill 1990; Robinson 2005), the DC is a formal institution constituted by its member-states, which has worked towards the coordination of MDIs' efforts to generate sustainable capitalist development since its creation. It is the multilateral organisation embodying *par excellence* the consolidation and expansion of the transnational elite bloc beyond its Lockean heartland. The DC, and to a lesser extent the OECD, through its subsidiary DAC, and the UNDP, have actively coordinated their activities to facilitate the expansion of both capital and capitalism (DAC 1989: 31-32; DAC 2006: 3; Cammack 2006). Neo-Gramscian and Marxist researchers have therefore identified a gradual convergence in MDIs' ideological approach to production relations since the Second World War and a shift in their approach to the global periphery in the wake of the debt crisis of the early 1980s (Cammack 2003; 2006; Robinson 1996; Cox 1987, 1992; Gill 2003; Augelli and Murphy 1988; Morton 2000).

The struggle of the transnational bloc was advanced by the implosion of the Soviet Union in 1989, which offered an unprecedented opportunity for MDIs to penetrate social spaces hitherto closed to, or restrictive for, the private ownership of the means of production. As the dissolution of the Soviet bloc was becoming manifest, new social spaces for private capital expansion incurred an unprecedented increase in the breadth and depth of MDI activities, rendering them increasingly indispensable as globally oriented, multilateral information-sharing and decision-making fora. Impediments to the expansion of the transnational bloc were disappearing, as the viability of Keynesian and Soviet-style central planning were apparently demonstrating their own limitations: the ideological thrust for PSD (via the provision of adequate conditions for business confidence, and public-private partnerships) seemed to be vindicated on the ground. The expansion of the Lockean heartland's frontiers induced a qualitatively significant increase in operations with a PSD component from 1989, aiming at the improvement of the business environment, public sector restructuring (consolidating central banks and government Ministries, restricting state activities to regulation and the provision of public goods, which signified the divestiture of state-owned corporations), and financial sector development (through the creation of stock markets and the consolidation of the private banking sector). These activities were considered, in a holistic fashion, to be mutually indispensable (IBRD 1993: 1-4). In order to address new social developments worldwide, the WBG launched the *Private Sector Development Action Program* in 1989. Since then, two thirds of the WB budget has been invested in activities related to PSD. By 1991, 152 WBG operations had a PSD component – including 40 Adjustment Operations and 99 Direct Investment operations (IBRD 1993: 18).

MDIs demonstrated impressive adaptation to the various national legal and institutional environments in which PSD reforms were implemented. The idea that a one-size-fits-all neoliberal project was applied is inexact. Their respective staffs have consistently expressed a highly reflexive and sophisticated understanding of the national legal, institutional, and economic constraints to restructuring. The IBRD thus admitted in 1993 that 'Because the magnitude and urgency of these privatization efforts are unprecedented, the WBG, other development agencies and governments alike are approaching them with an openness to learning from mistakes and to strengthening their design and implementation capacities as the process unfolds and new and unforeseen issues arise' (IBRD 1993: 10).

Finance ministers and central bank governors in the DC and DAC were also showing uneasiness about the frailty of business confidence and of privatised accumulation in the periphery. In its analysis of the debt crisis affecting Latin American social formations, the DAC asserted that 'they also helped to create political and economic uncertainties that have affected investment confidence', and by implication growth and living standards (DAC 1989: 24). WBG and DAC documents illustrate how fragile peripheral capitalist forces have historically felt in the face of 'the plebe' (García et al. 2002; García 2006). Established capital circuits can easily be undermined by political instability. 'A key variable is business confidence ... which ultimately is a long-term result of political stability and policy consistency. In Latin America, for example, preliminary results from PSAs suggest that when rules change, potential new investors first try to ascertain how permanent is the new business environment, a degree of caution understandable in a region that lacks a tradition of political and economic stability' (IBRD 1993: 5).

State-Building and the Promotion of Polyarchy

Against the conventional state vs. markets approach, MDIs have also demonstrated an awareness that accumulation can only occur through effective state organisation, legitimacy and stability. The political and the economic are internally related – the dialectical relationship between accumulation and its organisation have historically been at the centre of DAC and DC preoccupations.

The DAC and DC have demonstrated, in internal documents, an awareness of the potential contradictions between democratisation and SAP in Latin America. Yet they persisted in considering institutional and economic liberalisation as mutually supportive processes. 'With the recent trend towards democratic government in the region, establishing a political basis for effective and sustainable stabilization adjustment programmes is a delicate yet essential task for Latin America's leaders' (DAC 1989: 24). From the late 1980s onwards, MDIs and, especially bilateral development agencies pushed the third 'wave of democratisation' (Huntington 1990) by increasing the 'democracy promotion' component of Official Development Assistance (ODA) tenfold – from 0.5 percent of ODA in 1991 to 5 percent in 2000. Democracy promotion accelerated significantly under the Bush administration (Burnell 2005). Indeed 'democratization support is an established and growing industry' (Burnell 2005: 361). Yet commentators such as Robinson (1996) have demonstrated convincingly that this 'industry' promoted a historically specific form of authority and rule, which perpetuated existing and generated new forms of capital domination underpinned by the legitimacy bestowed by electoral representation. The following two chapters will demonstrate that the transnational bloc's promotion of polyarchy was correlated to the consolidation and depoliticisation of central banks, regulatory agencies and economic Ministries. Thus, the appearance of a democratic opening and power diffusion via regular and transparent elections veiled the concentration of power in key state agencies, which, in the context of a dearth of technocrats, were almost systematically led by the transnational leadership of the CEPB (Conaghan 1992).

The approach of MDIs to democratisation is reminiscent of Crozier, Huntington and others' (1975) warnings to the Trilateral Commission against 'excesses of democracy'. Representative democracy had to be promoted, but it was imperative that the *government* remain the dominant institution in all national states (Robinson 1996). This approach was adopted by the business leadership of the CEPB in the early 1980s, by securing 'the reestablishment of some corporatist mechanisms to ensure business access to state entities; the integration of high-ranking individuals from the private sector into government "economic teams" and; the strengthening of political parties on the centre-right and their attempts to alter the ideological climate of policy-making by injecting anti-statism into public discourse' (Conaghan 1992: 200). In other words, the issue was how to consolidate key government agencies (those involved in economic management), while weakening other state institutions. Indeed, 'For the Bolivian bourgeoisie, the question was not so much one of how to alter a regime type, but how to stave off the complete disintegration of political order' (Conaghan 1992: 212). Parliaments were either ignored or considered as a hindrance to necessary structural reforms. Constant emphasis was put on the empowerment and consolidation of the executive agencies of the state, since the government is the key interlocutor at the multilateral level and the executor of multilateral agreements. Thus 'Upgrading public administration capacity ... increasingly reflects recognition that trimming public sectors through privatization must be complemented with enhanced capacity in public agencies that are critical to development' (IBRD 1993: i).[11]

State institutions that 'play a key role in PSD' had to be upheld, if necessary through systematic MDI support (IBRD 1993: 3). The DC and DAC have thus recommended the systematic, coordinated involvement of MDI in the consolidation of central government agencies:

'Where developing country authorities lack the necessary policy-making resources and structures to assume in full their responsibility in designing policy programmes and in leading local aid co-ordination, donors should look for opportunities to encourage and support the upgrading of capacities in this central function. This must be a central priority for donor/recipient co-operation, with special responsibilities for the international institutions, especially the UNDP ... Support for policy reform efforts necessarily calls for substantial external support in the form of co-ordinated policy-related programme assistance' (DAC 1989: 33; see also DC 1996).

Beyond resistance by Keynesians and social democrats in OECD governments and legislatures, a fundamental concern of the transnational bloc was the ineffectiveness of governments and resistance from local elites and labour movements in peripheral formations, which hindered restructuring efforts. 'Institutional strengthening, and the development of an institutional culture supportive of PSD, are necessarily long and difficult processes, highly susceptible to failure and heavily dependent on unwavering government commitment in the face of conflicting demands from myriad domestic interest groups. The WB has made progress in supporting governments in this process, but continues to learn from experience' (IBRD 1993: 16). The DC demonstrated an awareness of implementation bottlenecks and distortions, but also of administrative (legislative, judicial, at lower echelons of administration) resistance to structural adjustment. The DC, three years later (1996) was emphasising again the need to consolidate governmental apparatuses, rather than legislative and judicial institutions because politically unpalatable nature of PSD.

The privatisations of state-owned corporations have systematically been accompanied by business-friendly macro-economic legislation facilitating investment; including flexible labour market and lower worker protection, lower taxation for businesses but also the creation and/or consolidation of rules-based (depoliticised) regulatory agencies. However, OECD policymakers, IMF and WB governors have revealed a profound awareness of the instability of capital-labour relations, and a genuine concern for the need to immediately deal with the social impact of privatisation (with initiatives such as the Emergency Social Fund in Bolivia – see chapter 4), because it was understood that the restructuring, liquidation or sale of state-owned companies would de facto involve a reduction of production costs through layoffs (WB 1989; 1998b). MDIs were careful to address the vital need to mitigate the political instability caused by rising unemployment: 'Mitigating direct social costs may involve implementation of measures to minimize the negative impact on job losses. While recent evidence suggests that the negative impact of privatization on labour may in some cases be limited, provision may well have to be made for employee ownership schemes or compensatory measures such as generous severance packages' (IBRD 1993: 10). Social safety nets, ad hoc employment generating infrastructure projects and investments in educational and health were thus considered to be vital stabilising complements of SAPs (DAC 1989: 38).

Furthermore, the need to achieve the hegemony of capital led to the publication of research emphasising that privatisation is empirically proven to have a minimal negative impact on the employees of state-owned companies, and hence is in society's general interest (Chong 2004). It was essential, however, that reluctant policymakers and trade union leaders be persuaded of the positive long-term impact, and on the relatively benign short-term impact of privatisation on both workers and consumers: 'In no case did divestiture make workers worse off, while in some instances they came out ahead, and in most cases, consumers were unaffected by or benefitted from divestiture' (IBRD 1993: 11). The post-privatisation institutional environment had to systematically stimulate competition and sustain business confidence through transparency, information sharing, the protection of private property and enhanced regulatory capacity; but it also had to inhibit the distorting tendencies of oligopolies or monopolies generated by privatisation (ie. economic concentration), to promote equitable income distribution and 'constructive labour relations' as an essential part of PSD (IBRD 1993: ii; DAC 1989: 36).

Expansion of the Transnational Historic Bloc in Bolivia

MDIs – at the forefront of which are the WB and the IMF – have been vital in sustaining transnational bloc expansion in Bolivia through the internationalisation of the state: while perpetuating hierarchical relations between states, they have also fostered correspondence and the consolidation of a network of interest between their cosmopolitan staff. In Bolivia this network of interest incorporated the leadership of the CEPB and the economic teams of the two dominant Conservative political parties, the MNR and the ADN. Despite recurrent conflicts between successive Bolivian Presidents and IMF staff (including the champion of restructuring, President Sánchez de Lozada [1993-1997; 2002-2003]),[12] 'consensus-building' via systematic policy-related technical assistance and 'dialogue' generated an ideological convergence between Bolivian modernisers and the staff of MDIs (Climenhage 1999; WB1998a, 1998b).

The expansion of a web of cohesive formal and informal business organisations, think tanks and research institutes since the 1960s (Bilderberg Group, Transatlantic Business Dialogue, Conference Board, European Round Table of Industrialists (ERT), World Economic Forum, Council on Foreign Relations, Trilateral Commission among others) is a corollary of transnational elite formation (Gill 1990, 2003; Robinson 2005). This transnational institutional network has expanded by thickening its ties with peripheral business organisations, incorporating and linking various levels – from continental and national confederations to regional and sector associations. It is in this context and under the impetus of competitive leaders such as Fernando Illanes, Gonzalo Sánchez de Lozada, Fernando Romero, Carlos Iturralde and Ramiro Cabezas that the CEPB, and since the mid-1990s the regional business organisation, the *Cámara de Industria y Comercio* (CAINCO), based in Santa Cruz, built ties with the Peruvian, Spanish (CEOE) and Latin American business confederations (the *Business Council of Latin America* [CEAL], which was presided over by Fernando Illanes in 2007-2008*)* from the late 1980s.[13] Created in 1990 and regrouping 510 business leaders and 16 national business confederations by 2009, the CEAL is a particularly relevant collective agent: by providing a regular forum for 'systematic information exchange' and the coordination of activities between national business confederations – through trimestral meetings by its board and annual plenaries –, it explicitly aims to 'stimulate the presence of private enterprise as an agent of transformations' (author's translation).[14] It has provided vital organisational support for the creation of private business networks that stimulate the organisation of transnational capital in Latin America, Europe, the US, Australia, Japan and China, but also for the transnational bloc's struggles for hemispheric commercial and institutional integration.[15] This network does not constitute a state *per se* but has played an instrumental role in fostering ideological and organisational cohesion in the transnational bloc.

Cohesion was also sustained by the internalisation of neoliberal strategies of economic management through a learning process in think tanks (*Unidad de Análisis de Politicas Económicas* [UDAPE], attached to the Ministry of Finance, *Fundación Milenio*, financed by the German development agency GTZ), workshops (the *Foros Económicos*) and transnational policy and educational networks (Climenhage 1999). Collective action by Bolivian monetarist economists in key governmental institutions and think tanks was key to the creative implementation of neoliberal reforms adapted to Bolivian conditions (Climenhage 1999).

In the mid-to-late 1980s, the ideological thrust of the staff of MDIs was primarily directed at Bolivian policymakers and high-level technocrats via Private Sector Assessments (PSAs),[16] annual consultative group meetings chaired by the UNDP and the WB, roundtables and workshops involving business leaders and policymakers in order to 'help the WBG and client governments gain a clearer view of the business environment' (IBRD 1993: i). A systematic educational campaign was undertaken by dominant transnational forces in MDIs to 'assist' national policymakers (in particular those on the frontiers of the metropolitan capitalist space) in internalising the business perspective. DC and DAC documents illustrate the struggle to form and consolidate a *global* (in outlook and form) capitalist bloc incorporating both businessmen and technocrats, and centred on public-private partnerships. This strategic campaign involved 'the development of an institutional culture supportive of PSD' (IBRD 1993: 16), a paradigm that had manifestly been fully internalised by policymakers in the metropolis by the early 1980s. The WB and other MDIs undertook a sustained ideological struggle to convince more or less sympathetic policymakers of the indispensability of PSD for global sustainability and elite reproduction. Government ministers and high-level civil servants were to 'gain a clear view of binding constraints that actually affect entrepreneurs' (IBRD 1993: 4) in order to undertake the required 'sustained period of consistent government actions aimed at creating a "market friendly" business environment ... to build sufficient confidence among private investors' (IBRD 1993: 5). Younger technocrats in Bolivia, involved in the private sector, were collectively working towards this objective:

'I wanted to favour the exporting sector. It was always my mission... The Ministry of Industry and Commerce was very powerful in the past... It controlled prices under Siles, of tomatoes, of eggs... A disaster. This Ministry was increasingly ailing. So when Jaime Paz [Zamora] invited me to the Ministry, I told Jaime "delighted", but I think that this Ministry no longer concords with the new structure that we are trying to create. Give me two months to see if I can propose something to you that makes sense, and if not I will propose to you that we leave it as it is...he said ok, ok, so within two or three months we created the Ministry of Exports and Economic Competitiveness. I'd say it was a mission. The Ministry of Industry did not make much sense anymore, it represented a system of preferences. We were at a time of "no industrial preferences at all now". We had to give advantages to no one... Yes, I was obsessed with one thing which was competitiveness. It was related to many other things, for instance tax neutrality for exporters'.[17]

The DAC was arguing in 1989 that 'The WB/UNDP sponsored consultative groups and round tables are appropriate fora to encourage and assist developing countries to plan and carry out strategies and programmes and projects for private enterprise development' (DAC 1989: 38). Consultative Group meetings have taken place annually in Bolivia since 1986 (WB 1998a), involving multilateral and bilateral development agencies and high level Bolivian technocrats. They played an essential role in facilitating 'consensus on the resolution of developmental issues' between MDIs and Bolivian governments, improving institutional coordination and fostering a division of labour between development agencies in accord with government officials.[18] Multilateral aid coordination bodies such as the Consultative Group were to work towards functionally relating state policies to capital accumulation in the periphery (DAC 1989: 39).

In the period under study hundreds of workshops and roundtables took place in La Paz and Washington DC – their frequency also increased between 1993 and 1997 (WB 1998b). The creation by the WB of national formal and informal 'advisory groups consisting of public and private sector representatives' (IBRD 1993: 8) was essential in incorporating business leaders and technocrats in the transnational bloc. Collaborative relationships between governments and businessmen with a 'high degree of personal standing in the business community, and a sound understanding of both domestic and global issues' (IBRD 1993: 9) were promoted via both formal and informal channels – these channels, needless to say, systematically excluded trade unions (Conaghan and Malloy 1995). 'Initial stages of the process are fragile and require substantial support by way of informal discussion and development of a framework for managing the consultative process ... Initially, the process should focus on reforms that alleviate discrete, readily identifiable concerns of the private sector in fundamental areas such as investment, taxation and regulation' (IBRD 1993: 9).

Such initiatives were undertaken in Bolivia, and involved primarily small entrepreneurs. Thus a joint commission of the Ministry of Industry, Commerce and Tourism and the Association of Small Entrepreneurs (FEBOPI) was set up in 1990 in order to reduce registration and operating procedures imposed by state institutions (WB 1991c: 59). The expansion of the transnational bloc beyond frontier areas involved the consolidation of public-private partnerships built on mutual trust and systematic information-sharing: 'Making the public sector better respond to the needs of the private sector also involves building a framework for collaborations between the public and private sectors, ... (by) establish(ing) in the context of a WB adjustment operation, an advisory group consisting of public and private sector representatives' (IBRD 1993: 8). However, while WB-sponsored mediation between small entrepreneurs and technocrats was deemed imperative to expand and consolidate the capitalist class as a whole in Bolivia, this was not required for transnationalised businessmen. From 1986 onwards, the dynamic leadership of the CEPB and, increasingly, of the CAINCO regularly filled key posts in economic Ministries, as had occurred under the Banzer dictatorship of the 1970s (Conaghan and Malloy 1995: 67).

The Anatomy of Capital in Bolivia

Between the National Revolution of 1952 and the enactment of the NEP in 1985, the state generated over two-thirds of all capital accumulation in Bolivia (WB 1985: ii) (see tables 4.1 and 4.2).[19] Most public investment decisions were determined by interest demands (patron-client networks radiating from the President and his government ministers). Such patrimonialism was particularly prevalent during the so-called *Banzerato* (1971-1978): 'Patron-clientelism became the glue that kept the Banzer government in place until 1978. It was the instrument that he used not only to create pockets of support for himself in the private sector but also among factions in the military and the urban middle-class. The proliferation of government bureaucracies and public employment was the fruit of the clientelistic dynamics undergirding the Banzer administration' (Conaghan and Malloy 1995: 67). Chronically unproductive and inefficient investment decisions by state-owned corporations were a manifestation of the exceedingly politicised form taken by the state since 1952, and illustrate the capacity of non-competitive capitalist elites surrounding the presidential cabinet to undertake ineffective or even phantom investments – conventionally with government guarantees and subsidised loans: 'Basically, any project backed by a strong lobby and with assured foreign financing has become part of the Public Investment Program. Easily granted Government guarantees, tempting terms from bilateral aid and suppliers credits have helped funds to flow into sectors or regions run by influential agencies (or local governments) rather than to sectors where returns would be higher' (WB 1985: ii). Lower interest rates for easily disbursed loans by the three state-owned banks (Banco Agricola Boliviano; Banco del Estado; Banco Minero), lack of auditing practices for businesses, government sanctioned tax evasion and the pardoning of debts by Presidential Supreme Decrees were expressions of a particularly rapacious and corrupt form of 'crony capitalism'. Bolivian private entrepreneurs were akin to 'fungi growing on the back of all state-owned corporations, which signed juicy contracts giving them quasi-monopolistic rights. There was no incentive whatsoever for efficiency and re-investment, as any surplus was either exported to foreign bank accounts or wasted by the consumption of owners and their managers. Importers benefitted a lot... Yes both foreigners and Bolivians. I know a man who became a millionaire because he was the only provider of dynamite to COMIBOL; the upper floors of the largest hotel in Oruro accommodated its managers and their entire families... Too many people lived off the state. By 1985 the situation had become completely unsustainable: it is rather surprising that this complete dependence on the state lasted so long'.[20]

Furthermore, as explained in the preceding chapter, the Barrientos and Banzer governments vastly accelerated the transfer of resources from the state-owned mining corporation COMIBOL in the highlands (*Altiplano*) to private agribusiness in the lowlands (*Oriente*) (production and export of sugar, soy, cotton and meat). Indeed, from 1968 and 1973, when a six-fold increase in guaranteed credits to farmers took place, the proportion allocated to agribusiness in the *Oriente* increased from 68 to 90 percent (Lavaud 1991: 208). On the one hand, the central administration effectively privatised and regionalised profits. On the other, it socialised risk by offering cheap (and rarely settled) credits to agribusiness through the state-owned *Banco Agricola*, and by guaranteeing agribusiness's largely irrecoverable debts to 118 foreign banks (Grebe 1983: 103; CEPAL 1983: 55-59).[21] Crucially, resources were allocated to companies whose owners were prone to taking advantage of the overvalued exchange rate to reinvest publicly lent or guaranteed capital abroad or deposit it in offshore accounts (WB 1991a: 2). The propensity of capital to strike in the face of recurrent social instability by exporting itself to safer countries generated capitalist interests that were not confined to Bolivia. The transnationalisation of Bolivian capital originated in the insecurity of investments in Bolivia itself and was facilitated by state guarantees.

The emergent agro-business elite, which rapidly diversified its activities into banking, construction, services and commerce (especially imports), organised itself through the *Cámara de Industria y Comercio de Santa Cruz* (Chamber of Industry and Commerce of Santa Cruz CAINCO) and the *Cámara Agropecuaria del Oriente* (CAO), and immediately projected its attention and efforts outwards through export-driven capital accumulation rather than domestic market formation. The CAO, by representing landowners as a whole, remained inferior in status, according to Lavaud (1991: 207) because 'in the vast ensemble of landowners, the entrepreneurs are few in numbers and because most farmers are placed in a situation of dependence towards industrialists who purchase their production' (author's translation). Export-led production integrated regional capital formation within transnational circuits, fuelling the consolidation of regional commercial houses articulated with Brazilian, Paraguayan and Argentinean merchants, but also the creation of private banks and other financial groups by agribusiness, generating a peculiar fusion of bankers, merchants and rural capitalists subsidised by the state into a primitive form of 'finance capital', according to Grebe (1983: 102-104).[22] Lavaud (1991: 207-208) concurs, arguing that by the 1970s, the neo-oligarchy of Santa Cruz did not encompass more than 100 families, which had *all* diversified their activities, were integrated precisely by banking, and constituted 'a nucleus of dependents that has only been able to take shape and survive in the shadow of the state' (author's translation). The financial power of *cruceño* capital was embodied in the *Banco de Santa Cruz*, established in 1966, largest commercial bank in the country and with a branch in Panama, and the *Banco de la Unión*, an offshoot set up by shareholders of the former.

Within the CEPB and Conservative political parties, private mine owners organised around the hitherto dominant Medium-sized Miners' Association (*Asociación Nacional de Mineria Mediana* [ANMM]), a small and highly transnationalised fraction of Bolivian capital based in La Paz and led by individuals such as Carlos Iturralde and Gonzalo Sánchez de Lozada, was by the mid-1970s on an equal footing with the rising *Cruceño* bloc of agribusiness, commercial and banking capital, while the domestically-oriented manufacturing and commercial fractions in La Paz were relegated to a subaltern position within the *criollo* bloc.[23] The concurrent deterioration of the tin industry – accelerated by the collapse of the world tin market in 1986-7 – and rise in oil and gas exports to Argentina since the early 1970s and later to Brazil (mid-1990s) further enhanced the economic weight of the region, hindered the Bolivian state's movement towards Andean macro-regional integration, and intensified *Cruceño* demands for autonomy against *Paceño* elites traditionally dominating the central executive agencies of the state from La Paz (Roca 1980).

Table 3.1: Relative Importance of Major State-Owned Enterprises, 1990 (prior to privatisation/capitalisation)

	1990 (percentage)								
	YPFB	ENTEL	COMIBOL	ENAF	ENFE	ENDE	LAB	AASANA	Total
Revenue	60.7	5.5	5.1	7.7	4.1	5	10.8	1.2	100
Exports	52.8	3.9	6.9	19.3	0	0.4	15.8	0.9	100
Capital investment	55.6	11.8	4.6	0.4	12.5	13.1	1.5	0.5	100
Value added	75.8	6.8	4.4	0.9	3.7	3.9	3.1	1.3	100
Wages	35.5	7.8	18.1	2.7	15.8	3.3	11.6	5.4	100
Employ-ment	22	7.6	25.6	2.9	27.8	2.9	6.9	4.4	100

Source: WB (1992d: 22).

Table 3.2: Relative Importance of Categories of State-Owned Enterprises, 1990, 1991 (percentage)

	Year	Enterprises attached to Ministries	RDC-controlled enterprises	Enterprises controlled by municipalities	Water companies
Revenue	1991	81.2	12.4	5	1.3
	1990	80.8	12.8	5.2	1.2
Exports	1991	99.1	0.9	0	0
	1990	99.2	0.8	0	0
Value added	1991	82	10.7	5.8	1.5
	1990	80.5	11.5	6.6	1.5
Capital investment	1991	58.7	31.9	7.5	1.9
	1990	59.7	29.8	4.4	6.1
Wages	1991	70.2	14.6	13.3	1.9
	1990	66.9	16.1	14.9	2.1
Employment	1990	84.4	10	3.4	2.2
Number of enterprises	1990	80 in 11 Ministries (1)	70 in the 9 RDCs (2)	20 (3)	170

(1) Of the 80 or so enterprises controlled by Ministries in 1990, only 8 were considered 'major' in terms of value and employment: YPFB (hydrocarbons), COMIBOL (mining), ENTEL (telecommunications), ENFE (railway), LAB (airline), ENDE (energy generation and transmission), AASANA (airport management) and ENAF (smelting and tin refining). Together they accounted for more than 80 percent of revenue, value-added and employment generated by SOEs. YPFB was by far the largest, accounting for 75% of value-added, 60 percent of revenues, 50 percent of exports, and 95 percent of transfers to the Treasury from major state-owned enterprises.
(2) The majority of the 70 RDC-owned enterprises were small, with 60 percent employing less than 25 workers. 11 RDC-owned enterprises employed more than 100 workers, mainly in agro-processing. Most of them were deficitary: 40 percent had ceased operations or were paralysed by 1991, and two thirds recorded an operating deficit in 1990 and 1991.
(3) Mainly provided services (transport, power, sewage, telephone). The largest was SAMAPA, the water and sewage company for La Paz, which employed 650 people and was purchased by Lyonnaise des Eaux in 1999 (renamed Aguas del Illimani).

Source: WB (1992d: 21)

The structure of the Bolivian economy has not changed significantly since 1985, with 'the distribution of enterprises in Bolivia largely skewed toward small-scale productive units' (WB 1991c: 43-44; see also Grebe 2002). To this day (Morales 2002, 2008, Grebe 2002), the vast majority of manufacturing activities remain characterised by informality and small size (less than 14 workers), and consist of family businesses with high levels of exploitation and undercapitalisation, and low productivity (see table 3.5). Of the 13,000 manufacturing businesses registered in 1988, only 200 employed more than 30 workers. The number of 'large firms' had increased to 1,000 by 2004, and generated more than 65 percent of Bolivia's formal GDP (WB 2005: 23). The manufacturing sector has primarily produced for domestic consumption, with foodstuffs, beverages, and clothing accounting for more than half of its output (IMF 1991b: 11). During the 1980-1985 crisis, manufacturing output contracted by close to 40 percent and failed to recover until the mid-1990s (see table 3.3 and 3.4), due primarily to a significant decline in demand accompanying a 60 percent decline in real wages between 1980 and 1986, and to the elimination of tariff barriers to trade in 1985 (Jenkins 1995; IMF 1991b), which opened up the domestic market to competition from cheaper imports.

However, more than 60 percent of Bolivia's real GDP is believed to have been generated by unregistered/informal firms since 1940, the highest level in the world (WB 2005: 23; UDAPE 2007a: 6). Informality is believed to have increased significantly with the development of cocaine circuits (late 1970s to mid-1980s) and the hyperinflationary crisis (1984-1985) (Doria Medina 1986); and to have remained stable since 1985, with more than 70 percent of firms and workers characterised by informality, i.e. unregistered with the tax office and unaffected by the *Ley General del Trabajo* of 1944 (Grebe 2002; UDAPE 2007a).[24] In the mid-1980s, 90 percent of agricultural workers, concentrated in the *Altiplano*, were employed in subsistence agriculture in so-called *minifundios* (small land plots) created in the wake of the 1953 land reform, although 'a majority of rural families obtain a substantial portion of their family income, between 30 and 60 percent, from activities conducted outside their farmsteads, and in almost all cases these activities include some form of wage labour' – in particular through seasonal participation in mining activities (Lora 1977; Godoy 1985: 137; Urioste 2001: 4). The modern, private agricultural sector, in turn, emerged in the late 1950s and has been concentrated in the *Oriente* (primarily Santa Cruz). It consists essentially of export-oriented medium and large landholdings (Gill 1987; WB 1991c: 43).

Table 3.3: Structure of Economy: GDP by Origin											
	1952	1970	1975	1980	1982	1985	1989	1993	1997	2001	2005
	(in percent)										
Primary sector	**43**	**28.1**	**27.9**	**35.1**	**36.9**	**35.9**	**36.7**	**27.7**	**24.9**	**23.8**	**25.3**
Agriculture	27	18.1	17.9	18.9	20.3	23	22	17.4	15.2	14.5	14.5
Extractive industries	16	10.3	10	16.2	16.6	12.9	14.7	10.3	9.7	9.3	10.8
Hydrocarbons	1	1	1.8	5.6	6.4	6.3	6.5	4.3	4.4	4.8	6.8
Minerals	15	9.3	8.2	10.6	10.2	6.6	8.2	6	5.3	4.5	4
Secondary sector	**16**	**18.6**	**19.2**	**18.8**	**15.5**	**15.3**	**16**	**19.5**	**20.2**	**19.8**	**19.1**
Manufacturing	13	14.5	15.1	15	12.4	12.2	13.2	15.2	16.7	16.6	16.5
Construction	3	4.1	4.1	3.8	3.1	3.1	2.8	4.3	3.5	3.2	2.6
Tertiary/services sector		**53.3**	**52.9**	**46.1**	**47.6**	**48.8**	**47.4**	**52.8**	**54.9**	**56.4**	**55.6**
General govt.	14	8	9.1	10.8	11.7	10.9	8.9	9.7	9.1	9.1	9.2
Commerce	12	17.6	16	11.1	11.5	12.1	13.2	11.7	8.7	8.4	8.2
Transport and communication	6	7.5	9.1	6.1	6.6	8.7	8.7	12.1	10.6	10.8	11
Banking	1	1.5	2	6	5.2	4.6	3.5	3.4	3.6	3.9	2.9
Electricity gas and water	1	1.4	1.4	0.7	0.8	0.9	1	1.8	2	2	2
Other (inc. services and ownership of dwellings)	8	17.3	15.3	11.4	11.8	12.3	12.1	14.2	20.9	22.2	22.3
GDP total (in millions Bol.)	**-**	**9,168**	**12,166**	**15,261**	**14,701**	**13,842**	**14,759**	**17,230**	**20,677**	**22,733**	**25,935**

Sources: Agreda (1969); WB (1989; 1994); IMF (1998b; 2003); UDAPE (2007b)

Table 3.4: Average Growth Rate by Sector, 1956-1984 (percentage annual change)										
	1956-61	1962-67	1968-73	1974-79	1980-84	1985-89	1990-93	1994-97	1998-2001	2002-05
GDP total	2	5.5	4.6	4.5	-4	1	4	4.7	2.4	3.4
Agriculture	2.8	2.3	3.6	3.5	-0.7	1	3.5	4.1	1.3	3.6
Mining	5.2	8.4	1.9	-3.8	-5.9	4.5	7.8	2.4	-1.7	2.6
Hydrocarbons	-0.2	-6.2	12.9	-10.6	-0.7	1.4	1.8	2.5	5.1	13.1
Manufacturing	7.1	7	4.3	6.7	-8.7	1	4.9	5.1	2.5	3.1

Sources: WB (1986; 1994; 2005); IMF (1998b); UDAPE (2007b)

Table 3.5: Contribution of Companies to GDP and Employment by Size, 1999

Size of firm (number of employees)	Output (% of GDP)	Employment (thousands)	Employment (% of total)	Productivity (thousand of bs.) (1)
Micro (1-9)	25.5	2,984	83.1	4
Small (10-19)	2.7	170	4.7	8
Medium (20-49)	3.3	123	3.4	13
Large (>50)	65.3	312	8.7	101
Adjustment	3.7			
Total	**100**	**3,589**	**100**	**13**

(1) Productivity is measured per employee. 1999 GDP was 48.156 billion bs.

Source: WB (2005: 23)

The small size of Bolivia's formal capitalist class has defined an extreme concentration in the ownership of productive assets, thereby stringently limiting market competition. The WB thus defined Bolivia's industrial sector as a 'tight oligopoly' in 1991.[25] However, as emphasised by Lavaud (1991: 225), there is no industrial fraction of capital to speak of in Bolivia. 'In the space of thirty years, the country has not been able to endow itself with a veritable industrial fabric. Industry has lived, or rather stagnated (*vivoter*), protected as it was by the diverse facilities provided by successive governments. There is no need to look for an industrial bourgeoisie in Bolivia: it does not exist' (author's translation). Bolivia's business elite has rather been concentrated in four circuits of capital accumulation: mining, agro-processing (the only two industrial circuits to speak of), banking and commerce. It has unsurprisingly led and projected its power through regional business federations – in particular the CAINCO, the CAO, the *Asociación Nacional de Mineria Mediana* (National Association of Medium-sized Mining [ANMM]) – along with the CEPB. Bolivia's elite has constituted, like oligarchic groups of the nineteenth and twentieth century, 'a small circle of individuals with a disproportionate share of the national wealth at their disposal' (Conaghan and Malloy 1995: 43). Furthermore, it has sustained its position at the apex of the Bolivian social hierarchy through close family ties (underpinned by racism towards the indigenous majority), the incorporation of white foreigners (Gill 1987; Lavaud 1991), and effective class organisation through the CEPB and, increasingly, the CAINCO.[26]

At the dawn of the polyarchic era, two sectors were highly transnationalised: mining and hydrocarbons production. The latter required large capital investments for exploration, extraction and distribution, and remained dominated exclusively by the state-owned *Yacimientos Petrolíferos Fiscales de Bolivia* (YPFB) (80 percent of oil and 70 percent of gas extraction) and foreign TNCs, until the privatisation/capitalisation process was undertaken in the mid-1990s, shifting ownership almost exclusively towards foreign capital (WB 1991c: 43; DPC 2004). Mining, in turn was characterised by the predominance of the state-owned *Corporación Minera de Bolivia* (COMIBOL) behemoth until 1987, on the fringes of which subsisted undercapitalised small enterprises and cooperatives; and a powerful, highly transnationalised and increasingly concentrated private *mineria mediana*, employing on average 200 workers. Indeed 'it is difficult to disentangle the hank of relationships between the *mineria mediana* and foreign interests' (Lavaud 1991: 226; author's translation).[27] Interestingly, both small and 'medium' mining enterprises continued to articulate capital accumulation with the *ayllu* in the mid-1980s, 'as though these capitalist entrepreneurs were adapting to the crucible of local folklore, rather than the other way round' (Godoy 1985: 158).[28]

Crucially, the initial impulse for political and economic liberalisation in the late 1970s came from the *mineria mediana,* a capitalist force which had not been particularly privileged by the patrimonial dynamics of the Banzer government.[29] Private mine owners, organised around the ANMM, accounted for 34 percent of Bolivia's total mineral production in 1977 and a not insignificant proportion of the state's fiscal resources, but only around one twelfth of total employment in mining – indicating significantly higher profit margins and productivity than COMIBOL (see table 3.6).[30]

The leadership of the ANMM dominated the CEPB in the 1970s and 1980s (Dunkerley 1990; Conaghan and Malloy 1995), but it was engaged in a protracted conflict with the Banzer administration over its introduction of a mining export tax superimposed on the existing system of royalty payments. The CEPB's calls for democratisation must be placed in the context of the political dominance of transnationalised mine owners resenting the 'milking' of their sector for the development of agri-business and banking in Santa Cruz (Conaghan and Malloy 1995: 63; Grebe 1983: 93).[31] The acute crisis affecting the mining industry in the early 1980s reduced significantly rents on mineral exports by COMIBOL, but also forced the state to virtually eliminate the tax burden on the *mineria mediana* (see table 3.7). The latter would thereafter no longer have to fear unfair treatment by the state in favour the *Oriente*. Crucially, dominant mine owners were involved in the extraction of a variety of metals and minerals (primarily zinc, silver, lead and gold) that had been less affected by declining prices in the early 1980s. They were able to use the tin crash and Bolivia's generalised state of crisis to lay off half of their employees (from 7,500 in 1983 to 4,100 in 1986) (see table 3.6), to purchase smaller companies and thereby concentrate mine ownership, and in the long run (from 1987 onwards) to benefit from marginally rising prices in order to massively expand production and exports. By 1990 they had more than trebled their total output compared to 1980 and more than doubled it again in the 1990s, while COMIBOL was being decapitalised, causing a 65 percent decline in its output between 1990 and 1997 (IMF 1991b:7-8; see also table 3.8). In 1991, they took advantage of a Mining Law (April 1991) enacted by the Paz Zamora government to engage in joint ventures with COMIBOL's remaining profitable operations, and to attract considerable FDI.[32] Following the enactment of the Privatisation Law (No.1330, 1992) mine owners further accelerated the integration of their companies into transnational production networks.

Table 3.6: Employment in Mining, 1980-1987

	1980	**1981**	**1982**	**1983**	**1984**	**1985**	**1986**	**1987**
COMIBOL	26,525	25,728	26,109	27,744	27,746	27,566	7,500	7,000
Mineria mediana	7,600	7,500	7,700	7,500	6,200	5,700	4,100	4,020
Mineria chica	27,800	26,200	24,800	23,500	22,800	19,400	11,000	10,000
Mining Coop.	22,800	21,000	24,700	26,200	27,100	28,900	28,700	25,500
Total	**84,725**	**80,428**	**83,309**	**84,944**	**83,846**	**81,566**	**51,300**	**46,520**

Source: WB (1989b: 79)

Table 3.7: The Tin Crash and Its Fiscal Effects: Contribution of Mining Sector to Government Revenues (in US$ million)

	1980	1985	1986	1987
COMIBOL	59.7	2.3	0.9	0
Private mining	28.9	0.6	0.7	2.5
Total mining	88.6	2.9	1.6	2.5
Total government revenues	589.7	114.1	461.8	479.8
Mining as % of government revenues	15	2.9	0.3	0.5

Source: WB (1989b)

Table 3.8: Bolivia: Volume of Mining Production						
	1993	1995	1997	1999	2001	2002
	(Index 1990: 100)					
Total	122.3	138.9	130.2	127.2	126.1	126.4
COMIBOL	76.9	38.2	33.8	41.4	0	0
Mineria mediana	159.6	218.9	213.7	190	226.1	229.1
Small private mines (inc. cooperatives)	115.6	126.1	113.3	114.9	99	96.5
	(percentage change)					
Total	19.1	17.6	1.8	-6.8	-2.3	0.3
COMIBOL	-18.7	-34.4	-7.4	30.9	0	0
Mineria mediana	45.8	8.9	5.7	-9.4	8.2	1.3
Small private mines (inc. cooperatives)	14	-6.5	-1.6	-8.5	-17.8	-2.5
Value of mining production (US$ millions)	315.4	315.3	413.4	329.7	290.5	275.5
Percentage change	-14.5	18.4	14.1	-8.2	-16.1	-5.2

Source: IMF (1998b: 43; 2003: 29)

Since the 1960s, business elites have increasingly unified capital fractions through economic groups, multi-firm conglomerates directly managed by family networks and other partnerships (Conaghan and Malloy 1995). These conglomerates have typically comprised bank ownership or minority participation in banks.[33] This was particularly the case in Santa Cruz, where the wealth of capitalists was rooted in land ownership and agro-processing (Grebe 1983; Gill 1987: 172-183; Lavaud 1991: 206-207).[34] Portfolio diversification has primarily been caused by a lack of business confidence in the face of real or potential competition by state-owned companies and of labour struggles (WB 2005). Not surprisingly then, owners of agro-industrial and commercial companies with more than 50 employees have typically been 'insiders' of commercial banks (represented on the Board of Directors of one or more banks), thereby obtaining cheaper long-term credit than 'outsiders'. Owners of outsider firms (typically less than 14 employees and employing 60 percent of Bolivia's manufacturing labour force since the early 1980s) have in turn been denied access to long-term credit and forced to rely on their own capital (WB 1991: 59). Bolivia's pivotal axis of accumulation in the 1970s and early 1980s articulated mining and commerce, the two most profitable activities since the National Revolution: Bolivia's largest (highly transnationalised) mining consortia owned shares in Bolivian or foreign commercial house, and vice-versa: COMSUR/MINESA, EMUSA/Rica-Cruz, Grace/PEMSA, Dowa

Mining/Kanematsu Gosho Ltd. They also increasingly invested in the lucrative commercial banking sector: for example, EMUSA owned shares in 32 enterprises outside of mining, including the *Banco Hipotecario Nacional*, while COMSUR was a minority shareholder of the IFC-supported Banco Industrial SA (BISA). These consortia have also been interlinked through shareholding in common companies and banks. Bolivia's wealthiest mine-owners have also been its dominant bankers, merchants and industrialists (De La Cueva 1983: 181; Lavaud 1991: 226-227).

Portfolio diversification challenges theories of objective fractional contradictions elaborated by the so-called Amsterdam school of transnational historical materialism (thereafter THM) (Van der Pijl 1984, 1998; Van Apeldoorn 2001, 2004; Overbeek 2000; 2004). The concept of capital fraction was initially coined by Marx in the second volume of *Capital* (2003), elaborated by Poulantzas (1975) and later used by Van der Pijl (1984, 1998), Gill (1990, 2003), Overbeek (1993, 2000, 2004), Van Apeldoorn (2001, 2004) and Robinson (2002, 2005) in their analysis of transnational elite formation. [35] Coxian IPE has tended to analyse transnational elites as a class *à part entière* (Cox 1996; Robinson 2002; 2005), thereby undermining the analysis of capital as a worldwide class integrated by productive, financial, and commercial circuits, and hence engendering a number of theoretical inconsistencies by jeopardising their avowed dialectical logic and forcing the use of a pluralistic methodology of the Weberian type (Burnham 1991; Bonefeld 2000). THM theorists, on their side, while remaining true to the dialectical method, have sought to return to Marx's original understanding of capital fractions as functional elements of the total circuits of capital to introduce a measure of pluralism in the Marxist metaphor of class struggle by questioning its status as the single trans-historical motor of social change (Overbeek 2004). They have emphasised the contradictions internal to the capitalist class, on the basis of its functional division (fractions), as a cause of structural transformations (Poulantzas 1975, Overbeek 2000, 2004; Van der Pijl 1984, 1998). These fractional struggles are essential, constituting 'a moment of the underlying process of class formation, rather than an aberration or insignificant epiphenomenon' (Overbeek 2004: 115). Capital-in-general as a (global) class is functionally divided between commodity, productive and money fractions, which concretely refer to merchant houses, industrial and financial (banks and other money investment) firms (Van der Pijl 1984, Holman and Van der Pijl 1993, Overbeek and Van der Pijl 1993; Overbeek 2004). The productive fraction is inherently less mobile than the others because it is territorially fixed, and therefore compelled to be *directly* involved in the disciplining of labour (Van der Pijl 1998). From these structural divisions are abstracted the circuits integrating these three fractions, which are defined as *finance capital* in its totality (Overbeek 2004). These fractions define concrete conflicts of interests within the bourgeoisie and leads congruent capitalist forces to temporarily congeal into social blocs ideologically organised around hegemonic projects. Van der Pijl (1998: 3) suggests that 'the concept of fraction makes it possible to reconstruct the historical growth of capital in terms of pluralism (or better, "polyarchy", since the range of options remains within narrow limits) of class strategies which articulate, ultimately, empirical constellations of particular fractions'.

Portfolio diversification and the formation of large capitalist consortia unifying financial, productive and commercial circuits in Bolivia unequivocally contradict THM's fractionalism, as the 'objective' line between money and productive capital is systematically being blurred by cross-shareholding structures. Assuming that fractional divisions ever defined intra-elite relationships – a contention convincingly refuted by Open Marxist theorists (Burnham 1991), struggles between transnationally integrated and domestic capitalist forces have overtaken strictly fractional struggles as the primary axis of elite contradictions worldwide, and certainly in Bolivia (Robinson 2005).

The nucleus of elites at the apex of the business community hardly constitutes a typical national bourgeoisie whose investments are domestically oriented and who defend a national identity and culture: they have historically shown a propensity for transnationalisation, observed by some researchers (Climenhage 1999; Mansilla 1994; Lavaud 1991). They or their parents have typically been immigrants or descendants of immigrants from European countries (primarily Spanish but also German, French, and Croatian), hence they tend to lack a purely national/Bolivian self-identification (Gill 1987).[36] They have grown up in the *Zona Sur* of La Paz, South of the Plaza Colón in Cochabamba, and the first *anillo* of Santa Cruz, often in gated communities exuding affluence comparable to wealthy neighbourhoods in US cities; they have conventionally been educated in bilingual schools located in the aforementioned neighbourhoods,[37] and have typically studied at US and European universities (see Climenhage 1999 for an in-depth analysis of these transnational educational networks in Bolivia). Their investments or savings have more often than not been located outside of the Bolivian space to ensure the security of their holdings (hence the regularly high level of capital flight in the early 1950s, again between 1969 and 1971, from the mid-1970s to the mid 1980s, and again from 1999 to 2005) (WB 1985, 2005). They often have worked abroad as researchers, business executives, or consultants;[38] often have demonstrated a denationalised (little or no dependence on contracts with state corporations, and on state subsidies) and competitive approach to capital investments in Bolivia (Mansilla 1994); and their domestic investments have sometimes been undertaken through joint ventures with US, European and Latin American TNCs. This is particularly true of the modern mining (COMSUR; Inti Raymi; EMUSA/Sinchi Wayra; IMCO; COMCO) and, to a lesser extent, banking sectors: the micro-credit bank Bancosol, established by Fernando Romero, includes foreign investors such as the NGO Acción International – which also engages in strategic partnerships with Citigroup, Visa International, and UPS among others; the Banco de Crédito involves both Bolivian and Peruvian investors, but is primarily owned by the Banco de Credito de Perú (86 percent), supported against expropriation and transfer restrictions by MIGA guarantees; the bank BISA has attracted a variety of institutional investments, for example by the IFC and the CAF, but also private Bolivian (León Prado) and foreign investors; Banco Mercantil, based in Santa Cruz, also involves minority foreign shareholders, and fused with the Banco Santa Cruz in 2006. The latter had been purchased in 1998 by Spain's Banco Santander. The BHN Multibanco (partly owned by Fernando Romero) and Banco de la Paz were both merged with Citibank and Grupo Credicorp in 1998).[39] Crucially, Bolivian banks are not merely passive recipients of foreign capital, but also actively engage in capital investments abroad.[40]

The formal commercial sector also has, by necessity, been reliant on, and promoted, transnational capital circuits (Gill 1987). Indeed, the five principal commercial houses in Bolivia were established prior to the 1952 Revolution as branches of multinational companies or by immigrants with contacts in international markets and establishing exclusive (and highly lucrative) distribution rights for imports (Lavaud 1991: 225). Notable examples are the *Casa Grace*, a transnational commercial house established by Irishman William Russell Grace in the 1870s and linking Peru, Bolivia, Chile and the US with British and US participation; *Hansa*, *Bedoya*, and the *Casa Bernardo*. The *Casa Grace*, Bolivia's largest commercial house was also the primary importer of mining equipment, and with *Hansa* (commercial house owned by the industrial enterprise *Barrosquira* and with shares in the Bank BISA) acted as exclusive agents of US and Swedish firms producing mining machinery. These exclusive commercial rights forced COMIBOL, for instance, to acquire capital inputs through these houses. Yet Bolivian governments themselves perpetuated the effective monopoly of the Casa Grace, by bestowing exclusive rights to it for the exportation of sugar and milk produced by the *Corporación Boliviana de Fomento* (Bolivian Development Corporation, effectively dissolved in 1985 with the decentralisation of state-owned enterprises). Like other dominant business consortia in Bolivia, the Casa Grace owned shares in over 50 companies, including several banks (*Banco Industrial, Banco Boliviano Americano, Banco Hipotecario Nacional, Banco de Inversión Boliviano*), insurance, agro-processing and industrial companies. Furthermore, like other commercial houses, it processed all its foreign currency revenues through foreign banks (*First National City Bank*; *Bank of America*), while its ownership of domestic enterprises enabled it to purchase Bolivian commodities in Bolivian pesos. This implies that commercial and financial circuits have served a covert function: capital flight (Lavaud 1991: 226-227; 249).

In 1974, the sale of the Casa Grace resulted in the formation of a transnational consortium with majority Bolivian ownership but incorporating Canadian and Swiss capital. The management, commercial circuits and credit lines of the 'Grace Empire' did not change until its fragmentation into a variety of business consortia fifteen years later, which were purchased by its Bolivian directors and shareholders. It is not incidental that prominent transnational businessmen/technocrats such as Ramiro Cabezas and Samuel Doria Medina built their fortunes through enterprises emerging from the breakup of the Casa Grace (see Appendix 3). Commercial capital unsurprisingly benefitted from the trade liberalisation initiated by the DS 21060, which favoured both importers and exporters.[41]

By the early 2000s, the transnationalisation of the banking, hydrocarbons and mining sectors was well under way (see table 3.9). However, as social upheavals and institutional backlashes against private ownership were intensifying, the business leadership of the CAINCO and the Banker's Association of Bolivia (ASOBAN) began a systematic effort to generate political alliances with purely foreign investors. The ASOBAN therefore incorporated foreign banks investing in Bolivia (Banco do Brasil, Citibank, Banco de la Nación Argentina, Banco Los Andes among others), while the CAINCO, via the Chamber of Hydrocarbons, incorporated TNCs investing in oil and gas extraction since the capitalisation process undertaken in the mid-1990s (Soliz 2004b; Claure 2008).[42]

Needless to say, the core of this transnational elite force is extremely reduced in size, constituted by a few dozens of individuals; and may seem like a small island in a sea of domestically-oriented uncompetitive businessmen and informal *burguesia chola* (chola bourgeoisie). Indeed, it is the case that a number of banks remain owned almost exclusively by family groups, such as the Banco Ganadero (Monasterio family), the Banco Nacional de Bolivia (Bedoya family), the Banco Económico (Marinkovic and Kuljis families) while the private bank Banco Unión involves a majority participation by the National Treasury (83 percent). It has been calculated that eight families of *Paceño* and *Cruceño* business groups control around 14 percent of Bolivia's banking assets (Bedoya, Monasterio, Kuljis, Marinkovic, Kempff, Petricevic, Tardío y Saavedra Bruno).[43]

Table 3.9: Foreign Investment in Bolivia's Banking Sector, 1998

Bank	Foreign equity (%)	Domestic equity (%)	Total capital (US$ millions)
Banco de Santa Cruz	90	10	515
Banco de Crédito	100	0	489.4
Banco Nacional de Bolivia	0.02	99.98	474.1
Banco Mercantil	2.78	97.22	465.1
Banco Industrial SA	73.8	26.2	455.1
Banco Unión	13.65	86.35	271.3
Banco Económico	27	73	191
Banco Ganadero	0	100	168
Banco Solidario	71	29	50.4
Banco Boliviano Americano	48	52	-

Source: ASOBAN

The WB calculated that in 1987, only four or five businessmen in the formal sector had assets valued over US$20 million (including Gonzalo Sánchez de Lozada and Carlos Iturralde), 'with most of the rest of the rich entrepreneurial class owning between US$1 million and US$2 million. With only a few entrepreneurs holding sizable stocks of assets, there is an important limitation to the investment capabilities of the private sector' (WB 1991c: 44). This transnational fraction thus required, and benefitted from, vital financial, ideological and institutional support by the transnational bloc, in particular by the staff of MDIs (through multilateral assistance for fixed public capital investment), to stimulate accumulation in the Bolivian space:[44]

'With *Nuevo Norte*, we have a group of around 20 entrepreneurs from La Paz incorporating all sectors,[45] people like Doria Medina... He doesn't participate much because he's very politicised, and we don't want to be contaminated by politics. People like Marcos Iberkleid, who owns Ametex [textile], the largest industrial company in Bolivia, with 3,500 employees. I am Vice-President of Ametex. Then, Emilio Unzuato of the Banco Mercantil, Fernando Illanes [see Appendix 3]. There's also Herbert Müller, who is President of Bancosol and has participation in it too. He's more of an intellectual but has been entering business, doing a couple of things here and there. Then there's Roberto Capriles, CEO of Sinchi Wayra [formerly Emusa, with 100 percent ownership by Pan American Silver Corp, a subsidiary of Glencore International AG]... Yes there is foreign capital, but it involves Bolivians... Right now, I don't have relations with outside investors. There isn't much need either... Today there are very few investors with foreign partners, before yes, there were a few more... Actually Telecel [set up by Fernando Campero] was one of the first foreign investments with local partners... We needed them, we had nothing at the time!... But truly, there are very few cases of Bolivians who have articulated an enterprise and brought in foreign partners, except in mining. In mining, yes there are quite a few. In services and manufacturing, nothing really. In the banking sector, only a little. In BISA, for example, you have the CAF, the IFC, etc. These are institutional investors, not private bankers, it's financial capital to favour companies. COMSUR and Telecel too received IFC investments, I negotiated and it turned out fine for me. There are not many cases like this'.[46]

Indeed, it was understood by the staff of MDIs that the heavy institutional and legal involvement of the IMF and WBG (IDA, IBRD MIGA, FIAS), as well as equity investments and loans by the IFC indirectly generates business confidence (IBRD 1993; DC 1996: ii). These institutions have offered guarantees for private investment, and their collaboration with successive Bolivian governments has demonstrated a commitment of the latter to PSD and public-private partnerships. The 'seal of approval' of the IMF is known to indicate a willingness on the part of the government to undertake politically unpalatable structural adjustment reforms in order to foster PSD (Körner 1986: 2). Moreover, they share information and provide technical assistance not merely to state agencies but *directly* to private capital; and offer guaranteed financing for private investments.[47] The IFC thus invested relatively small amounts, in relation to other Latin American countries (in line however with the small size of Bolivia's GDP) of capital via equity partnerships and loans in some of the most competitive Bolivian corporations between 1988 and 1998, for a total of $98 million, thus seeking to bolster business confidence in key sectors of the economy (mining, hydrocarbons, banking, telecommunications) and attracting further capital by TNCs (see table 3.10).[48]

Table 3.10: Statement of IFC's Committed and Disbursed Portfolio as of March 1998 (US$ millions)

		Committed			Disbursed		
Fiscal Year Approval	**Company**	**Loan**	**Equity**	**Quasi**	**Loan**	**Equity**	**Quasi**
1973	Minera	0	3.4	0	0	3.4	0
1976/88/ 90/91/95	BISA	14	2.7	0	14	2.7	0
1989/92/ 94/96	COMSUR	13.86	0	2.14	13.86	0	2.14
1991	Bermejo	0	5.9	0	0	3.47	0
1991	Central Aguirre	0.91	0.35	0	0.91	0.35	0
1992	Inti Raymi	12.5	0	5	12.5	0	5
1993	GENEX	1.08	0	1.19	0.64	0	0.9
1996	Mercantil-BOL	10	0	0	10	0	0
1996	Telecel Bolivia	10	0	5	6.67	0	5
Total portfolio		**62.35**	**12.35**	**13.33**	**58.58**	**9.92**	**13.04**

Source: WB (1998)

Table 3.11a: Fixed Investment, 1986-2004

	1986	1987	1988	1989	1990 (1)	1991	1992	1993	1994	1995
FDI (US$ million)	13	36.4	30	30	27.2	62	108	122	90.1	177
Net official transfers (US$ millions)	82	103	124	134	153	160	224	217	367	475
Investment as percentage of GDP										
Private	4.7	4	4.4	4.1	4.3	4.5	6.3	7.8	5.9	7.3
FDI	0.3	0.8	0.7	0.7	0.5	1	1.7	2	1.6	2.6
Public	3.2	3.1	6.6	6.8	7.6	9.3	7.7	7.5	9	8
Total	**7.9**	**7.1**	**11**	**10.9**	**11.9**	**13.8**	**14**	**15.3**	**14.9**	**15.3**

(1) Indicates wait-and-see reaction of business investors in the face of restructuring efforts by the Paz Estenssoro and Paz Zamora administrations

Table 3.11b: Fixed Investment, 1986-2004									
	1996 (2)	1997	1998	1999	2000	2001	2002	2003	2004
FDI (US$ million)	426	591	871	1,014	701	666	654	197	140
Net official transfers (US$ millions)	449	355	202	259	224	485	881	801	1,004
Investment as percentage of GDP									
Private	9	13.8	18.3	13.1	13.1	8.9	11.1	8.2	6.4
FDI	5.7	11.1	12.1	12.3	8.1	8.2	8.1	2.4	1.3
Public	7.3	5.9	5.3	5.7	5.1	5.4	5.5	5.2	6
Total	**16.2**	**19.6**	**23.6**	**18.8**	**18.2**	**14.3**	**16.6**	**13.4**	**12.4**

(2) From 1996 to 1999, private investment, in particular FDI, increased significantly, indicating the positive effects of PSD strategies on business confidence. Most of the private investment was a result of FDI in the five major state enterprises capitalised in 1995-6. In the period and subsequently, 45 percent of FDI was concentrated in the hydrocarbons industry.

Source: WB (1989c; 1991c; 1999c; 2005); Morales (1990; 1993, 1994).

The strategy was relatively effective from 1994 to 1998, as the proportion of private investment in GDP increased from 5.9 to 18.3 percent (it had only marginally increased from 4 to 5.9 percent between 1985 and 1994), and FDI responded to improving business conditions by expanding as a proportion of GDP from 1.5 to 12.1 percent, but concentrating capital almost exclusively in strategic corporations privatised by the Sánchez de Lozada (1993-1997) government: hydrocarbons, telecommunications, electricity, rail transport, smelters, water distribution (WB 1998b; IMF 2007; see also table 3.11).

The Jaime Paz administration had opened up the hydrocarbons sector in 1991, attracting thirteen foreign corporations to undertake joint ventures with state-owned YPFB (see table 3.12). Yet in absolute terms, investment in hydrocarbons remained relatively limited. The capitalisation of YPFB attracted another three corporations and generated a vast influx of FDI in hydrocarbons exploitation and exploration, which totalled $4.5 billion between 1997 and 2005 and averaged 6.5 percent of GDP. TNCs benefitted from the WB-sponsored construction of a gas pipeline to Brazil, producing primarily for export-led accumulation, and almost tripling the volume and value of hydrocarbons exports, while undergoing capital concentration (see table 3.12).[49]

Table 3.12: Number of Foreign Firms Involved in Oil and Gas Exploration	
Year	**Foreign firms**
1985	2
1987	2
1989	2
1991	7
1993	14
1995	13
1997	16
1999	9
2001	9
2003	8

Sources: IMF (1991b; 1998b; 2003; WB 2005)

Owners, shareholders and executive directors of corporations with minority or majority shareholding by foreign corporations have typically been prominent traditional party leaders, Ministers and Congressmen; or political independents appointed to head economic Ministries and superintendences (see Appendix 3). In light of the highly personalistic structure of capital in Bolivia – its excessively small size, its constitution by primarily *criollo* businessmen raised in the same neighbourhoods, educated in the same schools, with degrees from European and US universities, sharing a liberal worldview, participating in (or related as independents to) the same political parties, moving back and forth between private and public activities as well as academia, tending towards highly liquid investments (equity and savings) at home and abroad, and towards the diversification of their portfolios, those joint ventures or mergers that occur with foreign capital are not reduced to a single individual or a single company. Companies involved in joint ventures or the shareholding structure of which is not exclusively domestic are constitutive of broader business networks. The transnational bloc has ramifications in sectors considered to be domestic – whether directed towards the Bolivian market or for exports. This is, of course, the case in the *gran mineria*, but also in agro-business, commerce and banking. In other words, capitalists considered to be domestic, such as major exporters of agricultural commodities, have also a participation in banks (through family ownership or as minority shareholders of banks controlled by foreign capital); may have investments in manufacturing – either financed exclusively with Bolivian capital or with foreign capital;[50] and, as emphasised by the WB (see above), almost invariably have assets abroad, whether as equity or as savings in order to alleviate their exposure in Bolivia.

Conclusion

Our refutation of state-centrism is founded on the contention that what is considered as a US-controlled process should rather be viewed as a struggle by emergent transnational capitalist elites against global labour and other elite forces. National states have been constituted by and, in turn, re-configured this global power struggle. This chapter has placed post-1985 state and social restructuring in Bolivia within the context of transnational elite bloc formation in the late 1960s, and its expansion beyond its transatlantic Lockean heartland following the debt crisis of the early 1980s. It has deciphered the anatomy of capital in Bolivia since the early 1970s and argued that the tendency of dominant capitalist forces to diversify their portfolio entails a reconsideration of the validity of THM's 'fractionalism thesis'. However, struggles between transnationally-integrated and domestically-oriented capitalist forces became the primary axis of elite contradictions in Bolivia from the late 1970s onwards.

The consolidation of national capitalist elite blocs in the 1970s unfolded concurrently to the integration of dominant businessmen into the transnational bloc through systematic collaboration and engagement with MDIs, through IFC investments in privately-owned corporations in key sectors, and through joint ventures with metropolitan and Latin American TNCs. An appropriate image for this process is the dynamic formation of a constellation of national-in-global capitalist blocs radiating from transatlantic organisations and MDIs, and dominated by an expanding bloc of transnationally-integrated elites struggling for sustainable capital accumulation. The DC's global PSD blueprint expressed the attempt of this bloc to generate a new hegemonic strategy.

The increasing predominance of transnational elite forces in MDIs and in key Bolivian state agencies produced qualitative changes in policy preferences (see chapter 4). The WB and IMF increasingly emphasised fiscal and monetary stability, the privatisation of accumulation, public-private partnerships, business class formation in the periphery, state-building and multilateralism. Meanwhile, Bolivia's hyperinflationary crisis allowed an emergent transnational fraction of Bolivian capital to change the balance of forces within the three dominant political parties and vie for control of the state (see chapter 5).

This small elite nucleus, integrated into the transnational bloc primarily through official channels of development assistance, struggled to restructure economic relations, capital hegemony and the state in the Bolivian space. Capital hegemony entailed equating development, modernisation and *private* capital accumulation. Post-1985 restructuring may thus be understood as an attempt, by an enlightened elite formation integrated in the expanding transnational historic bloc, to graft modern capitalism and liberalism onto a corrupt, nepotistic and statist social organism, with the active support of MDIs.

The following chapter focuses on the internationalisation of the Bolivian state after 1985. Robert Cox and William Robinson's concepts of internationalisation and transnationalisation of the state have arguably not been sufficiently grounded in concrete historical relations. Chapter 4 executes this task: it relates neo-Gramscian abstractions with empirical evidence on the Bolivian state's deepening integration into a consolidating global governance complex. The Bolivian case forces a problematisation of Cox and Robinson's theoretical propositions, and the elaboration of an alternative understanding of internationalisation. The chapter demonstrates that internationalisation unfolded initially via an institutional articulation of key central government agencies (chiefly the Finance and Planning Ministries, the BCB and regulatory agencies), with MDIs and subsequently via a penetration of the lower levels of the administration by the staff of MDIs and private consultants as line managers and trainers. The internationalisation of the Bolivian state was internally related to depoliticisation and liberalisation efforts by the transnational historic bloc in Bolivia.

The mechanism underlying the articulation of key Bolivian government ministries with MDIs is one of social contradictions: in the disciplinary context of debt servicing, compounded by insufficient domestic capital formation caused by a lack of business confidence in the face of recurrent social instability, the Bolivian state actively upheld a relationship of dependence with MDIs for capital inflows. MDIs took advantage of the Bolivian government's dependence on their credit facilities to push through an increasingly integrated set of structural adjustment measures based on a reflexive and dynamic approach to past mistakes: macro-economic stabilisation via fiscal and monetary discipline; financial sector reform; and state-building. This dependence was in turn neutralised by the dependence of IMF and WB staff on the successful restructuring of social relations in Bolivia.

Nevertheless, restructuring efforts were undermined by protracted resistance in the streets and in the state, which validate the conceptualisation of the state as a site of social struggle, i.e. a contradictory organisation of subjection. As will be emphasised in the following chapters, Bolivian elements of the transnational bloc were part of and dependent on clientelistic social networks for the implementation of liberal reforms, which explains their failure to legitimise the high social costs of Bolivia's deepening integration into the world market. Chapters 4 and 5 demonstrate that attempts to restructure social relations in Bolivia must be understood as a dialectical process. Restructuring contained its antithesis in the systematic, variegated forms of resistance that the transnational bloc faced within and beyond the state throughout the period under study. Protracted institutional resistance to restructuring persisted in the management of RDCs and state-owned companies, in lower echelons of the central administration and welfare ministries (especially education; and integration/agriculture). The dialectic between restructuring and domestic Bolivian constraints helps to explain the street violence (Water Wars, Febrero and Octubre Negro, Gas War) that eventually led to the election of Evo Morales in 2005.

Notes

[1] The terms 'global' and 'transnational' must not be conflated: the former implies a whole, an *entity* incorporating and constituted by social relations in their totality, and hence cannot be reduced to the latter. In International Relations and IPE, the 'Global' therefore refers to world-wide forces and processes. However, the 'transnational' is 'a phenomenon that extends across, and thereby links as well as transcends, different (territorial) levels'. Transnational social forces therefore do not exist as a level beyond or outside the 'national' level but within and through it, 'in several national contexts simultaneously' (Apeldoorn 2004: 144-145). With reference to the transnational bloc – its constitutive members are not 'outside' national economic, ideological and institutional conditions but embedded in them and collectively acting within them.

[2] However, Cammack (2003: 39) in turn mistakenly contends that 'Rather, the two institutions are seeking to define and exercise a relatively autonomous role, promoting and sustaining a framework for global capitalism'. As pointed out by Taylor (2005) and as demonstrated in chapter 4, the WB and IMF must not be seen as unitary and devoid of internal contradictions, as 'entities' satisfying the 'need' to 'stand at a distance' from particular national states and from particular capitalist interests in order to 'secure competitiveness' (Cammack 2003: 39). In a sense, Cammack refers to an attempt at depoliticising the WB and the IMF, just as depoliticisation strategies have been employed in national state institutions. Nevertheless, MDIs, constituted as they are by national states, which are institutionalisations of social struggles, are themselves sites of struggle, systematically pulled back into capital accumulation's contradictory trajectory. The 'depoliticisation' of the WB and the IMF is

immediately contradicted by the political essence of worldwide production relations.

[3] Neo-Gramscian approaches echo Kautsky's (1970) heterodox suggestion that 'ultra-imperialism' transcending the rivalries between national capitalist blocs and national states is becoming a possible historical avenue.

[4] The fraction committed to the circulation of commodities is deemed less relevant to neo-Gramscian scholarship because it is functionally dependent on the other two fractions.

[5] A nation is a social formation, 'united' at a particular historical moment by the particular development of its language and kinship network. It has also been spatially bounded by its demographic history and by the territorial-institutional form taken by the state. 'National' specificities (fundamentally language, literature but also the arts) constitute top-down social constructs mediated by geography and infrastructural-technological development, and normatively underpinned by religious 'legality' (Anderson, 1991). In this sense, migratory controls and educational systems differentiated territorially and linguistically by national states have perpetuated an apparent inter-national 'diversity'. And yet, the burgeoning 'deterritorialisation' of identities caused by globalisation has loosened the link between nation and space (Scholte, 1996). Despite its peculiarities, the 'nation' is a fluid and changing social movement on the surface of the underlying structure of production and exchange of which it is a part and that interlinks it with other national formations.

[6] Morton rightly questions the 'core weakness' of the transnational state thesis: the contention that the 'particular spatial form of the uneven development of capitalism is being overcome by the globalisation of capital and markets and the gradual equalization of accumulation conditions this involves' (Robinson, 2005: 99). With reference to national contexts, see for instance Gramsci's analysis of 'combined and uneven development' of the Italian social space.

[7] Barber Conable, US Republican Congressman and President of the WB between 1986 and 1991, introduced the WB's bulky handbook on the Uruguay round of multilateral trade negotiations with these words: 'The fundamental truth that open markets spur efficient production and expanding prosperity is as sound today as it was 200 years ago, in Adam Smith's era... At Punta del Este and since, I have encouraged vigorous participation by developing countries in the upcoming Uruguay round. But why specifically is the WB anxious to keep open the avenues of trade? Development is our business. Economic growth in developing countries can more easily be achieved in the context of a liberal trade environment... Economic inefficiency has often been the price of protection, and trade liberalization the handmaiden of efficient development and growth' (WB 1987).

[8] The WBG is constituted by the Board of Executive Directors – formed by Ministers of Finance and Governors of Central Banks; and the International Bank for Reconstruction and Development (IBRD). The affiliates of the IBRD include the International Development Association (IDA), the International Finance Corporation (IFC) and the Multilateral Investment Guarantee Agency (MIGA). The Foreign Investment Advisory Service (FIAS), on its side, is an IBRD venture – providing loans and equity investments to credit-worthy and 'dynamic' corporations in peripheral formations (IBRD 1993). On FIAS see

http://www.ifc.org/fias. On MIGA, see http://www.miga.org/about/index_sv.cfm?stid=1588. On IFC, see http://www.ifc.org/about. All accessed 15 January 2008. Private Bolivian corporations began receiving IFC credits in 1973 (the mining company *Minera*) (WB 1998b: Annex B8). The Bolivian state began receiving IMF credits in 1956, and WB loans in 1962. It formally joined MIGA in 1990.

The WBG, increasingly dominated by monetarist economists from the early 1970s onwards, shifted its activities away from discrete, albeit conditional project-based lending towards programmatic Structural Adjustment Loans (SAL) in 1980. While conditionalities were related to sectoral or subsectoral policy change before 1980, lending began to be made for fiscal support, in order to sustain imports necessary for capital investments and accumulation; it became systematically conditioned on policy change at the macroeconomic level (Mosley 1991: 27-28).

[9] The DC is the apex of the WB-IMF administrative hierarchy. Its formal designation is the 'Joint Ministerial Committee of the Board of Governors of the WB and the IMF on the Transfer of Real Resources to Developing Countries'. Established in October 1974, it usually convenes two or three times a year; it thus had organised 65 high level meetings by November 2007. Its members are either Ministers of Finance or Central Bank governors of both metropolitan and peripheral states appointed for successive periods of two years by one of the governments or groups of governments represented on the WB's or IMF's Board of Executive Directors. 'The DC advises and reports to the Boards of Governors of the WB and the IMF on all aspects of the transfer of real resources to developing countries, and to make suggestions for consideration by those concerned regarding the implementation of its conclusions' (DC 1993: 1).

The DC involves a high degree of policy coherence not merely among these two large bureaucracies (IMF and WB), but more importantly still, among the finance ministries and Central Banks of all governments represented at the IMF and WB board of governors over time. It involves a high degree of ideological continuity and centralisation of administrative/technocratic power; it is used as a multilateral forum for the design of a global policy 'line', in coordination with the UNDP, the DAC, the regional development banks, and bilateral donors. This 'epistemic community' necessarily 'spills over' its institutional limits into the diplomatic realm by virtue of its allocation of budgets to other ministries – effectively disciplining of 'politicians' via money (see Taylor 2003; Haas 1992).

The DC is more directly involved in concrete issues of design and implementation (on the basis of WB and IMF activities) than the OECD's DAC. The DAC has increasing political clout (as demonstrated by its role as umbrella organisation for the Paris Declaration of 2005), but serves as a discussion forum for more general policy strategy elaboration rather than the implementation of policies specific to individual national states. It is constituted by high level civil servants and government ministers of OECD member-states.

In Bolivia, WB-financed SAPs, IMF-financed Enhanced Structural Adjustment Facilities were elaborated jointly with Bolivian governments. This coordination resulted in Policy Framework Papers (PFPs), which crystallised the strategic approach of Bolivian government to PSD in three-year plans.

[10] The 1956 stabilisation package implemented by the Bolivian government – and 1960s joint financing and technical assistance of the IMF and WB to military governments – illustrate convincingly this point (see Whitehead 1969; De La Cueva 1983; Climenhage 1999).

[11] On its side the DAC was arguing in 1989 that 'The machinery of government in OECD countries for ensuring consistent and effective overall policies toward developing countries needs to be strengthened' (DAC 1989: 18) and that 'Effective competition ... requires a strong and effective government' (DAC 1989: 36).

[12] Interview with Carlos Morales, 20 September 2007.

[13] Interview with Carlos Iturralde, 14 September 2007. See also http://www.ceal-int.org/ESP/estrutura.htm, accessed 20 January 2009.

[14] On the constitution and political objectives of the CEAl, see http://www.ceal-int.org/ESP/ceal.htm. Accessed 20 February 2010.

[15] The CEAL thus contends that 'regional integration has a greater possibility of success when entrepreneurs participate actively' (author's translation). See http://www.ceal-int.org/counter/ for list of 'International Network of Private Business Organizations', accessed 20 January 2009.

[16] Large-scale research projects (Private Sector Assessments – PSAs) were undertaken by the WB, focusing on business needs and constraints. The WB and International Finance Corporation (IFC), 'with inputs from MIGA and FIAS' (IBRD 1993: 4), jointly initiated PSAs in 19 countries in 1991, including Bolivia (IBRD 1993: i.; WB 1991). 'Many PSAs include in-depth interviews with entrepreneurs and firm-level surveys, which have provided insights into how entrepreneurs themselves – including small operators who normally lack a voice in the policy process – see the day-to-day world in which they operate... PSAs, which analyze the structure of, and constraints to, the private sector in given countries, and which lay out steps to advance PSD, have provided a sharper focus for analytical work at the country level' (IBRD 1993: 4).

Two PSAs were undertaken in Bolivia in 1991 and 2004 (WB 1991; 2005). PSAs, roundtables, aid coordination arrangements sustained the expansion and consolidation of the transnational bloc into Bolivia. The IBRD expressed satisfaction in 1993 at the fact that 'Progress was made in helping policymakers understand and address key constraints affecting private firms' (IBRD 1993: i), in order to generate a relationship of trust and mutual benefit between businesses and governments ('public-private partnerships'). 'To this end, the WBG has made gains over the past two years' (IBRD 1993: 4).

[17] Interview with Fernando Campero Prudencio, 20 September 2007.

[18] Interview with Mauro Mariani, 20 December 2007.

[19] By 1990, the state still owned 159 enterprises spread along its central and regional institutions: the Ministries of Defence (23 companies), of Energy and Hydrocarbons (7 companies, including the 'jewels' YPFB – hydrocarbons – and ENDE – energy), Trade and Industry (2 companies), of Information (radio, television and printing), of Transport and Communications (9 companies, including ENFE, the railway corporation, and ENTEL, the telecommunications corporation), of Aeronautics (including the Lloyd Aereo Boliviano airline), of the Interior (14 hotels), of Mining and Metallurgy (14 companies, including the 'jewels' COMIBOL – mining –, and Vinto – Iron and Steel smelting). The rest was distributed among the Regional Development Corporations created by

General Banzer in 1971 to decentralise production and transfer the state's fiscal resources towards Santa Cruz (WB 1991b: 113-116; Barragán 2008). The state's six jewels, COMIBOL (mining), YPFB (hydrocarbons), ENTEL (telecommunications), ENDE (energy), ENFE (railways), and LAB (passenger air transport) altogether accounted for over 60 percent of Bolivia's accumulation of capital, and 90 percent of Bolivia's exports and foreign exchange reserves.

[20] Interview with Ivo Arrias, 12 August 2007.

[21] Chief among them were the Bank of America (US – $116 million in loans between 1970 and 1979), Citicorp (US – $109 million in the same period), Banco do Brasil (Brazil – $87 million), Société Générale (Belgium – $76 million) and Dresdner Bank (Federal Republic of Germany – $57 million); but also Canadian and other European banks with loans not exceeding $40 million. The CEPAL (1983: 57) indicates that 'Bolivia represented a client of marginal interest for the international banking community... we can note the absence of a large number of institutions which tended to be very active in the financing of developing countries (and of Latin American countries in particular) during the 1970s...Bolivia did not benefit from significant acceptance in international credit markets. With regards to large creditors, we can observe that two of the four counted on the protection of their national export-promoting agencies; this is to say that they financed exports of their country of origin without assuming risks of their own. In fact, only Bank of America and Citicorp lent large amounts on their own account' (author's translation).

[22] Hilferding understood finance capital as a fusion of banking and industrial capital: "A steadily increasing proportion of capital in industry ceases to belong to the industrialists who employ it. They obtain the use of it only through the medium of the banks which, in relation to them, represent the owners of the capital. On the other hand, the bank is forced to sink an increasing share of its funds in industry. Thus, to an ever greater degree the banker is being transformed into an industrial capitalist. This bank capital, i.e., capital in money form, which is thus actually transformed into industrial capital, I call 'finance capital'." "Finance capital is capital controlled by banks and employed by industrialists." Cited by Lenin (1916).

[23] The *Paceño* commercial fraction focused predominantly until the 1980s on the exploitation of heterogeneous regional and local markets (buying cheap, selling dear) within the Bolivian space, hence failing to generate a unification of capitalist production relations around a single value structure but rather, in a parasitic manner, leaving pre-capitalist relations of production relatively untouched, despite their facilitation of monetisation in indigenous communities (Grebe 1983).

[24] The informal sector refers to economic activity that is not registered and pays no taxes. There are different degrees of informality: firms that are completely unregistered (50 percent of urban businesses in the 1990s and 2000s); that are not registered with the municipality (72 percent), that do not have a Tax Identification Number (79 percent in urban areas, rising to 90 percent in the countryside), and that are not registered with *FundEmpresa* (96 percent) (*FundEmpresa* was created in 2001 by the CAINCO and other business organisations to administer Bolivia's Commercial Register) (UDAPE 2007a; see also http://www.fundempresa.org.bo/. accessed 16 January 2009).

The proportion of the labour force confined to informality has been calculated at 60-65 percent in the mid-to-late 1980s, and rising to 65-68 percent in the 1990s. This includes the vast majority of labour in the agricultural sector, which pays no tax and holds no land title; and 74 percent of labour employed in manufacturing; 86 percent in commerce; 56 percent in construction; 43 percent in transportation; and 25 percent in services (WB 1989c: 43). The UDAPE (2007) contends that informality decreased as a proportion of urban labour between 1996 and 2006 (from 63 to 56 percent), but that considering Bolivia's population growth and urban migration, it increased in absolute terms from 1.2 to 1.5 million people. This also means that, if taking into account rural as well as urban workers, informality rises to more than 80 percent of Bolivia's labour force. This also signifies that, considering that between 8 and 13 percent of labour was employed by the state after 1985, no more than 12 percent of Bolivia's labour force has been employed in the 'formal' private sector.

[25] 'More than half of all 65 industrial subsectors were characterized by one-firm concentration ratios above 50 percent in 1988 (that is, the largest firm in each subsector accounted for more than 50 percent of total sales values) and all but 5 subsectors were characterized by four-firm concentration ratios above 60 percent... Industries characterized by four-firm concentration ratios exceeding 50 percent are generally classified as "tight" oligopolies (WB 1991c: 44).

[26] In the late 1990s, the CEPB, based in La Paz, degenerated into a 'provincial' organisation due to the ineptness and domestic orientation of its new leadership and its failure to incorporate new-coming TNCs investing in Bolivia's 'strategic' sectors. Interviews with Fernando Campero Prudencio, 20 September 2007 and Carlos Iturralde, 14 September 2007. Fernando Campero Prudencio argued that: 'In the era of the UDP, the CEPB was very powerful and well managed. Afterwards, employees were included, and then employees of lower rank, not even the owners of enterprises themselves. So the CEPB was devalued. So today, we have some pitiful *gremios*. The Federación de Empresarios de La Paz is a disaster, because people that preside over it, for example Roberto Mustafá, they enter ... to get access to the government and to obtain state contracts...CAINCO is different, a much better organisation... The CEPB is a paper tiger, it doesn't exist, it gets a lot of press but in reality it is very weak. Today, the CEPB no longer represents Bolivia's business community... Under Carlos Iturralde and Fernando Illanes, yes, it had some weight. **They truly had a participation in important decisions of the government**... It's possible that not incorporating TNCs was a factor. I see more problems though: except for the CAINCO, the leadership of federations has been weakening tremendously. With a couple of exceptions, it suffers from such intellectual and moral poverty! Some of them don't even have a company. They might have had something small in the past, they're waiting for the following elections, for the support of parties...'.

The power of the CAINCO is directly correlated to the transfer of resources from COMIBOL to agri-business in the *Oriente* since the 1960s and the promotion of export-led growth since the 1985, compounded by the discovery of hydrocarbons in Santa Cruz and Tarija, incentives for agricultural diversification, the transnationalisation of banking in Santa Cruz and the recent boom in soy prices.

In 2008, the CEPB was 'revamped' under the leadership of its new president, Gabriel Dabdoub, who is concurrently president of the CAINCO. This leadership role symbolises the recomposition of capital as a class-for-itself under the unquestioned dominance of *Cruceño* banking, commercial and agro-industrial capital. See http://www.cepb.org.bo/sitio/directiva_cepb.php. Accessed 15 November 2008.

[27] Until 1974, the transnational Commercial House Grace owned three of the largest private mines in Bolivia (*Avicaya, Estalsa, International Mining*), which produced 50 percent of tin and 85 percent of wolfram production in the private sector. Sánchez de Lozada's COMSUR, with 38 percent ownership by the *First National City Bank* , was the second largest mining company in Bolivia in the 1970s. EMUSA, with majority foreign shareholding was the third. Between them, Estalsa, COMSUR and EMUSA produced 44 percent of tin, 92 percent of wolfram, 88 percent of zinc, 67 percent of antimony and 40 percent of bismuth produced by the *mineria mediana*, indicating oligopolistic tendencies in the mining industry (Lavaud 1991: 226).

[28] Godoy (1985: 157) thus argues that mine owners, prone to portfolio diversification to reduce risk, 'cannot claim a share of equity to the mineral produced in his/her own property unless they participate in the venture materially, financially and morally and prove themselves munificent patrons'.

[29] Interview with Herbert Müller, 11 September 2007. By the mid-1980s, two 'medium' mining companies were foreign controlled, and five had minority foreign participation (WB 1989b: 5). The owners of these five firms dominated both the ANMM and the CEPB from the late 1970s to the late 1980s.

[30] From 17.8 percent of the value of mineral exports in 1980, the *minería mediana* expanded to 45 percent following the tin market crash of 1985-1986, and the subsequent decapitalisation of COMIBOL. The expansion of private mining continued into the 1990s, reaching 56 percent in 1996. Along with small-scale mining managed by cooperatives, private mining as a whole accounted for 80 percent of the value of mineral and metal exports in 1996 (Müller y Asociados 1996: 156-157).

[31] Deteriorating terms of trade for minerals and metals since the 1970s have taken their toll on the ANMM, and forced a process of capital concentration, primarily in the form of joint ventures or outright sales, which however enhanced the power of remaining mine owners within the CEPB. In the context of declining demand for tin and the appearance of cheaper production sites in South East Asia, Bolivia dropped from second to fifth largest world producer of tin. In 1985, the AMM comprised 29 affiliated companies employing 6,000 workers (from a peak of 8,500 workers in 1975). Two years later – after the tin market crash, 19 companies were left with a workforce of 4,020, and by 1999, there remained 13 affiliates of the ANMM: Andean Silver Resources, Arisur BAREMSA, Borrosquira Ltda. Empresa Minera Bernal, Cia. Minera Concepción, COMSUR, Empresa Minera Unificada S.A. (EMUSA), Empresa Minera Inti Raymi S.A., Cia. Minera "La Rosa," L & M Mining Co., Cia. Minera "La Solución," Empresa Minera Paitití, Empresa Santa Lucía, and Vista Gold Corp. However, the tin crash affected almost exclusively the state-owned COMIBOL, and market prices for other minerals declined slightly but did not collapse. The private sector took advantage of the DS 21060 and the discourse of hyperinflation and generalised 'crisis' to lay off one third of its workforce in

1985-1986. It thus managed to alleviate its structural decline, benefitting from higher prices for non-traditional minerals such as zinc and gold before resuming its growth in the late 1980s, its total output and the value of its exports far outstripping that of COMIBOL after 1987 (WB 1989b: 5-6; Velasco 1999). NB: Traditional minerals include silver, tin and antimony.

[32] In 1991, approximately $50 million was invested by Rio Tinto Zinc (US), Battle Mountain (US) and American Pacific (Canada) in three Bolivian mining corporations: (Sánchez de Lozada's) Comsur, Inti Raymi and Tiwanaku. These joint ventures resulted in foreign partners controlling respectively 25 percent, 85 percent and 45 percent of Bolivian companies' shares (WB 1992c: 7).

[33] For example, the Marinkovic family, one of the principal shareholders of the Banco Económico, also owns the company Industrias Oleaginosas S.A. (IOL), which produces the 'Rico' cooking oil. One of the principal shareholders of the bank BISA (17.6 percent), León Prado, also has investments in construction and soy processing. Andrés Petricevic, who is a minority shareholder in the Banco Unión, is also involved in construction. See 'Las Corporaciones en la Banca Privada', available on http://finanzasybanca.blogspot.com/2008_03_01_archive.html. Accessed 6 February 2009. See also Annex 3, listing transnational elites.

[34] In the case of mining, manufacturing, and agro-business, however, a significant portion of capital must be fixed. Importantly, the insecurity generated by recurrent labour strikes, higher investment costs, and competition by state-owned corporations rendered 'fixing' capital in manufacturing unattractive for economic groups, to the extent that it only accounted for 12 percent of GDP and 7.8 percent of the economically active population in 1985. In contrast, higher surplus value for mining and agro-business in the 1970s facilitated large-scale capital investments. Mining in particular attracted FDI. They therefore represented the bulk of exports and foreign exchange reserves from the late nineteenth century to the early 1980s, when mining was overtaken by hydrocarbons as the primary export commodity (WB 1991: 120-123).

[35] It is precisely through *fractionalism* that Poulantzas sought to overcome Miliband's instrumental understanding of the state: because of its functional division into competing fractions, capital cannot absolutely and completely control the state, which institutionally concentrates its internal contradictions. Thus by separating the institutional 'body' of the state from the control of any one fraction, the state sustains the reproduction of capital through the functional upholding of its 'general interest' despite, and against specific fractional requirements. Hence the 'relative autonomy' of the national state from specific class and fractional interests, through its functional fulfilment of the structural necessities of *transnational* capital circuits in their entirety (maintenance of social order, provision of infrastructure, economic policies sustaining capital accumulation) (Poulantzas 1975: 97, 1978: 127).

[36] In her analysis of the emergence of a *Cruceño* bourgeoisie (located in Santa Cruz) in the 1960s and 1970s, Lesley Gill (1987: 174) argues that 'the expansion of the regional economy not only allowed long-established Cruceño landowners to consolidate their position and reap large profits but also attracted a new group of investors and speculators to the eastern lowlands. The newcomers consisted of hacendados and mine owners from the highlands and

valleys, military officers, administrators, professionals and a substantial number of foreigners'.

[37] In La Paz, elite schools include the American Cooperative School, the Lycée Franco-Bolivien, and above all the Colegio Alemán; in Santa Cruz, these include the La Salle school, Cooperative School, the Colegio Alemán and International School. José Antonio Quiroga, editor-in-chief of Plural Editores, remembered a government meeting chaired by Fernando Romero under Sánchez de Lozada (1993-7), in which Romero joked that 'I can see that this is a Colegio Alemán government!' Interview with José Antonio Quiroga, 19 September 2007.

[38] This includes Xavier Nogales, Minister for Economic Development of the Mesa administration (Bolpress 2003).

[39] See WB (1999c; 2005) and MIGA (2009). See also Superintendencia de Pensiones, Valores y Seguros, http://www.spvs.gov.bo/reportes_asp/rmi/listaentidades.asp?tr=2, accessed 5 February 2009.

[40] For example, 26.8 percent of the Banco Mercantil's US$145 million investments in 2005 were directed towards 'safe' US Treasury bonds, other government agencies and MDIs (Banco Mercantil 2006: 3).

[41] Interviews with Ramiro Cabezas, 17 September 2007; Fernando Campero, 20 September 2007.

[42] See http://www.asoban.bo/asbanc.htm. Accessed 10 November 2008. The Chamber of Hydrocarbons incorporates more than 100 different firms – including foreign TNCs such as Petrobras, American Energy, Repsol, Total. See http://www.cbh.org.bo/es/index.php?cat=4&pla=5. Accessed 10 November 2008.

[43] This situation led Juan Antonio Morales (ex-governor of BCB) and other economists to criticise these family structures, which cause operations that do not take into account technical aspects: "the exception to the rule is the Banco Nacional de Bolivia, which is very well administered, but it is recommendable that banks be separated from the family. In other countries it is required that directors be independent in banks." Family ownership of banks generated problems of insolvency and forced the closure of eight banks in the 1990s. Available at http://finanzasybanca.blogspot.com/2008/03/8-familias-controlan-el-14-de-la-banca.html, accessed 7 February 2009.

[44] I was unable to find more recent data. However, it is not inconceivable that the number of 'very rich' in Bolivia has risen exponentially since 1985, and that the WB was simply not able to gather the information, considering the vast fortunes realised 'informally'. Possibly hundreds have built the large fortunes referred to by the WB, by benefitting from narcotrafficking and speculative activities during the hyperinflationary crisis (the typical example is that of Max Fernández, *mestizo* born in poverty, who built his fortune through currency speculation before creating Bolivia's largest industrial employer with 43,000 workers, the brewery *Cerveceria Nacional Boliviana*, and almost single-handedly financing the populist party *Unión Civica Solidaridad* in the 1990s), from foreign capital (including Official Development Assistance and private capital) investments in mining, telephony, banking and hydrocarbons in the 1990s; and from 'booms' in the price of commodities like soy, metals and minerals since 2004 (Gill 1987; Malloy and Gamarra 1987; Dunkerley 1990). On the fortunes of 'Goni' and Max Fernández, see *The New York Times* (1992).

[45] The business organisation *Nuevo Norte* was created in 2005. See http://www.nuevonorte.org. Accessed 7 February 2009.

[46] Interview with Fernando Campero Prudencio, 20 September 2007.

[47] Indeed 'the case for direct MDB financing of private sector activities needs to be strong...additional in the sense that a productive and profitable activity would not proceed without such support, and the share of the MDB's financial participation is such as not to displace private capital ... (and) must contribute to development or transition' (DC 1996: iii).

[48] Beneficiaries of various IFC loans and equity investments included the two largest private mining corporations in Bolivia, which have a transnational shareholding structure (Sánchez de Lozada's COMSUR in 1989, 1992, 1994, and 1996 – during his incumbency as President of Bolivia, creating a significant conflict of interest; and Inti Raymi, a 1982 joint venture between Bolivian capitalists and Houston-based Westworld Resources inc., since 1992); two banks (Banco BISA in 1976, 1988, 1990, 1991 and 1995; and Banco Mercantil in 1996); Central Aguirre, the administrator of Puerto Aguirre, an export processing free zone on the river Panamá (in 1991); Bermejo and Genex (hydrocarbons; respectively in 1991 and 1993), and Telecel, Bolivia's first mobile telephony service provider in 1996 (WB 1999: Annex 5).

[49] Investments in exploration and exploitation more than doubled between 1997 and 1998 (from $280 to $600 million in total), before gradually declining to $200 million by 2005. Expectably, heavy initial investments in exploration (in 1998 and 1999) subsided stringently after 2000 from two thirds of all investments in 1998 to one fifth by 2005 in favour of (declining) investments in exploitation (IMF 2007).

[50] This comprises, for example food-processing, textiles, or indeed small technological niches: Santa Cruz in particular has been witnessing a proliferation of small companies like *Cognos*, *ATI* or *Fundetic* since the mid-1990s, requiring little initial capital, engaged in technological certification, consulting, education and other services for enterprises, software and web-design, among other activities, and offering services to 'metropolitan' or 'Latin American' TNCs such as Microsoft or Axxon Consulting.

4
The Internationalisation of the Bolivian State

The early 1980s witnessed yet another global economic crisis expressed, this time, in the unmanageable external debt of Latin American, South Asian and African states, a profound disequilibrium between national price systems with world market prices and high inflation (Pastor 1987). This crisis generated potentially uncontrollable social instability which temporarily threatened the viability of global capital circuits but also offered an opportunity for a second wave of the internationalisation of the Bolivian state. The second wave of internationalisation was qualitatively different from the first, analysed in chapter 2, because 1) it was directed by a far more cohesive bloc of forces in transnational business organisations, multilateral organisations and national administrations; 2) it involved a struggle of unprecedented vigour for the privatisation of accumulation and institutional support for the expansion of capital in hitherto non-capitalist social spaces (i.e. primitive accumulation); 3) it was underpinned by the promotion of monetarist instruments of economic management, the depoliticisation of the BCB and of regulatory agencies, and the widespread use of private consulting agencies as well as the staff of MDIs to fill administrative-technical gaps in peripheral states; and 4) a systematic effort to coordinate the activities of MDIs and of successive Bolivian governments. MDIs and bilateral development agencies demonstrated, in the wake of this crisis, an admirable capacity for adaptation and a profound awareness of the unstable essence of capitalist relations of production (see chapter 3). Internal strategic documents of the 1980s and 1990s help to understand the approach of global centres of decision-making to global restructuring.

This chapter analyses the internationalisation of the Bolivian state from 1985 to 2005. The fiscal and monetary crisis faced by Bolivia since 1978 was accentuated by Mexico's defaulting on its external debt in 1982 (Pastor 1987*; Kuczinsky 1988). Mismanagement by, and elite resistance to, the UDP government plunged the country into an uncontrollable hyperinflationary and fiscal crisis (see chapter 2). The transnational business leadership of the CEPB had reached the commanding heights of the conservative ADN and MNR political parties with the sanction of party *caudillos* Hugo Banzer and Victor Paz Estenssoro. They formed neoliberal economic teams during the 1985 election campaign with the aim of radically restructuring production relations in Bolivia through the blitzing implementation of a comprehensive set of stabilisation and adjustment measures embodied in the DS 21060 (29 August 1985) (Conaghan 1990, Conaghan and Malloy 1995; Climenhage 1999). The DS 21060 secured the resumption of collaborative relations between the Bolivian government and MDIs, and the unconditional integration of Bolivia's small transnational fraction into an expanding transnational historic bloc of elite social forces. Increasing coordination between central government agencies and MDIs drove the internationalisation of the Bolivian state. Internationalisation, in turn, consolidated the structural power of the transnational bloc in Bolivia.

As hypothesised in chapter 1, the concept of internationalisation helps to explain the transformation of the state in Bolivia after 1985. Chapters 2 and 3 analysed the causes of internationalisation. The internationalisation of the Bolivian state complemented and sustained a radical program of social restructuring engineered and refined by MDIs' staff in collaboration with a small, transnational fraction of Bolivian technocrats, private managers and businessmen (in particular mining, banking and commercial capital) from 1985 to 2005, and implemented by successive governments during that period. Internationalisation is defined as the integration of the state into a global organisational or governance complex. As pointed out in the previous chapter, *global governance* is understood as worldwide, multilateral organisation, or institutional 'mechanisms for arriving at general policy consensus' through 'cooperation and dealing collectively with conflict' (Cox 1992: 27; Cox 1994: 100).

The consolidation of the global governance institutions created during or directly after the Second World War, and built upon pre-existing, yet internationalising national states has been elemental to global struggles for and against the restructuring of capitalist forms in the latest era of globalisation. However, chapter 5 shall demonstrate that state restructuring contained its antithesis in systematic resistance by domestically-oriented elites and labour forces, in the street and in the state.

Internationalisation is rooted in a *mutualistic symbiosis* between an expanding transatlantic elite bloc and a small, emergent nucleus of transnationalised business, technocratic and intellectual elites in Bolivia: a process whereby a fitness benefit for different social forces ensued from cooperation in the wider struggle for sustainable capital accumulation. By interlocking the executive institutions of the state with MDIs, the transnational bloc and its Bolivian constituents attempted to consolidate the capitalist form of the state and the hegemony of capital.

In order to build my case, I will proceed as follows: I begin by critically reflecting on Robert Cox's conceptualisation of internationalisation. Cox's approach must be problematised, firstly for its reversion to a national starting-point and secondly for its tendentious fetishisation of the form of the state preceding internationalisation: internationalisation in his view involves an *unprecedented* loss of power of welfare and domestically-oriented state agencies, which is determined by outside-in transnationalisation and paradoxically fits his national starting-point and his implicit fetishisation of the state (Cox 1981: 109; Bonefeld 2000). Crucially, Cox's approach to internationalisation turns the state into an instrument of transnational elite forces, undermining the functional *raison d'état* that is at the core of his theorisation of the state (Cox 1987). Internationalisation logically negates his own conceptualisation of states as relatively autonomous 'institutional structures', or 'limited totalities' (Cox 1981: 98, 100). The section offers an alternative conceptualisation and concludes by identifying the central attributes that help to measure, in a qualitative sense, its historical development.

The second section focuses on the concrete process of internationalisation, which occurred 1) via an institutional articulation of key central government agencies with MDIs (in particular the Ministries of Finance and Planning; the Bolivian Central Bank [BCB], the banking supervision agency – *Superintendencia de Bancos y Entidades Financieras de Bolivia* [SBEF] – and emergent sectoral regulatory agencies, the so-called *Sistemas de Regulación Sectorial* [SIRESE]); 2) via the payment of additional salaries by the IMF, WB and UNDP (the 'infamous' *sobresueldos*) to Government Ministers and high level civil servants throughout the period under study; and 3) via 'institution-building', which focused upon enhancing the effectiveness of state institutions beyond central executive agencies. Institution-building involved the penetration of lower levels of the state hierarchy by Bolivian and private consultants contracted by the Bolivian government and remunerated by MDIs, for training purposes (civil service reform) but also as line managers, to secure a transition towards an effective, depoliticised technocratic corpus. A strategic attempt to depoliticise state polity was integral to internationalisation, and involved a 'hollowing out' of the central organs of the national state, serving to shield particular executive agencies of the state, primarily the BCB, the SIRESE and the Ministry of Finance itself from political struggles (Burnham 2000; Jessop 1990). This hollowing out was only apparent and involved a paradoxical consolidation of these central agencies.[1]

Conceptualising the Internationalisation of the State

Any attempt to reflexively use the concept of internationalisation in the empirical analysis of national states must engage with the seminal work of Robert Cox (1981, 1987) and further developments made by Robinson (2002; 2005).

Assessing Cox and Robinson

For Cox, economic processes of transnational capital concentration have a social essence: they involve an emerging network of forces integrated transnationally and enjoying a social power that was hitherto inexistent in nationally fragmented capital. This power penetrates national formations through the internationalisation of national states. The internationalisation of the state has been interpreted by Cox and subsequent neo-Gramscian theorists as a new institutional mechanism sustaining the global hegemony of capital, which emerged in reaction to the global crisis of accumulation causing the effective dissolution of the Bretton Woods System in the early 1970s. The collapse of the Bretton Woods System was accompanied by the collapse of the norms defining international economic relations; this normative dissolution paradoxically reinforced the perceived need, by national administrations, to mutually harmonise the implementation of their respective economic policies, while it consolidated global regulatory institutions subsisting out of the breakdown of Bretton Woods. This institutional process did not constitute a structural break with the pre-existing order, but served to deepen, in the face of economic crisis, a historical convergence of policies (Cox 1981: 108-109).

Cox defined internationalisation as 'a mechanism' altering the 'structure of power' internal to state apparatuses, and hence transforming states into internally fragmented 'transmission belts' of the 'global economy', adjusting national economic policies to the requirements of transnational capital (Cox 1981: 107-109; Cox 1992:

154).[2] Bieler and Morton (2003: 489) expanded this definition by referring to globalisation as causing 'a restructuring of different forms of states through an internalisation within the state of new configurations of social forces expressed by class struggle between different (national and transnational) fractions of capital and labour'.

Internationalisation thus fragments states by 'giving precedence to certain state agencies' (Cox 1981: 109). It generates particular 'coalitions' of state agents directly involved in multilateral organisations and directly in contact with the private social forces involved in capital accumulation (such as the office of the Prime Minister and the Ministry of Finance), and pits these institutions against the government's welfare ministries and other domestically-oriented state agencies.

William Robinson (2002; 2005) borrowed heavily from Cox's (1987; 1992) concepts of economic 'globalisation' and state 'internationalisation' on the one hand, and Van der Pijl's (1984; 1998) analysis of transnational elite formation on the other, to argue that the transnationalisation of capitalist relations of production ('the economic') since the 1960s has been directly correlated to the transnationalisation of the state ('the political'). The latter is defined by the emergence of a transnational regulatory framework constituted by a 'multilayered' and 'multi-centred' supranational apparatus incorporating the 'transnationalised' agencies of national states. Robinson (2002: 215-216), like Cox, contends that transnationalisation has involved the fragmentation of national states, through which certain state institutions linked to emergent transnational accumulation processes become constitutive of the emergent instruments of global class rule. Robinson (2002: 211) goes further than Cox by asserting that state transnationalisation signifies the 'supersession of the nation-state system as the organising principle of capitalist development'.

Cox's approach to internationalisation suffers from a number of inconsistencies that have not been resolved by subsequent neo-Gramscian theorists. Most conspicuously, neo-Gramscian conceptualisations of the state embody profound tensions between Gramscian (1971) and early Poulantzan (1975) thought, implicit in the work of Cox (1987) and evident in that of Robinson (2002, 2005).

I emphasised in chapter 1 that neo-Gramscian scholars opened up Gramscian thought by reviving a holistic approach to political economy. Nevertheless, in Coxian thought holism has lapsed into domestic society-global economy dichotomies and consequently, to profound theoretical tensions at levels of abstraction below the ontological concept of production relations. On the one hand, globalisation is explained as a process external to domestic relations: emergent transnational capital circuits ('globalisation') supersede domestic circuits and cause the creation of 'multi-layered, multi-centred transnational state', the formation of a 'transnational class' above and beyond the international system and national complexes (Cox 1987, 1992; Robinson 2002: 216). This implies a relatively crude base-superstructure model whereby a new transnational base, externally related to national bases, causes institutional transformations.[3] On the other hand, Cox's theorisation of the internationalisation of the state and hegemonic world orders implied a reversion towards Gramsci's national starting-point, stimulating later attempts to 'combine Gramsci's emphasis on the national point of departure with a focus on emerging transnational forces but without lapsing in a one-sided view of internationalisation' (Bieler and Morton 2003: 485). Cox (1981: 96) considered national 'state/society complexes as the constituent *entities* of a world order', and cited Gramsci to explain his own methodological starting-point: 'do international relations precede or follow (logically) fundamental social relations? There can be no doubt that they follow' (Cox 1981: 120). Internationalisation is, therefore, a process logically unfolding out of national entities, and world (ideological) hegemony is struggled for by a economically and militarily dominant national ruling-class – thus Cox and Gill define the *Pax Britannica* and *Pax Americana* as historical forms of world orders sustained by a dominant national elite bloc.[4] The tension between outside-in and inside-out transformations remains, therefore, unresolved.

A related limitation in Cox's account (1987) is his fetishisation of the pre-neoliberal state: hegemonic historic blocs are constituted by a nationally-based alliance of forces that satisfy, through compromise, the *real* interests of labour. Hence the state, especially the Keynesian form prevalent in the Golden era of post-War reconstruction, served to protect its domestic society from the negative impacts of global capital accumulation: the modus operandi of the Keynesian state was therefore the functional maintenance of the general interest of national society.[5]

However, Cox's concept of internationalisation undermines his (however implicit) reiteration of the notion of relative autonomy originally articulated by Poulantzas (1978 [1968]). Internationalisation is a process whereby externally-oriented agencies of the state are instrumentalised by transnational forces to implement policies elaborated in multilateral organisations (behind closed doors), leading the state to lose the policy autonomy it had enjoyed in the idealised Keynesian past. Internationalisation thus signifies a process whereby the state imposes the neoliberal requirements of transnational capital and no longer protects society from external challenges. It logically erases the 'autonomy' of the structure of the state and thus negates its *raison d'état*: social reproduction.[6] Cox's theorisation of internationalisation implies an unwitting and un-problematised shift from functionalism to instrumentalism.

Cox rightly suggested, on one hand, that institutions reflect particular power relations, and on the other constitute 'particular amalgams of ideas and material power', although his vague notion of 'amalgam', just as that of 'nébuleuse', indicates a rather Smithian logical approach to the way in which institutions unite or bind economic and ideological struggles in their own contradictory social existence (Cox 1981: 99). He significantly undermined neorealist and conventional Marxist understandings of the state as a unitary actor or political form by positing that states are internally fragmented by social forces struggling not merely against it but *within* its institutional midst (Cox 1981: 106-107). The functional (regulatory and/or coercive) capacities of states, and indeed of MDIs (Taylor 2005), are therefore never fully nor perfectly realised because they are social relations themselves. Nonetheless, like Jessop (1990), Cox sees the state as a site of strategic-relational struggle *between elite forces*, precluding any consideration of labour forces *within* the state.

The Bolivian case does support Cox's contention that internationalisation accentuated the rivalries between state ministries, as substantive conflicts emerged between economic Ministers and the rest of the government, especially under the Paz Zamora (1989-1993) and Banzer/Quiroga (1998-2002) administrations. Nevertheless, this may be due to the peculiarity of its electoral system (Proportional Representation), which compels the dominant party to make certain concessions to its coalition partners; or to conflicts between modernising technocrats and the old guard of professional politicians forming part of the entourage of successive Presidents.[7] More importantly perhaps, one should question Cox's view that economic ministries have increased their power relative to welfare and politically-oriented Ministries. The question is: have economic ministries not always been dominant in capitalist states, precisely due to the abstract discipline of world money, and have finance ministries not increasingly become the pivot of governmental activities during the twentieth century? The autonomous power assigned to welfare ministries before neoliberal restructuring proves historically myopic (Burnham 2000; Bonefeld 2000).[8] In Bolivia, government *power* (an ability to achieve its ends, to constrain and pre-empt the actions of others) has systematically been centred on the President and economic Ministries since the 1952 National Revolution, which is generally considered as a bourgeois revolution expanding capitalism in its social space (Zavaleta 1983; Rivera 1983; Dunkerley 1984; Mansilla 1994; Moore 1990). This is not to deny that during Bolivia's entire modern history, repressive Ministries (Interior, Defence) and the army have had considerable power and *authority* within government (a claim to legitimacy) because capital hegemony was never achieved durably and systematic resistance within and outside the state regularly engulfed the organisational capacities of the state.

An Alternative Approach to Internationalisation

The previous chapter argued that transnational social formation must not be analysed as an unprecedented phenomenon, but as dialectically related to international relations. The expansion of a transnational bloc of capitalist forces beyond its Lockean heartland defined a protracted struggle for the restructuring of production relations, simultaneously in various national contexts. Restructuring involved the attenuation of the contradictions between global capital relations and the inter-state system (Lacher and Teschke 2008), precisely via the internationalisation of national states. Therefore, domestic struggles for and against restructuring have been constituted by and have constituted other domestic struggles.

Internationalisation cannot be conceptualised, as suggested by Robinson (2005: 92, 123), as constituted by any institution controlled by the transnational fraction, because any elite organisation can thus be indiscriminately considered part of it – the logical result of a Gramscian understanding of the state as 'extended' to 'political society'. In this light, not only is the state turned into a muddled 'nébuleuse' of institutions considered by Robinson to sustain transnational class rule (see also Cox 1992), but more importantly, the 'transnational state' apparatus can thus only be understood in instrumentalist terms, as an institutional device used by the 'political wing' of the transnational fraction in its interest (Robinson 2005: 88). This precludes an analysis of the state as a social relation traversed by intra-elite *and* class struggle (Poulantzas 1978:140-143). Instead of 'superseding' the international system as 'the organising principle of capitalist development', the internationalisation of the state is a social construct seeking to alleviate – but not fix – the fundamental contradiction between global capital and international fragmentation (Morton 2007: 149).[9]

The present study thus refers to internationalisation as the deepening integration of national states, originally via their central executive agencies, in particular economic Ministries and the Central Bank, yet increasingly through their entire institutional apparatus, into an organisational apparatus constituted by multilateral institutions that are global and regional in scope. Rejecting instrumentalism does not imply a reversion to functionalism: internationalisation involved the formation of a small elite vanguard integrated into the transnational bloc via systematic collaboration and consensus-building with the staff of MDIs; it defined, and was in turn distorted by a struggle against other forces in the state that shifted the balance of power internal to state institutions towards transnational capitalist forces (Climenhage 1999; WB 1998b: i).

How can one measure, in a qualitative sense, the deepening integration of the Bolivian state in the global governance complex? The search in primary evidence for systematic patterns of collaboration in policymaking over the period under study is a first step: at the central level of government, analysing policy-related negotiations between WB and IMF missions and respective governments, the degree of consensus on the developmental strategy for Bolivia, the recurrence and significance of policy-related technical assistance by MDIs' staff and private consultants, and the conditions under which the usage of credits and loans were bestowed by MDIs to the Bolivian government constitute the first attribute of the concept of internationalisation, i.e. an institutional articulation of key central government agencies (in particular the Ministries of Finance and Planning; the BCB; and emergent sectoral regulatory agencies) with MDIs. The payment of additional salaries by the IMF and WB (the infamous *sobresueldos*) to Government Ministers and high level civil servants throughout the period under study, in order for the state to be able to compete with the private sector in attracting competent technocrats, is a second attribute. The third attribute relates to institution-building, which focused upon enhancing the effectiveness and discipline of state institutions beyond central executive agencies. Institution-building involved the penetration of lower levels of the state hierarchy by private consultants contracted by the Bolivian government and remunerated by MDIs, for training purposes (civil service reform) but also as line managers, to secure a transition towards a depoliticised and disciplined technocratic stratum (WB 1998a; 2000c). The latter two processes are elemental to the notions of 'participatory development' (DAC 1989), 'public-private partnerships' (IBRD 1993) and 'country ownership' (WB 2005a), which facilitated the internalisation of the business perspective by civil servants in the central government in the late 1980s and early 1990s, and subsequently at lower (regional and municipal) levels of the state.

Internationalisation In Practice

Restructuring social relations in Bolivia involved the almost unconditional, systematic provision of financial, ideological and organisational support to successive governments by MDIs, but also systematic government commitment to restructuring. Internationalisation unfolded initially through a collaborative relationship between the staff of MDIs and of aforementioned key government agencies.

Quantity

Support to successive Bolivian governments came above all in financial form: throughout the period under study, the lifeline of the Bolivian state remained external public investment and fiscal support. More than half of state expenditures and investments were financed by MDIs and bilateral donors (see table 4.1). Between 1985 and 1994, ODA constituted well over half of all capital investments in Bolivia (above 7 percent of GDP).[10] In the 'booming' years of marginally improving terms of trade and the capitalisation of state-owned corporations between 1994 and 1998, this proportion declined from 7 to 4 percent. However, the unravelling of the restructuring process from 1999 onwards fostered a return to pre-1994 conditions. Total annual multilateral and bilateral aid to Bolivia ranged between $400 million and $582 million (in 2005) in the period under study, a particularly high level in relation to GDP and in comparative perspective, as illustrated in table 4.2 (WB 2005a: 88; Sida 2005).

The argument, of the dependency or world system theory kind, that multilateral credit was bestowed to Bolivia in order to increase its dependence on the global metropolis and maintain poverty and underdevelopment by helping US and European TNCs to squeeze profits out of Bolivian resources and labour is inadequate (Fernández 2003; Kohl and Farthing 2005; Chossudovsky 1998). As pointed out by Herbert Müller: 'Remember that in the era of Dr. Paz the debt to the banks was repaid at 11 cents to the dollar, it cannot be said that the FMI wanted us to repay the debt at all cost, it was effectively condoning 80 percent of the debt... There are margins, the proof is that it continued to operate here. The crux of the problem is not whether or not you repay your debts, but to *guarantee positive external flows*'.[11] Debt servicing does sustain money discipline. Furthermore, locked as they were in the vicious circle of social instability, lack of business confidence, and hence insufficient capital formation, which in turn fuels further instability, Bolivian governments did uphold a dependence on public

Table 4.1: Dependence of the Bolivian State on External Financing: Public Investment Expenditure by Source of Financing, 1989-1998 (in US$ thousands)

	Financing				**Total Public Investment Expenditure**
	Internal	%	External	%	
1989	151,755	45	182,242	55	333,997
1990	143,725	46	171,653	54	315,378
1991	227,703	54	192,797	46	420,500
1992	249,362	47	282,218	53	531,580
1993	197,144	41	283,423	59	480,567
1994	221,220	43	292,066	57	513,286
1995	249,432	48	270,300	52	519,732
1996	264,559	45	324,134	55	588,693
1997	322,900	59	225,381	41	548,281
1998	292,222	58	212,467	42	504,689

Source: WB (1999c: 40)

Table 4.2: Official Development Assistance to Selected Countries, 1996 (in US$)

	Bolivia	Honduras	Georgia	Zimbabwe	Ecuador	Paraguay	Lower Middle Income
% of GDP	13.3	9.5	7.3	5.5	1.8	1.1	0.7
US$ per capita	112	60	59	34	21	20	8

Source: WB (1999c: 42)

capital inflows. The disciplinary context of debt servicing thus seems at face value to have generated an unequal power relationship between Bolivian governments and multilateral donors. Yet debt servicing was not imposed from above on comprador lackeys and the Bolivian nation. Documentary analysis reveals that the relationship between the WB, the IMF and successive Bolivian governments was essentially *collaborative*: from the very moment the Paz Estenssoro government was elected in August 1985, Bolivia's transnational business elite fraction, positioned by Paz in economic Ministries, actively restructured Bolivian social relations and engaged MDIs. Once the essential problem of the Bolivian state in 1985-1986 (namely the servicing of principal and interest on debts to US and European private banks and, to a lesser extent, to the Paris Club) had been partially resolved through the IMF-sponsored repurchase of the private commercial debt on the secondary market (IMF 1986b; 1988) (see figures 4.1 and 4.2), a grace period of ten years for multilateral development loans had been agreed, and credits had been provided (WB 1986; 1998a), it became imperative for the IMF and WB staff to sustain Bolivia's integration in the capitalist production structure. The power relationship between the staff of MDIs and Bolivian elites was almost immediately equalised by the dependence of the former on the success of the latter in achieving first and second-generation reforms whilst maintaining political stability.

The above figures illustrate qualitative changes in the form of external credit provided to the Bolivian state: the channelling of development assistance through and by MDIs had the effect of gradually diminishing the fiscal dependence of Bolivian governments on transnational banks and the US State Department (or indeed, the Paris Club). Bilateral relationships of dependence were transformed by the second wave of internationalisation, defined by ideological convergence between transnational technocrats/businessmen, within and through state agencies managing economic relations and the staff of MDIs.

The staff of MDIs and the transnational bloc as a whole, including its Bolivian constituents, manifestly do not aim to increase poverty and to violently dominate labour. Rather, 'consensual growth' is the aim (DAC 1989): the viability of Bolivia's national accumulation process is deemed to require PSD (the consolidation of a capitalist class via FDI and joint ventures with local capitalists, but also via primitive accumulation) (Van der Pijl 1998: 38). It also required the reduction of the incidence of poverty and investment in 'human capital' through an improvement of welfare provision and an increase in formal employment, if only to stimulate demand, reduce political disorder (i.e. generate subaltern consent to restructuring) and increase tax returns for the state (WB 1990b; WB 1998b: 1; WB 2005b). 'There may be different paths. The objective, we all have a clear idea of what it is: the reduction of poverty'.[12] We may question the extent to which this assertion is true for 'all', but the transnational bloc's concerns regarding social stability were indubitably related to the alleviation of poverty (see chapter 3).

The rationale for WB and IMF involvement in Bolivia is encapsulated in their support of the post-1993 reforms: 'The proposed project is consistent with the Bank's country assistance strategy discussed by the Board on February 8, 1994 as well as the Government's

Figure 4.1: Distribution of Foreign Debt Stock by Creditor Type (Public and Publicly Guaranteed Only) in percent

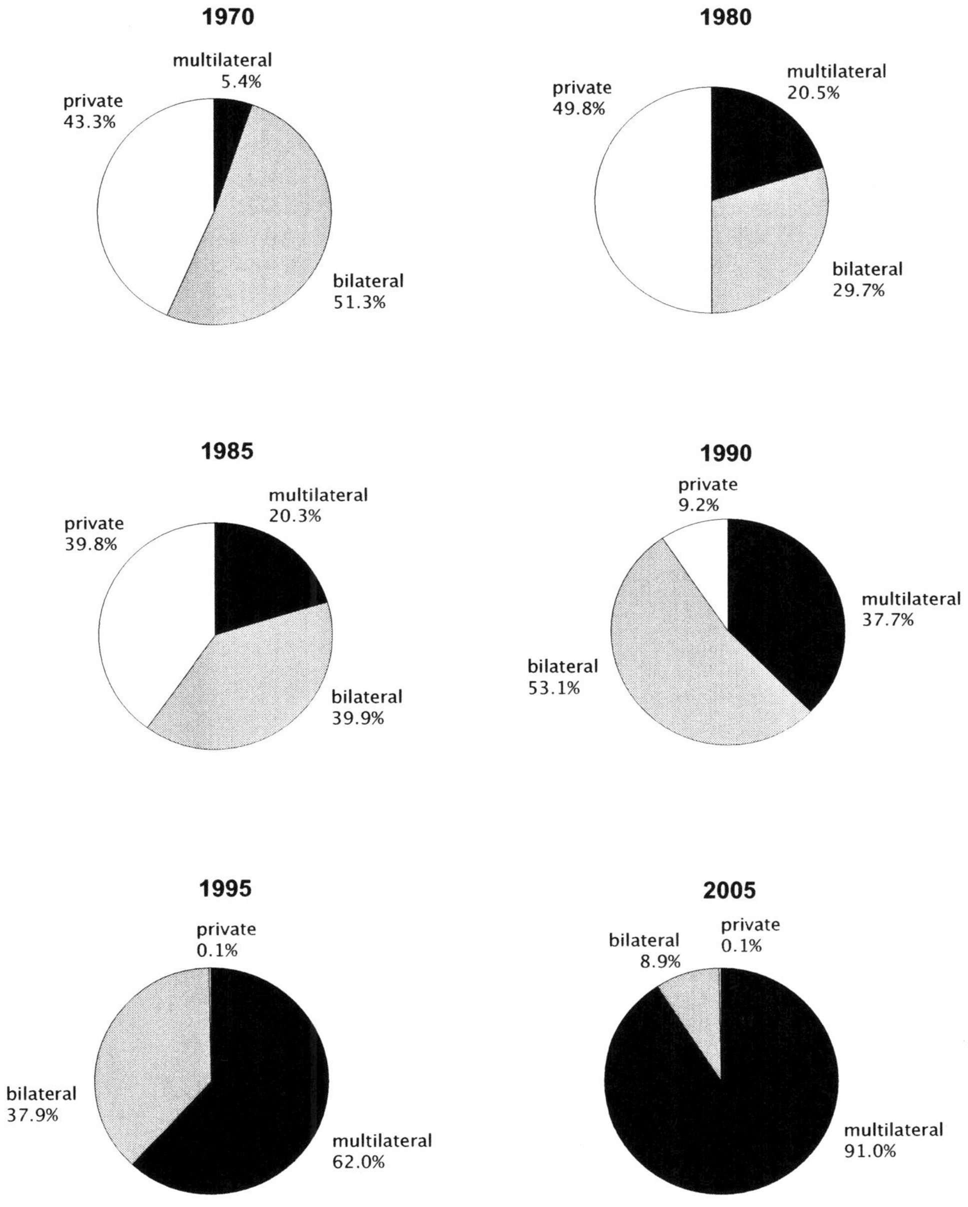

Source: WB (1986; 1999c); Morales and Sachs (1990); IMF (2007)

policy agenda, which aims to reduce the role of the state in productive and infrastructural sectors while improving the delivery of social services through efficient social sector expenditures' (WB 1994a: 6).[13] The fundamental contradiction underlying the empowerment of the capitalist class is that accumulation must be sustained through wages restrictions and the disciplining of 'human capital', generating systematic class struggle (Gill 1987; Conaghan and Malloy 1995; Malloy and Gamarra 1987). Indeed, as ex-Finance Minister Ramiro Cabezas points out: 'we couldn't attach ourselves to dogmas of the past ... Supreme Decree 21060 did not only liberalise the economy, it eliminated a series of conditions of a social type which were not convenient for the economy, such as the *estabilidad funcionaria*, which until then prohibited layoffs by employers. Although it seemed to them like a social conquest, it prejudiced workers by making employers excessively careful when contracting someone. And this applied especially, if not only, in the private sector because whenever a new government was formed, Ministers replaced their staff with their people'.[14] Despite a systematic struggle by the transnational bloc to build capital hegemony (WB 1994a; WB 1998b), Bolivia's persistent state of crisis entailed active resistance to restructuring, thereby compelling successive governments to unveil the coercive core of capitalist elite dominance, if necessary against organised worker movements within the state (Conaghan and Malloy 1995; Dunkerley 2007).

Figure 4.2: External Debt by Type of Creditor (in millions of US dollars)

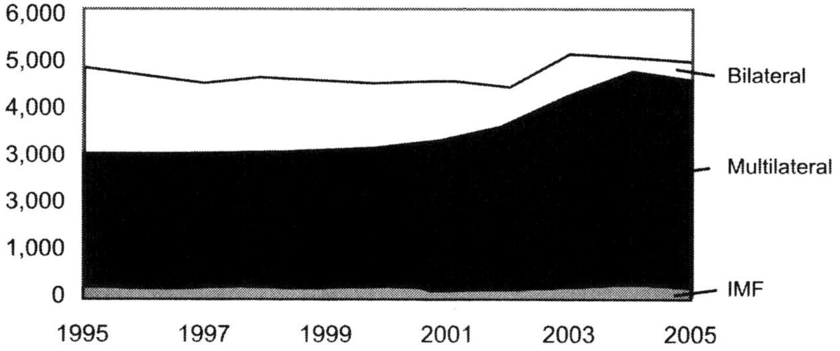

Source: IMF

Table 4.3: External Financing, Credits vs. Grants, 1989-1998 (in US$ thousands)

	Credits	%	Grants	%	Total
1989	129,268	71	52,974	29	182,242
1990	132,983	77	38,670	23	171,653
1991	148,879	77	43,918	23	192,797
1992	232,433	82	49,785	18	282,218
1993	217,460	77	65,963	23	283,423
1994	237,645	81	54,421	19	292,066
1995	222,710	82	47,590	18	270,300
1996	256,428	79	67,706	21	324,134
1997	174,238	77	51,143	23	225,381
1998	159,540	75	52,927	25	212,467

Source: WB (1999c: 41)

By 1998, when the executive director of the WB and IMF were recommending the application of the Heavily Indebted Poor Country (HIPC) initiative to Bolivia, only 16.6 million out of the $952 million in credits bestowed by the WB's IDA (26 credits in total) had been serviced because a grace period of 10 years was applied to concessional credits imparted to the Bolivian state (WB 1998d). Bolivian governments however, continued to service official bilateral debt and other multilateral creditors (such as the *Corporación Andina de Fomento*) accumulated prior to the 1984 moratorium on debt servicing and its 1987 rescheduling (IMF 1988). As indicated by tables 4.3 and 4.4, a significant proportion (37 percent) of all external financing in Bolivia prior to the HIPC initiative had taken the form of grants.

Table 4.4: Overall External Financing to 1999 (in US$ millions)

	Total External Financing	% of Total	Disbursed to the end of 1997	Disbursed in 1998	To be Disbursed
Grants	1,372	37	679.6	121.4	570.7
Credits	2,344.9	63	1,166.9	190	988.00
Total	3,716.6	100	1,846.5	311.4	1,558.7

Source: WB (1999c: 41)

Furthermore, the flow of 'official' capital remained positive for the Bolivian state prior to HIPC. On a yearly basis, prior to a wave of ODA under the Sánchez de Lozada administration, the Bolivian Treasury never repaid more than two thirds of multilateral development assistance disbursed from 1980 to 1992, as indicated in table 4.5.

The vast increase in the state's debt burden during the 1990s included debt that was eventually curtailed under the HIPC initiative ($448 million in 1998, representing 5 percent of GDP – yet only a fraction of its $4.5 billion foreign debt) (see table 4.6). 'The Bank played an instrumental role in sponsoring Bolivia for favourable debt obligation terms from the Paris Club, and for its more recent inclusion to the HIPC initiative. The weight and direction of the Bank's Consultative Group ... provided the forum for the international assistance community to muster concessional term funding sufficient to help finance a current account balance of payments deficit averaging 7.8 percent of GDP in 1986-1996. This assistance enabled successive governments to achieve and maintain macroeconomic stability. The results attained are even more impressive if one considers the severe adverse external conditions Bolivia was facing at that time – the terms of trade deteriorated 73 percent between 1980 and 1996' (and deteriorated further between 1996 and 2004) (WB 1998b:6).

Quality

However, the fiscal dependence of the Bolivian state on multilateral and bilateral credits and grants is not a sufficient explanation for the internationalisation of the state. The explanation is essentially qualitative and involves understanding the motivation of segments of Bolivian elites to pursue an increasingly close collaborative relationship with the staff of MDIs. Indeed, and I repeat here a meaningful citation, 'institutional strengthening, and the development of an institutional culture supportive of PSD, are necessarily long and difficult processes, highly susceptible to failure and heavily dependent on unwavering government commitment in the face of conflicting demands from myriad domestic interest groups. The WB has made progress in supporting governments in this process, but continues to learn from experience' (IBRD 1993: 16). From 1985 onwards, successive Bolivian Presidents and economic Ministers offered unwavering commitment to structural adjustment and PSD, despite instability and resistance in the state, in the street, and in government itself (IMF 1986b; WB 1998b; Dunkerley 1990; Climenhage 1999).

The regularity and intensity of formal negotiations at the central government level indicates institutional *cooperation* and is indicative of embryonic internationalisation: 1) regular missions (every three to six months) to Bolivia by WB, IMF, IDB, UNDP and, increasingly, European Commission officials; 2) annual Consultative Group meetings

Table 4.5: External Debt: Disbursements and Repayments, 1980-1992 (US$ millions)

	1980	1981	1982	1983	1984	1985	1986	1987	1988	1989	1990	1991	1992
Disbursements													
Multilateral creditors	**107.7**	**82.5**	**101.6**	**91.5**	**82**	**73.3**	**243.2**	**154.6**	**257.4**	**277**	**204.3**	**197**	**248.6**
World Bank (1)	74.2	45.2	30.1	12.9	15.7	12.2	7.3	43.2	111.5	78.8	48.7	47.9	55.6
IMF (2)	96.4	0.2	27	19.1	0	0	134.7	0	91.3	56.9	30.8	31	51.1
IDB	28.5	34.9	36.7	22.1	39	54.5	117.3	82.8	96.1	127.9	90.8	100	157.6
CAF	0.6	0.9	1.5	1.5	23.2	1.5	8.6	18.2	33.7	61.4	58.1	38.4	23.8
Bilateral creditors	**87.2**	**126.5**	**90.4**	**45.4**	**113.3**	**123.7**	**146**	**196.6**	**147.2**	**169.3**	**160.1**	**147.9**	**202.1**
Private creditors	**245.9**	**164.2**	**52.2**	**15.3**	**15.3**	**2.3**	**6.7**	**25**	**0**	**5.1**	**9.1**	**14.6**	**3.5**
TOTAL	**440.8**	**373.2**	**244.2**	**152.2**	**210.7**	**199.3**	**395.8**	**376.2**	**404.7**	**451.5**	**373.4**	**359.5**	**454.2**
Repayments													
Multilateral creditors	**7.2**	**10.4**	**14.1**	**17.2**	**35.4**	**72.7**	**71.3**	**60.8**	**71.3**	**110.1**	**116.9**	**81.2**	**86.8**
World Bank	2.9	4.3	9.3	9.7	14.2	12.7	18.9	19.7	23.9	20.1	22.5	27	23.3
IMF	0	2.2	8.3	11.5	24	23.5	38.2	34.5	59	12	45.6	44.1	37
IDB	2.3	3.9	2.1	3.9	4.1	7.4	7.9	9.1	9.8	14.8	25	28.6	28.9
CAF	0.8	1	1.8	3.2	3.5	2.6	20.9	5.1	9.5	47	40.9	21.9	31.2
Bilateral creditors	**33.9**	**37.5**	**39.2**	**44.1**	**59**	**63.3**	**21.1**	**224.1**	**137.6**	**95**	**150**	**138.4**	**129.1**
Private creditors	**85.2**	**62**	**54.7**	**45.5**	**19.9**	**12.7**	**11.2**	**6.8**	**31.2**	**6.8**	**5.8**	**5.6**	**7.6**
TOTAL	**126.3**	**109.8**	**107.9**	**106.7**	**114.3**	**148.6**	**103.6**	**291.7**	**240**	**211.9**	**272.6**	**225.2**	**223.4**

(1) Comprises IBRD and IDA loans and credit. Primarily IBRD until 1986. US$404 million disbursed from 1964 to 1985 on 26 projects. Thereafter exclusively IDA concessional credit.

(2) Indicates virtual boycott, by IMF and WB, of the economic policies undertaken by the Siles government (1982-1985), and 'wait and see' attitude for a year (IMF) or two (WB) under the Paz Estenssoro government (1985-1989). Despite dwindling amounts between 1980 and 1985, external financing was not completely cut, and IMF and WB missions continued to meet, if only sporadically, the economic team (MIR) of the Siles government. The year 1986 signals the financing of a new wave of technical assistance teams and development projects in Bolivia.

Source: WB (1994b: 185); IMF (1998b: 100)

Table 4.6: Foreign Debt Relief, 1999-2006 (in US$ millions)

	1999	2000	2001	2002	2003	2004	2005	2006	**Total**
HIPC I (1)	84.7	79	58.8	42.6	38.6	29.4	27.5	22.8	383.4
HIPC II	0	0.7	27.7	84.4	80.4	82.3	73.3	69.7	418.5
Total HIPC	**84.7**	**79.7**	**86.5**	**127**	**119**	**111.7**	**100.8**	**92.5**	**801.9**
Beyond HIPC			9.3	29.8	34.4	54.3	47.6	50.9	226.3
MDRI (2)								326.6	326.6
Total	**84.7**	**79.7**	**95.8**	**156.8**	**153.4**	**166**	**148.4**	**470**	**1,354.8**
Total outstanding foreign debt	**4,573**	**4,460**	**4,497**	**4,400**	**5,142**	**5,945**	**4,942**	**3,240**	

(1) Heavily Indebted Poor Countries: initially included a $450 million, equivalent to 13% of total debt outstanding in 1997.
(2) Multilateral Debt Relief Initiative created in 2005, and started taking effect in first half of 2006. Includes debt forgiveness by IMF, World Bank and IDB. IMF debt relief was immediate, while World Bank and IDB relief was phased over several years. World Bank and IMF relief totalled $1.8 billion, while IDB relief was worth $1.2 billion.

Source: WB 1999c. Central Bank of Bolivia. Reproduced in Morales (2008: 233).

involving multilateral bilateral donors (including the European Commission), government Ministers and high (increasingly mid-) level civil servants aiming to delineate annual development strategies and to foster multilateral institutional coordination in development assistance;[15] 3) after a six year hiatus in lending and following the signing of a standby arrangement (IMF 1986), by triennial Enhanced Structural Adjustment Facilities (ESAFs) involving IMF staff, the Ministers of Planning and Finance and the governor of the BCB (supplemented by annual Article IV consultations, Mid-term reviews and other ESAF and PFP annual or even monthly updates and extensions) (IMF 1988; 1991; 1998a); 4) two to three programme-based Structural Adjustment Programmes/Loans per year by the WB (1998b; 2005); and 5) indicating systematic strategic cooperation between successive governments, the IMF and WB, by triennial Policy Framework Papers (PFPs) prepared by Bolivia's Economic Ministers (Planning, Finance, Labour, Mining, Agriculture) and the Governor of the BCB 'in collaboration with the staffs of the Fund and the WB' and reviewed on an annual basis (IMF 1988: 4; IMF 1991a; 1998a). The strategic blueprints crystallised in these numerous agreements involved, furthermore, weeks of negotiations in La Paz and Washington (see for example, IMF 1991a: 1; WB 1998b); combined, they entail quasi-systematic meetings and negotiations.

More convincing evidence of internationalisation than systematic 'engagement' and government-level cooperation between distinct institutions is *coordination* – the harmonious functioning of institutional parts. The role of the resident offices and representatives of the WB, UNDP, IMF and later European Commission facilitated policy coordination between government Ministries and MDIs. One might appropriately define the relationship between the resident representatives of MDIs on the one hand and Bolivian economic Ministers and high-level technocrats on the other as intimate, as they engaged in day-to-day, backstage and formal dialogue on legal, institutional and economic reforms (WB 1998a: 4), but also on means to build capital hegemony (WB 1994a; 2000c). [16] However, the most fundamental attribute of internationalisation is *onsite, day to day policy-related technical assistance*, which helped to build a relationship of trust and mutual interest between Bolivian and foreign technocrats, certainly not devoid of conflict.[17] Systematic information-sharing sustained ideological cohesion, thereby buttressing the institutional articulation between MDIs and economic management agencies. 'The WB (in the form of IDA in Bolivia), the IMF and to an extent the IDB have provided important support from outside the country. The WB did this through a series of adjustment and technical assistance loans from 1986 to 1996, as well as continuing policy dialogue. It was, for instance, instrumental in the decision to separate banking supervision from the Central Bank in 1987 and it has played an important role, behind the scenes, in supporting the current Superintendent. The IMF has also played a similar role of support, in particular through its local office' (WB 2000c: 72).

Almost every policy-related agreement between successive Bolivian governments and MDIs in ESAFs (IMF) and Structural Adjustment Programmes (WB) contained a technical assistance component (WB 1998a; 1998b). Technical assistance is not a benign exercise; it required weeks if not months of onsite presence of IMF and WB staff or private advisors, whether one individual expert or teams attached to the BCB, regulatory agencies and economic Ministries (IMF 1994: 18-19). In order to satisfy specific benchmarks, it involved sometimes heated negotiations on almost every detail of legislative bills later presented to Congress by the government. It also generated protracted conflicts between WB technocrats and private consultants contracted by the WB for specific technical assistance projects, breaking up the view of the WB and IMF as monolithic entities (WB 1998c). The breadth and depth of multilateral technical assistance is quite astounding.[18] Prominent issues addressed by technical missions comprised, among others, financial sector reform, including banking and later insurance and securities market supervision and crisis management (late 1980s and early 1990s); civil service reform (1986-2005); the restructuring (1986-1990) and privatisation or liquidation of state-owned corporations (1990-1999); the administrative reorganisation of the BCB following its separation from SBEF in 1987 (1992-1994) competition and good practice in privatised sectors (1994-2005); streamlining trade and firm registration procedures (1986-2005); welfare provision (health and education from 1987 with the WB's approval of the Emergency Social Fund Credit, and pension reform from 1993); and administrative and fiscal decentralisation (1991-) (WB 1991b; WB 1992b, 1992c; WB 2000b; WB 2005; IMF 1994; IMF 1998b). The 'technical assistance' component of ODA, often provided as grants (IMF 1998a: 43), demonstrates a hands-on approach to restructuring, and requires a significant reconsideration of images of MDIs as distant imperialistic entities imposing neoliberalism from above (Fernández 2003, Kohl and Farthing 2005). It involved collaboration on a daily basis, fostering a relationship of trust and continuity in administration, thereby promoting a network of interest between high-level civil servants in the BCB, economic Ministries, SBEF, SIRESE and the staff of MDIs.

It is of fundamental importance that legislation central to the organisation of production relations was often passed in Congress several months, if not several years after being placed on the agenda of WB/IMF-government negotiations (WB 1989a, 1989c; 1991a; 1991b). Thus the WB and the IMF applied pressure on the government on issues such as the restructuring, privatisation or liquidation of state-owned corporation between 1990 and 1993,[19] and again in 1997-8 for the privatisation of the smelting company Vinto and for the privatisation of water distribution services (resulting in purchases by Bechtel [Aguas del Tunari] in Cochabamba and by Suez [Aguas del Illimani] in La Paz) (IMF 1998a: 25). They applied further pressure on the government to close down state-owned banks in the late 1980s and early 1990s (WB 1991a; 1991b), to trim the state through layoffs in the early and again late 1990s (IMF 1998a: 70), to maintain fiscal stability by containing increases in the wage bill, to simplify labour legislation in order to eliminate 'rigidities' in the labour market,[20] to accelerate civil service reform by enacting the law SAFCO (Ley No.1178 de Administración y Control Gubernamental, 20 July 1990) (WB 1989a, 1989c, 1991a;

1991b; IMF 1991a),[21] to establish depoliticised regulatory agencies during the second generation wave of privatisations/capitalisations (1993-1997), to separate the banking supervision agency (SBEF) from the BCB in 1987, and to depoliticise the BCB itself through SAFCO and through the Ley del Banco Central (1995): 'the IMF insisted heavily on the independence of the BCB from the early 1990s because they thought that it was the solution to institutional weakness in the country'.[22] The staff of MDIs thus took the initiative by raising key governance and economic issues and making recommendations towards their resolution. They often attached policy-related conditions to loans and credits – the allocation of credits in tranches contingent on the implementation of WB and IMF recommendations, measured according to precise 'benchmarks' and 'performance criteria' (IMF 1998a: 64).

'Conditionality' is a salient expression of leverage. According to Stallings (1992), market conditions, leverage and linkages are the three instruments used by the WB and the IMF to influence policy elaboration in the debtor country. Market conditions determine the vulnerability of national governments to external influence: peripheral countries' dependence on a single or a few export commodities render them particularly vulnerable to a decline in world prices or a recession in a dominant trading partner; especially in the context of a high debt burden, the dependence of a given government on multilateral credit increases. However, I agree with Climenhage's (1999) critique of the view that MDIs may instrumentalise market conditions in order to impose structural adjustment policies – WB and IMF documents do not support the view that they consciously harness detrimental market forces in order to force policies onto governments. In the context of transnational bloc formation however, adverse market conditions have tended to foster an ideational elite convergence on the appropriateness of policies to alleviate them.

Leverage, an agency-related, direct form of power, is the most visible form of external influence on national policymaking, i.e. the attachment of explicit policy conditions to economically vital loans and credit facilities. Leverage can be reduced to the idea that MDIs systematically promise or threaten the use of rewards (additional credit lines) and punishments (cutting-off external financing) in order to achieve the implementation of structural adjustment programmes by national governments. An important problem of this argument is that it is fundamentally based on a domestic-foreign dichotomy, which overlooks change in institutional relationships – for instance between coalition partners in government – and transnational elite formation. The notion of leverage is contradicted by declassified WB and IMF documents, which confirm the intimate relationship and high degree of consensus reached with economic Ministers, and by interviews with ex-Ministers of Finance. While leverage may have been prominent during the first two years of the Paz Zamora administration (1989-1993), economic ministers under the Paz Estenssoro (1985-1989), Sánchez de Lozada (1993-1997; 2002-2003) and Banzer/Quiroga (1997-2002) presidencies collaborated relatively harmoniously because an underlying consensus, a transnational network of interests or an 'epistemic community' (Haas 1992) had been consolidated by fully incorporating the leadership of the CEPB.

Pressure was thus applied in particular during the Presidency of Jaime Paz Zamora (1989-1993), for the enactment of a Privatisation Law and the closure of loss-making state-owned banks, due to its relative inertia (until 1991) in implementing reforms and its manifest 'sleaze' (WB 1991b; Dunkerley 2007 [1998]: 77, 84). However, the form in which recommendations were implemented, and to a certain extent their timing were usually a prerogative of Bolivian governments,[23] constrained as they were by the expectation of or actual resistance in Congress, in state corporations, at the lower levels of Ministries, sometimes in government itself and in the streets. Information sharing on the legal, institutional and ideological constraints on policy implementation was systematic and transparent.[24]

Furthermore, IMF and WB pressure was usually applied to well-disposed forces: 'when I took the position, the Central Bank was a direct dependency of the Minister [of Finance], if the Minister needed money he just needed to make a phone call and ask for it... The BCB had no independence whatsoever: half of its board of directors was appointed by the Minister. We realised that it was a real danger, because there is always a scarcity of resources and back then there was the temptation to ask and order. We knew that hyperinflation was caused by the weakness of the BCB, because the Minister could order the emission of new money. We realised, Juan Cariaga and myself, that the BCB needed to be independent'.[25] Similarly, layoffs (in the state-owned mining and hydrocarbons corporations, COMIBOL and YPFB in 1986-7, in the Finance and Planning Ministries and, again, in the YPFB in 1996-1997) and the restructuring of state-owned corporations were often planned or undertaken by the government prior to negotiations with the staff of MDIs – evidently satisfying the latter and resulting in 'almost no opposition to our programmes when we informed the IMF about them'.[26] WB plans for the complete privatisation of state-owned companies did face government resistance until 1992: 'Government commitment towards privatizations was not uniformly strong during this period – arguing that interim steps were necessary to downsize the public sector' (WB 1998a: 4). The WB recommended privatisation with an understanding that the 1986-7 collapse of the world tin market had already forced the government to close loss-making mines and lay off 23,000 miners (out of 30,000), that the Constitution prohibited private investments and ownership rights in COMIBOL and YPFB (WB 1991b; see also table 4.6), and that 'the issue of COMIBOL was very politically sensitive throughout the overall period, given the strong influence of the labor union, which systematically opposed reforms' (WB 1998a: 8).

The WB (1989b), whilst recommending privatisation, thus restricted itself, in its May 1989 'Mining Sector Rehabilitation Project', to support government plans for the restructuring of COMIBOL and YPFB, i.e. opening them to joint ventures with private (domestic and foreign) capital and curtailing financial support by the Treasury. Fernando Campero, Minister of Commerce in 1992-3, recalls the issue:

'Privatisation wasn't part of the government programme. Jaime Paz wasn't very clear on this. Of course, there were agreements with the IMF, we had to pursue the structural reforms, improve employment in the public sector, professionalise, things that we saw eye to eye on... Privatisation was on the table, but in reality we [the economic cabinet, including Samuel Doria Medina and Jorge Quiroga] took the initiative. It was a problem, there were all kinds of enterprises, producing tubes, matches, glass... a stupidity! So we decided to privatise them, at least these ones, because Jaime Paz had told us: "we are not going to touch the strategic sectors." It was very clear... If it had been for us, we would have gone all the way... For small companies everyone was more or less in agreement, maybe social democrats complained a bit. But I remember that we were apprehensive for Yacimientos [YPFB]. How to do it? It was big, messed up, and the Treasury lived off Yacimientos, especially after 1985... Afterwards Goni did it otherwise, with his capitalisation programme, and with good sectoral reforms through superintendencies...We also regarded the Bonosol as a positive thing. The system of pensions of the state was a disaster, totally corrupt.'[27]

Recommendations for layoffs in the state and trimming the state to reduce its wage bill and improve its fiscal balance were made throughout the 1980s and 1990s by MDIs, but usually to encourage and extend existing government initiatives, as in the case of staff reductions in the YPFB (2,000 layoffs in 1987-1988) and COMIBOL (23,000 in 1986-1988) in the late 1980s, the Central Bank (from 870 to 492) and the Ministry of Finance (from circa 1,200 to 1,000) in the mid-1990s (IMF 1998; WB 1999c: 12-14).[28] State employment in 1985 had reached 245,000 (see table 4.7). Despite the layoff of miners and of civil servants in the late 1980s, employment actually stabilised for the public sector as a whole (including government and state-owned corporations) to 209,082 in 1989 (WB 1999c: 13). In the following decade, state employment remained broadly stable despite the privatisation/capitalisation of state-owned corporations and the liquidation and restructuring of state-owned banks, which reduced employment in the former from 33,410 to 9,343 between 1989 and 1997 by transferring them to the private sector (additionally to the layoff of miners in 1986-1988), and from 4,711 to 792 in the latter (WB 1999c: 13). The restructuring of RDCs in 1996 also eliminated 4,713 workers from the state's wage bill. The WB considered this to be 'no doubt a tremendous accomplishment' (WB 1999c: 12), considering the 2.4 percent per annum population growth and the 4 percent annual GDP growth during that period, resulting in a reduction of the public share of total employment from 8 to 6.4 percent. However, decentralisation efforts (in health and education, for instance) in the 1990s involved a significant increase in municipal and prefectural employment (in the latter, from 96,804 to 124,160), signifying that 'In a sense, Bolivia missed an opportunity to downsize public employment', and that the Bolivian government had to resolve its 'serious overstaffing problem' by pursuing civil service reforms in order to contain the rise of real wages in the public sector (WB 1999c: 12, 14). The WB identified patronage and corruption as the fundamental causes of overstaffing and systematically urged widespread civil service reforms to improve the efficiency of state institutions (see below).

However, Bolivian governments also took the initiative within the matrix of stabilisation and structural adjustment, and then of PSD, and showed admirable creativity in the elaboration of legislation seeking to create the appropriate conditions for business confidence. The DS 21060, implemented two days after the investiture of Paz Estenssoro (29 August 1985) was a creation of the MNR and ADN's economic teams – including party leaders but also unaffiliated businessmen and monetarist economists.[29] The MNR and ADN teams working on a NEP did take into account recommendations of the WB's 1984 missions, its August 1985 *Economic Memorandum* (produced in the run up to the Presidential election) (WB 1985), and the comprehensive 1981 report on tax and fiscal reform of the Musgrave mission sponsored by the International Tax Program of the Harvard Law School (Cabezas 1990: 4). Nevertheless, their plans far exceeded the expectations of WB and IMF staff. The economic teams worked relentlessly for three weeks in quasi-total isolation during and directly after the general elections of

August 1985, seeking to elude media attention, which would politicise and dilute their plans (*La Prensa* 2005).[30] The DS 21060 was elemental to a shock and awe, comprehensive deflationary strategy, which would help Bolivia to restore business confidence and regain credibility among MDIs and bilateral donors (Cariaga 1990; Dunkerley 1990; Morales and Sachs 1990; Conaghan and Malloy 1994). Juan Cariaga, Gonzalo Sánchez de Lozada, Fernando Romero and other members of the MNR team had little hope that banks would resume lending, so they focused on engaging and convincing the IMF, the WB, the Paris Club and other multilateral and bilateral agencies that their plans were going to 'encourage self-sacrifice on the part of the Bolivian people', in order to reactivate concessionary credit lines (Cariaga 1990: 42).

Table 4.7a: Employment by the State, 1951-2003

	1951	1964	1975	1980	1985	1987
Total public sector	**40,000**	**90,000**	**182,000**	**201,240**	**245,000**	**212,442**
Central admin.	25,000	49,500	65,000	100,000	124,000	129,295
(percent)	62.5	55	35.7	49.7	50.6	60.8
Prefectures and municipalities (inc. RDCs)	-	-	-	-	11,990	12,038
Decentralised institutions (inc. universities)	-	-	-	-	22,132	22,132
State-owned enterprises	-	22,500	41,000	-	74,000	41,327
(percent)	-	25	22.5		30.2	19.5

The economic team brought their radical stabilisation measures to the attention of IMF and USAID missions in mid-August 1985,[31] and IMF and USAID officials did not take these drastic deflationary measures seriously. On its side, the Emergency Social Fund (ESF), designed in 1986 by the Bolivian government as a cushion for the devastating social costs of the closure of COMIBOL mines and layoffs in other state corporations in 1987-1990 (by employing about 30,000 workers in labour intensive infrastructural and social projects), was financed by the Bolivian Treasury before securing subsequent financial support by WB and IDB credits and grants (WB 1998a: 6-7).[32] The Paz Estenssoro government was indubitably the initiator of neoliberalism adapted to Bolivian conditions and had to demonstrate its determination – through two states of siege, its active repression of trade union leaders

Table 4.7b: Employment by the State, 1951-2003							
	1989	1993	1995	1997	1999	2001	2003
Total public sector	**209,082**	**205,986**	**201,666**	**217,733**	**219,620**	**217,375**	**219,287**
Central admin.	135,066	155,691	160,782	180,470	185,118	187,998	192,794
(percent)	66.2	75.6	79.7	82.9	84.3	86.5	87.9
Education	85,465	-	-	103,912	110,604	115,337	119,232
inc. Teachers	67,092	-	-	80,678	82,746	86,979	96,113
Health	10,970	10,270	9,414	13,210	15,278	15,868	16,271
Prefectures and municipalities (inc. RDCs)	9,716	12,848	11,727	18,467	20,635	15,217	15,187
Decentralised institutions (inc. universities)	21,699	4,254	4,247	743	681	882	-
State-owned enterprises	33,41	21,535	18,049	9,343	3,564	2,165	2,135
(percent)	16.4	10.5	8.9	4.3	1.6	1	1
inc. COMIBOL	-	4,308	1,419	1,231	658	110	-
Financial public sector (including BCB and state-owned banks) (1)	4,711	1,390	628	792	477	464	-

(1) Employment in the BCB declined from 870 in 1989 to 492 in 1997 (WB 1999c: 13). Following the closure of state-owned banks in the early 1990s, the financial public sector was almost exclusively constituted by the BCB.

Elaboration by author using WB (1986: 5; 1991c: 17; 1999c: 13; 2004: 19); IMF (1986a: 16, 18, 78; 1991b: 78; 1998b; 2003); and Berthin (1999).

and the introduction of labour market flexibility – initially to Bolivian businessmen and subsequently to MDIs in order to secure their unremitting support.[33]

Paz Estenssoro's economic team accurately traced the causes of hyperinflation to the massive fiscal deficit of the central government and state-owned corporations built up in the 1970s, financed by the BCB's printing of money. They therefore declared zero tolerance of state deficits and pursued a policy of tight fiscal and monetary discipline, increasing state revenue and reducing state expenditures via 1) a simplification of the tax system (reducing the number of taxes from 450 to 9, and focusing these taxes on consumption rather than income – with the introduction of a value-added tax – to facilitate its implementation), 2) a wage freeze and layoffs in the public sector, as well as the elimination of all subsidies and price controls – including the rates and fares for foodstuffs and public services such as transport, electricity and telephone, but also bonuses paid in cash and in kind to state employees,[34] 3) a currency devaluation to bring it to 'realistic levels', the introduction of daily currency auctions by the BCB, thereby virtually eliminating the black market in currency; the introduction of market-determined interest rates; and the authorisation of foreign currency deposits in private banks, thereby adding liquidity through capital repatriation and reducing lending and deposit rates; 4) the decapitalisation of state-owned corporations;[35] and 4) a liberalisation of international commerce, unifying import taxes and substantially reducing tariff and non-tariff barriers to imports (to 10 percent, effectively freeing capital movements) (Cariaga 1990: 43, 48; Morales and Sachs 1990; Cabezas 1990).

However, Paz Estenssoro's economic team did not implement pure orthodox policies: it refused to resume debt-servicing – including principal and interest – to foreign private commercial banks, aware that commercial credit lines had dried up since 1981 and anticipating that private lending would not resume in the foreseeable future. It also anticipated that an IMF- and WB-sponsored repurchase of the debt would occur on the secondary market, achieving a repurchase of 80 percent of the state's debt to commercial banks at 11 cents on the dollar (Cariaga 1990: 43, 50). It also, as already pointed out, resisted the privatisation of state-owned corporations and debt-equity swaps, preferring instead to restructure or decapitalise them (Conaghan and Malloy 1995).

Other examples of creative government responses to social instability, supported post-factum by MDIs, are observable in subsequent administrations: Jaime Paz Zamora, boasting some of his achievements as President (1989-1993), denied the 'originality' of the Popular Participation (Law No. 1551, 1994) and Decentralisation (Law No.1654, 1995) reforms implemented by his successor (Sánchez de Lozada) by describing the initiative of his government for the creation of a small, autonomous unit working on administrative and fiscal decentralisation, directly attached to the Presidency, financed by the WB and led by Carlos Hugo Molina, who was to subsequently manage the implementing agency for decentralisation, the *Unidad de Participación Popular* from 1993.[36] The Banzer/Quiroga 'National Dialogue', designed as a hegemonic struggle for the consensual reconfiguration of labour relations, was an initiative taken by a new wave of young, transnationalised technocrats surrounding Vice-President Jorge Quiroga, enthusiastically endorsed and supported by the WB (1999b; IMF 1998a).

The Sánchez de Lozada administration demonstrated outstanding hyperactivity and initiative: the creative 'Plan de Todos', organised around Constitutional, institutional (decentralisation) and privatisation reforms – the capitalisation programme interfaced by the creation of sectoral regulatory institutions (Law no.1600 SIRESE, 1994),[37] and by the complete privatisation of pensions (the Bonosol and its management by two private Administradoras de Fondos de Pensiones [AFPs], consortia of mostly foreign firms) (Law no.1732 of Pensions, 1996), was received coolly by WB staff.[38] Nevertheless, once the WB staff had been converted to the idea by Sánchez de Lozada and his team, it defended enthusiastically the concession of a capitalisation technical assistance credit (WB 1994a).[39] The bold program of privatisation of the six monopolistic jewels of the state tarnished by endemic corruption, patronage, deficits and over-staffing, YPFB (hydrocarbons), ENTEL (telecommunications), ENDE (electricity generation and distribution), ENFE (railways), LAB (airline), and EMV (smelter) was passed by Congress in the form of a Capitalisation Law in March 1994. Rather than an outright sale of the corporation's assets, and the transfer of the proceeds to the Treasury, capitalisation involved turning the state-owned corporations into private companies, transferring 50 percent of the private companies' shares to investors and requiring the latter to invest in the company itself, thus increasing the capital of the company by the purchase price, and transferring the shares corresponding to the state's ownership to fiduciary institutions. The trick of capitalisation was to require investors of the capitalised companies to sign a management contract; following the expiration of the contract, it offered the opportunity to the new manager of the company to purchase additional shares and thereby become majority owners (see table 4.8).

Table 4.8: Investment in Capitalised Companies Through 2001 (US$ million)						
	New Company	**Lead New Shareholder**	**Investment contracted**	**Total Investment contracted**	**Actual investment**	**% of target**
ENDE (Electricity) (1)	Corani	Dominion Energy (US)	59	140	160	114
ENDE	Valle Hermos	Constellation (US)	47			
ENDE	Huaracachi	Energy Initiative (US)	34			
YPFB (Hydrocarbons)	Andina	YPFB/Peres Compac(Arg.)	264	835	1,293	155
YPFB	Chaco	Amoco (US)	306			
YPFB	Transredes	Enron (US)	263			
ENTEL (Telecom)	ENTEL	Stet (Italy)	610	610	522	86
LAB (airline)	LAB	Vasp (Brazil)	48			
				87 (all transport)	104 (all transport)	120 (all transport)
ENFE (railway)	Andino	Cruz Blanca (Chile)	13			
	Occidental	Cruz Blanca (Chile)	26			
Total				1,672	2,078	124

(1) Each state-owned enterprise was broken up into a number of smaller units auctioned to the highest bidder: involved transferring management control and 50 percent of ownership to lead shareholder. Investors did not buy existing assets but made new investments in company, thereby increasing the equity base. Hence the term 'capitalisation'.

Source: WB (1998: Annex 2; 2005:3)

A super-Ministry of Capitalisation was created as part of the Capitalisation law, with the sole purpose of overseeing the entire process of sectoral reform. It was given significant autonomy and was disbanded following the completion of the capitalisation programme three years later (WB 1994a).[40] The Ministry of Capitalisation was interlocked with the WB. The credit facility made available to the Sánchez de Lozada government by the WB exemplifies the intensification of already close collaborative practice between central government agencies and MDIs: its objectives were 'to assist the Government in the planning, design and execution of its capitalization program and to ensure that the Government has at its disposal the varied and complex advice needed for such a program. At the same time, the project aims to design and establish the overall regulatory framework for the future development of key sectors'. More specifically, it aimed to 'strengthen the capacity of the Ministry of Capitalization ... help establish the regulatory agency ... develop specific reform strategies, legislation and regulations for the reorganization of the telecommunications sector' (WB 1994a: 2). The project complemented a large array of existing programmes (Export Corridors Project and Mining Sector Rehabilitation Project) or programmes under preparation (hydrocarbons, electricity, financial sectors, judicial reform) (WB 1994a: 2). The technical assistance project submitted to the Executive Directors of the WB had taken five months of preparation, involving both the Bolivian government and International Development Association (IDA) staff between December 1993 and April 1994, prior to, during and after its enactment by Congress. Further negotiations took place in May 1994 (WB 1994a: Schedule C). Sector specific working groups involving WB staff were constituted over that period to perform the technical work underpinning the Capitalisation law presented to Congress. A Procurement Unit was formed within the Ministry of Capitalisation 'to provide oversight and advisory services for the procurement of consultants and equipment to be financed under the various technical assistance operations' (WB 1994a: 3). The credit facility thus financed the employment, with WB resources, of 60 consultants and technical advisors to 'enhance the capacity of the Ministry to carry out its work' by training staff in the Ministry and by acting as counterparts to the Secretary of Capitalisation, at a cost of $7.5 million (WB 1994a: Annex 2 of 18).

The formation of the autonomous sectoral regulatory agencies (SIRESE) was not merely financed but also *designed* through systematic technical assistance. An in-house full-time technical advisor provided guidance to Superintendents and senior staff, while other technical advisors offered guidance on the organisational and administrative arrangements of SIRESE through consultant studies, and intensive training programs were formed for its staff. It was a fundamental objective of the WB and the Sánchez de Lozada government 'to protect the independence of the agency' (WB 1994a: 5). Furthermore, the WB arranged a 'twinning' programme with already established regulatory agencies in other countries, which would 'provide a source of ongoing support which can be tapped as technical assistance, training or staff-development opportunities' (WB 1994a: 6 of 18 Annex). Private consulting firms were also contracted by the government and financed by the WB, to assist in the valuation and legal counselling of capitalised corporations (Bauer and Bowen 1997). Effective supervision of the process was achieved through financial reporting and the submission, every six months, of a full progress report by the government to the IDA (WB 1994a: 7).

Once the institutional mechanisms had been put in place for a virtuous circle of transnational elite formation, it was possible to undertake the far more difficult task of sustaining social order through hegemonic endeavours designed to achieve a 'broad public understanding of needed reforms' (DAC 1989: 31) via 'mass communications to educate the public about the process and explain technical issues' (IBRD 1993: 10). The WB collaborated actively with the Bolivian government in the struggle to achieve hegemony. It provided 'assistance and materials for a public information campaign to design and explain the capitalization program and the distribution scheme' (WB 1994a: 3). The WB staff was well aware that 'successful capitalization in Bolivia will hinge in part upon effectively communicating both the costs of maintaining the status quo and the benefits of reform. An effective communication strategy must incorporate this broad message as well as educate various target audiences about specific aspects of the program, allay unwarranted fears, and build support among stake-holders' (WB 1994a: 2 of 18 Annex). For two years, the government employed a Public Relations Advisor within the Ministry of Capitalisation remunerated by the WB in order to 'effectively market the proposed program both domestically and abroad'. The Advisor worked closely with financial advisors and investment banks, and targeted Congressmen, company managers and employees in order to build Congressional and managerial support for the reforms. He undertook a research program based on focus groups and public opinion surveys in order to identify the issues generating public opposition, and 'tailor the communications effort to address and, where necessary, alter these perceptions' at a cost of $3.5 million (WB 1994a: Annex 3, 4 of 18; see Bauer and Bowen 1997 for an analysis of the actual implementation of this project). In the run-up to capitalisation and in order to convince reluctant economists in Bolivia, it was reiterated time and time again by transnational modernisers, including the WB executive director in Bolivia, that the privatisation/capitalisation of state-owned enterprises would indirectly generate hundreds of thousands of jobs (Cariaga 1994: 9-10).

Over a period of two decades, coordination between MDIs and central government agencies focused on the *political* struggle for the creation of a predictable, functional relationship between *depoliticised* (i.e. rules-based rather than discretionary) state agencies and capital accumulation, which transformed the state and its activities. These transformations were not unidirectional but resulted from restructuring efforts dialectically conditioned by systematic resistance outside and within the state, including in government (see chapter 5). Elemental to this dialectic was the political ascendency of the Ministry of Finance in relation to other Ministries, stimulated by its direct collaboration with MDIs and the discipline of money.

The Ministry of Finance and MDIs

Robert Cox argues that internationalisation has involved a qualitative enhancement in the power of economic Ministries at the expense of welfare Ministries. Evidence in Bolivia points not to a change in the relative weight between social and economic Ministries, but rather to a shift in power from the Ministry of Planning (a feature of state capitalism) to that of Finance, which became the principal interlocutor of the MDIs from the early 1990s (WB 2000c). The 'transversal' Ministry of Finance 'participates in all types of reunions in which decisions must be taken in relation to budgetary constraints. It is certain that the Minister of Finance must be constantly present ... Of course, the Finance Ministry was transversal because all ministries and state entities require budgetary resources ... I had to intervene in almost all institutions. The management of a Ministry is beyond the decisions of one person, it is contingent upon deliberation and above all upon broader restrictions on one's actions'.[41] The President, the governor of the BCB, superintendents of regulatory agencies and economic Ministers, originally led by the Minister of Planning and subsequently by the Minister of Finance, were the four primary transmission belts of collaborative policy strategies devised with MDIs. Together, they actively worked towards the depoliticisation of economic management.

Herbert Müller says: 'I think that there is a basic policy of conditionality on the part of multilateral organisations. But it is also true that the different Ministers of Finance, over the past twenty or so years, have played with the politics of conditionality in their favour. Ministers simply did not have the power to impose many of the measures that they implemented if it was solely based on the will of the Minister. So Ministers of Finance entered into collusion with multilateral organisations in order to set up a matrix of conditionality'.[42] The object of political opposition is no longer the Ministry of Finance, but becomes a remote and apparently overbearing multilateral organisation: a 'lightening rod' (Climenhage 1999).

'The Minister of Finance thus argues that "if we don't do this and this, we will not have any agreement with the IMF; and we therefore will not have access to international credit". We therefore have a functional use, by economic teams in the era of Dr. Paz, of Jaime Paz, of Banzer, of multilateral organisations. We (the Minister of Finance and the economic team) sat and debated what had to be done. The problem was: 'how can you sell this program politically to Congress, for example?' In order to sell it politically, we converted a program that *we* had decided into a policy of conditionality agreed upon with the WB. The capacity of negotiation of political forces in Congress, or even in the government itself, in order to undermine our measures was gradually lessened, because every time that the economic team signed an agreement with multilateral organisations and went in the cabinet to debate policies, at the end of the day it could say to the political sector: "*sorry my friend* (in English), this is part of the policy of conditionality. If we don't do this, there will be no money"'.[43]

Ex-finance Minister Edgar Millares offers a similar view. The disciplinary matrix of money and credit did restrict the Minister's range of policy options. There were a number of possible policy choices within the context of ESAFs, SAPs and PFPs. Nevertheless he points to a transnational consensus on the monetarist and austere fiscal foundations of poverty reduction in Bolivia. 'We did not discuss the "Positive Economy" while I was managing the Ministry, we were in agreement with multilateral organisations, thus the initiative was ours and they supported us. Neither did we engage in much debate over the "Normative Economy" because we were attached to global norms'.[44]

The predominance of economic ministries, in particular the Ministry of Finance, is correlated to the disciplinary effects of world money and the coordination of their activities with MDIs and bilateral creditors. Welfare (Ministry of Health, Education) and especially political (Ministry of the Presidency, of the Interior) Ministers tend to have a short-term perspective, a preoccupation with the maintenance of consent and social order, and the reproduction of the party leadership's in government by winning the following elections and remaining in office (see Grindle 1999 for a compelling discussion of rational choice/economic versus sociological approaches to policymaking). Their desire to make concessions to labour by increasing the wages and benefits of workers (including state employees), employment, pits welfare Ministers against economic teams (including the Ministers of Finance, of Planning, the governor of the Central Bank, and the directorate of the Ministry of Finance research institute, the UDAPE), who focus essentially on achieving or maintaining the appropriate conditions for growth. 'These two visions enter in contradiction: this ministry wants a wage increase, that ministry cannot finance that wage increase; this ministry wants an increase in social spending, that ministry cannot comply ... the welfare ministries never had much weight ... rather it is the direct entourage of the President (for instance the Ministry of Presidency, of the Interior, the party leadership) that we, the economic Ministers, had to confront'.[45]

Economic ministers (finance, planning, capitalisation, trade) placated opposition by professional politicians in the cabinet and in Congress to politically unpalatable economic policies by using the authority of MDIs. Decision-makers within the government and BCB used their formal or informal channels of access to MDIs to devise a policy, informed WB and IMF staff of their decisions, and then used the latter's authority to externally impose the policy in order to avert political conflicts with the institutions (whether state agencies or civil society organisations) that were likely to be opposed to these policies and to obstruct their effective implementation. The staff of MDIs were willing to take on the role of the bad cop if the Finance Minister's initiative seemed to improve the regulation of labour relations and the conditions for capital accumulation and PSD: 'paradoxically they acted as lightening rods for the opposition, which focused its wrath on the imperialistic foreigners rather than on the domestic reformers, allowing local policymakers to retain their support and popularity' (Climenhage 1999: 50). Thus Edgar Millares, in the face of potential opposition of *Aduanas* (Customs) staff but also business agents (exporters) whose interest would be jeopardised by his tax and auditing policies, decided to overtake the authority of President Banzer and Vicepresident Quiroga by negotiating directly with the IMF chief representative in Bolivia; he agreed with IMF staff that the next stand-by agreement should include the reform of the *Aduanas*. Subsequently Millares met the President and mentioned that the project of *Aduanas* reform is a condition of the standby agreement with the IMF. Banzer showed surprise but was not prepared to confront the IMF's authority, and therefore endorsed the reform despite the vertical and centralist organisation of Bolivia's presidential system.[46]

The tendency to use other institutions or individuals as culprits for politically difficult decisions may very well occur the other way round: MDIs staff regularly assign responsibility for the failure of the implementation of policies (for example, the partial failure of efforts to privatise the state-owned productive apparatus and welfare services in 1991, the failure to curb corruption and inefficiency in central, medium and local institutions of the state despite technical assistance provided for various civil service reforms) to particular Bolivian government Ministers or other state institutions (especially lower levels of the state hierarchy and Congress). Indeed, a Country Assistance Review undertaken by the WB's Operations Evaluation Department (OED) with the participation of USAID and the Swiss Development Corporation in 1998 argued that the WB's assistance strategy between 1986 and 1996 had been 'marginally satisfactory' in part due to 'poorly designed operations' (WB 1998a: vi), more specifically the WB's failure to adopt, until 1991, a 'forceful stance regarding the structural reforms needed to energize PSD and pursue poverty alleviation objectives', directing its efforts at 'restructuring rather than liquidating non-performing public banks ... and reforming public enterprises' while neglecting to 'formulate a specific strategy to tackle the fundamental problem' of poverty alleviation in the Altiplano (WB 1998a: v). However, the OED considered the WB's principal failure to be its insufficient attention to the 'lack of full commitment by the Bolivian authorities', Bolivia's 'lack of institutional capacity' and corruption (WB 1998a: iv; 2). The latter three points place responsibility for the relative failure of poverty alleviation and PSD efforts squarely on the Bolivian state, and indicate endemic resistance to restructuring at the highest levels of the administration: 'the political tensions implicit in [coalition governments] help explain the hesitant pace at which any ruling government has been able to execute comprehensive structural reforms' (WB 1998a: 2).

Bolivia's economic Ministers have had a precarious relationship with politicians throughout the period under study, in particular with Presidents, who have been able to hire and fire Ministers almost at will.[47] Just as MDIs have acted as lightening rods for social and intra-state opposition to structural adjustment and PSD (Climenhage 1999), Finance Ministers have systematically acted as 'fuses' by taking unpalatable decisions, sometimes against the wishes of politicians, and by remaining in position for a limited period of time; paradoxically, these fuses have sustained a continuity in economic management – to this very day – in part because of the BCB's monetarist bedrock provided by the long (eleven years, 1995-2006) tenure of Juan Antonio Morales as governor, and as already explained, because of the institutional linkages – through technical assistance teams – between economic Ministries and MDIs.

Sobresueldos

The *sobresueldos* are supplementary salaries paid by MDIs to the governor of the BCB, Ministers, Vice-Ministers and high-level technocrats, but also high and middle-level managers of state-owned corporations (Fernández 2003). Supplementary salaries were systematically paid to the Bolivian counterparts for specific projects financed by MDIs, which I interpret as a key attribute of transnational bloc expansion in Bolivia and the internationalisation of the state. While classified written evidence is available for the mid-to-late 1980s,[48] I have not yet encountered written evidence of sobresueldos paid after 1988. However, as emphasised previously, technical assistance projects were a regular element of SAPs and ESAFs and affected all economic Ministries from 1986 onwards. Considering that it has been a 'normal' policy of the UNDP, the WB and IMF, USAID and the IDB to 'equilibrate the remuneration of foreign technicians in relation to national technicians' (*El Deber* 1988; author's translation), we can assume that these *sobresueldos* remained a cornerstone of 'government commitment to reforms' until 2005, if not to this day. Although this fact was flatly denied by ex-President Jaime Paz Zamora and eluded by ex-Commerce Minister Jorge Crespo,[49] it was confirmed to me by well-informed staff in private development agencies and respected commentators of Bolivian politics that it is a continuing policy of aforementioned MDIs.[50] Gonzalo Sánchez de Lozada responded to the press in 1988 by asserting that 'these operations are *perfectly normal*. They respond to specific programmes of international entities that pay Bolivian personnel, *just as it occurs in all countries*. It is money that remains in Bolivia, which is better than if it was destined to other countries, isn't it? ... The UN, the WB and the IDB are *entities that are ours*, we belong to them. They are entities of technical assistance and we do not have an antagonistic relationship' (*El Mundo* 1988, emphasis added; author's translation).

The fundamental aims of MDIs, when granting *sobresueldos*, were for the state to be able to compete with the private sector in order to attract qualified professionals, to generate a community of equals in the state administration and MDIs, and to undercut corruption and high staff turnover in the state, thereby ensuring administrative continuity and the consolidation and coordination of the institutions of the state (*El Deber* 1988; *El Mundo* 1988). As mentioned previously, WB and IMF loans were primarily directed at fiscal support: more than half of the state's budget (between 7 and 10 percent of GDP) was financed with MDI credits and grants. Of MDI grants, a portion (between 3 and 10 percent) was directed towards *sobresueldos* of Bolivian technocrats, almost equivalent to the wages paid to the foreign private consultants employed by the Bolivian state and remunerated by MDIs – see next section. Indeed, the wages of 300 to 500 state managers were covered by IMF and UNDP financing at an annual cost of $5 to $20 million (*El Deber* 1988, *El Mundo* 1988; Fernández 2003). They targeted all Ministries and state-owned corporations, but were directed overwhelmingly towards economic Ministries, the BCB and the *Instituto Nacional de Estadisticas* (INE) (*Opinión* 1988).[51] Unsurprisingly, the local information media (*Hoy*, *El Mundo*, *Opinión*, *Presencia*), the leadership of the trade union confederation COB, nationalist and socialist members of Congress reacted to the news in 1988 that supplementary monthly salaries paid to technocrats were sometimes superior to the salaries paid by the state with proverbial nationalistic diatribes against imperialism: Bolivia was reduced to a 'shameful' dependence and subservience to MDIs and to the US (*Hoy* 28 July 1988: 8-9).

These payments, however, never achieved their objectives. It is not difficult to see why: *sobresueldos*, in the absence of significant civil service reform before the early 1990s, merely fuelled continued state patronage and corruption in the state. 'Public organisations were populated by a large number of politically appointed, unmotivated and underqualified public employees, at all levels of the organizational hierarchy' (WB 2000c: 9). A string of 'independent' Bolivian consultants in the direct entourage of the Finance Minister, subsecretaries, the Ministers' personal secretaries (!), drivers and doormen were paid additional salaries (from 4000 bolivianos paid to Fernando Cossio, the Subsecretary of Public Investment, to 40 bolivianos paid to the janitor of the Instituto Nacional de Estadisticas) (*Hoy* 1988). The managers of state-owned corporations, entrenched in their struggle against privatisation and restructuring efforts by MDIs and clients of politicians, were thus remunerated for perpetuating patronage and incompetence. Against the complaints of Willy Vargas, the President of the Lower House, and leftist congressmen such as Carlos Serrate Reich (*Vanguardia Revolucionaria*), the Minister of Information Hermann Antelo initially denied the facts at the time, before Sánchez de Lozada confirmed and justified the *sobresueldos*. Obviously, Willy Vargas's frustration was understandable, considering that *sobresueldos* were to bring Ministers' wages to the level of, if not above, that of Congressmen. Vargas's attempts, with the rest of Congress, to double the wages of Congressmen had just been frustrated by widespread popular outrage; in fact the attempt was inopportune, as 39,000 miners (out of 87,000 in total) were being laid off at that time (including 23,000 in COMIBOL) and paid a $1,500 to $2,000 bonus to finance their 'relocalisation' as a result of the collapse of the tin market, the closure of loss-making tin mines, and the decapitalisation of COMIBOL (WB 1989b: 3).

Penetrating the Lower Levels of the State Administration: Private Consultants

In order to short-circuit the problem of patronage and to reduce the state's wage bill, civil service reform was undertaken in various forms by successive governments with systematic financial and institutional support by MDIs. State-building, in particular *government-building,* understood as effective regulation and tax-collection, was already a cornerstone of first-generation reforms: an imperative condition for their successful implementation was the formation of an 'Administrative and institutional capacity adequate for SAP, which could be strengthened where necessary with the assistance of the Bank, the Fund and donors' (DAC 1989: 31). As pointed out in chapter 3, PSD required the systematic empowerment and consolidation of the executive agencies of the state (IBRD 1993: i). The DAC was arguing in 1989 that 'Effective competition ... requires a strong and effective government' (DAC 1989: 36). The DC and DAC have thus recommended the systematic, coordinated involvement of MDIs in the consolidation of central government agencies.

Civil service reform and training for technocrats were the cornerstone of institution-building. Facing endemic problems of corruption and politicisation in the institutions of the state, and the dearth of qualified technocrats, the economic team of the Paz Estenssoro government attempted to resolve the lack of organisational capacity by forming autonomous agencies or specially funded programs employing private consultants remunerated by MDIs, which were exempt from the cumbersome administrative procedures and control systems in place. These agencies worked on implementing the first-generation reforms elaborated in 1985. Nevertheless,

'Over time consultants took on line functions throughout the public sector, while their salaries continued to be paid by foreign aid programs, rather than the National Treasury or by the agencies' own revenues. This led to a "dual system" within the public administration. On one side were the poorly paid and often underqualified public employees, highly susceptible to political influence in order to retain their jobs. On the other side were the well-paid and generally well-trained "consultants", who suffered uncertainty because of their dependence on external financing. Moreover, as they did not enjoy the protection of a political "godfather", they were also vulnerable to arbitrary political decisions' (WB 2000c: 10).

The WB identified other issues raised by this dual organisational form, which nevertheless had preceded the new arrangement: 'high turnover and loss of institutional memory, ... conflicts of interest between consultants and their two employers, and lack of government control in channelling foreign aid' (WB 2000c: 10). More than 700 consultants remained in 'key posts' of the administration during the late 1980s and 1990s, remunerated by MDIs at a cost of $20 million per year, while the Ministry of Finance attempted from 1989 to 1992 to establish a special labour regime providing job stability for these 'key posts' (WB 2000c: 12).

Patching institutional gaps and bottlenecks through the use of autonomous agencies and private consultants (an 'island approach' to civil service reform) was insufficient, though (WB 1999c: 14), as many consultants felt '"sandwiched" between highly politicised upper and lower levels of public personnel' (WB 2000c: 15). Political party patronage in the state, while not supported by hard evidence, was deemed by the WB to cause significant distortions to the civil service reform process engineered jointly by the Bolivian government and MDIs. For example, in the late 1990s, political parties were perpetuating the illegal practice of obtaining funds by deducting up to 10 percent of civil servants' salaries: 'Parties therefore have an incentive to have large public payrolls. The stronger the party, the more ministries it controls. When a Ministry changes party, a large part of the payroll is changed to reward party loyalty and maximise funds' (WB 1999c: 14). The economic team of the Paz Zamora government, in collaboration with the WB, the IDB and the Swedish government, thus elaborated the so-called Economic Management and Strengthening Operation (EMSO) in 1989, which attempted to resolve the challenge of dual management by implementing a wide-ranging administrative reform programme, directly related to the enactment of the SAFCO law (1990) and the 1992 Administrative Reform Programme (DS 23326). 'This approach was to be incremental, starting with core central government agencies and gradually encompassing decentralized agencies, state-owned enterprises, and the large and medium-sized municipalities' (WB 2000c: 11). It posited the consolidation of a leaner, more effective, depoliticised, transparent and accountable public administration.

Fiscal constraints prevented the implementation of the reform, as the cost of competing with the private sector to train and attract a larger number of technocrats with high salaries was simply too high. The Sánchez de Lozada administration (1993-1997) thus abandoned the ambitious program of its predecessor and extended the key post approach to a Civil Service and Administrative Reform project founded on the concept of 'masa crítica' ('critical mass') consisting of 2,566 posts (covering all directors, middle managers, and professional posts in selected agencies), filled with intensely trained, well paid technocrats in nine state agencies (WB 1999c: 15). The critical mass was never reached. Only 248 of the 729 posts had been filled by 1997. By 2000, the key posts remained filled by donor-financed private consultants (WB 2000c: 15), prompting the WB to make desperate calls for 'deep political structural reforms' alongside civil service reforms to 'change the structure of party financing and patronage'; and to urge the abandonment of the 'island' or 'key posts' approach for a widespread and comprehensive reform 'covering the entire range of public officials' financed entirely by MDIs, and lasting another decade (WB 1999c: 14-15).

Expanding State-Building to the Municipal Level

Following 13 years of reforms, the WB was making a sombre assessment of restructuring in Bolivia: 'Bank assistance to Bolivia during the past ten years poses a fundamental paradox. On the one hand, the Bank's diagnosis and strategies to assist the country in dealing with the mid-1980s financial crisis were built on a *systematic engagement with successive governments*... Together with foreign aid, this assistance was instrumental in restructuring Bolivia, and helped the country achieve macroeconomic stability with moderate economic growth ... Yet side by side with this seemingly good economic performance over the last decade rests the other sobering hand of the paradox: Bolivia is still one of the most impoverished countries in the region' (WB 1998b: i; emphasis added). The disarticulation and ineffectiveness of the state beyond the central government was identified as one of the fundamental causes of continued high poverty rates (62 percent in 1999, 65 percent in 2005) in Bolivia (WB 2000c; WB 2005b). Therefore, the systematic engagement of MDIs with the central executive agencies of the state had to be expanded towards prefectures and municipalities.

This realisation was rendered all the more acute by the reforms undertaken by the Sánchez de Lozada administration. The work undertaken by the WB and other donors to sustain civil service reform and the implementation of the SAFCO law was undermined by the implementation of two important pieces of governance-related legislation in 1994 and 1995 by the Sánchez de Lozada government, the Constitutional Reform and the Law of Popular Participation, which introduced a plurality voting system to 50 percent of Parliamentary seats and extended the terms of the President, Congress, mayors and municipal council members from four to five years; and which transferred significant fiscal and administrative responsibilities to municipalities. WB staff (WB 2000c) pondered the possible consequences of these widespread institutional reforms: would they promote local-level democracy and participation or exacerbate regional cleavages; would they lead parties to fragment along regional lines; would they enhance the legitimacy and power of regional civic committees (WB 2000c: 7)? The measures were also undermining the SAFCO law and civil service reform, by fuelling patronage appointments through the devolution of fiscal and administrative resources and authority to municipalities. By that time, the 700 key posts remained a drop of water in a sea of corruption and patronage.

MDIs thus adapted to and articulated projects around the Popular Participation Law. From 1996 onwards, increasing coordination between MDIs, bilateral donors, municipal institutions and NGOs underpinned a widespread program of training for municipal managers to improve program elaboration and budgeting – i.e. extending money disciplining to the lower levels of the state and towards indigenous communities in hitherto isolated rural areas. It also involved a systematic engagement, via 'grassroots' NGOs, with the local constituency to generate 'local ownership' (i.e. legitimacy) of development projects (WB 2000b). The project was deemed a resounding success by WB staff. Again it focused on institution-building by enhancing the organisational effectiveness of the Secretariat for Popular Participation, the Small-Farmer Development Fund and the Secretariat for Popular Participation, but also – a relatively new development – on strengthening 'NGOs assisting municipalities and rural communities in identifying, formulating and implementing rural investments and managing their Municipal Development Plans' (WB 2000b: 2). It effectively conditioned PSD through primitive accumulation in rural areas by establishing 'bottom up, participatory processes of investment planning and implementation' (WB 2000b: 3).

As financial institutions providing micro-credit but also training to nascent businesses NGOs had a central role to play in grooming entrepreneurial social forces in both rural and urban areas: 'NGOs have a special role to play in the area of micro-enterprises' by sustaining money discipline and technical guidance at the municipal level (DAC 1989: 37). Again the project involved coordination between the WB task team, the government, and the participating bilateral development agency – the Swiss Agency for Development Cooperation. More than 265 municipalities had operationalised or started participatory planning processes with the support of NGOs, generating 'governability' (WB 2000b: 6) and 'consensus-building' (WB 2000b: 9). It 'provided training to numerous NGOs, consulting firms and technicians at all levels': 114 implementing agencies (NGOs and consultants) had received training by the end of the project and 800 training workshops were established. Roughly 600 NGOs were identified at the beginning of the project, with an annual turnover of over $200 million. Only 24 had planning experience and 149 were registered in the project area at the beginning of the project; by 2000, 301 had received planning experience and 400 had been registered. This sustained a 'progressively closer relation between NGOs and government' (WB 2000b: 8).[52]

The Popular Participation reform was a double edged sword: on the one hand it fostered 'inward-looking' and localised political conflicts (for municipal budget programming, the election of municipal councils and mayors, for instance), hence sustaining the depoliticisation of government polity, by 'shift(ing) part of the center of political gravity' (WB 2000c: 7). Nevertheless, it also offered unprecedented resources and organisational capacity for hitherto relatively isolated indigenist movements. Its depoliticisation effects internally contained their very contradiction in the form of revived politicisation (See chapter 5): it fostered genuine institutionalised struggle by labour against the interests of transnational and domestically-oriented capital, agro-business still structurally powerful in the *Oriente* of Bolivia, and the state managerial stratum linked to MDIs. The disjuncture between the emergent liberal state form and the socio-economic content defining the Bolivian space stimulated explosive social contradictions.

Conclusion

The internationalisation of the Bolivian state since 1985 has been defined by a double movement of contradictions: between capital and labour, between transnational and other elite forces. This chapter and the previous one located the primary cause of internationalisation in the emergence of a transnational historic bloc, which integrated a small nucleus of dominant business elites in Bolivia as equal partners in development and struggled, from 1985 onwards, to implement state reforms sustaining macro-economic stability and private capital accumulation. At the core of these reforms was the depoliticisation of economic management. The internationalisation of the state enhanced the structural power of the transnational bloc.

Bolivia's economic Ministries, the BCB and regulatory agencies have constituted *transmission belts*, not from the global economy to national society (Cox 1987), but rather of a strategy of liberalisation implemented through collaborative efforts between Bolivia's transnational fraction and MDIs. The internationalisation of the state has also involved the attenuation of the contradiction between global capital and the international system. This institutional attenuation has been manifest in the dialectical construction of a global governance complex reproducing class and intra-elite struggles within the institutions constituting it. This process fundamentally transforms the international system, and consolidates both supranationally and transnationally the internalisation of capital in all state-society complexes.

The institutional expression of global restructuring has been the transformation and reconfiguration of the state, undermining both the organisational powers and legitimacy of national forms of organisation and generating new sub- and supra-national forms. Increasingly sticky supra-national forms of organisation are manifest in the network of MDIs created by, financed by, and constituted by national states. Global governance reflects the social power of the transnational bloc and attenuates, if not transcends the fundamental contradictions between accelerating globalisation and national territorial divisions. MDIs attempt to achieve such attenuation by regulating global capital movements and attempting to solve constraints on the reproduction of capital (international labour movements, transnational organised crime and global ecological destruction). Since global organisations are constituted by internationalising states, which are institutionalisations of social struggles, global governance itself cannot but be twisted by the local, national and international contradictions defining it.

The following chapter analyses the emergence, consolidation and unravelling of Bolivian polyarchy from 1985 to 2005. It relates internationalisation to polyarchy and analyses transnational elite struggles to consolidate the latter in Bolivia. The attempt, by Bolivia's transnational elite fraction, to graft modern capitalism and liberalism onto a corrupt, nepotistic, and statist social organism by coordinating government activities with MDIs, was immediately undermined by the dependence of this fraction on clientelistic social networks for the implementation of liberal reforms, which explains their failure to legitimise the high social costs of Bolivia's deepening integration into global markets. As emphasised in chapter 2, structural adjustment and stabilisation strategies were not unprecedented in Bolivia. Such policies had been implemented in the 1950s and early 1970s, and entailed the disciplining of labour (Foxley and Whitehead 1980). In that sense, the post-1985 internationalisation of the state did not 'cause' resistance in Bolivia, but structural adjustment and PSD perpetuated 'social costs' that generated increasingly violent resistance.

Depoliticisation efforts were regularly undermined by the reproduction of both intra-elite and class conflicts outside but also within the institutions of the Bolivian state. The analysis of the process of internationalisation highlights systematic resistance to restructuring by domestically-oriented elite and subaltern social forces. The mechanism underlying the institutional interlocking between the national state and MDIs is thus one of social contradictions: in the disciplinary context of debt servicing, compounded by insufficient domestic capital formation induced by a lack of business confidence in the face of recurrent social instability, the Bolivian state actively upheld a relationship of dependence with MDIs for capital inflows. This dependence has sustained the discipline of world money which in turn has left a political space open for MDIs to collaborate actively, and sometimes pressure Bolivian governments into SAPs and the PSD blueprint. Yet Bolivian social conditions impeded restructuring efforts. Restructuring involved enacting politically unpalatable legislation, securing Congressional support, overcoming internal resistance to reforms and implementation bottlenecks, incompetence and endemic corruption in the state, and the institutional disarticulation between central, regional and local state agencies (Gray 2008; Barragán 2008). Yet the implementation of structural adjustment and PSD strategies required a reflexive adaptation to local conditions, i.e. to particular and ever-changing forms of resistance both within and outside state institutions. Continued collaboration between MDIs and Bolivian governments has, however, demonstrated that under the wider structural imperative of national-in-global accumulation, fiscal and monetary stability, and the servicing of the debt, the willingness of MDIs to condone, or their impotence in resolving corrupt and inefficient administrative practice has perpetuated, to this day, a sense of impunity by the old guard in government and lower levels of administration (see Wilmore 2007).

Systematic resistance in the street and in the state indeed forces a rethinking of historical materialist – including neo-Gramscian and Marxist – approaches to the state. Chapter 5 validates the alternative conceptualisation of the state as a contradictory organisation of subjection elaborated in the introduction: the state is social content rather than social form or structure (understood as totality), constituted by and constitutive of production relations. The state is a social relation embedded within broader relations and hence a terrain of social struggle. It must therefore not be seen as instrumentalised by capital (Robinson 2002, 2005), or as functionally related yet relatively autonomous from the production structure (Poulantzas 1975; Cox 1981, 1987). Rather, it is distorted by internal contradictions and can never perfectly manage social relations. The process of internationalisation is therefore neither linear nor unidirectional, but defines and is defined by state and broader social contradictions.

The dialectic between multilateral development assistance and domestic Bolivian constraints helps to explain the street violence (Water Wars, Febrero Negro, Gas Wars) that eventually led to the election of Evo Morales in 2005 and expressed the gradual unravelling of polyarchy in Bolivia.

Notes

[1] Although they do not refer explicitly to the concept of depoliticisation associated to rules-based (rather than discretionary) regulatory institutions, Conaghan and Malloy (1995: 13, 21) analyse attempts by civilian governments in Ecuador, Bolivia and Peru to 'maintain economic policy making as a sphere insulated from direct societal pressures, so as to allow maximum autonomy to the economic team'.

[2] Cox (2002), in the face of widespread criticism, subsequently retracted his concept of 'transmission belt'.

[3] Robinson's (2002: 215-216) argument that emerging transnational capital circuits are superimposed on existing national circuits is conceptually and historically questionable. Van der Pijl (1998) and Van Apeldoorn (2004) demonstrated convincingly that capital emerged *as*, if not *in*, a transnational social space: its very emergence and expansion traversed, re-constituted and contradicted the territorialisation of pre-existing inter-state relations.

[4] I concur with Burnham's (1991: 75) take on the Coxian theorisation of 'world hegemony as an outward expansion of internal national hegemony established by a dominant social class'.

[5] See Bonefeld (2000) for an effective rebuttal of Cox's idealisation of the Keynesian mode of regulation.

[6] Cox's 1981 distinction between 'material', 'inter-subjective' and institutional structures in his abstract triad creates an ambiguity around the materiality of ideology (and indeed institutions) and more generally around the materialist basis of his theory.

[7] A relatively high degree of cohesion may be observed in the MNR-led governments (1985-1989; 1993-1997). However, economic ministries

(Planning, Finance, Commerce, Mining, and Energy and Hydrocarbons) have been defined by extreme cohesion and continuity in Bolivia since the late 1980s.

[8] Picciotto (1990: 29) criticised both Cox and Poulantzas for assuming an essential contradiction between the logics of domestically- and externally-oriented state institutions.

[9] For a compelling Marxist critique of the logical inconsistencies of Robinson's concept of a transnational state, defending a conceptualisation of MDIs as relatively autonomous from worldwide production relations, see Cammack (2007). In turn, for a compelling critique of Cammack's (2003, 2007) analysis of the 'governance of global capitalism' by relatively autonomous – hence unitary and devoid of internal contradictions – MDIs, see Taylor (2005).

[10] Indeed, the share of private investment actually declined between 1985 and 1995, from 80 to 45 percent of total investments (WB 1998a: iv).

[11] Interview with Herber Müller, 11 September 2007.

[12] Interview with Edgar Millares, 13 September 2007.

[13] WB and IMF projections calculated in coordination with economic Ministries have, nevertheless, regularly been grossly over-optimistic: thus the WB was contending in 1994 that the capitalisation programme would 'free up to 25-35% of the Government's annual investment budget to invest in human capital and basic infrastructure', while in fact the fiscal impact of privatisation of state-owned corporations and pensions was negative – increasing the budget deficit by 3 percent and reducing tax receipts by $300 million (WB 1994: 7; 1999a; 2004). Fiscal constraints have, not surprisingly undermined the improvement of welfare delivery since the mid-1980s.

[14] Interview with Ramiro Cabezas, 17 September 2007.

[15] Interview with Mauro Mariani, 20 December 2007. 'With this strong donor support for a Government that was fully committed to a new reform program came the revival of the Consultative Group, which met in December 1986' (WB 1998a: 3).

[16] In January 1999, a three-day workshop on Bolivia's Comprehensive Development Framework, involving the 'Bank Bolivia Country Team' and a delegation led by Bolivia's Vice-President and Minister of Finance, other Ministers and 'vice ministers from some of our counterpart agencies' concluded that there was 'general consensus that Bolivia exhibits very favourable initial conditions to launch this effort', considering that 'Bolivia is a top IDA performer' and the 'Trust and a strong sense of partnership between the Government and the Bank teams, and fertile ground for strong partnership with donors and civil society' (WB 1999: 10).

The IMF has had one senior Resident Representative in La Paz, acting as a counterpart to the Minister of Finance and the governor of the BCB, and engaging in almost daily dialogue with them since 1986. Interviews with Juan Antonio Morales, 28 September 2007; Ramiro Cabezas, 17 September 2007. The location of the IMF office in La Paz, on the 17th floor of the Edificio BCB (the tallest building in La Paz) symbolises its power at the heart of the institution controlling the flow of money and foreign exchange. Fernando Campero Prudencio also confirmed that the government's economic mini-cabinet (see below) was in regular contact with the IMF: 'in those days, I can sincerely say there were no real conflicts with the IMF, because we saw it as a way to fortify what we were trying to do. [The IMF] included, in agreement with us, a number of covenants that we discussed internally but on the essence, there was a complete consensus... There was nothing really for which they were telling us: "you have to do a little bit more". The only theme they were pushing was privatisations, something we regarded as common sense. Really it was in no way a conflictive relationship. It was more accurately: "Well done! We are doing everything *comme il faut*" [in French]. Rather we were discussing how actors were going to react'. Interview with Fernando Campero, 20 September 2007.

[17] Interview with Carlos Morales, 20 September 2007.

[18] For example, the technical assistance component of the 1991 WB structural adjustment credit (co-financed by USAID and the Swiss development agency), cost $5.037.500 million, and involved the employment and training (onsite and abroad, with provisions made for more than a hundred trips at costs ranging from $2,500 to $6,000 per trip) of the staggering number of 427 consultants in banking supervision, public enterprise reform, and capital market development; but also for the purchase of computer systems (WB 1991b: 132-133).

In 1998, a Memorandum letter to the IMF Managing Director by the Minister of Finance gives a sectional image of a much broader process of institutional interlocking by mentioning a new tax collection system devised by the Ministry of Finance 'with the support of the IDB', the Minister of Finance's request for technical assistance by the IMF's Department of Fiscal Affairs for an improvement of Bolivia's Customs Administration, the improvement by the BCB of the registry of private external debt with 'the technical assistance of the IMF's statistics department', or the government's dialogue business and labour organisations for the reduction of market 'rigidities' 'with the assistance of the IDB' (Gobierno de Bolivia 1998: 5; 8, 9, 14).

[19] President Paz Zamora had endeavoured to generate business confidence following his election in August 1989. He caused significant uneasiness in the business community because of his social democratic credentials and participation in the UDP government of 1982-1985. A run on deposits and capital flight in late 1989 was only curbed by addressing the 'credibility issues' of the government via the introduction of DS 22407 in January 1990 (see DS 22407 – 11 January 1990). DS 22407 ratified the preceding administration's efforts (DS 21660) to lock-in structural adjustment and to stimulate an 'economic reactivation' that depended on tackling 'shyness in private investment' (Morales 1990: 10). See table 3.11.

However, Paz's efforts, though laudable, were deemed insufficient by the WB: 'Current reform efforts intended to improve the environment for private investors (supported by the Structural Adjustment Credit) have included eliminating transfers to public enterprises. While this is a step in the right direction, the fiscal situation would improve more if those public enterprises involved in public activities were completely privatized' (WB 1992c: 2).

Considering the dearth of capital in Bolivia (WB 1991c: 44), worsening terms of trade, the fiscal deficit incurred by the state because state-owned corporations persisted in constituting 'a drain on Government current expenditures, specially wages and salaries' (WB 1992c: 2), and the need to redirect state investment towards social welfare in order to alleviate the dismal condition of households and thereby generate political stability (hence attracting private capital investments) (WB 1990; WB 1991a, 1992b; 1992c), WB staff had been pressuring the Paz Zamora government for two years to implement second-generation PSD reforms. They expressed satisfaction at the government's introduction of three new pieces of legislation, which, 'if implemented correctly, may help attract foreign investors to Bolivia. The Investment Law guarantees equal treatment of foreign and domestic investors, places no restriction on repatriation of profits and provides for full payment in the case of expropriations', while the Hydrocarbons and Mining laws opened state-owned companies to private capital and stimulated Bolivia's convergence with international norms in taxation law (WB 1992c: 3).

[20] The IMF continued to complain in 1998 that the labour market legislation was antiquated and inconsistent. 'The current labor legislation inflates the cost of labor, creates uncertainty, and reduces the incentive for investment in the formal sector' (IMF 1998b: 26). The basic labour legislation (the Ley del Trabajo) was devised in 1937, and has been complemented by 500 pieces of separate labour-related legislation, and 2,500 relevant Supreme Decrees, generating numerous contradictions between pieces of legislation (in particular between the DS 21060 and preceding laws and Supreme Decrees), and significant space for different interpretations of the law (IMF 1998b: 27). 'Consequently, several regulations in the labor law are either not enforced or unenforceable because regulators and the judiciary alike find it nearly impossible to apply them comprehensively and coherently. This has created mutual mistrust between workers and employers... In Bolivia, the protection for workers features prominently under the existing law at the expense of employers' flexibility in hiring, contracting, and firing of workers. The bias in favor of labor protection heightens labor cost and limits employers' ability to respond rapidly to changing market conditions.' (IMF 1998b: 27).

[21] The law SAFCO, passed in Congress in 1990 under the Paz Zamora administration but already negotiated in 1988-1989 between the WB and the Paz Estenssoro government, established common accounting procedures in all state agencies, the establishment of a General Comptroller's Office for auditing purposes and the elimination of the ex-ante control function, in order to hold state managers accountable for their decisions, thereby aiming to create a transparent, responsive and efficient state and preventing corruption.

[22] Interview with Juan Antonio Morales, 28 September 2007. The depoliticisation of the Central Bank was effected by the *Ley del Banco Central de Bolivia* (1995), which formally established its 'autarchic character' (article 1), and the restriction of its relationship with the government to a single intermediary, the Minister of Finance (article 4), effectively sheltering it from political pressure.

[23] Interviews with Edgar Millares, 13 September 2007; Ramiro Cabezas, 17 September 2007; and Herbert Muller, 11 September 2007.

[24] The commitment of Bolivian governments to 'provide the Fund with such information as the Fund may request in connection with the progress in implementing its program' was, in contrast to the situation in 1980-1981, not a *lettre morte* (IMF 1998: 50).

[25] Interview with Ramiro Cabezas, 17 September 2007.

[26] Interview with Ramiro Cabezas, 17 September 2007.

[27] Interview with Fernando Campero, 20 September 2007.

[28] Interviews with Edgar Millares, 13 September 2007 and Carlos Morales, 20 September 2007.

[29] The *Acción Democrática Nacionalista* (ADN) party publicly campaigned for a radical deflationary plan in the 1985 elections, while the MNR 'had been distinctly pusillanimous about it' (Dunkerley 2007: 74). As already emphasised in chapter 3, Jeffrey Sachs had initially been invited by the ADN economic team and began working on a stabilisation plan from April 1985.

[30] English translation available at http://www.naomiklein.org/shock-doctrine/resources/part3/chapter7/decreto-coyuntural, accessed 15 October 2008.

[31] It was only after the implementation of DS 21060 that the NEP was discussed with WB, IDB and CAF officials, who announced publicly their support but waited a full year before resuming lending to Bolivia (Cariaga 1990: 42).

[32] Interview with Fernando Campero, 20 September 2007. 'From the outset, the ESF generated a mixture of interest and scepticism at the WB: interest because it marked the Bank's first intervention aimed directly at easing the social costs of adjustment, an area where the Bank had been strongly criticized for being too slow to act; scepticism because employment generation was the main purpose of the ESF, and Bank staff generally frowned upon supporting "job-creation" schemes' (Jorgensen 1992: 6).

[33] The government thus achieved rapid capital repatriation totalling $260 million in 1985-87. It signed a standby arrangement with the IMF and obtained an 'Import Reconstruction' facility with the WB in the summer of 1986 (WB 1986; IMF 1986).

[34] According to Cariaga (1990: 47), 'Bolivian mine workers had benefitted from an absurdly subsidised comisariat system that represented one-half of Comibol's 1984 operational deficit', including large quantities of subsidised bread, rice, meat and sugar, while YPFB employees received 400 litres of free gasoline per month, and state employees enjoyed bonuses in cash and in kind that multiplied wages by a factor of 1.5. These subsidies must however be placed in relation to the low wages of state employees (especially miners) (Crabtree 1987), and in relation to inflationary pressures: real wages declined by 50 to 60 percent between 1980 and 1985, and contracted further during the implementation of first generation reforms. The rise of gasoline prices (from 1 cent to 30 cents a liter) was particularly damaging to the population and fostered recurrent strikes and marches in 1986.

[35] COMIBOL, for instance, was incurring losses exceeding $248 million in 1985. These losses spiralled out of control with the collapse of the world tin market in December 1985 (WB 1991c; Crabtree 1987). In order to pursue its stabilisation programme, the Paz government gradually reduced operations in 1986 before closing 7 large mines and laying-off 23,000 miners in December 1986 and January 1987, paying them severance payments totalling $60 million (about $2,000 per employee) and forcing their re-localisation in major cities and in the coca-producing Chapare region. The government subsequently prohibited new credit facilities to COMIBOL by state-owned banks (Cariaga 1990; WB 1989b).

[36] Interview with Jaime Paz Zamora, 28 September 2007. See Grindle (1999: 117) for the contention that work on decentralisation began in September

1993 under the newly elected Sánchez de Lozada administration and that Molina's 'was a voice in the wilderness – nobody was listening'.

[37] As already pointed out, plans for the privatisation of state-owned corporations were been devised by Paz Zamora's economic team, with technical assistance from WB officials, prior to the election of Sánchez de Lozada, especially in the telecommunications sector (transforming the 'autonomous' state cooperatives providing local telecommunications services into joint stock companies, and 'restructuring/privatizing ENTEL', which managed long-distance communications) (WB 1992d: iii, vi). Furthermore, with the enactment of the Privatization Law (No.1330, 1992) state-owned YPFB had engaged in joint ventures with a significant number of private companies for the exploration of new and development of existing hydrocarbon reserves, paving the way for the enactment of the Capitalization Law in 1994. These private companies included Chevron, Texaco, Maxus, Santa Fe, Exxon, Bolivian Oxy, Tesoro Bolivia, Pluspetrol, Solpetrol and Perez Companc (WB 1992d: 122).

[38] See Bauer and Bowen (1997) for a well-informed description of the key issues discussed by government and WB staff in numerous workshops in 1993 and for an insight into other political parties' opposition to capitalisation.

The privatisation of pensions was integral to the whole 'battery of reforms' (Whitehead 1997) implemented by the Sánchez de Lozada government under the Plan de Todos: on the one hand it provided for a (rather optimistic) *creation and distribution* of additional resources by private pension funds (AFPs) through the investment on financial markets of 50 percent of the capital invested by the new owners of capitalised corporations. The strategy also sought to resolve the fiscal burden of existing public pension schemes. On the other, it was devised as a way to generate liberal hegemony by 'addressing a major preoccupation of the very groups most opposed to straightforward privatization, ... attempting to convert a zero sum conflict (domestic nationalists versus foreign exploiters) into a convergence of material interests' (Whitehead 1997: 78). By entitling roughly Bolivia's 270,000 pensioners to annual bonus payments (supposedly paid with the profits made by AFPs on financial markets), it was designed to create a constituency pressuring for capitalisation.

AFPs were transnational consortia mainly constituted by foreign firms. The first was formed by Argentaria (Spanish, with 57% holding), Invesco (US/British with 10%), Magister Internacional (Chilean, 13%) and Sidesa (16%, Bolivian). The second was owned by the Banco Bilbao Viscaya (Spanish, 67%) with Banco Bilbao Viscaya Pensiones SA (33%) (Slade 1997: 356).

There were some caveats: the scheme was socially regressive, as it was only distributed to people above 65 years of age. Considering that the average life expectancy in Bolivia was 60.5 years old in 1997, the poorest sectors – especially in rural areas – were not going to benefit from it. Furthermore, only individuals in possession of an identity card were eligible for the bonus. A large proportion of peasants in the Altiplano were not formally citizens, as they did not have an identity card and sometimes did not know their exact age. 'In rural areas, the task of locating, documenting, and paying a dispersed population of aged and often immobile people, many of whom are illiterate, and more than half of whom do not speak Spanish as their first language, [was] formidable indeed' (Whitehead 1997: 81).

Things did not go according to plan. The distribution of the first bonus ($247) occurred only one month before the general election of 1997, leading opposition parties, the COB and informed observers to accuse the MNR government of using the Bonosol as an electoral instrument, and therefore did not manage to transform the image of Goni as a 'vende-patria' nor to entrench popular support for the capitalisation programme. Only two AFPs were constituted, and the formation of a general superintendency (*Sistema de regulación Financiera [*SIREFI]) regulating four financial sectors (pensions, insurance, banking, securities market) was unable to create effective prudential regulation nor to oppose itself to the formation of an effective monopoly by AFPs. AFPs were immediately (and remained) deficitary, and the state had to cover their payment of pensions. The Bonosol had to be replaced by a far less generous pension scheme dubbed *Bolivida* by the following government (Banzer/Quiroga). The administrative costs of pension reform (partly accentuated by corruption and fraud) were underestimated and increased the fiscal deficit of the state in 1998 and 1999, just as the worldwide financial crisis was beginning to affect the Bolivian economy.

For an analysis of the limitations of pension reform, see IMF (2003).

Projected and Actual Pension Costs (US$ millions)

	1997	1998	1999	2000	2001	2002
	Initial projections					
Total costs	226	214	203	193	183	173
	Actual costs					
Total costs	254	307	308	344	356	366

Source: IMF (2003)

[39] The $14.7 million concessional credit was supplemented, as had become the norm, by other bilateral and multilateral credits: a $2.3 million Technical Cooperation Facility by the IDB, and a $700,000 credit line by the French government.

[40] Sánchez de Lozada, furthermore, passed the DS 24806 two days before the end of his presidential term (4 August 1997), which legalised the ownership of subsoil hydrocarbon reserves for private investors. See *Tribunal Constitucional de Bolivia* (2003).

[41] Interview with Edgar Millares, 13 September 2007. Millares, Finance Minister in the Banzer administration, suggests that the gradual sidelining of the Ministry of Planning accompanied the dissolution of a state-led economy: 'el ministerio de planificación dejo de existir, porque la planificación responde a un esquema mental de organización politica de diferente forma a la que es el pensamiento del libre mercado. El momento de haber eliminado el Ministerio de Planeamiento tenía que asumirse las funciones que pasaron al Ministerio de Hacienda'. Fernando Campero Prudencio concurs: 'When I was invested with the Ministry of Commerce, the Ministry of Planning was still the most important at the time. Samuel Doria Medina had that position, and he had been

preceded by Enrique García, who had been President of the CAF. As *primus inter pares*, let us say, Doria Medina was more important in the economic area. But we often convened with the Ministries of Finance, Planning and Foreign Trade. Planning clearly had more weight... By decree he was the chief of the economic cabinet, a mini-cabinet presided by the Minister of Planning'. Interview with Fernando Campero, 20 September 2007.

[42] Interview with Herbert Müller, 11 September 2007.

[43] Interview with Herber Müller (emphasis added), 11 September 2007.

[44] Interview with Edgar Millares, 13 September 2007.

[45] Interview with Herbert Müller, 11 September 2007.

[46] Interview with Edgar Millares, 13 September 2007.

[47] Conaghan and Malloy (1995) argue that this precariousnesss defined the *Banzerato*. Furthermore, Paz Estenssoro (1985-1989), Paz Zamora (1989-1993) and Banzer (1997-2001) represented the pre-1985 relations of forces in Bolivia, permitting continuity – in the form of patronage and corruption – within the process of state transformation. As such their authority bridged modernising transnational capitalists and technocrats and the domestically-oriented politicians and businessmen (Malloy and Gamarra 1987; 1988; Dunkerley 1990).

[48] These include letters from various government Ministers to the UN Resident Representative in Bolivia or the UN International Coordinator, referring for example to Projects BOL/84/016, BOL/87/006 or BOL/87/012, with reference to agreements ATN/SF-2353-BO or ATN/SF-2942-BO with the UNDP on supplementary salaries, to be paid in future months or retroactively (Serrate Reich 1989, Annexes 6 to 27: 136-156).

[49] Crespo said: 'This was not something I was involved in'. Interviews with Jorge Crespo, 28 September 2007 and Jaime Paz Zamora, 28 September 2007.

[50] Interview with José Antonio Quiroga, 19 September 2007.

[51] 31 percent of the supplementary salaries were allocated to the Ministry of Finance; 17 percent to the INE, and 15 percent to the Ministry of Planning.

[52] On the proliferation of NGOs in Bolivia since the mid-to-late 1980s, see Van Domelen (1992). There were 477 NGOs in 1997; the number had risen to 723 in 2004, before rescinding under the Morales administration to 434 (INE).

5
Polyarchy in Bolivia

The previous chapters analysed the mechanisms and processes underlying the internationalisation of the Bolivian state between 1985 and 2005. It indicated the strategies employed by the transnational bloc to functionally relate state activities with capital accumulation, through the depoliticisation of executive agencies interlocked with MDIs, and by attempting civil service reform. The present chapter relates internationalisation to the contradictions of liberal democratisation, which unfolded in conjunction with and was sustained by transnational bloc expansion and the integration of the state into a global governance complex. It analyses specifically the emergence, consolidation and unravelling of Bolivian polyarchy from 1985 to 2005. The focus of this chapter is, hence, on the liberalisation of the Bolivian social space – in particular of the state – and resistance to liberalisation. It seeks to empirically ground the conceptualisation of the state elaborated in the introduction as contradictory organisation of subjection in empirical evidence: as a social relation constituting and constituted by broader production relations, the Bolivian state is a terrain of both intra-elite and class struggles.

As emphasised in chapter 1, institutional reforms in Bolivia after 1985 have been measured according to minimalist, procedural conceptualisations of democracy, understood as *polyarchy*, (Dahl 1971). Scholarship focusing on democratisation in Bolivia has been overwhelmingly informed by *problématiques* restricted by a closed system of meaning and norms, and although political analysts readily acknowledge the limitations of minimalist definitions of democracy – in particular the potential contradictions between economic restructuring and political democratisation – they have taken them as a starting-point for the purpose of empirical measurement (O'Donnell 1992, Valenzuela 1992; Mansilla 1994; Domingo 1993; Whitehead 2002a; Van Cott 2000; Grindle 1999).

Marx and Gramsci exposed the classical liberal ideal-type form of state-society relations as a legally and ideologically buttressed form of governance subjecting labour to capital (see chapter 1), and Gramsci's critique of liberal democracy underpinned Robinson's (1996) reinterpretation of the meaning of *polyarchy* as a form of social organisation defined by the use of procedural means of representation to legitimise capital domination. (Almost) transparent elections based on (not quite) universal suffrage were certainly a feature of Bolivia from 1985 to 2005 (Domingo 1993; Dunkerley 2007[1998]), as were competition and alternation between two party blocs (ADN-MIR and MNR), and the possibility for an alternative bloc to win elections opened the way for the electoral victory of Evo Morales in 2005. Yet there persisted a systematic negation of basic civil liberties through recurrent states of siege, and systematic legal encroachment of labour rights (Mainwaring 1992: 297-298; Navarro 1999; García et al. 2000, 2002). Polyarchy was defined by the attempt to concentrate power and authority in opaque (unaccountable and non-representative) state agencies 'at one remove' from popular demands and acting on the basis of 'market rules' rather than at the 'discretion' of elected representatives (Burnham 2000).

The present study adopts this meaning of liberal democratisation, but unequivocally rejects the instrumentalism informing Robinson's analysis (see chapters 1 and 4). It argues that a systematically *relational* understanding of the state helps to explain more adequately the development of polyarchy in Bolivia.

As emphasised in chapters 1 and 3, a holistic approach entails placing the liberalisation of the Bolivian state within the context of the latest phase of capital globalisation since the early 1970s. I mentioned in chapter 1 that I understand liberalisation as social restructuring, involving struggles to adjust the Bolivian space to global market prices and to privatise accumulation; to achieve the hegemony of capital via the diffusion of neoliberalism; and to achieve the viability of polyarchy. The central attribute of this phase has been the increasing predominance of a transnational historic bloc of elite social forces.

The widespread collapse of military regimes in Latin America in the late 1970s and early 1980s is correlated to the profound economic crisis affecting the global periphery at the time, which stripped existing business-military elite blocs of any capacity to generate hegemony. An expansion of the transnational bloc from its transatlantic heartland occurred at the very moment and in part *because* state capitalist models of development were unravelling under deteriorating terms of trade and the inability to use fiscal instruments to manage the economic downturn

(Dunkerley 1990; Conaghan and Malloy 1995). The expansion of the transnational bloc in Bolivia unfolded primarily through the internationalisation of the state (see chapters 4 and 5). This process was not imposed from above but concurrently involved competitive elites domestically-rooted in different national contexts: the cause of liberalisation in Bolivia is located in collaborative practice between the expanding transnational bloc and a small nucleus of Bolivian business, technocratic and intellectual elites. Liberalisation and internationalisation are thus directly correlated.

This chapter is structured as follows: it begins by analysing the transition to and consolidation of polyarchy since 1978, arguing that, in the absence of a separate technocratic stratum and in the midst of economic crisis, Bolivia's transnational capital fraction took matters in its own hands by struggling, within and through the CEPB and conservative political parties (MNR, ADN and MIR) for the liberalisation of the state and the viability of polyarchy. A strategic attempt to depoliticise state polity was integral to polyarchy (see chapter 4). Depoliticisation involved a struggle to consolidate particular executive agencies of the state, primarily the BCB, the SIRESE, the SBEF and the Ministry of Finance. Privatisation was also perceived by liberalisers to depoliticise the state (Mansilla 1994); and fiscal and administrative decentralisation since 1994 have been interpreted by Kohl (2003) and Gustafson (2002) as depoliticisation efforts – which must be problematised because *intent* to depoliticise must be validated.

Nevertheless, depoliticisation and liberalisation encountered systematic resistance to restructuring by domestically-oriented elite and subaltern social forces *within* and *beyond* the institutions of the Bolivian state. The second section demonstrates that the tension between liberalisation and domestic Bolivian constraints helps to explain the reorganisation of labour and indigenist forces in the mid-to-late 1990s that eventually led to the election of Evo Morales in 2005.

Businessmen in Government: The Rise and Consolidation of Polyarchy

Following a seven-year economic, institutional and ideational crisis characterised by a rising debt burden and drying up of recycled petro-dollars, democratic outbursts and military repression, and the dissolution of the hegemony of state capitalism, liberal democracy seemed to be taking hold in Bolivia by the summer of 1985. The long crisis of democratisation witnessed a succession of civilian and military governments, which attempted to manage more or less coercively antagonistic social relations *sur fond de* fiscal and monetary crisis. The socialist-leaning Siles government, elected in 1980 and invested two years later after a particularly bloody military interlude (Dunkerley 1982), was overwhelmed by the crisis and declared a moratorium on debt servicing in March 1984, before calling elections half a year later (see chapter 2). By then, inflation had reached 23,000 percent in annualised terms, inducing the implementation by the Paz Estenssoro government elected in August 1985 of socially costly stabilisation and structural adjustment measures, subsequently followed by attempts to create the conditions for PSD (see chapter 4). The crux of the problem of democratisation between 1978 and 1985 is that democratic impulses – the unleashing of organised labour demands – rendered the fiscal and monetary crisis affecting the Bolivian state 'unmanageable' (WB 1985). Hyperinflation and the quasi-bankruptcy of the state, as the essential manifestations of money discipline, were the structural antitheses of democratisation in the Bolivian space.

The year 1985 was a watershed for Bolivia because it apparently concluded a period of crisis-as-rupture that effectively marked the formal collapse of its pre-existing economic, ideological and institutional relations: capital accumulation articulated around the pivot of state-owned extractive corporations; the nationalist ideology of state capitalism legitimising this form of economic development; and the form of the state binding economic and ideological relations in an institutional frame defined by authoritarian presidentialism, personalism (*caudillismo*) and patronage (Malloy and Gamarra 1988; Domingo 1993; Gamarra 1994). Until 1985, the state had been torn apart by two poles of organised violence claiming governing legitimacy beyond the formal executive, legislative and judicial organs of the state – the army on one hand, characterised by praetorianisation (Gamarra 1988); and armed labour militias articulated around the trade union confederation, the COB and the emerging indigenist farmers' union, the CSUTCB on the other (Lavaud 1991).

The 1985 elections seemed to be foundational in the sense that they apparently broke this polarisation through a consensual, representative system of rule: they were 'the first to produce a peaceful transfer of power under democratic conditions' (Domingo 1993: 109) establishing 'a surprisingly conventional and stable democratic regime' (Whitehead 2002b: 28). Nevertheless, it will be demonstrated below that both the stability of this 'democratic' regime, and the *transition* from authoritarian military rule to civilian democracy have arguably been exaggerated in the academic literature (Mayorga 1991; Domingo 1993; Crabtree and Whitehead 2002; Whitehead 2002b).

The economic crisis inherited by the Siles government (1982-1985) was exacerbated by mismanagement, internal strife in the government, recurring strikes by the COB, capital flight and systematic opposition by the CEPB and a conservative parliamentary bloc led by the MNR and the ADN; 'we formed a responsible anti-communist bloc of ADN and MNR Congressmen who endorsed reasonable legal projects but opposed those that would further economic deterioration and social disintegration'.[1] This legislative bloc would later cement party leadership support for the 1985 *Pacto por la Democracia* (Pact for Democracy) accord between the ADN and MNR. According to Hugo San Martin, 'Political liberalisation emerged with the *Pacto por la Democracia*. The government of Siles Zuazo had demonstrated that it was impossible to govern without a parliamentary majority. This is what the *Pacto* achieved. This is well regarded by political scientists, because its electoral system permits agreements, which is the basis for democracy. Democracy is a pact. Democracy is dissent, but it also offers the possibility of consensus. Bolivia's political system permitted this after 1985'.[2] The hyperinflationary crisis, which de-legitimised the socialist discourse of the UDP and the COB, offered an unprecedented opportunity for burgeoning transnational business elites to vie for the control of the MNR and ADN parties, and to radically restructure social relations after 1985.

The 1985 general elections were, then, won by the nominally antagonistic MNR and ADN parties, whose economic teams had worked in parallel on an orthodox programme of stabilisation during that summer (Climenhage 1999; Conaghan 1990; Conaghan and Malloy 1995).[3] Following protracted post-electoral negotiations, Paz Estenssoro, the leader of the MNR, obtained the Presidency, while the ADN was granted control of a number of state agencies (for example, of AASANA – Customs), state-owned corporations (such as the state-owned airline LAB) and RDCs.[4] General Banzer was promised the Presidency in the following general elections – hence perpetuating patronage in the state, despite the modernising discourse of both parties: after all, 'we had to give jobs to our people'.[5] The DS 21060 (and its follow-ups, the DS 21660 and 22407, which ensured continuity in the economic management of the Paz Estenssoro and Paz Zamora governments), induced a re-engagement of the WB and IMF, which signed a standby agreement and two 'Reconstruction Import Credits' providing lines of credit to key state-owned corporations for imports of capital inputs and concessionary credits to private mining companies (see chapter 4). These – and subsequent – credit facilities provided the necessary fiscal support for the government's stabilisation and structural adjustment programmes. Concurrently, the *Pacto por la Democracia* ensured legislative support for this shock treatment of hyperinflation and the accompanying ratification of a state of siege (Conaghan and Malloy 1995; Dunkerley 1990).

The history of Bolivia's polyarchic era is one of behind-closed doors pre- and post-electoral pacts and coalitions between party leaders (increasingly dominated by transnational businessmen despite the continued presence of professional politicians and uncompetitive, domestically-oriented capitalists), the so-called *Democracia Pactada*. Formal negotiations, but also informal dinners and meetings, drinking binges and family links were instrumental for consensus- and alliance-building.[6] It may seem paradoxical that two of the three dominant political parties after 1985 – the ADN and MNR – were respectively led by dictator-turned-democrat General Hugo Banzer, and an early collaborator of Banzer (between 1971 and 1974) and Conservative political mastodon, Victor Paz Estenssoro. It rather signals continuity in Bolivia's organisation of subjection. The constant ambivalence of the CEPB leadership towards democracy throughout the 1978-1985 period is a manifestation of such continuity.[7] It has been contended, for instance, that civilian elites, in particular the CEPB, constituted a pivotal force for the transition towards civilian democracy since 1978 (Mansilla 1994). The evidence suggests otherwise: it points to the support of business elites for authoritarian *juntas*, even for the narco-government of García Meza in 1980-1, at least until its deleterious effects on accumulation, monetary stability and the subjection of labour had become too manifest (Dunkerley 1990; Mansilla 1994; Conaghan and Malloy 1995). Indeed, the 'promotion of democracy' by the CEPB after 1978 (Conaghan 1992) was contradicted by its overt support of the García Meza narco-dictatorship following the 1980 coup d'état.[8]

The third party, the MIR, a Christian socialist turned social-democratic party, created during the *Banzerato* and repressed heavily by Banzer and subsequent military *juntas*, eagerly crossed the 'river of blood' separating it from Banzer following the 1989 elections in order to obtain the Presidency, after tense negotiations with the ADN leadership in which Banzer was (yet again) promised the Presidency in the following elections:

'This situation [the electoral negotiations with the ADN following the 1989 general elections] occurred in a different global context... When we entered the government, the denouement of the twentieth century was taking place in favour of the market... The project of worldwide revolution was unravelling... Reagan, Thatcher were at the apex of their power, and likewise for neoliberalism... We had to adjust, we didn't want the wall to fall and to crush us so we had to jump over it, to the other side of the wall!'[9]

The success of the coalition government, cemented by a quasi-supra-governmental National Political Council (CONAPOL) constituted by the leadership of the MIR and ADN (including Banzer and executive secretaries Guillermo Fortún [ADN] and Oscar Eid [MIR]), led the two parties to subsequently participate in elections as a political front, under the banner of a Patriotic Accord (*Acuerdo Patriótico*) (Gamarra 1994).[10] In each party (especially the ADN and MIR), an old guard of professional politicians persisted in dealing with pre- and post-electoral negotiations with coalition partners, and elaborated the appropriate political strategies to remain ahead in the polls and to secure the domination of the party in Congress, in the judiciary and in the executive itself. This instrumentalist approach to politics, inducing a domestically-oriented struggle *for power* very much imbued the discourse of MIR and ADN *subjefes* Oscar Eid and Guillermo Fortún in interviews.[11]

Yet change was symbolised in modernising, outward-looking movements within the three dominant parties, underpinned by the financial power of prominent businessmen. The large and growing budgets allocated by political parties to finance increasingly sophisticated electoral campaigns (involving various media outlets) since 1985 have been covered essentially by the modernising leaders of the CEPB.[12] The MNR, under the leadership of Gonzalo Sánchez de Lozada ('Goni') in the early 1990s managed to build and promote an image contrasting starkly with the corruption, nepotism and inefficiency of the ADN and MIR parties in power, securing an ample victory in the Presidential election of 1993 (with 36 percent of the vote) and significan political space to liberalise the party and the state. This image was built by conflating democracy, modernity, and the market:

'Goni was able to establish himself as an innovative man, an efficient technocrat, a politician who represented what he had generated in 1985 with the DS 21060, but with new ideas. We, the intellectuals in the centre-left collective of the MNR, denominated this a "revolution in democracy", an "intellectual and moral reform", exactly the same concepts used by the Morales government today. Goni represented change, with a new discourse, he opened the party up in 1992. So businessmen entered the party because they saw him as an efficient technocrat, we democrats did too. Goni brought Americans to change the party statutes, to reorganise the party no longer along corporatist lines (corporatist centres of farmers, miners) but along territorial lines (neighbourhoods, etc.). This is when MNR cells were generated. This was a complete change... Many new people entered then, there were new faces, with new ideas more in tune with democratic modernity rather than revolutionary nationalism... For instance, I came up with the idea of uninominal deputies to perfect the electoral system. I was inspiring myself from the German system, the double vote system... Others came up with the Constitutional Court [established in 1994]... Of course there was a lot of resistance in the party against Goni, old leaders like Garrett, Sandóval, Bedregal. But Goni was the man. They stayed but Goni no longer paid heed to them. He gave them crumbs. For example, he gave Bedregal the Presidency of Congress, which was nothing. Bedregal wanted to be Chancellor (Minister of Foreign Affairs). Many of them wanted to be ambassadors, and he didn't give them anything'.[13]

The era of democratic consolidation was thus founded on two political party blocs, each led by a coalition of competitive businessmen financing electoral campaigns and a rescinding old guard of professional politicians sharing control of the executive, legislative and judicial organs of the state. By the early 1990s, the balance of power had manifestly tilted towards the former.

The internationalisation of the state involved the positioning of prominent, competitive businessmen at the head of economic Ministries. Resistance to structural adjustment and PSD in government by the old guard of the MNR, ADN and MIR was rapidly placated by successive Presidents through their marginalisation from key government positions. The sidelining of Guillermo Bedregal, who led the MNR's old guard, from the Ministry of Planning in 1986 offered the opportunity for Sánchez de Lozada, at the head of an eventually victorious rival movement of modernisers in the MNR, to establish a more business-minded and entrepreneurial outlook in economic ministries (WB 1989c; Dunkerley 1990; Domingo 1993; Conaghan and Malloy 1995).

Sánchez de Lozada in the MNR, and later Jorge 'Tuto' Quiroga in the ADN, Samuel Doria Medina and Jorge Crespo in the MIR, supported by a well-organised movement of modernisers in those parties, parachuted prominent businessmen and professionals, some of whom had formed part of the MNR and ADN economic teams in 1985, at the head of economic Ministries (including Planning, Finance, Commerce, Hydrocarbons, Mining): 'Goni thought that the state could and should be managed just like a private company'.[14]

In the context of a dearth of skilled technocrats and researchers and the *va-et-viens* of political parties in government following elections – always accompanied by a high turnover in Ministries, to which I will return – businessmen regularly moved back and forth between the state and the private sector, sometimes teaching or undertaking research in the

Universidad Católica Boliviana, the UDAPE or abroad, participating in the formation of a new breed of liberal Bolivian technocrats and researchers.[15] The banking regulator (SBEF), the BCB and the Ministry of Finance have typically been filled by business executives, monetarist academics and technocrats trained abroad and within the three agencies themselves, considered by the WB – in contrast with the rest of the government – to be 'effective agencies dominated by technocratic staff' (WB 2000c: 71).[16] The Paz Zamora government followed the same pattern, especially after 1991, when growth and inflation were respectively subsiding and increasing, and WB and IMF staff were beginning to grow impatient at the lack of progress of the PSD programme (WB 1991a). As pointed out in the previous chapter, the Paz Zamora government was regularly accused of sleaze, of excessive politicisation, and Paz himself refused to generate social conflict through the privatisation of Bolivia's strategic enterprises (YPFB, COMIBOL, ENDE, ENFE, LAB).

'I had nothing to do with the Paz government that entered in 1989. Paz invited me in January 1992, he called me and said: "I thought of you, I want to create a cabinet that is totally technocratic", because he had a very politicised cabinet. So Samuel Doria Medina [Planning], Tuto Quiroga [Finance], Ronald Maclean [Chancellery], myself [Commerce], and a couple more people came in; we were young people, with little political experience, coming from the private sector... Jaime Paz was realising that with politicians, things were getting out of control... There was social tranquillity and coordination in Ministries, it was a good transition, but Jaime Paz realised that there weren't many achievements. And politicians are slightly conservative, so there wasn't much movement... Yes absolutely, there was a process of depoliticisation and Jaime Paz completely supported this... When I entered the Ministry, there was a highly politicised Vice-Minister, of the ADN, and I had to replace him with someone closer to my line of thought regarding efficiency... I also had to kick out 12 secretaries the day after I arrived, and Jaime Paz supported me. I replaced them with trustworthy and reasonable people. The problem is that I had very little time. If I was going to completely reorganise the structure of the Ministry, I was not going to implement any policy. So I didn't undertake any profound transformation. I brought in two or three consultants, and we worked with a small team of 8 or 9 people, and we did everything with this group'.[17]

These small technocratic teams, around the leadership of Samuel Doria Medina, Jorge Quiroga and Fernando Campero accelerated the reform process in 1992-3 and laid the groundwork for Sánchez de

Lozada's reforms. By the late 1980s transnational business and technocratic elites had achieved the necessary predominance in the state to implement second-generation PSD reforms. The WB in 1991 could therefore take comfort in the fact that despite political risks and state ineffectiveness in implementing reforms, 'the (MIR-ADN) economic team is firmly committed to the program, has obtained the support of the President and already has taken many of the most politically difficult measures... Any failure to maintain macroeconomic stability could endanger the success of the reform process. This risk is judged to be low, since the Government has maintained stability since taking office and the program has broad support across the major political parties' (WB 1991: ii-iii).

The 'patriarch' President Paz Estenssoro, who commanded respect and obedience from modernisers and traditionalists alike, managed to craft a particular form of governance which 'straddle(d) the patrimonial dynamics of the parties and the technocratic dynamics of his economic team, and then to meld these contradictory logics into a coherent system of rule' (Malloy 1991: 55). General Banzer and Jaime Paz played similar roles in the ADN and MIR parties. Guillermo Bedregal, who was bestowed the Ministry of Foreign affairs by Paz Estenssoro as compensation for his removal from direct economic management, acted as a *de facto* Prime Minister who dealt with political conflicts and resistance within and outside the state, while economic Ministries remained relatively insulated from day-to-day partisan squabbling and could concentrate, almost unhindered, on stabilisation and structural adjustment (WB 2000c: 5). Indeed, the 'hybrid' form of Presidentialism (Gamarra 1991) created by Paz Estenssoro was to inform the organisation of subsequent governments until 2005: the old guard, the professional politicians and minor coalition partners were confined to political (interior, foreign affairs) and welfare (education, health and sanitation) Ministries while transnationalised businessmen and technocrats collaborated with the WB and IMF to elaborate policies, implement them via Presidential Supreme Decrees, and subsequently present them to Congress as a *fait accompli.* In the meantime, under Juan Antonio Morales's governorship (1995-2006), the Bolivian Central Bank (BCB) sustained an uninterrupted, depoliticised and highly effective management of monetary and exchange rate policy, which buttressed the liberalisation of the state through monetary discipline and debt servicing.

The Fall of Polyarchy

Social and state restructuring encountered systematic resistance by domestically-oriented elite and subaltern social forces *beyond* and *within* the institutions of the Bolivian state, forcing a distortion of the transnational bloc's modernisation strategies. This tension helps to explain the reorganisation of labour and indigenist forces in the late 1990s that eventually led to the election of Evo Morales in 2005.

Resistance to Restructuring in the State

The successive MNR-ADN (*Pacto Por la Democracia* 1985-1989: 84 out of 130 seats), ADN-MIR (*Acuerdo Patriótico* 1989-1993: 71 seats) and MNR-MRTKL (*Plan de Todos* 69 seats, with 7 seats added by the *Movimiento Bolivia Libre* (MBL) in post-electoral negotiations) political blocs,[18] enjoyed clear – if declining – majorities in Congress, and were defined by cohesion in and between the executive and legislative branches. The 1997 elections, won by the MIR-ADN *Acuerdo Patriótico* (with 55 seats) but short of a majority, forced their leadership to negotiate the incorporation of populist parties – *Unión Cívica Solidaridad* (UCS) (21 seats) and *Conciencia de Patria* (CONDEPA) (19 seats) – in order to obtain the election of General Hugo Banzer and achieve a semblance of legitimacy and representativeness (see tables 1.1 and 5.1). The year 1997 signalled a manifest unravelling of the transient legitimacy of traditional political parties and, arguably, of the liberalisation process itself, by preventing the *Acuerdo Patriótico* from obtaining an absolute majority in Congress.

By 2002 anti-systemic parties, in particular the MAS led by Evo Morales had dented the dominance of the ADN, MIR and MNR parties – systematic resistance in the streets and in the state to restructuring was translated into electoral challenges to polyarchy. It demonstrated the inability of the MNR, ADN and MIR to achieve, even between the three of them, a majority in Congressional elections; and indicated the partial dissolution of the transnational bloc's struggle to achieve hegemony in Bolivia, a dissolution confirmed one year later in the October 2003 'Gas War' (Assies and Salman 2003). The incapacity of a political party to win elections following its government tenure; the shrinking number of votes obtained in elections by the two dominant political party blocs, MNR on one side and MIR-ADN on the other, and their need to incorporate an ever-growing number of disparate, smaller political parties in order to achieve a majority in Congress and hence the election of their Presidential candidate are indications that polyarchy was an insufficient condition for the entrenchment of neoliberal hegemony.

Government and Legislature

The hyperinflationary crisis that affected Bolivia in 1984-1985 had stringent disciplinary effects: it fostered a certain measure of institutional order within the central executive agencies of the state, in contrast to the recurrent institutional conflicts defining all levels of the state hierarchy and distorting the stability of the state since the 1930s (Dunkerley 1984; Malloy and Gamarra 1988). Nevertheless, the appearance of normalcy in the electoral process and the relative stability and cohesion of economic Ministries and regulatory agencies contrasted with the convulsions of all other state institutions, throughout the period under study. Despite the cohesion characterising economic Ministries and despite their modernising discourse, Presidents had to accommodate clients in the legislature and in ministries. Patronage in welfare and repressive Ministries undermined administrative continuity and entered in contradiction with the relatively technocratic Finance, Planning, and Trade Ministries. The contradictions internal to central governments undermined the functional maintenance of capital reproduction and accumulation.

As emphasised in the previous chapter, the predominance of economic ministries, in particular the Ministry of Finance, is directly related to the disciplinary effects of world money and their privileged, direct interlocution with MDIs and other creditors. The economic cabinet had to discipline welfare (Ministry of Health, Education) and especially political (Ministry of the Presidency, of the Interior) Ministers, whose preoccupation with the maintenance of hegemony and order for electoral purposes induced them to make concessions to labour.

The continuity in policy-related dialogue transcended the turnover of individual members in governments' economic cabinets and, indeed, in IMF and WB missions (WB 1998a). This continuity also shows a profound understanding, on the part of WB and IMF staff, of legal, institutional and wider societal constraints on the implementation of reforms. For instance, the privatisation of infrastructural services (water and energy distribution) was rendered difficult by legislation on municipal administration and ownership (WB 1992b), and the privatisation of mining and hydrocarbons corporations (COMIBOL and YPFB) was rendered almost impossible by the Constitution, which effectively prevented their outright sale and necessitated legal acrobatics by economic teams (bestowing management rather than ownership

Table 5.1: National Elections Results, 1985-2005 (Major Parties Only)

	(Percent of valid votes)					
Parties	**1985**	**1989**	**1993**	**1997**	**2002**	**2005**
MNR	30.4	25.7	35.6	18.2	22.46	6.5
ADN- (1)	32.8	25.2	21.1 (2)	22.3	3.4	
MIR	10.2	21.8		16.8	16.3	
PODEMOS						28.6
FUN						7.8
MAS					20.94	53.7
NFR					20.91	0.7
MIP					6.1	2.2
CONDEPA		12.3	14.3	17.2	0.4	
UCS			13.7	16.1	5.5	
MNRI	5.5					
MBL	0.7 (3)	8	5.4	3.1		
IU			1	3.7		
PS-1 (1985/1989)	2.6	2.8				
PS					0.7	
Others	17.8	4.2	8.9	2.6	3.3	5
Valid votes	1,504,056	1,415,869	1,647,710	2,177,171	2,778,808	2,873,801
Blank	7.3	4.4	2.1	3.3	4.4	3.4
Null	5.6	5.7	2.7	2.9	2.8	4
No. of registered Presidential candidates	18	10	14	10	11	8
Vote in Congress						
Elected	Paz E. (94)	Paz Z. (97)	Sánchez (97)	Banzer	Sánchez (84)	Morales
Loser	Banzer (51)	Sánchez (50)	Palenque (16)	(unopposed)	Morales (43)	(no vote: absolute majority)
Total population	5,885,000	6,431,000	6,897,000	7,653,000	8,815,000	9,427,000
Registered voters	2,108,458	2,136,560	2,399,197	3,252,791	4,164,909	3,671,162
Votes cast	1,728,365	1,573,790	1,731,309	2,321,117	2,994,065	3,102,417
Abstention rate	18	26.3	27.8	30.1	27.9	15.5

(1) ADN in electoral fronts with Partido Demócrata Cristiano since 1989.
(2) ADN and MIR ran in pre-electoral front: Acuerdo Patriótico.
(3) MBL part of IU coalition front in 1985 and 1989.

Source: Corte Nacional Electoral

rights to foreign investors) in order to undertake their capitalisation (see chapter 4).

In Bolivia, the legislature has more often than not constituted a reactive, rubber-stamping and legitimising rather than dynamic institutional force in relation to government policies. A historical exception to this rule is the populist Siles Zuazo administration (1982-1985), which was unable to govern primarily because of the obstruction it faced by the conservative majority in parliament and the senate, which undermined both its wage concessions to labour and stabilisation packages (see chapter 2). Parliament, since 1985, has only taken centre stage in the context of general elections or in delaying and amending legal projects submitted by the government. Bolivia's system of Proportional Representation is distorted by an important peculiarity, which allows Congress to elect the President (among the three candidates obtaining the largest proportion of votes) when no candidate obtains an absolute majority of votes (Whitehead 2002b: 23). Hence Congressional authority in appointing the President has fostered backstage party-leadership negotiations and accords between dominant and smaller parties, leading to the formation of increasingly uncoordinated and unstable coalitions involving both transnational elites and professional politicians (see tables 1.1, 5.1, 5.2 and 5.3).[19]

Typically, pre- and post-electoral negotiations resulted in the allocation of Ministries and posts to coalition partners and party clients. President Paz Zamora's *Acuerdo Patriótico* (Patriotic Accord) (1989-1993), initiated a deleterious practice that Banzer reproduced following his election in 1997. It undermined the conventional form of coalition-building, and the cohesion of the government itself by dividing the same Ministry by levels (for example, an ADN Minister and a MIR vice Minister, and vice versa) instead of letting each party control Ministries in their entirety. Although it fostered peaceful co-existence between the MIR and ADN, which cemented their joint participation in the 1993 general elections, this co-existence was also founded on the promotion of patronage and ineffectiveness (WB 2000c; Dunkerley 2007 [1998]). In order to accommodate coalition partners, full Ministries were created, fully staffed with clients of the Ministers and Vice Ministers (President Paz Zamora thus created three Ministries and sixteen Vice Ministries during his incumbency) (Domingo 1993). Despite embodying modernisation *par excellence*, President Gonzalo Sánchez de Lozada (1993-1997; 2002-2003) himself was compelled by the Proportional Representation system to perpetuate the policy of bestowing one Ministry to each of the minor political parties forming part of his government, and of allocating posts in welfare and political Ministries to

Table 5.2: General Elections, 1985-2005: Upper House Seats

Senate: 27 senators (1)

Number of seats						
Party	1985	1989	1993	1997	2002	2005
MNR	16	9	17	4	11	1
ADN-	10	8	8	11	1	
MIR	1	8		7	5	
PODEMOS						13
FUN						1
MAS					7	12
NFR						0
MIP						0
CONDEPA		2	1	3		
UCS			1	2		
MBL	0	0	0	0		
IU	0	0	0	0		
PS-1	0	0	0	0		
Others	0	0	0	0		0

(1) Each of the country's 9 departments returns three senators in a party-list electoral system: first-placed party in each department returns two senators, second-placed party returns the third senator.

Source: Corte Nacional Electoral

his party clients.[20] However, the persistence of patron-client networks has typically spilled over the executive agencies of the state, affecting the judiciary and its independence: this was manifest (among other examples of illiberal practice) in the judiciary's almost complete dependence on the politically-determined appointment of judges, resulting in the disregard for, or political manipulation of, judicial decisions; fraudulent elections in 1989 due to the politicisation of the National Electoral Court; and a protracted struggle in 1990-1991 between the Supreme Court, dominated by judges previously appointed by the MNR government, and the MIR-ADN government of the day, which undertook a *juicio de responsabilidades* (impeachment) to replace its political adversaries (Domingo 1993). Struggles by the transnational bloc to achieve transparency and the elimination of privileges were immediately undermined by dominant and smaller parties' utilisation of Proportional Representation to secure leadership positions in Ministries, and employment in the state. Professional politicians in governments were certainly not 'committed to pay the price of reform, including loss of control, patronage and sometimes illegal benefits through the introduction of realistic pricing, competition and accountability' (DAC 1989: 36; 38).

Table 5.3: General Elections, 1985-2005: Lower House Seats						
Parliament: 130 deputies (1)						
	Number of Seats					
Party	**1985**	**1989**	**1993**	**1997**	**2002**	**2005**
MNR	43	40	52 (2)	26	36	7
ADN-	41	38	35 (3)	32 (4)	4	
MIR	15	33		23	26	
PODEMOS						43
FUN						8
MAS					27	72
NFR					25	0
MIP					6	0
MRTKL	2		52 (2)			
FSB	3					
CONDEPA		9	13	19		
UCS			20	21	5	
MNRI	8					
MBL	0 (5)	10	7	5		
IU				4		
PS-1	5					
Others	13	0	3	0	1	

(1) Proportional representation electoral system: D'Hondt formula used until 1986, favouring proliferation of smaller parties; thereafter St Laigue system, which favours larger political formations. Under Electoral Law of 1996, introduction of 'additional member' mechanism: half the deputies are elected from a party list ('plurinominal' deputies); the other half as individual candidates for 68 constituencies. For in-depth analyses see Domingo (1993) and Dunkerley (1998).

(2) MNR-MRTKL electoral front in 1993

(3) MIR-AND electoral front in 1993: *Acuerdo Patriotico*

(4) ADN-NFR-PDC electoral front in 1997

(5) MBL and other parties as part of *Izquierda Unida* electoral front

Source: Corte Nacional Electoral

The struggle for depoliticisation, transparency and accountability forced economic Ministries, the BCB and the SBEF (banking regulator) to distance themselves from business organisations in order to sustain the structural viability of capital as a whole; and to fend off challenges by other business forces within the institutions of the state, for instance in Congress. DS 21060 undermined the power base of domestically-oriented capitalists and managers of state-owned corporations by eliminating barriers to trade and subsidised prices and credits, and by implementing an austere fiscal policy involving the decapitalisation of state-owned corporations (Cariaga 1990; Conaghan and Malloy 1995). From 1985 to 1988, the transnational bloc faced organised manufacturers who lobbied strongly against the reduction of tariff and non-tariff barriers to trade, but also exporters, who struggled to maintain quantitative barriers to imports. Economic Ministers were able to fend off these challenges, in part because new-found competition was generally considered by business federations as a small price to pay for monetary stabilisation, cheaper credit and the disciplining of labour.[21] The only sector able to resist trade liberalisation was the sugar producing *gremio*:

'Manufacturers no longer pressured my Ministry, because the elimination of barriers to trade began with Goni, or the government of Paz Estenssoro... In his time, Goni confronted the industrial sectors, by the time I entered the Ministry there was no more damage to the industrial sector. Of course, there was always some random sector that was coming to us to ask us to increase tariffs... like cigarettes, manufacturers here and there, but nothing strong, nothing well-articulated, nothing for which we had to struggle. I was telling them: "look, we're in a process, you'll need to reconvert, you have to be more competitive". They left slamming the doors, but things were as they were and they couldn't change them much. The confederation [CEPB] was in agreement with us, manufacturers had made more noise in there in 1985-1986, but afterwards it was clear that there was *"no return"* [in English], and they all adjusted, they became more efficient and survived... With regards to imports and foreign investments, we had the lowest tariffs in Latin America, so who was going to complain?... But a sector which has always been successful at this [maintaining tariff barriers], with all governments, is the sugar-producing sector. To this day, it is the *only* sector which benefits from tariff advantages. It is still forbidden to import sugar into this country!... Extremely powerful! They were very skilful, they mobilised the sugar-cane owners, who were numerous and always scared governments. Nobody else managed to achieve this. Here we had expensive sugar, why? Because sugar-cane owners managed to impose this. The couple of times when I tried to address the matter Jaime Paz said: "no, listen Fernando, this is a long-term issue, there are long-standing agreements"... This was one of the themes that we couldn't touch upon... Goni had managed to open up everything, except sugar!'[22]

Domestically-oriented bankers were also effective at resisting modernising reforms.[23] The liquidation by the SBEF (banking regulator) of state-owned and private banks (four private banks in 1987, one in

1988, the three state-owned banks in 1991, two banks in 1994, one bank in 1997, one in 1999 and one in 2000) (see table 5.4), signified an end to the conventional Bolivian practice of bailing out, subsidising or recapitalising bankrupt banks, which was however perpetuated by Jaime Paz Zamora until 1990 via Supreme Decrees, and against the advice of the IMF and WB (WB 1991a, 1991b). Mandatory closures generated protracted opposition from managers and employees in state banks and from ASOBAN, the banking federation, at least until the late 1990s and despite the fact that foreign banks and shareholders were being incorporated in its directorate (see chapter 3). Power sharing between domestic (family-owned) and transnational banks, as well as the penetration of the state by prominent bankers was reflected in attempts by ASOBAN to obstruct regulatory measures by the SBEF. WB staff expressed frustration at the situation in several documents:

'It is likely to be the banks themselves – small in number and usually well-organized for collective action – who will be able to exert more power over the regulator... The main opposition to the work of the SBEF has come from some of the banks – those banks whose ability to make profits has been most threatened by the application of prudential rules. These banks have often been adept at political infighting and effective in using different branches of government to press their cause. The most notable case concerns the liquidation of a bank [*Bidesa*] in 1997. The bank's principal owners used their positions in Congress – one of them was elected deputy in 1998 – to conduct a campaign against the Superintendency. They also sued a number of the senior officers of the SBEF, including the Superintendent' (WB 2000c: 70-71; see also WB 2005: 100).

Institutional order in central government agencies thus *necessitated* endemic patronage and outright corrupt practices by the elite old guard of political parties (professional politicians) (Malloy and Gamarra 1988; Dunkerley 2007 [1998]). Minor coalition partners of President Banzer's *megacoalicíon* government (1997-2002), on their side, in particular populist parties such as CONDEPA and UCS, created bastions of resistance to PSD strategies within government itself, by failing to internalise the business perspective and the movement towards a functional capitalist state. The very legitimacy of CONDEPA and UCS rested on an 'anti-politics' discourse and a cult of personality of their respective *caudillos* (Mayorga 1995; Dunkerley 2007 [1998]), which seem to validate O'Donnell's (1993:1) concept of 'delegative democracy', which he considered as a 'new animal' or emerging 'subtype of existing democracies': the disenchantment of labour and marginalised social forces with the capacity of representative institutions

Table 5.4: Financial Developments, 1987-2003		
Year	**Event**	**Measures**
1987-1991	Mandatory closing of 8 banks (4 in 1987; 1 in 1988; 3 state-owned banks in 1991). Run on bank deposits prior to and directly following 1989 general elections.	DS 22407.
1994	Bank run. Mandatory closing of two banks (Banco Sur and Cochabamba) representing 11 percent of total assets of commercial banks. General weakness of banking sector	
1995	Severe liquidity problems	Policy to restructure banks; improvements in prudential regulation; New Central Bank Law
1996		Official cost of bank restructuring: 4% of GDP.
1997	Run on deposits of one restructured bank in February. Bank purchased by foreign bank. Closing of bank BIDESA	Setting of minimum capital/assets ratio.
1998	Run on deposits of largest commercial bank (Banco Santa Cruz). Purchased by Banco Santander Central Hispano. Multibanco and Banco La Paz merged with foreign banks (Citibank and Grupo Credicorp).	Law strengthening power of Superintendency of Banks (SBEF)
1999	Mandatory closing of Banco Boliviano Americano representing 4% of total bank assets. Sold to Banco de Credito.	New law modifies regulatory framework of financial system that buffers impact of bank closures. Gradual tightening of provisioning requirements
2000	Banco Santa Cruz in trouble: losses represent 84% of losses of all national private banks.	Measures to encourage reprogramming of loans. Restructuring of Banco Santa Cruz. Transparency in interest rates. Change in loan classification criteria to improve quality of bank portfolio
2001	Non-performing loans up at 16.0% from 6.6% in 1999	Launching of FERE that provides credit to banks that reprogram loans to clients with the capacity to repay. Launching of PROFOP to provide one-time credits to capitalised banks.
2002	15% drop in bank deposits in context of elections	
2003	High level of non-performing loans (19%). February run on deposits in context of social uprising.	Laws to strengthen bank resolution mechanism and facilitate prompt corrective action for banks with problems in Congress.

Source: WB (2005: 100)

to address their demands fosters withdrawal and apathy, and further marginalisation, which in turn leads them to 'delegate' their grievances to leaders whose commitment to representative democracy is questionable in light of their tendencies towards personalism – a direct relationship between the leader and his constituency – and patrimonialism – the distribution of favours by the *caudillo* (O'Donnell 1993; Gamarra 1996: 76). Gamarra (1996:79) was making the accurate observation in the late 1990s that these parties, by participating in coalition governments, 'may have played a crucial role in the stability of Bolivian democracy and may have become the only mitigating force that has prevented the emergence of radical groups among the marginal sectors of Bolivia'. Nevertheless, their stabilising social function was profoundly deficient: subsequent events prove that they only transiently achieved the prevention of more radical social mobilisation by indigenist forces and *cocaleros* (see below), primarily because they actively undermined the effectiveness of policies that their leaders were helping to legitimise by their very presence in government. Although the disruptive Max Fernández, who was initially part of the Sánchez de Lozada government, was isolated within a year (Gamarra 1996), the combined presence of the UCS and CONDEPA in Banzer's *megacoalición* – without their founding *caudillos* – severely undermined its internal cohesion by intensifying the tendentious corruption, patronage and inefficiency generated by Banzer's pursuance of Paz Zamora's policy of carving Ministries and Vice-Ministries up between coalition partners.

While the first Sánchez de Lozada government (1993-1997) had been manifestly home to the pioneer transnational business confederation leadership (Fernando Illanes and Fernando Romero – see table 3.13) and was able to achieve unprecedented efficiency and depoliticisation, the Banzer/Quiroga (1997-2002) administration was more eclectic, in part because numerous smaller parties formed part of the *megacoalición* and had to be accommodated with Ministerial positions, but also because economic Ministries were dominated by more provincial manufacturers, bankers and agro-industrialists from Santa Cruz, Banzer's city of origin and historical stronghold.[24] Restructuring was, therefore, immediately disfigured by the social forces and organisations constituting governmental coalitions.

Administration, Civil Service Reform and 'Key Posts'

Corruption and patronage were notoriously endemic in (but certainly not restricted to) the Paz Zamora government (1989-1993), Banzer's *megacoalición*, and Sánchez de Lozada's short-lived second administration (2002-2003) (Gamarra 2003). Patron-client relations sustained a high staff turnover in executive agencies and hindered the effective implementation of reforms: according to WB data (WB 1999c; 2000c), turnover in all Ministries after elections ranged between 20 (Ministry of Justice) and 50 percent (Ministry of Housing). As elaborated in the preceding chapter, civil service reform was undertaken in various forms by successive governments in order to short-circuit the problem of patronage, with the systematic financial and institutional support of MDIs. *Government*-building was a cornerstone of first- and second-generation reforms, and civil service reform was at the heart of government-building.

The employment of more than 700 private consultants in key posts was designed to consolidate a leaner, more effective, depoliticised, transparent and accountable public administration. Nevertheless, the fiscal costs of comprehensive civil service reform were simply too high for governments facing a growing budget deficit plugged up by ODA, which in turn signified a ballooning foreign debt. The liberal corporate tax regime established in 1985 to stimulate PSD was relatively unsuccessful at attracting private capital (Jenkins 1995), and signified very low tax returns for a government which, however, did not have the fiscal resources required to finance the improvement of its tax collection agency – and thereby tap into other fiscal resources, or address contraband. Furthermore, the Banzer government faced unexpected costs in 1998-1999 generated by the privatisation reforms implemented by the preceding Sánchez de Lozada administration (including the transfer of management rights to TNCs and the unexpected deficits generated by the AFPs administering the Bonosol [privatised pensions]) (see table 4a).

Crucially, and this was a problem identified by the WB (1994b; WB 1999c) prior to the capitalisation process, the heavy dependence of the Treasury on the YPFB (rents on hydrocarbon exports) signified that, just as capitalisation and pension reform were incurring heavier costs than expected, rents on oil and gas exports were significantly declining due to capitalisation itself (which reduced taxes on exports to the record-setting rate of 18 percent), thereby squeezing further the resources available for civil service reform (along with welfare expenditures). Fiscal resources were further siphoned off via the perpetuation of patronage in political parties, corruption and inefficiency (WB 2000c). This vicious circle, alleviated by the HIPC initiative and systematic fiscal support by MDIs (through grants and concessionary loans), became unsustainable following the 1997 financial crisis.

At the same time, a series of institutions were established to enforce a merit-based civil service. Nevertheless, the last of them, the *Servicio Nacional de Administración de Personal* was understaffed, underfinanced, and its position in the Ministry of Finance was so marginal that its staff did not even have access to basic data from other Ministries. The General Comptroller's office, on its side, never managed to fully review government activities and failed to hold state managers accountable for their activities, due to systematic resistance to internal audits and lack of transparency (WB 2000: 16-17).

IMF and WB staff quickly realised that the lack of institutional capacity would undermine the processes of privatisation and capital markets formation. Privatisation and the imposition of market discipline in privatised corporations were perceived to depoliticise the corporations themselves (WB 1991b). However, the shift away from direct state participation in production needed to be filled institutionally by the direct formation of depoliticised regulatory institutions. The regulatory *Superintendencias* were set up post-facto, and failed to control effectively newly privatised corporations while some contracts demonstrated improper procedures – the Enron contract for oil distribution and the sale of the state-owned airline Lloyd Aereo Boliviano (LAB) are exemplary.[25]

'Capitalisation was misunderstood by people... I was actually on the other side, and I can tell you that the process was totally transparent. Except maybe for ENFE, and LAB, but after all LAB was hard to sell. ENFE they gave it away. There's no longer any railway to speak of in this country... I participated in two capitalisations of ENDE, with a US company called AES, and we finished fourth in one and third in the other. ENDE had been turned into three units and we participated in two... With AES, although we had a fantastic relationship, we lost, and we had to win... For ENTEL, I brought in some Italians... ENTEL did not yet have mobile phones, and it was being sold with all concessions. I proposed to my partners [in Telecel, Bolivia's first mobile telephony company] to participate in the capitalisation. They said no, so I said: "then I will do it, and if I win I'll sell my participation in Telecel". So I spoke with AT&T, which ran off, with Springtel MCI, which was very interested, and finally Telecom Italia... For ENTEL I had a 15 percent participation in the offer, I had signed an agreement with Stet International in Rome...After winning the bid, we realised that they weren't really trustworthy... They made us sign the agreement at the last minute... We decided to leave, actually took them to court and we won... They did make a lot of money by selling overpriced equipment to ENTEL, through companies that they themselves created, and by selling services at Italian prices. The Directorate that Goni put in place was a disaster, saying yes to all these overcharges. And they have definitely made a profit out of the $610 million that they invested' (see table 4.8).[26]

Transnational elites acted within wider elite and client networks, which constrained their freedom of action and the transparency of appointments. One may conceivably accuse modernisers of having consciously perpetuated patronage in order to muster Congressional and administrative support for the implementation of the most difficult reforms, including privatisation. 'It is possible that Sánchez de Lozada needed to ensure he could "pay" for support (from his own party as well as from others) for these initiatives by maintaining control over distribution of a number of valuable patronage posts in the central administration'. Furthermore, 'in a show of on-going deference to the spoils system, some of Sánchez de Lozada's new Ministers tried to fire civil servants hired (under the)... previous administration. One notorious case occurred at the Ministry of Agriculture' (WB 2000: 13). It was thus necessary for the Ministry of Finance to withdraw WB funds from the Ministry of Agriculture in order to counteract extreme examples of patronage.

Liberalisation and its complementary depoliticisation process contained their antithesis in the perpetuation of patronage, corruption and resistance to layoffs in the state.

Linking Resistance in the State and in Civil Society

It is all too often forgotten in Critical research on Bolivia that the organisational vanguard of social resistance to stabilisation measures in the mid-1950s, early 1970s, and from the mid-1980s onwards was invariably state employees, in part because, unlike 70 percent of workers confined to the informal sector, they enjoyed permanent contracts enshrined in the *Ley General de Trabajo* (1944) and retained their membership in the COB (García 2007). Empirical evidence systematically undermines historical materialist views of state managers and employees as agents of state repression and instruments of the *criollo* ruling-class, or part of a functional mechanism for the reproduction of capital. As relatively protected and stable labour, civil servants are perceived as less likely to rebel. Yet as restructuring efforts were directed primarily at the *formal* economy and particularly at the state, state employees (miners and YPFB workers in the mid-to-late 1980s, managers in state-owned enterprises and banks from the early 1990s, and teachers from the late 1980s) were more immediately affected by layoffs, wage freezes and productivity requirements than labour in the private and informal sectors. They therefore spearheaded resistance to restructuring in the 1980s and 1990s. While the COB was their primary instrument of resistance, they were the lifeline of the COB itself, despite the crippling closure of COMIBOL mines and the layoff of miners, who had constituted the organisational core of the COB.[27]

It ought to be pointed out that despite systematic resistance from the COB to restructuring efforts, it was palpably ineffective in influencing policy until the election of Banzer which coincided with the initation of a profound and long-lasting regional economic crisis in 1997. The year 1997 is a turning point in the fortunes of the labour movement, because, and as will be elaborated below, it undermined neoliberal hegemony beyond repair and opened up new spaces for resistance, which facilitated the subsequent victories of labour and indigenist forces from 2000 onwards.

The promulgation of DS 21060 on 29 August 1985 immediately triggered the mobilisation of all labour federations by the leadership of the COB. The announcement of an indefinite general strike was respected, according to the COB, by 90 percent of workers in the formal labour market – of which 40 percent were employed by the state in 1985 (IMF 1986; Navarro 1999: 41; 46). Government Ministers and the President responded to the general strike with the legalistic and anti-communist discourses that had characterised the pre-1980s military dictatorships – signalling a relatively unsophisticated attempt to build hegemony. They also threatened an institutional impasse through the President's abandonment of his post if he was not allowed to resolve the crisis – a technique used almost two decades later by President Mesa in the face of unmanageable instability in 2004 and 2005. Hence Fernando Barthelemy, the Interior Minister, declared publicly that 'the law will be applied rigorously'; Guillermo Bedregal, Minister of Planning, that 'the essential content of the economic policy will not be negotiated. President Paz Estenssoro is disposed to leave his post before abandoning his decision to overcome the crisis'. On his side, President Paz announced that "the ultras intend to create chaos, the conditions for a social agitation that allows that the communists, the extremists seize power (cited in Navarro 1999: 42, 46). Interior Minister Barthelemy ordered the detention of six cadres of the BCB who participated in the strike; police raids in the headquarters of the COB to prevent the subversive activities of communist 'agitators' and of the COMIBOL (state-owned mining corporation) to force its employees to return to work; and the arrest and confinement of prominent union leaders in the isolated camps of Rubén Darío and Puerto Rico. Twenty days of escalating confrontation between the COB and the government resulted in the declaration of a state of siege by the latter. Guillermo Bedregal recalled the event: 'Everyone in the cabinet was afraid and nobody dared to act. I therefore took upon myself to sign the decree (No.21069)'.[28]

The most blatant expressions of restructuring in the 1980s and 1990s, the decapitalisation of COMIBOL (1986-1987), the privatisation or liquidation of minor state-owned corporations (1991-1992), the privatisation/capitalisation of major state-owned corporations (1994-1996), and education and pension reform (1995-1996) almost exclusively affected state employees, who were understandably at the forefront of campaigns, marches and strikes against these policies. The prescient expectation of layoffs in privatised/capitalised or restructured corporations (see table 5.5) generated nationalist outrage in the state administration (including among managers of affected corporations) and in the media (Bauwer and Bowen 1997; Kohl and Farthing 2005; Gamarra). In 1986, the closure of six tin mines was challenged by 20,000 miners in Oruro and Potosí, whose strikes were unlikely to be effective in the face of closures. However, the so-called *Marcha por la Vida* by laid-off miners, which generated considerable popular sympathy, began to trigger large-scale marches involving urban workers, and induced the government to declare a second state of siege, which definitely broke the back of the miners' union. Paradoxically though, their relocation to cities and to the coca-producing regions fuelled the diffusion of their organisational skills and of the culture of *sindicalismo* to other regions.

Table 5.5: Capitalisation and Direct Employment Creation

	1991	1994	1997	2000
ENTEL	1,888	1,689	2,089	1,004
ENDE	180	195	196	174
YPFB (YPFB residual from 1997)	5,594	4,927	1,977	954
Andina	0	0	179	154
Chaco	0	0	-	1,385
Transredes	0	0	413	380
ENFE Total	6,367	5,254	1,042	783
Red Occidental	4,262	3,415	439	322
Red Oriental	2,114	1,839	603	461
LAB	1,694	1,537	1,713	1,735
Total direct employment	15,723	13,602	-	6,189

Sources: Salinas et al. (2002); Fundación Milenio (2002)

The capitalisation of state-owned corporations between 1994 and 1997, in particular that of hydrocarbons company YPFB ('the mother of all battles') and of LAB (which had come to be perceived as regional patrimony by labour and managers based in Cochabamba), was virulently opposed in the written press, by the COB leadership, and in particular by managers, who 'resisted efforts to capitalize state enterprises by holding back information, denying access to company files, and even developing alliances with labor and with customers' (Gamarra 1997: 117). The workers directly affected by capitalisation, organised by their sectoral unions, marched in La Paz and Cochabamba, engaging in violent clashes with riot police (Kohl and Farthing 2005; Crabtree 2005).

The most violent instances of resistance to reform, however, were generated by the teachers' union in the late 1980s and 1990s. The latter remains, to this day, linked with the highly secretive Trotskyite party POR and has been at the forefront of general strikes and marches in urban areas, which escalated on four occasions between 1985 and 1995 to the point where states of siege had to be imposed by governments.[29] It is certainly true that despite the teachers' militance and spearheading of urban resistance to reform, they did not exercise the same power over the union movement as had the miners until the dismanteling of the COMIBOL. Yet it is teachers' marches and hunger strikes in 1989 and 1995 that induced the third and fourth states of siege, indicating an undeniably capacity for social mobilisation beyond sectorial interests. The inability of the government to generate hegemony – despite expensive media campaigns to sway the public at large rather than the vested interests affected by the reforms – indicated popular distrust towards the Sánchez de Lozada's exclusionary form of decision-making (Gamarra 1997: 119; Van Cott 2000). It also signified that the state of siege remained the most effective instrument to quell growing dissent against the battery of reforms (capitalisation-cum-pension privatisation, education, decentralisation) implemented between 1994 and 1997 (Gamarra 1997; Whitehead 1997).

The Ministries of Education, Agriculture and Mining remained fighting grounds for socialist, communist and indigenist organisations throughout the period under study. Resistance and agitation, primarily but not exclusively in these Ministries, severely undermined the effectiveness of the executive agencies of the state. The nucleus of collective resistance to stabilisation measures in 1985 and 1986 was miners employed by the state-owned corporation COMIBOL; by 1989, they had been replaced by the teachers. The enfeeblement of the COB after 1985 is correlated to the privatisation of state-owned corporations, and to the extension of the informal labour market: its organisational power became overwhelmingly reliant on the membership and activism of state employees. The fact that it retained some political clout into the 1990s was essentially due to the paradoxical stability in state employment (from 212,000 employees in 1986 to 219,000 in 1999): the elimination of workers on the state payroll through privatisations was offset by staff increases in welfare Ministries, especially in Education (from 85,465 to 103,912 between 1989 and 1997 – including 67,092 to 82,286 teachers; indeed the number of teachers continued to increase significantly into the twenty-first century, to 96,113 in 2003) (see table 4.7; WB 1999: 13).

With public sector wages below the average real wage (see table 5.7 below), teachers were the most adept at increasing their share of the state's wage bill: their activism not only secured increases in staff numbers (thereby increasing their mobilisation capacity), but also achieved a 7.9 percent annual increase in salaries in the 1990s (following a 65 percent decrease in real wages between 1982 and 1989 – from 282bol. per month in 1990, teachers reached 468bol. in 1997) (WB 1999: xxi). The state's wage bill remained roughly stable (12.8 percent in 1980, 6.6 percent in 1986, 8.5 percent on average in the 1990s, 9 percent between 2000 and 2007) (see annex 1), which signifies that 'the rest of the General Government employees saw an average increase of only 1 percent per year, of half the average per capita growth rate' (WB 1999: v).

In short, until the late 1990s, subaltern resistance to restructuring was spearheaded by underpaid state employees, including the management and workforce in state-owned corporations and in the administration facing layoffs or wage freezes. However, teachers' activism and organisational cohesion effectively turned them into the backbone of the urban COB.

Resistance Out of the State: Social Change, Instability and Business Confidence

As emphasised in chapter 3, policymakers and staff in MDIs have certainly not undertaken policies designed to perpetuate underdevelopment, and have shown an obsession with the acceleration of sustainable capital accumulation. They have demonstrated a profound awareness of the polarising tendencies of capital accumulation and the need to alleviate the instability of labour relations. Despite appearances to the contrary – a mere preoccupation with numbers – Finance Ministers and Central Bank governors have been acutely aware of the frailty of business confidence and of privatised accumulation in Bolivia. Bolivia's capitalist forces, in turn, have felt particularly vulnerable to the disruption of capital circuits by political instability, and shown an understanding that the containment of labour power requires the disciplining of organised labour and marginalised forces.

The 2004 Private Sector Assessment undertaken in Bolivia focused on interviews with the chief executives of 15 medium-size or large scale firms, employing 20 to 400 workers. Bolivian capitalists emphasised the consistency and effectiveness of macroeconomic policy, which supported PSD in Bolivia. In particular the BCB exchange rate management successfully maintained the competitiveness of the Bolivian currency and maintained monetary stability: the annual inflation rate usually remained below 10 percent between 1986 and 2005 (WB 2005: 24). Nevertheless, the primary limitation of macroeconomic policy was the persistent and worsening fiscal imbalance and hence the public debt, which perpetuated the state's dependency on fiscal support by MDIs and constrained PSD. Other problems identified by businessmen were regulatory constraints such as the ineffective protection of property rights (especially intellectual property) by the state and endemic corruption in the judiciary and customs service. However, the central constraint on business confidence in Bolivia throughout the period under study has been unmanageable social instability (WB 2005: 25).

Resistance to structural adjustment and PSD in civil society has been systematic, taking a variety of forms, including strikes and hunger strikes, marches, and violence. It has been organised by an increasingly large constellation of indigenist unions and political parties, neighbourhood associations, along with the COB. Recurrent marches, roadblocks and violent skirmishes with the police and the army indicate that attempts to achieve hegemony through polyarchy and attempts to 'help' the population 'understand' the disadvantages of the *status quo* unsuccessfully veiled the coercive essence of capital accumulation: repression remained the essential means of sustaining order. Labour unrest was not deemed by the IMF to affect production as only about 1.4 hours per year were lost between 1993 and 1995. Unemployment in the formal sector was also deemed satisfactory, at 5 percent. Nevertheless, underemployment (20 percent) and employment in the informal sector (65 percent) persisted in destabilising production relations by sustaining extremely low wages and job insecurity (IMF 1998; see table 5.6).

Table 5.6a: Labour and Employment, 1960-2005

	1960	1970	1975	1980	1982	1985	1987
	(in thousands)						
Population	3,428	4,325	4,888	5,355	5,564	5,885	6,157
Labour force	1,195	1,359	1,479	1,826	1,909	2,057	2,101
Employed	-	1,236	1,404	1,720	1,708	1,686	1,670
Unemployed	-	123	75	106	201	371	431
	(in percent)						
Urban population	34	40.7	-	44.7	46.1	48.2	49.5
Rural population	66	59.3	-	55.3	53.9	51.8	50.5
Unemployment and unde-remployment rate	-	9.1	5.1	5.8	10.5	18.0	20.5
Urban informal sector em-ployment (1)	-	-	-	25.5	24.2	25.9	31

Table 5.6b: Labour and Employment, 1960-2005

	1989	1992	1995	1998	2001	2003	2005
	(in thousands)						
Population	6,431	6,897	7,481	8,039	8,624	9,024	9,427
Labour force	2,216	2,69	3,628	3,802	4,099	4,466	4,502
Employed	1,772	2,157	3,550	3,638	3,884	4,222	4,257
Unemployed	443	533	78	164	215	244	245
	(in percent)						
Urban population	50.8	58	59.4	-	61.8	-	64.2
Rural population	49.2	42	40.6	-	38.2	-	35.8
Unemployment and underemployment rate	24.4	19.8	17.5	18.8	25.1	28	23.3
Urban informal sector employment (1)	30	65	63	-	61.3	63.2	59.1

(1) The informal sector refers to economic activity that is not registered and pays no taxes. The figures for 1980 to 1989 are contested. They have more often been calculated at 60-65 percent of the urban labour force in the mid-to-late 1980s, and rising to 65-68 percent in the 1990s. This includes the vast majority of labour in the agricultural sector, which pays no tax and holds no land title; and 74 percent of labour employed in manufacturing; 86 percent in commerce; 56 percent in construction; 43 percent in transportation; and 25 percent in services (WB 1989c: 43). The UDAPE demonstrates that the proportion of informal labour depends on the attributes of informality that are measured (registration of business: 65 percent of labour in 2006; social protection: 79 percent; size of business: 59 percent). Up to 1995, the statistics offered here refer to unregistered businesses. From 1996, they refer to the size of businesses.

Source: WB (1991c: 30); IMF (1986, 1991b); INE

However, the Bolivian microcosm became far more complex as it underwent accelerating change from the early 1980s. The image of urban islands of *criollos* (white) and *mestizos* (mixed-race) dominating a rural indigenous sea was altered beyond recognition by rapid urbanisation, the expansion of an informal market economy, the rise of the coca-cocaine circuit centred on the Chapare region, the decline (and recent resurgence) of mining, and the preponderance of gas exports, which shifted the economic (and increasingly demographic) centre of gravity of Bolivia towards the hydrocarbons-rich departments of Santa Cruz and Tarija. These social transformations conditioned a proliferation in the 1990s and early 2000s of neighbourhood associations, single issue Coordinators (the Water Coordinator in the Cochabamba Water Wars of 2000 is a salient example), regional Civic Committees, mining cooperatives and *gremios* (guilds and trade unions) in both formal and informal sectors (Kohl and Farthing 2005; Crabtree 2005). The COB has thus had to share the centre stage of resistance with a plethora of smaller associations, giving a multifaceted and fluid form to civil subaltern resistance and consequently to *criollo* domination itself (Lemoine 2005). As pointed out by Crabtree (2005: 6), the weakening of the COB, and the need for it to connect its activities with an expanding array of organisations has rendered it increasingly unable 'to defend or coordinate the activities of other social organisations as in the past'.

These social transformations defined a fundamental shift in discourses of resistance since the early 1980s, from critiques of capitalism and imperialism, to critiques of neoliberalism and of indigenous exclusion and repression. The latter discourses are however rooted in older contradictory discourses: nationalism and indigenism. The former continues to inform domestically-oriented capitalists, trade unions, socialist parties, the army, and the media, in a variety of forms. The latter, partly fuelled by the emergence of a so-called *burguesia chola*, or indigenous bourgeoisie,[30] but also by the reorganisation of the 540 or so remaining *ayllus* of the *Altiplano* around the *Consejo Nacional de Ayllus y Markas del Qullasusyu* (CONAMAQ) in the mid-1990s, has generated a variety of communitarian discourses recovering and contriving the roots of contemporary indigenous formations in an idealised pre-colonial past.

While class-based discourses and nation-wide labour organisation were undermined by the 1978-1985 crisis, the expansion of the informal economy, and subsequent structural adjustment, the social costs of restructuring were so high (in terms of layoffs, wage freezes, labour market flexibility) and its benefits invisible (real wages only marginally increased between 1985 and 2004, after plummeting during the hyperinflationary crisis [see table 5.7]) that Bolivia remained on the brink of social explosion almost throughout the era of restructuring, despite the social cushion of coca and cocaine production (see table 5.8),[31] large-scale employment generation by the ESF and its follow-up, the *Fondo de Inversión Social* (Jorgensen et al. 1992, Van Dijck 1998), and the recycling of narco-dollars in the formal banking sector in the 1980s (Dunkerley 1990).

Mauro Bertero thus contended that: 'Few economists in Bolivia want to admit that the process of stabilisation in 1985 was successful in part thanks to what was instituted as booty in the Central Bank, by buying and selling dollars without asking where the dollars came from...Coca and cocaine production and trade had a significant weight in the Bolivian economy during the hyperinflationary period. We can speak of 12 to 14 percent of GDP, or between $250 and $450 million per year... During the "golden era" of narco-trafficking, we were strongly dependent on the informal economy, which played a function of absorption of unemployment... Here we had an informal economy which financed the process of economic re-construction by generating employment and by importing electro-domestic products'.[32]

Different geographical and social sites of labour re-composition thus emerged. The early 1990s witnessed the surfacing of two rural bastions of resistance, in Achacachi (close to the lake Titicaca) and the Chapare, areas controlled respectively by indigenist organisations (the farmers' union, the CSUTCB) and the *minero-cocalero* unions, rearticulating and congealing revolutionary nationalist and indigenist discourses and currents of opinion, and generating new lines of conflict in the COB (Antezana 1983; Crabtree 2005; Rivera 2007; Webber 2008).

President Gonzalo Sánchez de Lozada (1993-1997) managed to co-opt an important fraction of indigenist organisations (the *Movimiento Revolucionario Tupac Katari de Liberación* [MRTKL]) by bestowing the Vicepresidency upon its leader, Victor Hugo Cárdenas (Albó 1994),[33] and by implementing the Laws of Popular Participation (1994) and Decentralisation (1995) (see chapter 4). The concession of the Vice Presidency was a small price to pay to achieve the consent of at least a fraction of the indigenist movement, as Goni and his team were well aware. President Paz Estenssoro, a few years earlier, had told one of his Ministers 'why are you wasting your time debating with the Vice President? He has no authority and no power. He does not matter'.[34] Indeed, the formation of a MNR-MRTKL front effectively 'limit(ed) the mobility and influence of the Katarista movement within a broad coalition', and accentuated ideological rifts between indigenist currents

Table 5.7: Wages, 1982-2005											
	1982	1985	1987	1989	1992	1995	1998	2001	2003	2005	2007
Nominal min. wage (bol)	8470	30,000,000	50	60	135	205	300	400	440	440	525
Real min. wage index (1982 = 100)	100	33	39	35	51	60	69	69	75	69	
Real avg. labour wages (1991 bol)				480		540	660	490			

Sources: IMF, WB, UDAPE; author's calculations.

Table 5.8: Coca Farming and the Illegal Economy								
	1975	1985	1988	1991	1996	2000	2003	2005
GDP total (in US$ millions)	3,346	3,748	4,299	5,263	6,140	7,182	8,030	8,765
Value of coca production as percentage of GDP		7 to 11	6 to 10	2 to 4	2 to 4	0.7 to 2	0.7 to 2.7	2 to 3
Population directly and indirectly dependent on coca trade (in thousands)	100-150	250-500	250-500	200-300	120-250	100-120	100-120	
Area under cultivation (ha)	11,000	33,700	59,000	47,900	48,100	14,600	23,600	27,500
Eradicated (ha)					7,512	7,953	10,087	6
Area (ha) allowed by Law 1008 (1988)			12	12	12	12	12	12

Sources: WB (2005); UNODC (2005); Doria Medina (1986); Van Dijck (1998)

(Albó 1994: 72). The MRTKL was de-legitimised by its participation in the 'anti-national' MNR government; nevertheless the indigenist movement, centred primarily on the new leadership of the CSUTCB (at the head of which was the *Mallku* – Condor or supreme leader – Felipe Quispe) and its new political party offshoot, the *Movimiento Indigena Pachacuti* (MIP) as well as the CONAMAQ, persisted in organising, marches, roadblocks and outright rebellions and guerrilla attacks on the police in the region of Achacachi in the mid-to-late 1990s and early 2000s (Kohl and Farthing 2005).

As emphasised in chapter 1, decentralisation has been seen as a response to democratic demands of indigenist movements, a means of diffusing power and even a 'liquidation of the past' by sympathetic observers (Van Cott 2000; Grindle 1999). Others have interpreted it as a depoliticisation strategy (Gustafson 2002; Kohl 2003; Kohl and Farthing 2005) (see chapter 1). I have not encountered evidence proving a Machiavellian plot to shield the government from subaltern demands (Gustafson 2002). Nevertheless, it is possible to infer that a particularly astute businessman and technocrat such as Sánchez de Lozada, who regularly cited Machiavelli (Climenhage 1999), did not devise the *Plan de Todos* as a patchwork of unrelated policies, but as a coherent and comprehensive plan (Whitehead 1997). It is more than likely that there exists a relationship between the enactment of the Capitalisation Law and that of the Popular Participation Law only a month later. The depoliticisation of the Central Bank and of the Ministry of Capitalisation, the intensifying coordination between economic Ministries and MDIs (see chapter 4), can simply not be disconnected from decentralisation measures. The concentration of institutional power in the BCB and economic Ministries, and their insulation from subaltern demands, cannot be seen as autonomous from the 'irrational' decision to defuse political power towards lower levels of the state (Grindle 1999).

Whether there was a relationship between decentralisation and the government's depoliticisation strategy is beside the point: as emphasised in the preceding chapter, the WB observed the depoliticisation *effects* of decentralisation – inward-looking and localised political conflicts. Yet, depoliticisation was directly undermined by subaltern disenchantment with General Banzer's subsequent attacks on coca production and the informal sector, and his government's inability to distribute the Bonosol (pension) (WB 2005). The unprecedented provision of fiscal resources to indigenous municipalities (see table 5.9) effectively financed the revival of indigenist organisations and discourses, as the CONAMAQ, an umbrella organisation for *ayllus,* which struggles for the formation of a Kollasuyu sovereign state, amply demonstrates.[35] The depoliticisation effects of decentralisation contained their antithesis in what had become intra-state struggles of municipalities, increasingly dominated by indigenist organisations, against liberalisation.

Table 5.9: The Fiscal Effects of Decentralisation and Capitalisation: Investment by Administration Levels (in percent)

	1992	1993	1994	1995	1996	1997	1998
Central govt.	71.8	72.5	65.5	53.4	24.1	18	29.4
Ministries	32.4	38.3	37.5	33.3	10.5	11.8	28.3
of which SNC (1)	22.5	22.7	30.8	22.3	0	0	15.1
State-owned companies (2)	39.3	34.3	28	20.1	13.6	6.2	1.1
of which YPFB	22	19.7	20	11	9.1	4.9	0.5
of which ENDE	11.9	6.5	5	7.3	4.2	1.1	0.1
Departmental administration	19.6	17.9	12	13.4	34.8	38	27
Prefectures	0	0	0	0	14	22.7	24.9
RDCs (3)	19.6	17.9	12	13.4	0	0	0
Local administration (4)	1.9	2.4	9.4	24.4	21.8	24.7	25.5
Municipal govts.	0.2	0.4	7.9	22.8	19.9	23.2	25
Water enterprises	1.8	2	1.6	1.6	1.9	1.5	0.5
Other	6.7	7.2	13.1	8.8	19.3	19.2	18.2
Total	100	100	100	100	100	100	100
Total (in thousand US$)	531,579	480,570	513,288	519,731	588,694	548,280	504,689

(1) Servicio Nacional de Caminos (National Road Service). This institution was temporarily decentralised between 1996 and 1998.
(2) Indicates decapitalisation of privatised state-owned corporations over three years preceding the signing of new management contracts with private investors (capitalisations in 1996-1997).
(3) Regional Development Corporations (RDCs) eliminated in 1996.
(4)Decentralisation and increasing weight of prefectures and municipalities in overall state budget after 1995.

Source: WB (1999c: xiii)

DS 1008, enacted in 1988, had directly antagonised miners-turned-*cocaleros* by restricting the cultivable area of coca and fostering a large-scale militarisation of the Chapare region, involving a significant contingent of US troops (Painter 1994; Van Dijck 1998). The militarisation of the Chapare, and the heavy repression of coca farmers that it entailed, fuelled their reorganisation and transformed the region, and the department of Cochabamba, into a stronghold of *minero-cocalero* resistance to the repressive apparatus of the state. This base became the training and fighting ground of Evo Morales and the hard core of the MAS. I would tend to agree with Mauro Bertero's analysis of the recomposition of labour in the Chapare: 'President Morales was successful in his antagonism to US policy rather than to the executors of these policies. His success in building a union leadership has to do with his opposition to US policies the country perceived as imposed onto local administrations'.[36]

It is by articulating a discourse opposing US-led neo-colonialism (related to the coercion of *cocaleros* in the Chapare), rather than the elaboration of a clear alternative societal project, that the *cocalero* union, the nucleus of the MAS political party, was able to muster broader popular support and eventually become a national political force.

These two rural bastions (Achacahi and Chapare) extended their reach into cities, in particular El Alto (slum-turned-city overseeing La Paz), sometimes galvanised by the *burguesia chola*. The continuing vulnerability of informal workers, the unemployed and underemployed in cities, and a constellation of urban neighbourhood associations and *gremios* – what Mamani (2005, 2007) referred to as 'neighbourhood micro-governments' (*micro-gobiernos barriales*) in El Alto –, thus started to form a third, urban clutch on Bolivian elites. It is worth reminding, though, that the organisational capacity of labour to rebel and re-compose itself over the two decades of restructuring was kept alive and disseminated by state (or former state) employees.

By 1998 a sense of urgency was apparent in WB documents (WB 1998a, 1998b, 1998c, 1998d), as real wages were stagnating, unemployment and underemployment rates were beginning to increase considerably, indicators of poverty remained dismal, subaltern impatience and nationalist sentiment were intensifying in reaction to the capitalisation and pension reforms. Insipid GDP growth had barely matched population growth, signifying stagnation in real wages. Furthermore, Bolivia registered a marginal increase of its GDP-per-capita, from almost $950 in 1977, the year in which Bolivia enjoyed its highest rate, to circa $1,000 in 2003). However, inequality was perceptibly increasing as a consequence of welfare privatisation and capitalisation, and the application of a liberal and regressive indirect tax regime (centred on the VAT [see chapter 4]) – the GINI index had thus increased by more than three percentage points since 1995, stripping the redistributive effects of pension privatisation and Popular Participation of any legitimacy (see figure 5.1 and table 5.10).

Figure 5.1: Bolivia's Relative Growth Performance

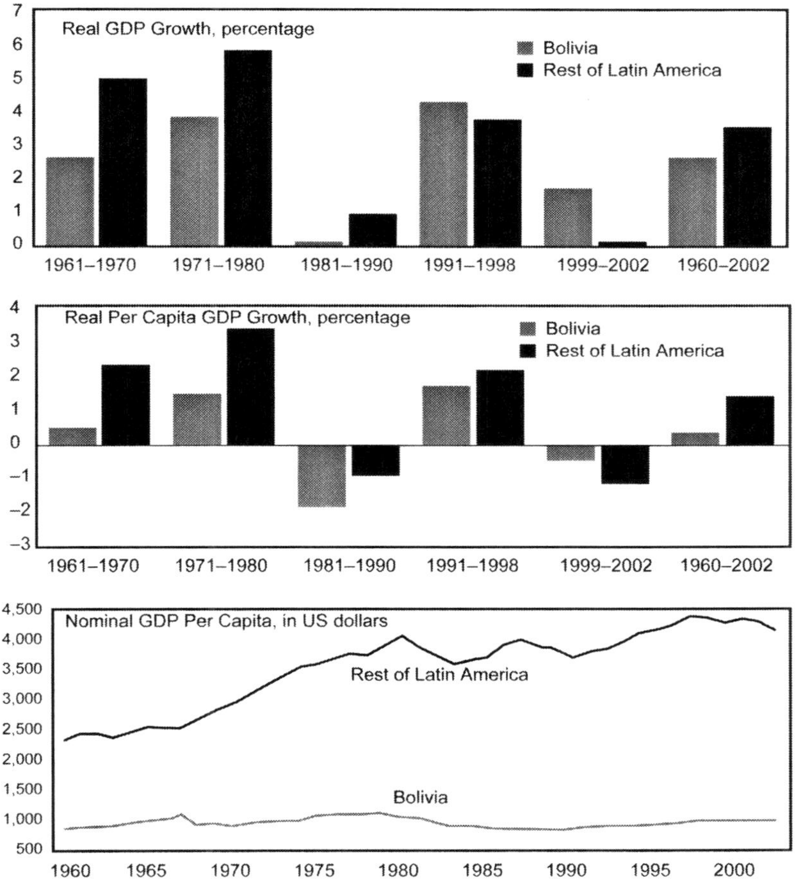

Source: IMF (2007)

Moreover, the government-sanctioned massacre of 10 miners in the Amayapampa mines in December 1996 (the so-called 'Christmas massacre') had converted unstable social conditions into potentially unmanageable and escalating rebellions. Killings of coca growers by military forces were increasing (10 deaths in 1997), and the National Dialogue organised by the Banzer/Quiroga administration in 1998 had failed to mediate the relationship between labour and capital and institutionalise labour unions and indigenous organisations. Close collaboration between transnational elites and MDIs persisted and intensified in the 1998-2005 period – with the HIPC initiative, a substantial increase in MDI financing (the WB increased its annual disbursements from $30 million between 1986 to 1991, to $50 million between 1992 and 1996, and between 50 and $100 million from 1998). In the meantime an evaluation report (WB 1998a) was criticising the WB's inefficiency in fostering privatisation (and PSD) and a more flexible labour market, and advising further efforts in those directions. A massive increase in multilateral credit facilities, a new army of consultants and staff train all levels of administration, and the generalised use of NGOs as partners in development was supposed to revitalise fledging PSD, to no avail.

The volatility surrounding the election of Banzer in 1997 was compounded by additional destabilising dynamics. By 1998, capital accumulation and its trickle down effect in Bolivia started to slow, due to five shocks, two of which were generated by government policy: 1) the Russian and Asian financial crises (1998), which led to a significant increase in interest rates and affected negatively the Bolivian banking sector and by extension manufacturing and construction; 2) the Argentine and Brazilian devaluations and recessions (1998-2001), which reduced the dollar value of remittances from Bolivians living in Argentina, and affected negatively the competitiveness of Bolivian export commodities, leading to a reversion of the trade flows for some products, and compelling compensating depreciations of the boliviano, which in turn increased non performing loans and public debt service in national currency; 3) El Niño (1998), which reduced agricultural production by an estimated 4.4 percent; 4) the fiscal costs of the pension reform, which accounted for 70 percent of the fiscal deficit; and 5) the coca eradication programme of the Banzer administration, under the pillar 'Dignity' of its four-pronged programme, which reduced the area under cultivation from 48,000ha in 1996 to 14,600ha in 2000. From a peak of 5.6 percent of GDP in 1988, coca fell to 0.7 percent in 2000, hurting farmers and their families in the context of an economic slowdown and a decrease in real wages (WB 2005a: 5-6). Coca eradication and the relative failure of the alternative development programme financed by USAID and the European Commission, in the context of unravelling liberalisation, fuelled the determination of mineros-cocaleros.

'What happened with Banzer's "Plan Dignidad"? He attacked narco-trafficking on one side, and on the other he enacted a law against contraband, so he was attacking two key factors for the survival of informal workers. This, in conjunction with the economic crisis in Brazil in 1998, which caused a significant deceleration of the economy, had such a grave impact on the informal economy that it generated a breeding ground for the social explosions in 2000, such as the Water War'.[37]

From 1998 to 2003 a perceptible unravelling of restructuring efforts occurred: the economic crisis was further intensifying income inequality, as an 11 percent increase in the wealth of the highest decile of the Bolivian population could be contrasted to a 20 percent decline for the poorest decile: by 2001, the former was appropriating 46 percent of GDP while the latter 0.17 percent (270 times less) (UDAPE 2007b). Furthermore, the illegitimacy of the *megacoalición* due to ineffectiveness, patronage and corruption in government and the wider institutions of the state had become manifest (WB 2005). This problem affected the MNR party, which had epitomised modernisation and liberalisation since 1985-6 under the leadership of Sánchez de Lozada, in particular after his victory in the party elections of 1989 against Guillermo Bedregal. The MNR's demoralising defeat in the 1997 general elections triggered internal dissent vis-à-vis the leadership's electoral strategy and programmatic approach to political economy, as well as the organisation of the party itself. Dissent was placated by Sánchez through the marginalisation of social democrats in the party:

'Goni, from 1993 to 1997 was a very lucid guy. The breaking point occurred in 1999, after the collapse of the process of democratisation internal to the (MNR) party. After the end of his term, the polls presented Goni as a *'vende-patria'* [traitor, who sells out the country to foreigners], and the ADN and MIR were also using the *'vende-patria'* discourse, which hurt us a lot. Goni realised that it would be very difficult to return to the Presidency. We were seeing that things were not going well, and were telling him that we needed to operate a change within the MNR. Everything was indicating that we needed to shift towards the centre-left. He didn't want to hear any of it, and he was wrong. He was too orthodox, and this orthodoxy really killed him politically. Orthodoxy and his entourage. José Justiniano on the technocratic side, and Carlos Sánchez (Berzain) whose dictatorial

Table 5.10: Poverty and Inequality in Bolivia, 1970-2005								
GDP per capita growth 1970-1990 (%)	-1.1							
GDP per capita growth 1990-2007 (%)	1.3							
Pop. under $1 a day 1995-2005 (%)	23							
Year		**1970**	**1975**	**1985**	**1990**	**1995**	**2000**	**2005**
GDP per capita (US$)		610		574	747		952	1,016
GINI index (0 = Perfect equality; 100 = Perfect inequality)			52			59.4	62.6	60.4
Income earned by richest 20% of pop. (%)			59		56.4	56	59	63.5
Income earned by poorest 20% of pop.(%)			4		4	4	4	1.3
Total poverty rate (% total pop.)			80	74.7	77.3	68.6	66.4	59.6
Poverty incidence (1)			40	29.1	30.6	20.8	21.2	22.9
High and extreme poverty incidence			40	45.6	46.7	47.8	45.2	36.7
Urban			66		60.6	49.8	27.9	20.5
Rural			99		95	90	75.0	62.9
Life expectancy at birth (in years)			47	50	54	60.5	62	65.5 (2)
Males		38	45	48	51	59	60	64 (2)
Females		42	49	52	56	63	63	67 (2)
Infant mortality rate (per 1000 births)		166	151	98	102	75	67	53
Urban					83		50	44
Rural					120		90	67
Median age		18.4			18.4		20.1	20.8
Access to safe water (% of population)			34	53	55	60	69	
Urban			81	81	82	75	86	96 (2)
Rural			6	27	27	27	39	69 (2)
Households with piped water (%)					60		73	76
Urban					89		92	90
Rural					31		39	52
Households with sanitation (%)					23	58	69	73
Urban					42	78	86	89
Rural					3	29	40	45
Net primary school enrolment rate (% of age group)								
Male				84		95	95 (3)	94 (3)
Female				74		87	95 (3)	96 (3)
Total			73	79	91	91	95 (3)	95 (3)
Adult illiteracy rates (% of pop. above 15 years of age)			36.8		21.9	17.9	14.6	12.8 (4)
Male					13.2	10.4	8.1	7 (4)
Female					30.2	25.1	20.8	18.5 (4)

(1) A household is defined as poor if income covers 70% or less of a basic needs basket. Two subcategories of poverty can be identified: the very poor and extremely poor. The income of the very poor covers 80% or less of the basic food basket, and that of the extremely poor covers 30% or less of the food basket (WB 1990b: 8). (2) Data is for 2006; (3) Data is for 2004; (4) Data is for 2003. *Sources: WHO, WB, IMF, UDAPE, UN data.*

political management proved deficient in 2003.[38] In the 1990s, Sánchez Berzain was influential but not responsible for political guidance. By the early 2000s, Goni became a man who let himself be guided by these two arms, precisely because he had lost self-confidence with respect to what he had represented in the past. By then, even the quality of our political programme had worsened... Profound change was needed. In the party, there even emerged plans to find a substitute for Goni... people from outside the party, even José Justiniano himself... We had been critical of Goni from 1999, when it was no longer permitted to have democratic elections in the MNR. From then on, there was a problem with the leadership of Goni himself. I was in permanent contact with Goni until 1999. Afterwards I no longer formed part of his entourage. Horst Grebe, who managed the foundation *Milenio*, also a left-wing intellectual, was also sidelined. Carlos Hugo Molina and Roberto Barberi, who had formed part of the process of Popular Participation, were now out. The left-wing of the party was thereafter marginalised, and Carlos Sánchez, who represented the hard line, who had an utterly negative view of democracy, took control... The process of democratic renovation that the party needed at the time was a farce. Instead of revitalising the party structure, to generate new leaderships, everything was a fiasco, a lie. Goni began to manipulate the polls, to impose his own favourites – such as Justiniano as *subjefe* – as candidates'.[39]

Goni, determined to secure a victory in the 2002 general elections despite his abysmal ratings in opinion polls, contracted the US political consulting firm GCS (for its founders Stanley Greenberg, James Carville and Robert Shrum), which had successfully directed the electoral campaign of US President Bill Clinton in 1994. The 'GCS package', to cite Carville, used advanced qualitative and quantitative research methods – opinion polls, focus groups – to elaborate an electoral strategy that systematically shifted the attention of voters away from the image of Goni as a *vende-patria* by buttressing simple issues and campaign mottos ('Yes we can' [*Si se puede*], a motto applied successfully in the latest US Presidential election by the Obama campaign team). Meanwhile, it engineered a sophisticated negative campaign against other Presidential candidates (in particular Manfred Reyes Villa, Mayor of Cochabamba and leader of the *Nueva Fuerza Republicana*, but also Evo Morales). Despite Goni's crude honesty and manifest aloofness,[40] the GCS team achieved a just-in-time transformation of his image and secured an unexpected, but excessively fragile election victory (22.5 percent; followed by Morales and Reyes Villa, tied at 20.9 percent).[41] The close victory of Goni effectively broke up the MNR/*Acuerdo Patriotico* party blocs by compelling the formation of a second *megacoalición* involving the MNR, MIR and several smaller parties.

The Last Straw: Contradictions in the Repressive Apparatus of the State

While two fragile, internally divided and unpopular governments (Banzer/Quiroga and Sánchez de Lozada) were attempting to manage a profound economic crisis, the instability of the state, compounded by upheavals in civil society, was increasingly affecting its repressive apparatus. As pointed out by a legal consultant of the armed forces in 2003, the bulk of soldiers and policemen have been among the most exploited employees of the state, 'surviving in precarious conditions, with "hunger salaries", without social benefits or promotions. In the barracks, exploitation is greater than in factories, and every day it fuels discontent and the class struggle' (Trigoso 2003: 28). A number of mutinies occurred within the police in the mid-1990s for wage increases or to protest delayed wage payments; these mutinies had to be repressed by other police or military forces (Trigoso 2003: 29). In April 2000, a police hunger strike in La Paz over delayed wage payments, which escalated into demands for a 20 percent wage increase, was generating increasing media and popular sympathy. The police strike occurred simultaneously to the Water Wars in Cochabamba and peasant rebellions in Achacachi,[42] causing significant unease on the part of the government. The latter, alarmed by these various foci of rebellion, declared Bolivia's fifth state of siege in democracy, and ordered special police forces (the *Grupo Especial de Seguridad* [GES]) to disperse the policemen on strike. The latter refused, triggering a mass mutiny by police garrisons (10,000 strong) in La Paz, and the reinforcement of the GES barracks by armed policemen. The government, panicked, sent military forces against the 2,400 policemen defending the GES barracks. The inability of the troops to defeat the rebellious policemen compelled the government to announce the suspension of the state of siege, the annulment of the Ley del Agua privatising water distribution for the city of Cochabamba, and a 50 percent wage increases for policemen (far surpassing the 20 percent increase they had solicited). The fifth state of siege therefore fuelled rather than quelled organised subaltern violence: 'Until that moment, people were respecting the authority of the state. Afterwards, they started sticking out their tongue at the state'.[43]

Other hunger strikes by policemen occurred between 2000 and 2003 (Trigoso 2003). In 2003 the GES was again at the forefront of class rebellions within the state. New wage demands by police forces had been unmet by the government by early 2003. However, the imposition of a new tax on middle income workers (monthly salaries above bol.880) to cover the fiscal breach in February 2003 directly affected the police, fostering a rebellion by the GES in La Paz, who laid siege to the Presidential Palace, fighting against (some of them killed by) special military forces on the Plaza Murillo (Kohl and Farthing 2005). The tax proposals, which indirectly affected larger family or client networks inflamed the local population and resulted in various expressions of rage, such as looting. The government subsequently retracted the project of law, buying itself a few months before the following social explosion, the Gas War of October 2003.[44]

The reorganisation of subaltern movements around the anti-systemic political parties MIP and MAS, and around reinvigorated trade unions (in particular the CSUTCB) and their melding of nationalist, classist and indigenist discourses against neoliberalism, accelerated the retraction of key reforms designed to foster business confidence. The Water Wars in 2000, Febrero and Octubre Negro in 2003, signalled a moment of social rupture (Kohl and Farthing 2005; Hylton and Thomson 2007). Two years of further instability, including a referendum on the nationalisation of hydrocarbons in 2004 – on which President Carlos Mesa did not act,[45] and another Gas War the following year (which forced his resignation), was concluded by the election of Evo Morales to the Presidency with an unprecedented, absolute majority (53.7 percent) in December 2005 (Dunkerley 2007).

Conclusion

The consolidation of a transnational fraction of capital in peripheral national settings developed concurrently to its respective integration into the transnational bloc through systematic collaboration and engagement with MDIs, through IFC investments in dynamic private national corporations and through joint ventures with metropolitan TNCs. An appropriate image for this process would be the dynamic formation of a constellation of transnational capitalist fractions in various national settings, radiating from MDIs and informal elite organisations. The transnational bloc has struggled for the transition to and viability of polyarchy.

Polyarchy in Bolivia, which was part of the so-called third wave of democratisation in the early 1980s (Huntington 1990), has been characterised above all by a concurrent centralisation of decision-making power and authority in central governmental agencies (nationally) and in multilateral (i.e. intergovernmental) institutions (globally). The globalisation of liberal democratic institutions – legitimised via a reductionist understanding of democracy as a regular holding of carefully and transparently managed national and local elections – has been correlated to the internationalisation of national states and the depoliticisation of state polity. Internationalisation has involved the diminution of substantial policy-related conflicts among denationalised technocratic and business elites, in a formal and informal institutional setting shielded from direct subaltern policy inputs and imposing the discipline of world money.

The period under study can perhaps be conceived (without lapsing into oversimplifications) as a protracted struggle between four highly fluid and hierarchically related historic blocs, each torn apart by internal contradictions: transnationalised and domestically oriented elites, socialist-oriented/urban-based and indigenist/rural-based labour. Elite blocs – despite manifest antagonisms, which systematically threatened a breakdown of their unity in the struggle against labour – perpetuated an effective alliance in the broader struggle against subaltern blocs, while the latter suffered a series of defeats (in the workplace, in the state, in the streets, in the minds) before re-organising in the second half of the 1990s and achieving a series of victories from 2000 onwards culminating in the election of Evo Morales in 2005. Transnationalised elites reached and have remained at the apex of the national hierarchy since 1985. Meanwhile, the backbone of the COB and the vanguard of urban-based resistance, the miners' federation, dissolved after the tin crisis of 1986-1987. They interestingly became a *rural* force and their relocalisation in the coca-producing Chapare region, leaving to teachers the role of an urban vanguard. The indigenist bloc, increasingly penetrating urban spaces via migration from the Altiplano countryside gradually dominated the labour movement, entering in ad hoc alliances with the COB, the *cocaleros* and radical parties, but always in a climate of suspicion. This suspicion persists in undermining the effectiveness of the Morales administration.

The legitimacy and effectiveness of restructuring efforts was perceived by the MDIs' staff and Bolivian modernisers to be dependent on the functional relationship between state polity and accumulation (i.e. via rules-based, depoliticised agencies, which would provide the conditions for investment, growth and employment), but also on clear and transparent rules of the game for elite rule and reproduction, embodied in polyarchy. Attempts by the transnational bloc to depoliticise state polity contained their immediate antithesis in systematic re-politicisation by domestic elite networks, on which Bolivian transnational elites were dependent to achieve restructuring.

The perpetuation of corruption and patronage by domestically-oriented elites systematically undermined the transparency and legitimacy of polyarchy. The legitimising function of polyarchy was, in turn, immediately discredited by resistance to restructuring by state employees. State employees, in particular teachers, kept the flames of labour organisation alight throughout the 1990s, until the *Plan Dignidad* of General Banzer, compounded by worldwide economic crisis and unprecedented levels of sleaze and corruption in government, triggered a blaze that overwhelmed it and successive administrations.

Liberalisation was an elite-driven attempt to facilitate the transition from an authoritarian military-capitalist oligarchy to civilian representation based on electoral competition (polyarchy), a protracted and violent process which lasted seven years (from 1978 to 1985). Overwhelmed by subaltern demands and power – yet without collapsing into a structural break with global capital –, the transition process resulted in the re-disciplining of labour through fiscal and monetary crises. It subsequently involved the struggle to render polyarchy viable, i.e. to generate neoliberal hegemony by conveying legitimacy to the restructuring of production relations in Bolivia. Thus institutional reforms towards representation and accountability, including the transparency of state institutions, the separation of state powers, the nominal defence of basic individual and collective rights and freedoms (expression, association, strike), the formation of a technocratic corpus interfaced economic reforms elaborated and implemented in an institutional setting created in collaboration with MDIs and shielded from subaltern interference. These are the central attributes of the liberal graft onto the Bolivian social organism by the transnational historic bloc.

Has the graft stuck beyond 2005? The evidence remains contradictory, suggesting on the one hand that resistance – by domestic elites and subjugated forces – to restructuring was systematic from 1985 and increasingly effective after 2000. The transnational bloc failed to entrench neoliberal hegemony, and an ever-fleeting social order was maintained only through coercion. The victory of Evo Morales in the 2005 Presidential elections potentially signalled a radical break with the two preceding decades, with promises to engineer a new Constitution and an overhaul of production relations. Nevertheless, the Bolivian state has been legally locked in the global governance complex and attempts by the current MAS administration to radically overhaul the organisation of social relations in Bolivia have been substantially neutralised through the discipline of world money and the integration of the Bolivian production nexus into the world market (IMF 2007). Although its election, for some, signalled the beginning of the end of accumulation strategies, the Morales government has paradoxically been furthering the transnational bloc's struggle to consolidate the capitalist form of the Bolivian state by maintaining fiscal and monetary stability, by recapitalising nationalised corporations and by undertaking legal actions towards increased transparency and accountability in the state, thereby entrenching the hegemony of capital in the Bolivian social space. This entrenchment of capital domination has perpetuated the class constitution of the state and opened the floodgates of wage and other demands; while elite struggles against the redistributive reforms implemented by the Morales government have regularly threatened to overwhelm it.

Notes

[1] Interview with Hector Ormachea, 5 September 2007. The evidence offered by Dunkerley (1990), Conaghan and Malloy (1995) and Malloy and Gamarra (1988) blatantly contradicts this assertion. See chapter 2.

[2] Interview with Hugo San Martin, 22 September 2007. See also Gamarra (1991).

[3] The Vice President, Jaime Paz Zamora (leader of the MIR) abandoned the sinking UDP ship in 1984 and instructed MIR Congressmen to support the election of Paz Estenssoro against Banzer to the Presidency in 1985, despite the fact that Banzer had nominally won the elections by 40,000 votes (Domingo 1993; Dunkerley 1998).

[4] Interview with Mauro Bertero, 10 September 2007.

[5] The *Pacto por la Democracia* was broken by Gonzalo Sánchez de Lozada a few months before the 1989 elections. His famous 'ya no tengo las manos *atados'*, ridiculed for its gringo-like grammatical mistake, signalled a 'hunger for power' that is still generating frustration on the part of the ADN's leadership. Interview with Guillermo Fortún, 21 September 2007.

[6] Interviews with Guillermo Bedregal, 5 September 2007; Oscar Eid, 13 September 2007; and Guillermo Fortún, 21 September 2007. Considering the small size of elite forces, Congressional, Senatorial and administrative dynasties are a recurrent feature of polyarchy, observable in governments themselves: the Paz family produced two Presidents under polyarchy – Victor Paz Estenssoro [1952-1956; 1961-1964; 1985-1989] and Jaime Paz Zamora [1989-1993].

[7] An unnamed member of the CEPB Consulting Group formed in the late 1970s to elaborate a political strategy expressed this instrumentalist approach to democracy: 'We always looked at the military as an important force to save us from extreme leftist groups in this country. And the less prestige they have, the less we could count on them…And we knew that this meant that the longer they [the military] stayed, the bigger the chances that the extreme left would have in getting in the country with a coup. And when that happened we thought it would

be very hard to remove them. They would take measures like Nicaragua and it would be hard for us to take them out. So we could not allow the prestige of the military to suffer, so we started a campaign to go into a true democratic process...We decided to come out with a document *!Democracia Ya!* And this was the first document that came out openly for such a position' (cited by Conaghan 1992: 212-213).

[8] The President of the CEPB, Marcelo Pérez Monasterios, announced in the Press in February 1981 the full institutional support of the business community to the so-called Government of National Reconstruction, emphasising that 'the postulates recommended by the government in economic terms completely coincide with those that the Bolivian private enterprise has constantly been pursuing', and assuring the military junta of 'the support and backing and permanent assistance of the private enterprise to the projects of the "reconstructors"' (cited in Mansilla 1994: 133; author's translation). By that time, the WB and IMF had disengaged from Bolivia despite attempts to cooperate with the *junta* on a SAP, as it had become obvious that the latter was sheltering narco-traffickers, wasting ODA and emptying the Treasury to purchase luxury commodities for its personal benefit (see chapter 2). Mansilla (1994: 133) generously interprets this announcement as 'excusable opportunism' in the face of a particularly repressive government. The CEPB felt obliged in August 1982 to deny García Meza's allegation, during his trial, that the CEPB had not only supported but instigated and cooperated with the military officers involved in the coup d'état of July 1980.

[9] Interview with Oscar Eid, 13 September 2007.

[10] 'It was a tranquil administration'. Interview with Carlos Borth Irahola, 17 August 2007. Fernando Campero agrees: 'The vision was very optimistic. Furthermore, really after the disorder of hyperinflation, everything was seen as marvellous. Stable prices, there was work *no más*. It was Goni who struggled with everything, with everyone, with the problem of free employment... No, there were no longer any conflicts with the COB [by 1990]. The COB was nothing anymore. Of course there was something here and there, but there weren't big marches and social conflict, it was a happy era'. Interview with Fernando Campero, 20 September 2007.

[11] Interviews with Oscar Eid, 13 September 2007 and Guillermo Fortún, 21 September 2007.

[12] Exact figures are almost impossible to obtain: Domingo (1993) gives the figure of $19 million spent on the 1989 electoral campaign, 80 percent of which was provided by business members of the MNR and ADN.

[13] Interview with Hugo San Martin, 22 September 2007. San Martin makes reference to Edil Sandóval, Guillermo Bedregal and Julio Garrett. Bedregal was the leader of the revolutionary nationalist faction in the MNR. Member of the economic team devising the DS 21060, Minister of Planning (1985-1986), Chancellor (1986-1989), elected Deputy from La Paz (1985-1989; 1989-1993; 1993-1997; 1997-2002), and President of Congress (1993-1997). Sandóval, senior MNR member, was Minister of Agriculture and Campesino Affairs in 1985, elected Senator from Santa Cruz in (1985-1989); Deputy from Santa Cruz (1989-1993, 1993-1997 and 1997-2002). Garrett was ambassador to the USSR (1969-1973), President of the Senate (1982-1985), Vice-President of the Republic (1985-1989), elected Senator for Oruro (1966-1969; 1979; 1980;

1989) and Chuquisaca (1993-1995) and Chancellor of the University Andina Simón Bolívar (1992-).

[14] Interview with Horst Grebe, 17 September 2007.

[15] Interviews with Fernando Campero Prudencio, 20 September 2007; Edgar Millares, 13 September 2007; Ramiro Cabezas, 17 September 2007; and Jorge Crespo, 28 September 2007 who described their own experiences as businessmen and technocrats.

[16] The Ministry of Finance has almost systematically been filled by business executives and the leadership of the CEPB in the 1980s, or private consultants and long-term participants in the economic teams of the MNR and ADN. The list includes almost invariably the most prominent members of Bolivia's transnational fraction described in chapter 3: Juan Cariaga (1986-1988); Ramiro Cabezas (1988-1989); David Blanco (1989-1991); Jorge 'Tuto' Quiroga (1992-1993); Fernando Illanes (1992-1993); Fernando Cossío (1994-1995); Edgar Millares (1997-1998); Herbert Müller (1998-2000); Ronald McLean (2000); Luis Carlos Jemio (2004-2005).

The strategic Ministries of Planning, Energy and Hydrocarbons, Mining and Commerce followed a similar pattern. Sánchez de Lozada positioned business community leaders and members of the modernising wing of the MNR at the head of economic Ministries from 1986 onwards, and this precedent was perpetuated by the following governments. The Ministry of Planning has been invariably led by Bolivia's most prominent businessmen (again, listed in chapter 3), including Gonzalo Sánchez de Lozada himself (1986-1988), Fernando Romero (1988-1989), Samuel Doria Medina (1991-1993), and José Guillermo Justiniano (MNR and leader of the *Federación de Ganaderos* 1993-1995).

Ministers of Energy and Hydrocarbons included the usual suspects Fernando Illanes (1988-1989) and Carlos Morales (1986-1988) (see chapter 3). Two wealthy, domestically oriented, and relatively unprincipled businessmen, Ivo Kuljis (Banco Económico) and Jorge Pacheco (football club El Strongest), were Ministers of Economic Development between 1997 and 1999. The Ministry of Commerce was to be led by two important businessmen Jorge Crespo (1997-1999) and Fernando Campero Prudencio (1991-1993). Close collaborators of General Banzer in business, including the ex-President of the CEPB Carlos Iturralde and David Blanco were conferred political Ministries.

[17] Interview with Fernando Campero, 20 September 2007.

[18] For Alfonso Ferrufino, one of the national leaders of the *Movimiento Bolivia Libre* (MBL), the decision of party boss Antonio Aranibar, against Ferrufino's and other leaders' advice, to enter into a post-electoral alliance with the MNR, which embodied 'anti-national' neoliberalism, was the 'bear hug' that broke the internal legitimacy and cohesion of the party. Aranibar's decision was perceived as particularly fraudulent considering that the MBL leadership had split from the MIR eight years earlier precisely because of the latter's repudiation of its socialist identity and strategy. Interview with Alfonso Ferrufino, 10 September 2007.

[19] This electoral system has allowed two Presidents (Paz Estenssoro in 1985, Paz Zamora in 1989) to be appointed by Congress despite finishing second and third in elections, with the support of professional politicians in the legislature. Oscar Eid was acutely aware of this peculiarity, but also of the personal frustration felt by Banzer at Sánchez de Lozada's repudiation of the

1985 Pact for Democracy (in which Paz Estenssoro had promised the 1989 Presidency to General Banzer with MNR Congressional support). This personal animosity rendered the election of either leader impossible in Congress without the support of the MIR. Eid took advantage of this stalemate by making the famous declaration in national media that the 1989 general elections had resulted in a *Triple Empate* ('triple tie') between Sánchez de Lozada (23.1 percent of total votes), Banzer Suárez (22.7 percent) and Paz Zamora (19.6 percent), thereby incorporating the MIR leader, Jaime Paz, who had finished third, in the Congressional race for the Presidency. After protracted post-electoral negotiations with the ADN leadership, Oscar Eid was able to block Sánchez de Lozada's bid for the Presidency *and* to achieve the election of his *jefe*, Paz, under a Patriotic Accord. Interviews with Oscar Eid, 13 September 2007 and Guillermo Fortún, 21 September 2007.

[20] Goni's modernising image and the contrast built between his first administration and the MIR-ADN *Acuerdos Patrioticos* (1989-1993; 1997-2002) should be tempered by widespread evidence of corruption during his incumbency: in 1997, Bolivia was thus rated 49th out of 50 countries surveyed by Transparency International for its 'corruption perception index', with a score of 2.05 out of 10 (the score actually improved in 1998 and 1999, to 2.8 and 2.5 respectively) (Domingo 2001: 157).

[21] See Conaghan 1990; Conaghan and Malloy 1995; interviews with Herbert Müller, 11 September 2007; Carlos Iturralde, 14 September 2007 and Fernando Campero Prudencio, 20 September 2007.

[22] Interview with Fernando Campero Prudencio, 20 September 2007.

[23] There were 13 private domestic banks (owning 70 percent of assets); 4 foreign banks; 3 state-owned banks (Banco Agricola, Banco Minero, Banco del Estado) and 12 savings and loans cooperatives in 1989.

[24] Interview with Herbert Müller, 11 September 2007.

[25] Interview with Francesco Zaratti, 11 September 2007.

[26] Interview with Fernando Campero Prudencio, 20 September 2007. Campero added that: 'I was really happy not to have entered in this with the Italians... Yes, I could have made a lot of money out of it. But frankly, I am an entrepreneur, I like to make money, but there are things that I don't like to do, and I would have felt very uncomfortable with this. So they entered the mobile telephony sector, and we competed with them... Thankfully, I sold all my shares in Telecel at the right moment, because afterwards all markets in the world collapsed, I didn't expect it to come so hard. The shares of my former partners went from $86 to $1.5. Many other telecommunications companies in the world also collapsed'.

[27] The political demise of the mining union *Federación Sindical de Trabajadores Mineros de Bolivia* (FSTMB) was facilitated by the collapse of the world tin market in March 1986, which structurally constrained the decapitalisation of the COMIBOL. The closure of six mines was accompanied by mass redundancies and the relocation of miners to cities and the coca-producing region of the Chapare. Layoffs effectively reduced both miners' membership in the FSTMB and the union's political clout (see Crabtree 1987; WB 1989b).

However, it could be argued that the weakening of the unions began prior to 1985, since the unions demonstrated their inability to protect their members' living standards from the onslaught of hyperinflation (Malloy and Gamarra 1988).

[28] Interview with Guillermo Bedregal, 5 September 2007.

[29] Four states of siege were ordered over a 10 year period conventionally seen as 'stable': between 19th September to 04th October 1985; 28th August to 15th September 1986; 15th to 24th November 1989; *18th April to 17th July 1995!*) (Navarro 1999).

[30] The *burguesía chola* is a highly exploitative, urban-based commercial fraction of capital constituted by Aymara and Quechua merchants and retailers, which emerged and thrived in the extensive informal economy since the 1980s. They have maintained close ties with their clans in the countryside and have supported a revival of indigenous identity against *criollo* domination. The promotion of indigenous nationalism by the *burguesia chola* may be interpreted as an externalisation of potential antagonisms arising from relations of exploitation within the clan or the community itself (Lavaud 2007).

[31] Bolivia is the third largest producer of coca in the world, after Colombia and Peru and is far more dependent on the coca-cocaine circuit than its Andean neighbours (Painter 1994). Coca production is considered traditional and intrinsic to Andean culture and history. Under the first Banzer administration (1971-1978) coca production increased significantly, generating fortunes for agro-businessmen in the departments of Cochabamba and Santa Cruz (Gill 1987). The 1978-1985 economic crisis triggered a boom in production, before the enactment of Law 1008 (1988) restricted the growth of coca production. Coca production is believed to have increased from 27,000 to 151,000 tonnes between 1975 and 1987, while the area under cultivation expanded from 11,000 to 60,000 hectares in the same period, before sharply declining prices for cocaine on the US market facilitated the implementation of Law 1008 (Painter 1994). Doria Medina (1986) was inferring in 1986 that the gross product of the informal sector ($3.147 billion) was superior to that of the formal economy ($3.055 billion), that more than $350 million per year was generated by the coca economy after 1980, and that 80 percent of the value added generated by the cocaine trade left Bolivia as capital flight. Although the proportion of informal activities in Bolivia's GDP was not fundamentally altered in the 1985-2008 period, that of coca and cocaine production is believed to have declined significantly from the late 1980s onwards.

Indeed, coca production appears to have provided a vital social cushion for the implementation of DS 21060 and subsequent liberalisation policies: it is estimated that the coca-cocaine circuit indirectly employed between 250,000 and 500,000 people in the early 1980s (from 120,000 and 250,000 in the 1990s), and generated $350 to 450 million per annum during the 1980s (circa $250 million in the 1990s). It has been estimated that coca production accounted for 7-11 percent of GDP in 1985, 6-10 percent in 1988, and 2.7 in 1993 (Van Dijck 1998: 41-43).

The IMF, on its side, calculated that from a high point of 5.6 percent of GDP in 1988, coca and cocaine production decreased to 0.7 percent in 2000. Mauro Bertero, Minister of Agriculture (1989-1991) argues that: 'From 1988 to 2000, there was a kind of "balloon effect". Bolivia had reduced its production of coca [due to eradication policies implemented by the *Unidad Móvil de Patrullaje* (UMOPAR), established in 1983 and acting in coordination with the

US Drug Enforcement Agency, and 'Operation Blast Furnace' with the participation of US troops in 1986, which triggered the militarisation of Chapare, as well as a relatively ineffective Programme of Alternative Development] while Colombia's production had increased exponentially. There was a reverse effect after the implementation of the Plan Colombia at the end of the Clinton administration. This balloon was squeezed in Colombia, inducing a migration of narco-trafficking to regions of low institutional resistance, basically the Bolivian Amazon, and eventually we witnessed a substantial increase in coca production... There is a macro-structure of narco-trafficking that cannot be reduced to *cocaleros*... Furthermore, the primary destination of cocaine produced in Bolivia is no longer the US, but the second largest consumer in the world, Brazil, and from there to the ports of Gdansk and Rotterdam, for consumption in Europe and Asia... There is therefore a dark side in all this process of narco-trafficking, which is related to worldwide tendencies'. Interview with Mauro Bertero, 10 September 2007.

[32] Interview with Mauro Bertero, 10 September 2007. The figure offered by Bertero is perhaps inflated, in part to justify the war on drugs in Bolivia.

[33] It is indicative of the role played by the MRTKL in the Sánchez de Lozada administration that Cárdenas was bestowed the Vice-Presidency (head of Partiament), a position caricatured as the 'spare tire of the car' (Albó 1994: 74). No other member of the Katarista movement held a cabinet position and the party's highest post in the executive branch was bestowed to the Vice-President's brother, as director of the Peasant Development Fund, a rank below that of Under-Secretary. In part, the lack of organisational and technical capacity of the MRTKL signified that the President's 'closer circle includes very few who are really from the naciones orginarias' (Albó 1994: 74). Crucially, the government's reorganisation under Sánchez de Lozada involved the formation of three Superministries (Sustainable Development, Economic Development and Human Development). The first two were headed by Guillermo Justiniano, who represented the agro-business sector, and Villalobos, also associated with large-scale private capital. The third, accused of being a 'superministry for the poor' dealing with mall-scale rural production (Albó 1994: 73), was directed by Fernando Romero, prominent member of Bolivia's transnational fraction (see table 3.13), former manager of the ESF, and banker who had spearheaded micro-credit in Bolivia, a disciplining instrument considered in Marxist thought as elemental to the violence of primitive accumulation (Van der Pijl 1998; Bonefeld 2000).

[34] Interview with anonymous Minister in the government of Paz Estenssoro, September 2007.

[35] See CONAMAQ's mission and history at http://www.conamaq.org.bo/. Accessed 28 January 2009.

[36] Interview with Mauro Bertero, 10 September 2007.

[37] Interview with Mauro Bertero, 10 September 2007.

[38] José Guillermo Justiniano Sandoval, close confident of Goni and long-time member of the MNR secretariat, had been invested with the Ministry of Campesino Affairs (1987-1989); the Ministry of Sustainable Development (1993-1995); before directing the Ministry of the Presidency (1995-1997, and again in 2002). He was elected Senator for Santa Cruz in 2002. Together with Carlos Sánchez Berzain, the *zorro* (fox), Justiniano managed the political

strategy of the MNR and acted as the voice of the President from the early 1990s onwards. They led behind closed doors pre- and post-electoral negotiations with coalition partners, organised media attacks against the MIR leadership in the early 1990s (accusations of links to narco-traffickers, which forced Oscar Eid to protect Jaime Paz by spending four years in prison), and internal party discipline, while Fernando Illanes, Fernando Romero (see table 3.13) and Alfonso Revollo (as Minister of Capitalisation between 1994 and 1997) dealt with economic management, attempting to remain at one remove from political struggles. Sánchez Berzain and Justiniano were the MNR's equivalent of Guillermo Fortún (ADN) and Oscar Eid (MIR), managing day-to-day politics (understood as struggles for power rather than power struggles) in Bolivia. Sánchez Berzain (Minister of Presidency 1993-1995) and Justiniano alternated at the Ministry of the Presidency (the voice of the President), but as Minister of Government (1995-1996, 1997) and Minister of Defence (2003), Sánchez Berzain was directly involved in the organisation of the government's repressive activities in the two Sánchez de Lozada administrations.

[39] Interview with Hugo San Martin, 22 September 2007.

[40] In the run up to the 2002 general elections, Goni was asked by a reporter: 'which foreign port would be the most appropriate to export our natural gas? Are you planning on a national consultation?' His response was a negation of democracy: 'No, you cannot ask the people about such complex technological and economic issues. That would be an injustice, like using a blunt knife for surgery' (Boynton 2005).

[41] For vivid insights into the MNR's 2002 Presidential campaign, see Boynton (2005).

[42] The privatisation of water distribution in the city of Cochabamba and their sale to the TNC Bechtel, led to price increases of 300 percent, and widespread rebellion. Water distribution services were therefore re-nationalised. In Achacachi, indigenist guerrillas attacked police forces and declared their territory 'free' from internal colonialism, before being repressed by the army (Assies 2003; Crabtree 2005; Kohl and Farthing 2005).

[43] Interview with anonymous high-level civil servant, September 2007.

[44] The first Gas War (Octubre Negro) was triggered by Sánchez de Lozada's declaration of a project to export gas via Chile (the 'historic enemy'). Widespread upheavals and repression resulted in 80 killings by the military, the collapse of the government and the escape of the President and some of his Ministers to Miami and Washington DC (Kohl and Farthing 2005).

[45] The wording of the five referendum questions was convoluted and biased towards the creation of joint ventures between YPFB and capitalised corporations, rather than any form of re-nationalisation of the hydrocarbons sector. It was therefore duly boycotted by the CSUTCB and the COB (Hylton 2004). However, a majority of voters answered positively to each of the questions (see table 5a). Only the 50 percent royalty of gas exports, with which the MAS leadership was in agreement (fuelling accusations of reformism), was implemented. However, the inaction of the Mesa government triggered demands for the full nationalisation of the hydrocarbons industry in 2005 (McNeish 2006: 221-222; it must be pointed out that McNeish's translation of questions 3 and 4 is inexact, and actually changes the meanings of the referendum questions).

Referendum 2004, Questions and Results

	(in percent)			
	Yes	No	Blank	Null
Question 1	67	10	11	12
Question 2	72	6	10	13
Question 3	67	10	12	11
Question 4	40	33	17	11
Question 5	44	27	17	12
Registered voters	4,461,198			

Question 1: Are you in agreement with the reform of the Hydrocarbons Law No.1689 introduced by Gonzalo Sanchez de Lozada?

Question 2: Are you in agreement with the recovery of the hydrocarbon well-holes as the property of the Bolivian state?

Question 3: Are you in agreement that YPFB should be 'refounded' in order for the Bolivian state to recover the property of the Bolivian people's shares in capitalised oil companies, such that it can continue to participate throughout the productive chain of hydrocarbons?

Question 4: Are you in agreement with President Carlos Mesa that gas should be used as a strategic resource in order to secure practical and sovereign access to the Pacific Ocean?

Question 5: Are you in agreement with the export of gas as part of a national policy that: covers the consumption of gas by Bolivians; helps to develop the industrialisation of gas in the national territory; charges taxes and/or royalties from the oil companies up to a level of 50 percent of the productive value of gas; and uses resources from exports primarily for education, health, roads and employment?

Source: CNE

6
Evo Morales, the MAS and Elite Resistance to Change

The preceding chapter demonstrated how restructuring efforts began to unravel in the late 1990s, despite an increase in multilateral financing, and an intensification of the coordination between MDIs and the Banzer/Quiroga and Sánchez de Lozada governments. The recomposition of labour and indigenist movements in times of dwindling growth and government repression of coca growers and contraband generated a series of labour victories, which eventually led to the landslide election of Evo Morales to the Bolivian Presidency in December 2005.

The election of Evo Morales signalled the conclusion of a long crisis that had defined, for a quarter of a century, the inter-related developmental cycles of liberalisation and internationalisation.The discourse of the MAS leadership, in particular of Vice President Alvaro García Linera and the group of intellectuals surrounding him (the collective *La Comuna*), and the manifest sympathy shown by Venezuelan and Cuban Presidents Hugo Chávez and Fidel Castro towards the MAS government led Conservative European and US pundits to throw the MAS into the basket of an immature radical left instrumentalised by Chávez, into which Ecuador's Rafael Correa and Nicaragua's Daniel Ortega were later thrown (*Financial Times* 2006; *The Economist* 2006a; 2006b; 2006c).[1] This 'crypto-communist' left was contrasted to the mature social democratic governments elected in 2006 in Brazil, Uruguay, Peru, Argentina and Chile on the one hand and to the conservative allies of the US government in Mexico and Colombia on the other. The map of Latin America thus was redrawn by well-established organisations quantifying democracy and freedom as 'red', 'pink' and 'blue', each carrying varying degrees of 'democracy', 'freedom' and 'stability'.[2]

Four years have passed since the 2005 elections. This time span offers us the opportunity to pause and reflect on the incumbency of Evo

Morales, the achievements and shortcomings of his administration. It allows us to discern patterns of continuity and change in Bolivia's domestic and foreign relations, and to measure the extent to which the conceptualisation of the state offered in the introduction of this book holds up to empirical evidence. The Morales-sponsored reforms have generated vigorous and sometimes violent resistance by Bolivian elites, both within and beyond the state, spearheaded by business organisations, regional Civic Committees, and conservative political parties (Eaton 2007). Bastions of the opposition in the state – the senate, the prefectures, municipalities – have also hindered and redirected social change (Do Alto and Stefanoni 2008). How have broader social struggles transformed the Bolivian state in the past three years (2006-2008), and how has the penetration of government agencies by indigenist, nationalist and socialist forces represented by or allied with the MAS affected the institutional balance of social forces in Bolivia? How has, in turn, the MAS leadership been transformed by its newfound capacity to organise subjection in Bolivia? What was the electoral programme of the MAS and what were the aims of its supporters? How has it attempted to lay the groundwork for a 'movement towards socialism', and to what extent has it achieved its aims? What have been, in turn, the aims and identity of the Bolivian opposition and what political strategy have they employed in resisting or redirecting change?

These domestic developments – traversed by transnational elite collaboration with domestic forces to oppose MAS-sponsored reforms – should be placed within worldwide and macro-regional processes of social and institutional change. We must break internal-external dichotomies by investigating how domestic and foreign relations intersect in the institutions of the state. The election of Evo Morales forms part of a hemispheric rejection of neoliberalism and imperialism. It has therefore significantly changed relationships between the Bolivian state, the US, and MDIs. How have the US government, the multilateral donor community and transnational capital reacted to Morales's investiture and his reform project and how has the Morales government managed its relationship with transnational elite forces? How have alternative macro-regionalist projects such as the *Alternativa Boliviariana Para los Pueblos de Nuestra America* (ALBA) transformed Bolivia's foreign relations? There is no space to address the issue of how the intensifying regionalisation of commerce and growing Chinese demand for Bolivia's commodities (including lithium for the car industry) is changing the geoeconomics of Bolivia's production relations (see table 6.8), and how the worldwide economic crisis will affect, in the medium term, the nationalisation project of the Morales government, and its relationship with MDIs.

Addressing these questions will facilitate an understanding of the extent to which the incumbency of Evo Morales and the policies that his government has implemented signal a radical shift away from, or a structural rupture with, the reforms undertaken by successive administrations since the hyperinflationary crisis of 1985.

A clear distinction must be made between the destabilising tactics of the US State Department, the DEA and USAID on the one hand, and the engagement of the Morales administration by the rest of the donor community. The latter has been far more effective in sustaining the Bolivian state's protection of private property as well as fiscal and monetary discipline. The process of internationalisation of the Bolivian state under way since the 1950s, and intensified since 1985 seems to be persisting, and seems to be redirecting Morales-sponsored reforms in Bolivia. However, the continued integration of the Bolivian state into global governance institutions enters in contradiction with the alternative macro-regional project built in collaboration with Venezuelan, Cuban, Nicaraguan and Ecuadorian governments. Concurrent internal and external institutional struggles are thus placing the Bolivian state on new and unpredictable developmental paths, however within the restricted bounds of alternative capital accumulation projects.

In order to address aforementioned questions, the chapter has a sevenfold structure: it begins by assessing the emerging balance of social forces in Bolivia, focusing on the increasing polarisation between indigenist and criollo movements and their respective societal projects and hegemonic strategies. It then analyses the programme of the MAS and the conflicts that surrounded and defined the ratification of a new Constitution. Thirdly, it focuses on the substantial sticking-points of the MAS's constitutional project: land reform and the re-nationalisation of Bolivia's strategic jewels, emphasising that these issues are the nexus between the Bolivian government, other state agencies, foreign capital and the donor community. It then focuses on the struggles surrounding the various referenda (on Autonomy Statutes, revocation of President and Prefects, and finally Constitution) that took place in 2008 and January 2009. It subsequently analyses US interference in Bolivia's domestic politics and the multilateral lines of conflict generated by TNCs, the donor community and the ALBA. I conclude that the Morales government has retained its authority in part thanks to the transcendence of its bilateral relationship with the US government, its engagement of MDIs and the necessary transformation of imperialistic relations within the Latin American space. Contemporary state transformations validate a conceptualisation of the state as a contradictory organisation of subjection.

The Emerging Balance of Social Forces: Revisiting Indigenism and Social Transformations

The contemporary development of Bolivian social relations and state are inextricably tied to what Braudel (1980) conceptualised as the *longue durée*. The causes of the 2005 election of Evo Morales must concurrently be sought in the restructuring efforts of the 1985-2005 era, the struggle for democratisation between 1978 and 1985, the National Revolution of 1952, the economic depression and Chaco War political struggles of the 1930s and 1940s, but also in post-independence, colonial and Incaic history. As pointed out in chapter 2, the essential contradiction defining Bolivia since colonial times has been one between a dominant *criollo* (white, of European descent) bloc of forces co-opting urban *mestizos* (mixed-race), and subaltern indigenous nations.[3] This antagonism fuses production and race relations of domination. It is defined by and is constitutive of the broader contradictions underlying capital globalisation on the one hand and international relations on the other, in particular between Bolivia, neighbouring states, the US and lately the emergent South and East Asian powers.

As demonstrated in chapter 2, organised resistance to *criollo* dominance and foreign imperialism has taken a variety of shapes since the colonial era. In the second half of the twentieth century and until the late 1980s, the struggle was spearheaded by the miners' union (FSTMB), which controlled the trade COB, and to a lesser extent by Leninist, Trotskyite and socialist political parties (Lora 1987). A third substantive political front opened in the late 1970s with the formation of the CSUTCB. Indigenous communities were transformed by military repression in the mid-1970s from a conservative social force into revolutionary movements allied in 1978-1979 with the urban proletariat against the *junta* led by General Banzer (Zavaleta 1983; Rivera 1983). The CSUTCB and its political party offspring (the latest being the *Movimiento Indigena Pachakuti* [MIP] headed by ex-CSUTCB leader Felipe Quispe), while cooperating with the COB and FSTMB, undermined their Marxist-based discourse by articulating a new ideology of *revolutionary indigenism* (Rivera 2007). This communitarian discourse has contrived the roots of contemporary indigenous formations in an idealised pre-colonial past, and has somewhat paradoxically been bolstered by the emergence of a *burguesia chola* (see chapter 5).

Indigenous nationalism runs against Bolivian nationalism, which is historically a *criollo* construct serving to repress indigenous identity and organisation, especially since the 1952 integrationist National Revolution, and which continues to inspire domestically-oriented capitalists, urban-based trade unions, socialist parties, the army and much of the written press, in a variety of forms (Sanjinés 2004). In the Self-Other logic of zero-sum nationalist rivalries, indigenous nationalism can only realise itself by suppressing the Bolivian construct, or by dissolving itself further within the Bolivian hegemonic ideal of independence. This is the fundamental line of discursive contradiction within the MAS administration, which concurrently advocates nationalist and indigenist forms of emancipation (Lavaud 2007). The indigenist discourse seems to have overshadowed traditional nationalist ideologies in the past decade, generating a tectonic shift in the discourse of organised labour from Marxist critiques of capitalism and foreign imperialism, to critiques of neoliberalism and of indigenous exclusion and repression.

However, just as a third front was opening up in the 1980s, the Bolivian microcosm was becoming far more complex as it underwent accelerating change. These social transformations effectively conditioned the reconstitution of a self-consciously working class movement into a heterogeneous and multiple *plebeian mass* (García 2000, 2001).

The emergence of a 'plebeian mass' caused the proliferation of organisations forcing the COB and CSUTCB to share the centre stage of resistance with a plethora of smaller associations, giving a multifaceted and fluid form to subaltern resistance and consequently to *criollo* domination itself (Lemoine 2005; Crabtree 2005). The organisational core of the MAS, the union of coca farmers from the Chapare region – many of whom were laid off and relocated miners who retained their organisational capacity through the 1990s and early 2000s (see chapter 5) –, is only one element of this wide array of movements. The MAS won the elections at a point in time when the lines of conflict had palpably multiplied into innumerable struggles for the defence of local, sectoral and national/ethnic interests, and become potentially unmanageable.

The principal achievement of the MAS has been to harness these various lines of resistance and become the overarching organisational force opposing neoliberal restructuring, internal colonialism and indigenous exclusion (MAS 2008a). The MAS leadership achieved the seemingly impossible feat of channelling the symbolic power of nationalist, class-based and indigenist discourses into a persuasive discursive whole centred on two fundamental issues reminiscent to those of the National Revolution of 1952: agrarian reform and the re-nationalisation of privatised corporations (Do Alto and Stefanoni 2008). The MAS received 53.7 percent of the popular vote in the 2005 general elections (combining congressional and presidential elections), with a turnout of 84.5 percent, the highest in Bolivia since 1978 (Zavaleta 1983: 26; see tables 5.1, 5.2 and 5.3).

Bolivia's governing conservative political parties, entrenched in the Upper and Lower Houses of Parliament since the collapse of the second Gonzalo Sánchez de Lozada government (see previous chapter), were utterly disorganised. While the MNR was positively delegitimised by the massacres of *Octubre Negro*, the transnational leadership of the MIR and ADN was attempting to remodel these political parties in order to avoid a landslide by Morales. The foundation of the political parties *Poder Democrático y Social* (PODEMOS) by ex-President Jorge Quiroga (September 2005) and *Frente de Unidad Nacional* (thereafter *Unidad Nacional* [UN]) by ex-Minister of Planning Samuel Doria Medina (December 2003) was designed to create a facade of novelty and of rejection of the past (unpalatable political figures and policies, corruption and repression). Nonetheless PODEMOS and UN were not effective enough to conceal their manifest agglutination of *criollo* and *mestizo* businessmen, politicians and technocrats that had respectively filled the ranks of the ADN and MIR. Quiroga (ADN-PODEMOS) obtained 28.6 percent of the vote in the 2005 presidential elections and Doria Medina (MIR-UN), was a distant third with 7.8 percent (See tables 5.1).

The MAS thus obtained an absolute majority in the lower house of parliament (72 out of 130 deputies) yet the Senate remained an institutional stronghold of Conservative forces (15 out of the 27 seats), controlled by PODEMOS (13 seats) in a conservative alliance with the much diminished MNR (1 seat) and the UN (1 seat). Furthermore, the MAS failed to win Bolivia's first departmental/prefectural elections, taking control of only 3 out of 9 prefectures (Oruro, Potosí and Chuquisaca) (see table 6.1). This institutional fragmentation has been a thorn in the side of Evo Morales, as prefectures and the senate remain bastions of institutional resistance to the political programme of the MAS (Do Alto and Stefanoni 2008).

Table 6.1: Prefectural Elections, December 2005

Department	Prefect elected (previous/current party)	Percentage of Votes	Participation rate (%)
La Paz	José Luis Paredes Muñoz (MIR/PODEMOS)	38	86.6
Potosí	Mario Virreira Iporre (MAS)	41	80.6
Oruro	Alberto Luis Aguilar Calle (MAS)	41	88.7
Chuquisaca	David Sánchez Heredia (MAS)	42	82.7
Cochabamba	Manfred Reyes Villa (NFR/AUN)	48	86.1
Santa Cruz	Rúben Costas Aguilera (APB)	48	81.4
Tarija	Mario Cossío Cortez (MNR/ERCC)	46	84.1
Beni	Ernesto Suárez Sattori (ADN/PODEMOS)	45	81.3
Pando	Leopoldo Fernández Ferreira (ADN/PODEMOS)	48	83.6

NB: APB (Autonomía Para Bolivia): formed by Ruben Costas to allow him to participate in the 2005 Prefectural elections. AUN refers to Alianza de Unidad Cochabambina, and ERCC to Encuentro Regional: Camino al Cambio. These two departmental electoral fronts agglutinated business and civic organisations, and the NFR and MNR party apparatuses respectively.

Source: CNE.

As emphasised in preceding chapters, Bolivian *criollo* elites are not devoid of internal power struggles, as transnational and domestic elite blocs have been traversed by spatially differentiated subaltern challenges in the regions of the *Altiplano* (Western highlands), the valleys, and the *Oriente* (Eastern lowlands). A significant fraction of *Cruceño* elites has advocated sovereignty for 'their' region since the 1950s by forming the *Comité Civico Pro-Santa Cruz* (CCPSC) in 1957 to defend the (successful) appropriation of 11 percent of rents on oil exports. The latter have generated significant fiscal resources for the departmental administration and maintained latent the regional bloc's separatist sentiments as their predominance in the national administration, political parties and business confederation was increasing. The CCPSC leadership has barely veiled its white supremacist ideology and the close relationship of its members with the fascist political party FSB is well documented (Zavaleta 1983; Antezana 1983; Dieterich 2006).

Overshadowing these regional elite rivalries, the election of Evo Morales has arguably unified the capitalist class interests of domestically-oriented and transnational business fractions on the one hand, and the caste/racial consciousness of *Paceño* and *Cruceño* elites on the other. Economic and ideological convergence against a broader enemy fostered their coalescence around civil and state institutions such as PODEMOS, the FUN/UN, the senate, the prefectures, the CCSPC and business organisations. Indeed, a National Democratic Council (CONALDE) has been formed as an opposition bloc made up of five provincial governors, business associations, conservative civic groups, and legislators of the PODEMOS party.[4] The strategic nucleus of resistance to the Morales government has become the CCPSC, led by Germán Antelo – signalling that resistance to the MAS, in the streets and in the state (including the two houses of parliament but especially at the departmental and municipal levels of the administration), is now spearheaded by *Cruceño* businessmen and landowners, while professional politicians of the Altiplano persist in the Senate and Congress to undermine the legal projects of the MAS. The CCPSC is articulated with the political parties that dominated the executive and legislative organs of the state until 2005,[5] but also with business organisations congealed in the CAINCO and the CAO, among other organisations.[6] Since the early days of the capitalisation process (post-1995), high level managers of the transnational hydrocarbons corporations, through their membership in Bolivia's Chamber of Hydrocarbons, have also participated in the board of directors of the CAINCO (whilst ignoring the national business confederation located in La Paz, the CEPB, aggravating the increasingly provincial status of its leadership and rendering it politically irrelevant until 2008) (Claure Quezada 2008; Soliz 2004b), and lobby against central government taxation, whilst supporting regional developmental policies (see also chapter 3).

These business federations thereby constitute an elastic institutional fabric cultivating the strategic/programmatic union of foreign TNCs (investing primarily in hydrocarbons and banking) and export-led agribusiness, and a formidable platform for the projection of their power against the MAS government. The CAINCO, CCPSC and CAO have also engineered a strategy of 'direct diplomacy' whereby delegations of business leaders visit the European Commission, the US government, Brazil and Argentina to muster international support for the protection of private property but also for the autonomist demands of the *Media Luna*.[7]

The CCPSC does not merely attempt to resist the MAS through formal institutional actions and the deployment of an autonomist discourse, but also employs terroristic tactics in the streets via its youth organisation, the *Cruceñista* Youth Union (*Unión Juvenil Cruceñista* [UJC]). The UJC was set up in 1957 as the CCPSC's shock troops, a quasi-paramilitary organisation using 'extra-legal' means to defend the '*Camba* identity' and fight the government-induced debasement of the Camba 'nation' (*El Deber* 2006; Eid 2008).[8] Its leader boasted 80,000 members in 2007 (145,000 according to newspaper *La Razón*) between 14 and 35 years of age (Eid 2008), and a 'guard of honour' made up of 200 youth in peace time – which increases to 1,500 in times of crisis – (*El Deber* 2007), who all receive military training and own fire weapons (*La Razón* 2008b). The UJC has actively participated in the intimidation of indigenous immigrants and particularly MAS supporters in Santa Cruz since 2003 – going, for example, on a pre-dawn rampage in *Kolla* markets in Santa Cruz in August 2007, attacking vendors with baseball bats and racial slurs; sending death threats to the President of the *Assemblea Permanente por los Derechos Humanos* (Permanent Human Rights Assembly) who had excessively defended indigenous rights in the region,[9] kidnapping and beating Cuban doctors bestowing medical services to low-income patients in Santa Cruz; and on the 10th of September 2008, raiding state-owned institutions in the city, including its television station, the telecommunications corporation Entel, and the tax-collection agency. These operations, mediatised as 'isolated' acts by 'uncontrolled' youth are designed by the CCPSC to provoke a coercive response by the government and thereby muster international sympathy and domestic support for the CCSPC (COHA 2008b).

The concurrent upheavals in the *Altiplano* (Highlands) and entrenchment of *criollos* in the *Media Luna* (East and South of the country) have augmented the centrifugal tendencies of the Bolivian national formation. The *criollo* bloc, facing the possibility of its own demise, has successfully galvanised a significant fraction (potentially a majority) of the urban population in the Media Luna by emphasising the racial distinction between *Cambas* (natives of the lowlands) and *Kollas* (indigenous peoples from the Highlands) and denouncing the 'invasion' of their territory by the latter, proposing internal migration controls. A discourse contrasting a backward and reactionary Altiplano on the one hand, and a dynamic and modern *Oriente* on the other, has been particularly effective in generating substantial popular support among urban dwellers in Santa Cruz.[10] *Criollo* secessionist ambitions are nevertheless undermined by pervasive Aymara and Quechua immigration from the Altiplano since the 1970s, whose support for the

MAS, at least in rural areas and in the extensive shantytowns surrounding the city of Santa Cruz, is potentially secured by Morales's universal pension, minimum wage and land reform programmes, to which I will return (Inter Press Service 2008b).[11]

The Constituent Assembly and the New Constitution

Evo Morales was elected on the political platform of rolling back neoliberalism, and decolonising Bolivia's society and state. The electoral programme of the MAS, couched in nationalist rhetoric – with sometimes inconsistent classist, indigenist and internationalist undertones – reasserted Bolivia's sovereignty in the international system, founding the 'movement towards socialism' upon seven pillars: 1) above all, and as way to legally ground the MAS's 'revolutionary' and 'democratic' struggle, the election of a Constituent Assembly; 2) an 'agrarian revolution' to redistribute unproductive state- and privately-owned landholdings to indigenous communities; 3) the re-nationalisation of privatised corporations in strategic sectors (in particular hydrocarbons and mining) as a pivot for industrialisation in other sectors; 4) an ambitious social welfare programme to redistribute the income generated by gas and mineral exports; including an increase in the legal minimum wage (see below), the implementation of a *Renta Dignidad* (universal pension scheme involving a monthly payment of bol.200, or $26 for pensioners, financed by gas receipts, at an annual cost of $260 million for the Treasury), the *Bono Madre-Niño*, which provides for free healthcare to pregnant women and bol.1800 over two years for the child, expected to cost $100 million per year, and which recently secured WB financing, and the *Bono Juancito Pinto,* which allocates bol.200 to parents per child in primary school in order to stimulate child schooling (*Reuters* 2006; *El Deber* 2009); 5) a creative administrative and fiscal decentralisation articulating various forms of 'autonomy' – departmental, municipal, indigenous; 6) the submission of two laws ('Tijera' and 'Marcelo Quiroga Santa Cruz', approved by Congress in August 2007) to generate government accountability, fight corruption, reduce waste in state administration, and bring to trial Gonzalo Sánchez de Lozada and his Government Ministers, responsible for massacres in the Gas War of October 2003; and 7) support the alternative regionalist movement promoted by Venezuelan President Hugo Chávez, enshrined in the ALBA (Stefanoni 2005; *Bolpress* 2006; MAS 2008a; 2008b).

In order to address popular demands for the radical overhaul of the social and institutional structure of Bolivia, the MAS took a legalist approach, whereby the creation of a new Constitution would synthesise various social interests and create a new ('refound') Bolivia (*El Mundo* 2007a).[12] The constitutional bet of the MAS was a dangerous one because it signified playing on the turf of the opposition by confronting sometimes barely literate farmers against hardened lawyers and politicians – whilst positioning their best and brightest in the government and the legislature.[13] The Constituent Assembly was invested on the 2nd of July 2006 and began its deliberations on the 6th of August, Bolivia's Independence Day. Based in the capital city of Sucre, it was assigned a mandate of twelve months to agree on a draft Constitution. From the very beginning, the assembly suffered delays caused by procedural issues, in particular the majority needed to adopt Constitutional articles. In the face of attempts by MAS delegates to change the rules of the Constituent assembly (by authorising the adoption of the Constitutional text by an absolute majority), the minority opposition insisted that a two thirds majority be required for the approval of individual articles of the Constitution. Riding a wave of support following its nationalisation of extractive industries a couple of months earlier, the MAS had obtained a majority of seats in the election of the assembly – 137 out of 255 seats, but 34 seats short of a two thirds majority.

After five months of procedural deliberations, the MAS caved in, conferring an effective veto right to the opposition over contentious articles. Left with seven months to write a Constitutional text, the minority opposition caused subsequent delays through protracted struggles over issues of fiscal and administrative decentralisation and the legal status of departments, municipalities and indigenous communities (Do Alto and Stefanoni 2008: 104-107). The issue of rents from hydrocarbons exports (the *Impuesto Directo a los Hidrocarburos* – IDH), of which 11 percent (of massively increasing gas revenue) is allocated to prefectures, was particularly contentious, because the MAS sought to transfer it to the central government's *Tesoro General de la Nación* (Treasury) to finance a universal pension scheme (see below). Just as the fiscal resources devolved in the mid-1990s to municipalities financed indigenist organisations (Kohl and Farthing 2005), the IDH financially bolsters one of the institutional bastions of the opposition and effectively fuels autonomist discourses: indeed, 'Without the IDH, autonomy is a vehicle without gasoline' (Inter Press Service 2008a). These lengthy delays forced the Assembly to postpone the deadline for the approval of the Constitution to the 14th of December 2007.[14]

The delays of the Constituent Assembly bought the opposition time to reorganise itself and leave its trenches by systematically undermining any article that would challenge the status quo while rearticulating a discourse centred on departmental autonomy as a democratic counterweight to the centralising and authoritarian tendencies of the MAS government.[15] The opposition also introduced the not-so-superficial theme of the *capitalía plena* (full capital), the transfer of the executive and legislative branches of the state from La Paz to the dormant city and nominal capital of Bolivia, Sucre. The logic of the opposition was that the *capitalía plena* would shift the administrative centre of gravity away from the La Paz-El Alto agglomeration and undercut Aymara influence. It also serves the geopolitical aim of adding prefectural support to the Media Luna and hence dividing the MAS (considering that the prefecture of Sucre is controlled by the MAS). Besides its unviable financial cost, the strategy was highly successful in galvanising the Civic Committee of Sucre and creating a violent mass movement coalescing around parochial interests (Crabtree 2007a).

The Civic Committee of Sucre duly insisted on the incorporation of the issue in constitutional deliberations of the Constituent Assembly, which convened in the city of Sucre. The refusal of the MAS delegates to do so incensed the Civic Committee, which organised violent protests in the city (leading to four deaths and hundreds of injuries) in August 2007 and forced the President of the Constituent Assembly, Silvia Lazarte, to suspend the deliberations for one month in September 2007 (Do Alto and Stefanoni 2008: 107-109). As violence was spiralling out of control in Sucre, Morales announced publicly the holding of a revocatory referendum on his Presidency and the Prefects in 2008, placing hope on his high charisma and popularity.[16] By extension, this referendum would fully legitimise his Presidency and bolster a Constitution now associated with the MAS administration. Violence was nevertheless only partially quelled, inducing the government to order the relocation of the assembly in Oruro on December 8 in order to approve the Constitutional draft before the 14 December deadline. The opposition duly boycotted the proceedings in order to undermine the legitimacy of the Constitutional text, although delegates of the small political party UN did attend the vote (153 delegates in total were present) (*Al Jazeera* 2007). With the absence of the opposition, the assembly speedily approved the 411 article Constitutional text proposed by the MAS by an overwhelming majority – expectedly well in excess of the two thirds required for the adoption of the text; however, the majority of the new Constitution's articles were passed with more than 140 delegates in favour, indeed close to the two thirds majority that the opposition had insisted upon.[17]

Following months of struggles by the opposition to undermine the legitimacy of the Constitutional text and the effectiveness of the Morales administration (see next section), the Morales government accepted to revise some of the more unpalatable articles of the Constitution in order to swing PODEMOS and the FUN (or parts of them) behind approval of the Constitutional referendum. Under the auspices of the *Fundación Boliviana de Democracia Multipartidaria* (FBDM), financed by the SIDA, and the German-funded Instituto Latinoamericano de Investigaciones Sociales (ILDIS), behind closed doors negotiations were undertaken by moderates Carlos Börth (Senator for PODEMOS), Carlos Romero (MAS, current Minister for Rural Development) and Samuel Doria Medina (FUN) with the active participation of foreign ambassadors and representatives of MDIs. By consciously isolating hardliners from the negotiating table, the MAS and CONALDE achieved a consensus on a revised constitutional text (*La Prensa* 2008). The revisions of the Constitution focused primarily on limiting Presidential terms (to two), maintaining plurinominal constituencies rather than the exclusively uninominal constituencies propounded by the original Constitutional text, and clarifying the definitions of the different types of autonomies.

The Constitution, approved on 25 January 2009, enshrines various key principles which will significantly reshape Bolivia's institutional form and consolidate the power of Evo Morales while undercutting that of the opposition (Asamblea Constituyente de Bolivia 2007). It defines Bolivia not merely as a multicultural (as the previous Constitution defined it) but a *multinational* state (article 1 of the Constitution), which entails the defence of indigenous communities' right to territorial sovereignty – the complete control over renewable resources and shared control with the state over non-renewable resources (article 2). Indigenous sovereignty, despite arguments to the contrary, indubitably enters in contradiction with the cohesion of the national state, but may indeed reflect the state of affairs in rural areas – it also serves the strategic purpose of undermining departmental autonomy through municipal powers but also through the creation of a new sub-national administrative level of 'democratically-defined', autonomous *provinces* constituted by contiguous municipalities (article 281), which inevitably cuts across departments and undermines their capacity to enjoy full legislative and executive authority over their (article 282). Another concession to indigenists is judicial reform, which gives equal weight to indigenous and existing justice systems through the principle of 'juridical pluralism' (article 179). The 'plurinational' Constitutional Court (*Tribunal Constitucional Plurinacional*) will be formed by an equal number of judges representing indigenous and non-indigenous justice systems (article 198). Judges of both the Constitutional Court and the Supreme Court (the latter being the highest court of 'ordinary', as opposed to 'indigenous' justice) will be elected by universal suffrage rather than appointed by the Parliament (articles 183 and 199).

The shape of the upper house of parliament has been transformed: while the Chamber of Deputies has been left unchanged (130 Congressmen), that of Senators – renamed Chamber of Departmental Representatives increased (36 – four per department – from 27). The mixed system of uninominal and plurinominal constituencies has been maintained, although a small number of seats in the lower house are now reserved for indigenous representatives. The proposal to eliminate the Senate – in which politicians of the *Media Luna* (Tarija, Beni and especially Pando), are over-represented – was abandoned at the last minute. Presidential elections has also be reformed: rather than being elected by Congress in case no candidate obtains an absolute majority, the President will be elected through a second round of elections, a system of 'doble vueltas' already adopted in most other Latin American countries (article 167).

Furthermore previous restrictions on consecutive Presidential terms have been removed, permitting the participation of Evo Morales and of his Vice President, Alvaro García Linera (article 169) in the 2009 general elections.[18] This latter proposal – although far from aberrant in placed in relation to advanced liberal democracies –, does demonstrate a tendentious *caudillismo* (reliance on an authoritarian strongman) in the MAS, and arguably signals a fundamental weakness of the government: the constellation of social forces that voted for Morales has been united at least as much by his charismatic personality as his programme. It is not incidental that the slogan accompanying every new governmental policy is *Bolivia cambia, Evo cumple* ('Bolivia changes, Evo performs'). Indeed, the government 'of social movements' witnesses a concentration of power in the person of Morales, who not only remains party leader but heads a coordinating body for each institution with a MAS presence (government and parliament, national party leadership, Constituent assembly, associated social organisations) (Do Alto and Stefanoni 2008: 113). It is accordingly doubtful that the MAS can politically outlive Evo Morales.

Nationalisation and Land Ownership: The Sticking Points

The ownership of means of production and land are arguably the most fundamental issues tackled by the Constitution. Nationalisation and land ownership have expectedly emerged as the nexus of the showdown between Conservative and indigenist forces. The Constitution promotes a mixed economic structure, or rather the articulation of two structures – capitalist and communitarian. As a concession to domestic and transnational business interests and to multilateral governance institutions, it enshrines collective ownership in indigenous communities (*ayllus*) but defends private property in the rest of the national territory. It however reasserts the state's ownership of natural resources, indicating the government's aim to enhance the state's grip on the mining sector (MAS 2008c).

Land reform (Morales's 'agrarian revolution') has constituted by far the most problematic issue, leading observers to contend that 'the class struggle in Bolivia is taking the form of an agrarian confrontation' (Antón 2008): under the terms of the reform, eventually 124,000 km2 of state-owned and, eventually, unproductive privately-owned land larger than 5,000 hectares,[19] mostly located in Santa Cruz, are to be redistributed to *ayllus* or colonists from the Altiplano over the next five years. It signals a strategy by the government to intensify indigenous migration from the *Altiplano* towards the *Media Luna* in order to undercut the secessionist ambitions of *Cruceño* elites while directly antagonising agribusiness, which finances and organises the CCPSC and has spearheaded the autonomist movement.[20] It also responds to an excessive concentration of land in a few hands, which violates the Constitution currently in force (the latter warrants the expropriation by the state of private land exceeding an area of 50,000ha). Indeed, according to the National Institute for Agrarian Reform (*Instituto Nacional de Reforma Agraria)*, 15 families own an area exceeding altogether 550,000ha, while 35 families own areas exceeding 10,000 ha each. A small landowning fraction will therefore be affected by the land reform.[21]

Nationalisation, on its side, has infuriated Prefects and the CCPSC not because of nationalisation *per se*, which has significantly increased the rents from gas exports (the IDH) allocated to the prefectures (from $291 million to $737 million, 440 of which are directed to gas-producing regions), but because the Morales government and the new Constitutional text link nationalisation to pension reform. It thus uses a significant portion of the IDH towards the direct financing of a pension system based on universal entitlement. At an estimated annual cost of $260 million, 676,000 Bolivians above 60 years of age began to receive monthly payments of 200bol ($26) on February 1st 2008. The direct transfer significantly undercuts the resource base of one of the opposition's strongholds and increased the popularity of the government at a crucial point in time, prior to the referenda on departmental autonomy. The CONALDE and CCPSC, whilst accusing the central government of 'confiscating' their rightful windfall rents, have been unable to effectively challenge this progressive and popular policy (*Inter Press service* 2008a).

Referenda: Constitution and Autonomy Statute

Congress voted in February 2008 to hold a referendum on the Constitution on the 4th of May. MAS supporters gathered around the building and prevented several opposition Congressmen from attending the vote, fuelling accusations by the opposition that the Constitution was illegal and anti-democratic (International Crisis Group 2008). The Civic Committees and Prefects of the Media Luna retaliated by announcing the holding of referenda on a departmental Autonomy Statute in Santa Cruz on the same date, and later in other departments. The Autonomy Statute provides for the election of prefects and of a regional parliament, with powers to legislate on issues ranging from taxation, telecommunications, housing, land and transport. This would thwart the government's plan to redistribute fallow land in the region. Furthermore, the governor would be endowed with the right to sign international agreements, run its own police force and be given immunity from prosecution by national tribunals. The Statute also recognises indigenous rights of Santa Cruz natives, the Chiquitanos and Guaranis, but denies those rights to Aymaras and Quechuas, who have migrated en masse from the Altiplano to Santa Cruz since the 1970s. Despite *criollo* contentions that it 'unifies' Bolivia via decentralisation, this approximates a declaration of independence (*Inter Press Service* 2008c).[22]

The CCPSC, the Prefect of Santa Cruz and the Mayor of the region's capital devoted substantial funds in order to mobilise the Departmental Electoral Court to hold the referendum despite its illegality. By endorsing and organising the referendum, the latter openly disobeyed the CNE in La Paz, indicating an open fracture in the state. The information media – which are overwhelmingly owned by *criollo* elites and have systematically criticised government policies – also mobilised to defend the democratic nature of the referendum (Do Alto and Stefanoni 2008). Despite violent confrontations in Santa Cruz between MAS and autonomist activists, resulting in 30 casualties (including one death), the vote took place as anticipated while the rest of the country was holding its breath. The success of the Statute referendum was to be measured through turnout, considering that the government had advocated a boycott of the referendum. The latter was a relative success for the opposition: a 66 percent turnout resulted in an 86 percent victory for the 'Sí' to departmental autonomy. This signifies close to 50 percent popular support for the discourse of Conservative forces, short of an absolute majority in Santa Cruz but sufficiently high to form an institutional bloc against the government and to legitimise the referenda taking place in Beni, Pando and Tarija the following month, which were all won by autonomists with similar turnouts and results (Crabtree 2008a). The national press (*El Deber, La Razón, El Nuevo Día, Los Tiempos*) expectedly considered the result as a 'triumph for democracy' against MAS authoritarianism, while interestingly the foreign press was divided, either siding with the Bolivian press (*El País, The Economist*) or offering a more sober analysis of the results (*New York Times, Le Monde, Libération*). The relatively high turnout indubitably embodied the most powerful challenge yet to the government, as it de-legitimised and potentially neutralised the Constitution itself. A reconfigured institutional balance of forces emerged which damaged the authority of the MAS and undermined the implementation of further reforms.

The revocatory referendum announced in October 2007 to quell the violence in Sucre was reiterated a few days after the referendum on the Autonomy Statute, in order to overshadow future referenda on regional autonomy. Nevertheless, the opposition astutely struck the government again almost immediately after the government's announcement: the 28 members of Santa Cruz's Departmental Council used the results of the referendum to constitute themselves as a provisional legislative assembly, announcing legislative elections in ninety days. The Prefect of Santa Cruz, Rubén Costas labelled himself 'governor' of the 'autonomous government of Santa Cruz', leading Vice President García Linera to declare that such actions amounted to a coup d'état, legitimising retaliatory coercive action by the government (Fuentes 2008).

Prior to the revocatory referenda, the government seemed to be overwhelmed by blows coming from an increasing number of directions: on the 24th of May 2008, Evo Morales was prevented from entering the city of Sucre for the apparently benign announcement of the distribution of 50 ambulances, credits for the region of Chuquisaca and the construction of 1000 social housing by a large crowd led by Sucre's municipal authorities; the crowd forced a highly symbolic retreat of indigenous supporters of the MAS, the army and the police from the city centre (resulting in 50 casualties); it echoed a similar conflict that had taken place in Cochabamba in January 2007 between urban youth and coca farmers, which had then been tamed by police forces (*El Deber* 2008b). The comparison is relevant in showing that the government and the coercive apparatus of the state, hitherto able to manage violent conflicts, were being torn apart by opposition strongholds in the state. *Criollo* elites were apparently demonstrating more cunning strategic and organisational capacities than the government, as the ideological balance was tipping towards counter-hegemonic regionalist discourses, although they were never able to effectively soil the image of Evo Morales himself. The government, facing a battered opposition, had the initiative until the election of the Constituent Assembly. From then on, the Morales government was forced to react to elite initiatives, but also, yet to a lesser extent, by organised labour (see below). After a short honeymoon period, the state, torn as it was by various lines of resistance, thus struggled to manage social forces that have systematically threatened to overwhelm it. Recent evidence thus validates the conceptualisation of the state proposed in the present research (see chapters 1, 5).

Faced with challenges in the state and in the streets spearheaded by opposition Prefects and regional Civic Committees in the Eastern Provinces, Evo Morales attempted to reassert his authority and legitimise his rule by holding revocatory referenda on his Presidency and for Prefects on the 10th of August 2008, an unprecedented occurrence in Bolivia's history. The personal showdown between Morales and the Prefects of the *Media Luna* was a clear measure of the current balance of social forces. Although highly unlikely in light of the popularity of the welfare policies implemented by the government in preceding months and the aura surrounding Morales's person, a revocation of Morales's Presidency would have probably signified the political collapse of the MAS, the abandonment of the Constitutional project, and the resumption of multiple, unmanageable lines of conflict. The MAS leadership's awareness of this fact began to fissure the government in the run up to the election, as some leaders suggested that the amendment of some of the Constitution's articles would be necessary. The recurrent and ever-increasing calls for dialogue with the opposition over the Constitutional text by a hitherto defiant government demonstrated its vulnerability. Three opposition parties eventually agreed (in late May) to discuss amendments to the Constitution, referred to in the preceding section (Crabtree 2008b).

Morales was ratified in office with 67 percent of the vote, and two prefects of the opposition (in La Paz and Cochabamba) lost their mandate. This crucial electoral victory was nonetheless tempered by the success of four Prefects in the *Media Luna*, including an equally significant victory for Santa Cruz's Prefect Rubén Costas (almost 67 percent of the vote). Moreover, Evo Morales only obtained slightly over 40 percent of the electorate's support in Beni and Santa Cruz, indicating an entrenchment of existing social antagonisms and the relative effectiveness of regionalist discourses in those regions (see tables 6.2 and 6.3). By explicitly associating his persona with the government's Constitutional project, Morales manifestly succeeded in its revitalisation, mobilising tens of thousands of miners, indigenous peasants and trade union leaders to undertake a 200km march on Congress, and obtaining, after long and tense negotiations with opposition Prefects and the CONALDE (*La Razón* 2008a), the ratification by Congress of a revised Constitutional text and of a date (25 January 2009) for two concurrent referenda, on the Constitution itself and on the maximum size of landholdings (either 5,000 or 10,000 hectares) (*Inter Press Service* 2008d).[23]

However, as John Crabtree (2008b) recently pointed out, the referenda were manifestations of the current balance of power in and beyond the state. They signalled that the lines of conflict drawn by Bolivia's forces during Morales's incumbency have been crystallised by the referenda. Most importantly, they indicate that the autonomist discourse of the opposition for the Eastern provinces is currently taking hold. Yet, bolstered by Morales's victory in the revocatory referendum, which reflected the legitimacy of its welfare and economic policies, the unpopular activities of the UJC and the continued support of neighbouring governments and MDIs for the MAS, the population ratified the new Constitution in January 2009.[24] The Constitutional referendum entrenched preceding voting patterns, with a majority of the electorate rejecting the Constitutional text in the *Media Luna*, but indicated a weakening of the opposition in the crucial regions of Tarija and Pando, while the electorate of the contested region of Chuquisaca ratified it (see table 6.4). However, the issue of *latifundia* was far less contentious, as an overwhelming majority of the electorate, in every department, supported a reduction of the maximum legal size of landholdings to 5,000 hectares (see table 6.5).

Cornered by the significant victory of Morales in the revocatory referendum in August 2008, and instead of rearticulating a counter-hegemonic discourse through its media outlets, of consolidating its institutional bastions, and of securing its economic acquis through negotiations and temporary agreements with the government, the opposition declared open war by unleashing its UJC and other autonomist shock troops onto supporters of Morales and conspicuous symbols of central government presence in the *Media Luna* in early

September 2008. The takeover of various factories, roadblocks and sabotage of gas pipelines allowed the government to use force legitimately in order to contain the ultras and to maintain order. Evo Morales declared a state of siege in the north-eastern region of Pando in the face of 30 unprovoked killings perpetrated by individuals accused by the government to be hitmen employed by the opposition Prefect Leopoldo Fernández, who rejected the claim and, undermining his credibility, fled to Brazil before being taken into custody (*The New York Times* 2008c; *International Herald Tribune* 2008).

Table 6.2: Revocatory Referendum: President and Vice-President of the Republic of Bolivia, 10 August 2008.

Question: ***Are you in agreement with the continuation of the process of change led by President Evo Morales Ayma and Vice-President Álvaro García Linera?***

	Yes	No	Participation rate (%)
	(in percent)		
National (9 depts.)	**67.41**	**32.59**	**83.28**
Potosí	84.87	15.13	84.45
La Paz	83.27	16.73	88.37
Oruro	82.99	17.01	87
Cochabamba	70.90	29.10	86.01
Chuquisaca	53.88	46.12	80.72
Pando	52.50	47.50	84.17
Tarija	49.83	50.17	79.8
Beni	43.72	56.28	75.86
Santa Cruz	40.75	59.25	75.94
Valid votes	3,120,909		
Blank	134,098		
Null	115,973		
Registered voters	4,047,706		
Votes cast	3,370,980		
Abstention rate (%)	16.72		

Source: CNE

By overestimating its own hegemonic potential and by underestimating the government's ability to contain the most radical elements within its midst, to project an image of responsibility and to exercise measured coercion, the opposition fuelled its dissolution. In Gramscian terminology, it failed to understand the temporary need to engage in a protracted war of position, and instead it declared an all-out war of movement, which it rapidly lost. The increasingly brutal onslaughts of the opposition eroded the legitimacy of their temporarily (between early 2007 and mid-2008) effective attempts to dissolve the hegemonic bloc built by the Morales administration. The hegemonic cycle initated by the MAS in 2002 is now in full swing, as elite forces prove divided, disorganised and discouraged, and Morales and the MAS won the general elections in December 2009 by a landslide, effectively marginalising left-wing alternatives set up by former allies and facing a conservative electoral bloc hastily constituted behind the controversial and delegitimised figure of Manfred Reyes Villa, Prefect of Cochabamba revoked in the August referendum (Hatheway 2009; see tables 6.6 and 6.7; see also previous chapter).

Table 6.3: Revocatory Referendum: Prefects, 10 August 2008

Question: ***Are you in agreement with the continuation of the policies, actions and management of the Prefect of the department?***

Department	Name of Prefect (Previous/Current Party)	Yes	No	Participation	Result
		(in percent)			
La Paz	José Luis Paredes (MIR/PP)	35.48	64.52	88.33	Revoked
Oruro	Alberto Luis Aguilar (MAS)	50.85	49.15	87.01	Maintained
Potosí	Mario Virreira (MAS)	79.08	20.92	84.42	Maintained
Cochabamba	Manfred Reyes Villa (NFR/AUN)	35.19	64.81	85.96	Revoked
Santa Cruz	Rubén Costas (APB)	66.43	33.47	75.92	Maintained
Tarija	Mario Cossío (MNR)	58.06	41.94	79.8	Maintained
Beni	Ernesto Suárez (ADN/PODEMOS)	64.25	35.75	75.93	Maintained
Pando	Leopoldo Fernández (ADN/PODEMOS)	56.21	43.79	83.75	Maintained

NB: PP (Plan Progreso), formed by Paredes to be allowed to participate in elections.

Source: CNE.

Table 6.4: Constitutional Referendum, 25 January 2009			
Question: ***Are you in agreement with the project of the Political Constitution of the State presented by the Constituent Assembly, and adjusted by the Special Commission for Reconciliation of the National House of Representatives, which includes the consensus reached in the dialogue between the national government, prefects and municipal representatives on autonomy, incorporating the result of the consultation on article 398 to be resolved by the present referendum, and to be promulgated and in force as a new Fundamental Law of the Bolivian State?***			
	Yes	**No**	**Participation rate (%)**
	(in percent)		
National (9 depts.)	**61.43**	**38.57**	**90.24**
Potosí	80.07	19.93	87.51
La Paz	78.12	21.88	92.32
Oruro	73.68	26.32	91.90
Cochabamba	64.91	35.09	92.23
Chuquisaca	51.54	48.46	88.98
Tarija	43.34	56.66	87.20
Pando	40.96	59.04	82.77
Beni	32.67	67.33	84.66
Santa Cruz	34.75	65.25	88.13
Valid votes	3,360,592		
Blank	59,524		
Null	91,583		
Registered voters	3,891,316		
Votes cast	3,511,699		
Abstention rate (%)	9.76		

Source: CNE

The results of the general elections were a clear manifestation of the existing balance of social forces, which is tilting further towards the MAS and its allies. It indicated a consolidation of the overwhelming dominance of the MAS in the Altiplano and valleys, in particular in La Paz, where more than 80 percent of voters supported the MAS. Crucially however, the absolute majority achieved by the MAS in Tarija and the 40 percent vote in Santa Cruz and Pando indicated a clear recession of the Conservative opposition throughout the *Media Luna* and the geographical expansion of the MAS's hegemony. Crucially, the MAS now controls more than two thirds of both houses of representatives, effectively preventing the opposition, by Conservative parties, to any legislative project it might put to the vote. As indicated in table 6.7, the votes by expatriates, which was far more significant in demographic terms than the departments of Beni and Pando, clearly benefitted the

MAS, especially in Argentina. Such clear support by Bolivia's diaspora is enhancing the transnational dimension of the MAS's hegemony.

Table 6.5: Referendum: Maximum Size of Landholdings, 25 January 2009

	5,000 hectares	10,000 hectares	Participation rate (%)
	(in percent)		
National (9 depts.)	**80.65**	**19.35**	**90.14**
Potosí	86.66	13.34	87.48
La Paz	86.25	13.75	92.36
Oruro	83.54	16.46	91.90
Cochabamba	82.44	17.66	92.25
Chuquisaca	79.62	20.38	88.94
Beni	69.72	30.28	83.73
Tarija	68.63	31.37	87.20
Pando	67.10	32.90	82.83
Santa Cruz	65.91	34.09	88.13
Valid votes	2,425,981		
Blank	893,198		
Null	188,551		
Registered voters	3,891,316		
Votes cast	3,507,730		
Abstention rate (%)	9.86		

Source: CNE

US Interference

The domestic onslaughts of the opposition to Morales have been partially defused by the revocatory referenda in August 2008, the ratification of the new Constitution by the population and the landslide victory of the MAS in the general elections of December 2009 (Crabtree 2008, 2009). Domestic struggles, however, did not occur in an international vacuum and must be directly related to US foreign policy in the region. US-financed repression of coca farmers and its vocal support of repressive Bolivian governments in the late 1990s and early 2000s have turned the US government into an obvious culprit for persistent poverty and inequality in Bolivia. Despite its indubitably secondary role in the restructuring of Bolivian social relations, the US state department has remained a powerful symbol of external colonialism. It has propelled charismatic political leaders such as Evo Morales onto the national and international political stage and led the

Morales administration to indiscriminately – and perhaps inappropriately – relate neoliberal restructuring with US dominance in multilateral institutions (IMF, WB, IDB). Since the election of Morales, the US government has maintained a relatively low public profile, leading observers to interpret it as a wait and see approach towards the MAS (Gamarra 2007: 3). Empirical evidence nonetheless demonstrates that the US State Department has remained impressively active in seeking to covertly undermine the Morales administration. On the 11th of September 2008, Morales expelled Philip Goldberg, the United States (US) ambassador to Bolivia, on the grounds that he is 'conspiring against democracy and wants Bolivia to break apart' (*The Guardian* 2008), prompting Venezuela's Hugo Chavez to follow suit in solidarity with Morales (*Reuters* 2008f), and the US to respond by declaring the Bolivian envoy in Washington DC 'persona non grata' (*BBC News* 2008a). Morales later expelled the Drug Enforcement Agency (DEA), and the substitute of Philip Goldberg (*Reuters* 2008g). On its side the Bush administration responded with a series of antagonistic actions, further souring relations with the Bolivian government, by placing Bolivia on a counter-narcotics blacklist on September 16 2008 and later announcing the suspension of the Andean Trade Promotion and Drug Eradication Act (ATPDEA), for failing 'to cooperate with the United States on important efforts to fight drug trafficking' (COHA 2009).[25] How have, then, US ambassadors and the DEA 'conspired' against democracy?

A string of gaffes by US embassy staff has brought light on the covert activities of the United States Agency for International Development (USAID), leading Evo Morales to declare in a diplomatic gathering in August 2007 that 'I cannot understand how some ambassadors dedicate themselves to politics, and not diplomacy, in our country. . . . That is not called cooperation. That is called conspiracy' (Dangl 2008a). In early 2007 the relative of a senior military advisor in the US embassy was detained at the La Paz airport with 500 bullets, purportedly for hunting purposes. In July and again in November 2007, at least three Peace Corps volunteers and a Fulbright researcher were asked by US embassy staff to 'keep tabs' on (provide information on the identity, whereabouts and residence of) Venezuelans and Cubans they met in Bolivia (*ABC News* 2008; *Democracy Now!* 2008). Philip Goldberg engaged in secret meetings with the Prefect of Santa Cruz, Rúben Costa, and the leadership of the CCPSC directly prior to a wave of opposition-sanctioned violence in August 2008, which forced Morales to declare martial law in the department of Pando. These

Table 6.6: General Election Results, 6 December 2009

Party	Presidential candidate	Percent of valid votes	Lower House seats		Upper House seats	
			Seats	Percent	Seats	Percent
MAS	Evo Morales Ayma	64.22	88	67.7	26	72.2
PPB - Convergencia (1)	Manfred Reyes Villa	26.46	37	28.5	10	27.8
UN	Samuel Doria Medina	5.65	3	2.3		
AS (2)	René Joaquino Carlos	2.31	2	1.5		
MUSPA (3)	Ana María Flores	0.51				
Gente	Román Loayza	0.34				
PULSO (4)	Alejo Véliz	0.28				
BSD (5)	Rime Choquehuanca	0.22				
Total Congressional seats			130	100	36	100
Total population (2009)	10,227,299					
Total registered voters (6)	5,139,554					
Foreign registry (7)	170,067					
Votes cast	4,859,440					
Blank votes	156,290					
Null votes	120,364					
Abstention rate (%) (8)	5.05					

(1) PPB (Plan Progreso Bolivia): created in July 2007 by the former Prefect of La Paz, José Luís Paredes - revoked by referendum in August 2008. Managed to attract the support of PODEMOS and other opposition parties in order to form a bloc against the MAS. The absence of Jorge Quiroga in the elections must be noted: heavily criticised for advocating the revocatory referenda, which consolidated the power of Morales and led to the revocation of Prefects Reyes Villa and Paredes, Quiroga left the Presidential race in September 2009.
(2) AS: Alianza Social. Co-founded by René Joaquino, populist mayor of Potosí, and Filemón Escobar, ex union leader and former MAS senator until broke from party in 2005.

(3) MUSPA: Movimiento de Unidad Social Patriótica. Initially led by Loayza, a MAS founder, campesino congressman and key MAS representative in the Constituent Assembly. Loayza, allied to former government spokesman Alex Contreras repudiated by the MAS, left the party in April 2009, accusing Morales of surrounding himself with neoliberal cabinet members and announcing his intent to challenge him in the elections. MUSPA retracted its support for Loayza, who came to replace Victor Hugo Cárdenas at the head of the party Gente, substituting him with businesswoman Ana María Flores.
(4) PULSO: Pueblos por la Libertad y la Soberanía
(5) BSD: Bolivia Social Demócrata
(6) Registration en masse and within an exceedingly short period of time through the *padrón biometrico* (biometric registry) involved a 28.5 percent increase from the 2005 registry and (unproven) allegations by the opposition of fraud.
(7) For the first time in Bolivia's history, Bolivian expatriates were allowed to register and vote in the general elections.
(8) By far the lowest abstention rate in Bolivia's 'democratic' (post-1978) era.

Sources: CNE, INE

meetings induced well-documented allegations that the autonomist shock troops engaged in these terror activities had at least received the blessing of Goldberg for their coordinated activities, if not financial and organisational support by the US embassy (COHA 2009; ABN 2008; ABI 2008).

In light of its success in the 2002 general elections (Evo Morales came second), the MAS was identified by the US government as the most powerful anti-systemic force in Bolivia. A declassified memo released that year explained that a 'USAID political party reform project aims at implementing an existing Bolivian law that would ... over the long run, help build moderate, pro-democracy political parties that can serve as a counterweight to the radical MAS or its successors' (Dangl 2008b). For the past six years, the Bush administration has provided direct financial support and strategic advice to Conservative parties and associations in order to undercut the influence of the MAS. USAID recently established a special Office of Transition Initiatives (OTI) in Bolivia which, in the words of USAID, 'intervenes rapidly and undertakes quick-impact interventions through short-term grants that catalyze broader change' (Weisbrot 2008). Since 2006, this 'support for democracy' has taken the form of strategies promoting administrative and fiscal decentralisation, in order to consolidate state institutions that challenge the central government. The OTI has transferred at the very least $4.5 million to foundations and NGOs used by the Conservative

Table 6.7: General Elections, Valid Votes by Department for the Four Main Parties, 6 December 2009									
	MAS		PPB-Convergencia		UN		AS		Number of total valid votes
	Number	%	Number	%	Number	%	Number	%	
La Paz	1,099,259	80.28	119,248	8.71	110,292	8.05	21,185	1.55	1,430,312
Santa Cruz	441.705	40.91	567,974	52.60	46,451	4.30	13,025	1.21	1,131,779
Cochabamba	569,237	68.82	203,041	24.55	34,804	4.21	9,469	1.14	883,358
Potosí	243,855	78.32	13,238	4.25	7,375	2.37	41,767	13.42	343,669
Chuquisaca	127,995	56.05	76,722	33.60	12,998	5.69	5,885	2.58	253,992
Tarija	114,577	51.09	85,84	38.28	16,513	7.36	3,847	1.72	243,75
Oruro	178,363	79.46	20,17	8.99	13,87	6.18	8,431	3.76	237,887
Beni	60,671	37.66	85.631	53.15	11,897	7.38	1,062	0.66	171,317
Pando	16,334	44.51	18,739	51.07	1,099	3.00	281	0.77	38,275
Expatriates									
Argentina	58,959	92.13	2,039	3.19	911	1.42	647	1.01	66,504
Spain	16,487	48.21	14,719	43.04	2,076	6.07	320	0.94	35.744
US	2,571	31.05	5,055	61.04	506	6.11	62	0.75	8,565
Brazil	13,196	94.95	379	2.73	179	1.29	46	0.33	14,288
Total valid votes	2,943,209	64.22	1,212,795	26.46	258,971	5.65	106,027	2.31	4,859,440

Source: CNE

opposition and white separatist organizations, and to the four autonomist prefects of the *Media Luna* (the departments of Santa Cruz, Tarija, Beni and Pando). Juan Ramón Quintana, Minister of the Presidency, has given the figure of $89 million out of the $134 million of USAID financial assistance in 2007, a quite tremendous sum (*Bolpress* 2007). It might very well be inflated, but certainly even $4 million at Purchasing Power Parity can do significant damage in Bolivia. This funding is spent undermining the legitimacy of the government through media campaigns soiling Evo Morales's image and introducing issues (*capitalia plena*, departmental autonomy, the Venezuelan 'conspiracy') that galvanise parochial popular movements and foster political instability (*Center for Economic and Policy Research* 2008).

Meanwhile, the US-based National Endowment for Democracy, active in the coup d'état against Venezuelan President Hugo Chávez in 2002, has also supported regional polarisation by organising workshops and panels promoting decentralisation and challenging the nationalisation of strategic sectors. The US ambassador's role in the independence of Croatia and Bosnia in the 1990s, and the active participation of *criollos* of Croatian descent (Branco Marinkovic, prominent businessman and head of the CCPSC, is exemplary) (*The New York Times* 2008d), but also Catalan researchers in those workshops has fuelled accusations of attempts to Balkanise Bolivia (Chossudovsky 2008; Garcia Merida 2008).[26] Additionally, both USAID and the DEA pursue to this day their long-standing policy (since the late 1980s) of funnelling assistance funds and providing training and weapons to special police units, purportedly to fight narco-trafficking; yet in light of its spying and subversive activities, one may infer that the US government has sought to fissure and destabilise the coercive apparatus of the state (Weisbrot 2008; *Democracy Now!* 2008).

US financial and strategic support for the three pillars of domestic opposition to the MAS government, (PODEMOS, Civic Committees, and Departmental Prefects) revitalised, if only temporarily, an elite movement on the defensive since *Octubre Negro*.

On its side, the MAS has taken various coercive measures which have ensured its political survival until now. It signed a 'Complementary Accord to the Basic Technical Cooperation Agreement in Defence between the Republic of Bolivia and the Bolivarian Republic of Venezuela', a mutual defence agreement which entails the provision of Venezuelan military support to the Bolivian government in case of an invasion or a civil war (COHA 2006). Numerous Venezuelans and Cubans are undertaking humanitarian work in Bolivia; about 600 Cuban doctors are providing free services in rural areas, in particular in the

Santa Cruz region, the bastion of *criollo* opposition to land reform (Girvan 2008: 6). It is certainly possible that some of these activities are not strictly humanitarian and are rather designed to provide military and strategic support to the government in the *Oriente*. According to sources close to the President interviewed in the summer of 2007, at least 50 Venezuelan economic and military advisors are active in the Presidential palace and key Ministries.[27] The extent of Venezuelan aid and consequent influence on policymaking in Bolivia has been vastly exaggerated in Conservative media, but the diplomatic support offered by Chávez to the Morales government did provide a buffer against more aggressive measures by the US-supported opposition.

The government has begun an ambitious military procurement programme, using Venezuelan funds (at least $50 million in loans since 2006) and windfall tax resources to build two military bases in Santa Cruz and Beni, purchase 100 vehicles, 3 planes and 4 helicopters and other military equipment; it sent 2,500 elite Bolivian troops for training in Venezuela (*The Washington Times* 2007); it increased the salaries of military officers and replaced 56 senior military officers overtly complaining about the 'anti-democratic socialist absolutism' and the 'Cuba-Venezuela orientation' of the Morales government over a 2005 scandal in which they were accused of allowing the dismantlement of 25 anti-aircraft missiles by US technicians, Bolivia's sole anti-aircraft defence (*The New York Times* 2007; COHA 2006). Furthermore, Venezuelan President Chávez announced repeatedly in the media that he would intervene militarily in Bolivia in the event of a civil war (*International Herald Tribune* 2008). The government also signed various agreements on technological cooperation with China, Peru and Argentina. Securing the support of the army has been the cornerstone of the government's struggle against the destabilising activities of the opposition and the US government. Until now, the army has obeyed Morales's orders – taking over the facilities of private hydrocarbons corporations upon the announcement of their nationalisation in May 2006, deploying in mining areas to restore order in the face of violent skirmishes between mining cooperatives and state-employed miners in February 2007, and implementing the state of siege ordered by the government in Pando in September 2008. The army apparently supports the nationalist project of the government in the face of the secessionist ambitions of Media Luna *criollos*, as Bolivian Army General Luis Trigo issued a rare statement the day preceding the holding of the referendum on regional autonomy organised by the CCPSC in May 2008 that condemned it as a threat to national security (*The New York Times* 2008a).

Furthermore, Vice President Alvaro García Linera retains close ties with the radical indigenist *Ponchos Rojos* (Red Ponchos), a guerrilla movement active in the Achacachi region (close to the lake Titicaca) since the 1970s. Its leaders boast, exaggeratingly, 100,000 armed men and have struggled since the late 1970s for the reconstitution of the Aymara territory, the *Jach'a Uma Suyu* (The Omasuyos) which extends from Peru to the North of Chile (*El País* 2007). Evo Morales urged 'our Armed Forces along with the "Ponchos Rojos" to defend our unity and our territorial integrity' at a rally in January 2007 (*Los Tiempos* 2007), and García Linera threatened to mobilise thousands of them in order to defend the Constituent Assembly and the land reform. In November 2007, a shocking video was widely diffused in Bolivian media, showing leaders of the Ponchos Rojos beheading two dogs in front of a large and cheering Aymara crowd in Achacachi, and threatening the same fate to the leadership of the CCPSC and of the Prefects of the *Media Luna* (*La Razón* 2007).

Its association with the Ponchos Rojos has undermined the MAS's progressive image and its popularity in urban areas. Racist lines of antagonism are being drawn and territorialised, fuelling the potential to overwhelm the MAS administration in the process.

TNCs, the Donor Community and the ALBA: Multilateral Lines of Conflict

In stark contrast to subversive US activities in Bolivia, European policymakers and the staff of MDIs have demonstrated a more subtle understanding of the Morales government and have worked towards stabilising the Bolivian space (BBC News 2006a).

MDIs and the Morales Administration

The short-term tactics of MDIs (engagement and cooptation) and the US State Department (elimination) towards the new Bolivian administration have demonstrated profound contradictions. There appears to be reluctance on the part of the donor community to endorse the fragmentation of Bolivia into two or several sovereignties. Instead of antagonising the new democratically elected government, they have systematically engaged it, waiving more than half of Bolivia's foreign debt in 2006 and 2007 (from $4.942 billion in 2005 to $2.142 billion two years later), including the entire stock of debt outstanding to the World Bank, the IMF and the IDB (Gamarra 2007: 43; see also table

4.6). The European Commission, in the meantime, is increasing the $50 million yearly grants it has been offering to the Bolivian Treasury and NGOs since the mid-1990s.[28]

While respecting the will of the people, MDIs have restricted their efforts to locking Bolivia in the global capitalist production structure by fighting the expropriation of Transnational corporations' (TNCs) assets and promoting public-private partnerships between private corporations and the state-owned COMIBOL and YPFB (IMF 2009, 2010). Yet the Morales government's commitment to fiscal and monetary stability, free trade and the defence of private property was never in doubt, in part because the favourable macroeconomic conditions that surrounded its investiture, compounded by the 'generosity' of MDIs. As will be elaborated subsequently, the unprecedented fiscal surplus generated by the rising value of its primary exports and the need to alleviate the inflationary pressures resulting from increased state spending conditioned its commitment to 'responsible' macroeconomic management. However, in order to dispel myths diffused by the media, it ought to be pointed out that the MAS never characterised itself as an avowedly socialist party – unlike Chávez in Venezuela – despite the radical rhetoric of some of its leaders. One can arguably consider the economic programme of the MAS administration as deepening the structural discipline of capital in the Bolivian space, rather than undertaking a movement towards socialism.

Depoliticised state agencies, chief among them the BCB, have remained relatively unscathed, as the incumbency of Juan Antonio Morales until mid-2006 perpetuated a monetarist economic management and price controls which persists to this day.[29] The exchange system remains free of restrictions on current international payments and transfers, and no significant controls on capital flows have been imposed (IMF 2009: 1). Interestingly, one of the pillars of the MAS's programme has become macroeconomic stability, in stark contrast with its more radical electoral rhetoric (MAS 2008c). The ghost of hyperinflation and the debt crisis of the early 1980s continue to haunt the present Bolivian government, which is 'fully aware of the need to maintain macroeconomic stability' and 'to continue with fiscal consolidation efforts' (IMF 2009: 3). Far from delinking from the multilateral institutional complex into which his predecessors had integrated the Bolivian state, the Morales government cooperates with MDIs and the European Commission, partly to accentuate the transcendence of Bolivia's bilateral relationship with the US government.[30]

The macroeconomic programme of the MAS reminds us painfully of Bolivia's pre-1985 state capitalism model, couched in new rhetoric regarding the invention of a rather blurry transition to socialism in the form of 'Andean-Amazonian capitalism' articulating large private and public corporations, primitive capitalism centred on family and kinship networks (artisanship, small commerce), and a 'communitarian' economic organisation as autonomous territorial sovereignties (*Bolpress* 2005).[31] The cornerstone of this form of capital accumulation remains, as in the 1930s, 1950s and late 1960s, the nationalisation of strategic resources. Vice-President García Linera was thus boasting in 2007 that "the Bolivian state has thus increased its control of the GDP by 6 to 7 percent, to 19 percent today. Our objective is to reach 30 percent" (Do Alto and Stefanoni 2008: 99). Arguments that state-ownership and organisation of production through nationalisation constitute a qualitatively distinct form of production (potentially providing a transitional platform towards socialism) fallaciously assume that state and market are two separate and contradictory entities, as both (re)produce the exploitative containment of labour power (Picciotto and Faundez 1978; see chapter 1). State subsidies and price distortions for nationalised sectors are usually branded socialist policy instruments, but are themselves determined by the value of the commodity to be marketed. Such practices are characteristic of capitalist states.

Not incidentally, the IMF (2007, 2009, 2010) has lauded the MAS leadership's fight against corruption and waste in the institutions of the state and the increased efficiency of tax-collecting agencies, although the government has not been able to prevent persistent patronage. In his speech on Bolivia's national day in 2007, President Evo Morales emphasised that IFIs are no longer imposing conditions for economic and state restructuring because Bolivia is already achieving the 'responsible' fiscal and monetary policies advocated by them. The core tenets of neoliberalism – monetary and fiscal discipline, free trade – remain intact.

This does not preclude an improvement in the conditions of workers – as long as terms of trade remain positive – the Gini index decreased to 0.563 in 2007 (no data is yet available for 2008-2009) and is likely to pursue its downward trend with continued growth, controlled inflation and the continuation of the welfare policies expounded earlier. As emphasised in the preceding chapter, low GDP growth between 1985 and 2005 barely matched population growth, signifying a stagnation of real wages. The principal historical constraints on accumulation in Bolivia have been deteriorating terms of trade, corruption and legal insecurity, and above all *social instability*. Returns on investment beyond the hydrocarbon and banking sectors have historically been hindered by tense Bolivian labour relations. Low FDI and domestic capital formation as a proportion of GDP is characteristic of the entire 1985-2005 era, reflecting low business confidence.

TNCs and the Morales Administration

What does this mean for the relationship between the Morales administration and transnational capital? Firstly, that the investiture of Morales did not cause low business confidence and did not destabilise already highly volatile social relations, as argued by the Conservative media referred to earlier. More importantly, that the threat of capital flight and economic collapse brandished by right-wing newspapers and European leaders in May 2006 in the face of nationalisation remains low considering the quasi-exclusive dependence of Bolivian growth on hydrocarbons and mining, and the unprecedented global upsurge in demand for oil, gas, minerals and metals.[32] Even without significant private domestic capital formation – a situation prevalent before Morales's election and not caused by the MAS government, GDP growth has been more robust (circa 4.5 percent in 2006 and 2007, 6 percent in 2008) as the value of exports tripled from $1.6 billion in 2003 to $3.9 billion in 2006, $4.8 billion in 2007 and $6.4 billion in 2008 (50 percent of the value of exports being constituted by hydrocarbons and 30 percent by minerals and metals), generating an unprecedented positive trade balance of $1.409 billion, just as corporate taxation was increasing significantly allowing foreign exchange reserves to grow to $8.317 billion by late 2009 (see tables 6.8 and 6.9).[33]

These windfall profits generated an unprecedented fiscal surplus in 2007 ($1.206 billion) which has turned the Morales administration into a responsible partner of the IMF and the WB. Increasing foreign exchange reserves and liquidity on one hand, and escalating fiscal expenditures on the other, however led to an inflationary upsurge (11.7 percent in 2007, 11.8 percent in 2008), which affected negatively real wages despite a 10 percent increase in the minimum wage by Presidential Decree (DS 29473, 5 March 2008) to 577bol (77 dollars), following a 5 percent increase in May 2007 to 525bol (DS 29116) and a 13.6 increase in May 2006 (DS 28700), in part to secure popular support for the government before the Constitutional referendum, and to demonstrate to trade unions that '*Evo cumple*' (*Fundación Milenio* 2008; INE 2009a). Inflationary pressures were neutralised by the world crisis, which stabilised prices in 2009 and stripped the opposition of its pivotal criticism of the government's economic management. However, wage and other demands by labour have had to be reined it because Morales can simply not, and arguably

Table 6.8: Exports by Product Group, 1970-2007 (in US$ millions)										
	Minerals / metals	Tin	Gold	Zinc	**Hydro-carbons (1)**	**Non-traditional exports (2)**	Manu-factured goods	**Adjustments (3)**	**Total**	**GDP**
1970	205	102	0	-	13	10.5	0.5	23	206	2,521
1975	314	171	0	-	159	63.5	3.5	31.5	505	3,346
1980	639	378	0	41	245	156	39.5	3.5	942	3,916
1985	264	186	5.5	29.5	374	32.5	-	44	628	3,748
1987	207	69	37.5	33	256	106.5	36	51	519	
1989	403	127	44.5	132	214	204	40	98	723	4,511
1991	356	99.5	39	140	241	251	68	88	760	
1993	362	83	76	120	96.5	296	91	44.5	710	5,382
1995	480	89	131	151	130.5	479	141	14.5	1,075	
1997	499	82	111	200	107	647	209	-87	1,166	6,660
1999	397	69	89	154	65	521.5	191	-88	1,051	
2001	340	56	92	119	289	501	167	-71	1,284	7,304
2003	369	75	72	124	491	622	203.5	-87.5	1,598	
2004	457	147	34	152	839	788.5	178	-115	2,146	8,421
2005	546	126	79	201	1,428	709	240	-130.3	2,791	
2006	1,061	145	127	549	2,040	767	366	-371.3	3,863	10,300
2007	1,034	-	-	-	2,268	1,233	-	245	4,780	13,290

(1) Gas has constituted between 80 and 95 percent of all hydrocarbon exports since 1985.

(2) Includes agricultural and manufactured commodities. Chiefly sugar, cotton, coffee and timber in the 1970s and early 1980s. Thereafter soy and rice became prominent exports. Soy boom in early 2000s: Soy exports accounted for $420 million in 2004 - but highly dependent on US-Andean Free Trade Agreement.

(3) Includes exchange rate adjustments, minerals processing, insurance, freight and leased aircraft, re-exports

Sources: BCB; Morales (2008: 226).

does not wish to evade the discipline of the market, at least for the time being. There is some value in the Conservative critiques of Morales contending that remains in power thanks to windfall tax returns, high oil and mineral prices and the generosity of the IMF, the World Bank, and the IDB. These conditions have permitted temporary increases in nominal wages and a quite massive increase in GDP per capita in 2008 which have served to mollify organised labour, if only temporarily.[34]

Table 6.9: Selected Economic Indicators, 2004-2008

	2004	2005	2006	2007	2008
GDP (millions of 1990 US$)	8,421	9,574	10,300	13,292	17,198
GDP per capita (1990 US$)	935	1,016	1,293	1,352	1,661
Exports (merchandise and services) (US$ millions)	2,146	2,791	3,863	4,780	6,448
Imports (merchandise and services (US$ millions) (1)	1,845	2,334	2,809	3,361	4,674
Real growth rate (%)					
GDP	3.6	4.4	4.8	4.6	6.15
Population	1.6	1.5	1.5	1.4	1.4
GDP per capita	4.6	4.9	5.7	4.8	22
Inflation (accumulated at year end)	4.6	4.9	5.4	11.7	11.8
Official exchange rate (Bol/US$) (end of year)	8.04	8.09	8.06	7.90	7.07
Terms of trade (1980 = 100)	21.7	22.8	27.5	28	
Terms of trade (1990 = 100)	66.6	69.9	84.3	85.8	

(1) Indicates negative effects of Brazil's financial crisis on trade relations in 2001; commercial surplus from 2004 with increasing prices for key commodities (oil and gas, soy, minerals and metals) and tremendous export growth from 2005.

Sources: IMF, INE, UDAPE, BCB

Nationalisation does have international repercussions, as it affects the interest of TNCs controlling the strategic hydrocarbons, telecommunications, and electricity sectors.[35] The nationalisation of extractive industries by Supreme Decree (28701) symbolised the assertiveness of subjugated forces in Bolivia and is regarded as an exercise in redistributive justice against abusive exploitation by TNCs.[36] Resistance by US and European governments to the May 2006 nationalisation of oil and gas was lukewarm, in part because of the awareness that privatisation contracts signed in 1996 grossly underestimated natural gas reserves and TNCs have already multiplied the returns on their investments, while infringing worker rights and causing large-scale environmental damage.[37] Most importantly, nationalisation does not constitute a full-on expropriation of foreign property: Morales has justified the decision not to compensate foreign investors by saliently distinguishing between expropriation and nationalisation: the Bolivian administration implemented a Venezuelan-style nationalisation in which TNCs operating gas fields (and relinquishing ownership of the gas produced to YPFB) must pay 82% of their profits to the state, instead of 50% before nationalisation and 18% before the 2004 gas referendum, an agreement signed by all parties in October 2006 following intense negotiations (Gray 2007). 'The days of superprofits are over. But even at 18 percent of the value of gas being produced, the foreign companies will enjoy 20-25 percent profits', argued Jorge Alvarado, president of the YPFB, in 2006 (Lewis 2006). Moreover, the government has recently sought to consolidate its national support base prior to the referendum on regional autonomy by taking a controlling stake in four TNCs operating in the energy sector in Bolivia (through the purchase of $214 million worth of shares, giving the state a 50 percent stake plus one share in the companies) (*Reuters* 2008c), and by decreeing the re-nationalisation of the telecommunications company Entel on the 1st of May (*Reuters* 2008d). The latter move antagonises more directly the European Commission and the Italian government. The government withdrew in 2007 from the World Bank's International Center for Settlement of Investment Disputes (ICSID), evading arbitration in favour of Stet's claims (*International Institute for Sustainable Development* 2007). The timing of these waves of nationalisation demonstrates an assertion of government power and commitment to reform in the face of the referenda on regional autonomy.

Despite threats of capital flight and legal challenges in the ICSID, all TNCs investing in the hydrocarbons sector have remained in Bolivia and accepted the new contractual terms. Instead of a capital pullout, the opposite has been occurring, signalling an important political victory for the Morales government. FDI, at US$581 million in 2006, US$739 million in 2007, and $1.302 billion in 2008 – with, as illustrated below, the signing of joint ventures in the mining sector –, fully recovered from the record levels of the years of capitalisation/privatisation of state-owned corporations (from US$90 million in 1994 at the start of the capitalisation process, FDI reached $1.026 billion in 1998 and 1.010 billion in 1999). In 2007 it was close to 30 times greater than in 1990 (US$27 million), and significantly higher than in the years preceding the investiture of Morales (US$567 million in 2003, US$488 million in 2005) (INE 2009b). Although FDI was significantly lower than in previous years in 2009 (it totalled only $322 million by the end of the second quarter, including $58.99 million in the second quarter), it remains relatively high by Bolivia's standards. TNCs seem to have understood that the legitimacy of the new Bolivian administration, despite significant increases in corporate taxation and the obligation to sign joint ventures with state-owned corporations, will paradoxically enhance the social stability necessary for profitable investment. Most importantly, booming Chinese and Indian demand (see *The New York Times* 2009b; table 4) has rendered such ventures highly profitable. Indeed, with oil prices well above $70 (affecting the price of gas too), legal conflicts between the MAS and the opposition compounded by roadblocks and regional protests have not affected TNC investment plans and have barely impinged on output in the energy industry (*Reuters* 2008b).

TNCs have also been lining up to invest in the mining sector, with contracts for future investments worth $2.9 billion: the Indian corporation Jindal Steel and Power Ltd signed a $2.1 billion contract with the new administration in 2007, including the construction of a steel plant and the employment of 10,000 people – the largest capital investment in Bolivia's history (*Reuters* 2007); other investments include the $700 million San Cristobal silver, zinc and lead project by Apex Silver Mines Ltd, the $141 million reopening of the Karachipampa lead-silver smelter, and the $220 million San Bartolome silver plant by Coeur d'Alene Mines Corp (*Reuters* 2008e). This is immense for a national economy weighing $18 billion in 2009. Crucially, the current revival of Oruro and Potosí (with regional growth rates approximating 18 and 24 percent respectively in 2008), which may be further uplifted by its unmatched lithium deposits in the Salar of Uyuni, partially rebalances the economic weight of *Altiplano* and *Media Luna* (*Reuters* 2008a; *New York Times* 2009a; ABI 2009).

The extent to which the global economic crisis will affect Bolivian production relations beyond 2009 – including employment, wages, infrastructural development but also the hegemonic and counter-hegemonic struggles and the form of the state – remains to be seen, but it is bound to undermine the transient hegemony achieved by the MAS

(*El Deber* 2009). Bolivia's limited integration into global capital markets has insulated it partially from the global financial turmoil – signifying that GDP growth softened to 3 percent in 2009 rather than recede. Sharp if temporary declines in commodity prices for its main exports (hydrocarbons, minerals and metals, except gold) are beginning to negatively affect FDI and fiscal revenue, although exports maintained adequate levels through 2009 and a trade surplus was achieved ($5.001 billion compared to $4.467 billion in imports in 2009), while Bolivia closely avoided deflation for the year [0.29 percent inflation rate at year end]) (INE 2009c; BCB 2010). However, the IMF is expecting growth to rebound in the coming year, accompanied by moderate inflation (IMF 2010). A probable current account deficit in 2009 will reduce the government's margins of manoeuvre for its ambitious social programmes. This may very well signify that the government, to control inflation and sustain GDP growth, will be disciplined into implementing 'wage restraints' and 'improving the investment climate' (IMF 2009: 4).

The ALBA

However, the continued integration of the Bolivian state into global governance institutions enters in contradiction with the alternative macro-regional project built in collaboration with Venezuelan, Cuban, Nicaraguan, Dominican Ecuadorian governments: Hugo Chavez's alternative to the FTAA, the Alternativa Boliviariana Para los Pueblos de Nuestra America (ALBA),[38] is founded on a creative approach to regional integration that aims to dissolve the cash nexus binding the world market through the creation of alternative, de-monetised and expanding circuits of international exchange based on solidarity and welfare provision (the exchange of oil for medical services is the conventional example) (Harris and Azzi 2006). The ALBA system of integration purposely prioritises social needs and poverty reduction above private accumulation and private ownership. Its guiding principles are solidarity, complementarity, and the reduction of asymetries through compensatory financing. It principal lines of activity have been direct support for projects directly benefitting the poorest social strata; non-reciprocal and compensated trade arrangements (i.e. direct product exchanges); and concessional financing for the reduction of energy import bills for state-owned enterprises and for social and physical infrastructural projects (Girvan 2008). ALBA's expansion has signified the dissolution of the FTAA, and is an indication of a profound reconfiguration of bilateral relationships between the US and Latin America. However, three fundamental constraints have undermined this project. Firstly, ALBA's exchanges of services continue to intersect with established circuits of capital, and are quantitatively too limited to undermine money discipline. They constitute drops of water in a sea of market relations. Secondly, the other regionalist Chavez-Morales initiative, the *Banco del Sur,* which seeks to provide an alternative to IMF lending, unwittingly undermines the ALBA by incorporating a notoriously Conservative government (Colombia) and by offering micro-credit to small entrepreneurs, a striking example of the expansion of capital – through a process of primitive accumulation into rural areas, including indigenous communities, hence undermining communitarian production purportedly defended by the MAS.[39] More importantly, its capital of $8 billion is dwarfed by that of conventional development institutions and its political impact is likely to be minimal. Third, the ALBA is a top-down initative that has no roots in labour and indigenous movements, affecting both the depth and breadth of its impact on transnational production relations. Fourth, the Bolivarian bloc intersects with a multilevel regional and global governance complex which dwarfs its size and potential success. Bolivia remains integrated in global institutions – the United Nations, the IMF and the World Bank Group – along with other regional organisations (Mercosur, Andean Community), which legally constrain government policies. Furthermore, most Latin American governments have refused to join ALBA, and rather worked towards the consolidation of Mercosur and continental energy integration (the construction of a pipeline from Venezuela to Argentina, for instance).

It is worth reminding that the most fundamental economic constraints faced by Bolivia's government have historically been – especially since the late 1970s – generated by Argentinean, Brazilian and Chilean imperialism rather than strictly US dominance.[40] Bolivia's commodity exports (agricultural products and gas) are primarily directed towards its direct neighbours, and its principal source of foreign exchange since the late 1970s has been the export of natural gas to Argentina and, since the late 1990s, to Brazil (see table 6.10); Brazil's 'national interest' in sustaining a cheap, steady supply of gas depends on the extended exploitation of Bolivian gas fields by state-owned *Petrobras*.[41] In geoeconomic terms, Brazil and Argentina are far more relevant than Venezuela and Cuba, or indeed Chile (the historic enemy), a reality that is borne out by the increasing cooperation between the Bolivian government and Mercosur.

Petrobras, the Brazilian state-owned corporation, has been the most vocal critic of nationalisation efforts by the Morales administration. The principal impediment to Bolivia's economic development remains its

Table 6.10: Direction of Exports, 1978-2006 (in percent)												
	1978	**1980**	**1982**	**1985**	**1989**	**1993**	**1997**	**2001**	**2003**	**2004**	**2005**	**2006**
US	31.1	25.7	26.2	15.1	18.4	25.7	20.3	13.9	14.1	15.9	14	9.6
EU	24.4	24.5	15.1	20.8	27	29.6	24.5	10.5	6.7	7.2	5.6	5.8
Europe other	-	-	-	1.8	3	2.5	9.2	13.1	10	2.4	3.8	5.1
ALADI (inc. CAN, Brazil, Argentina, Venezuela, Chile)	27.3	36.7	51.8	59.7	42.6	40.4	41.8	58.4	63.7	64.3	65.8	63.6
Brazil (1)	4	3.5	2.2	0.6	6	3	2.9	22.1	30	31.7	38.3	37.6
Argentina	17.1	23.7	44.5	55.6	28	17	14.1	5	3.4	5.8	9.2	9.2
Venezuela	0.2	0.1	0.1	0	0	2.4	1.1	7.3	10.5	10.8	5.5	4.6
Chile	2.9	4.5	1.2	0.9	3	2	4.4	2.4	2.6	2.3	1.4	1.6
CAN	2.8	4.7	3.5	2.6	5.6	16	19.3	27.2	26.1	22.5	10.6	9.8
Colombia	0.7	0.9	0.7	0.6	0.6	5.2	6.8	14.1	9.4	5.3	6.2	3.7
Peru	1.6	3.1	2.6	2	5	10	12.2	5	5.4	6.1	4.3	5.9
Asia (inc. China, Japan)	-	-	-	0.9	0.5	0.6	0.5	1.4	4	8	8.3	11.6
China	0	0	0	0	0	0	0	0.2	1.1	3	4.6	8.9
Japan	2	0.9	1.8	0.4	0.2	0.3	0.3	0.4	0.7	1	0.7	0.9
Rest of world	15	12.2	5.1	3.5	8.5	3.7	3.9	2.7	1.5	2.1	2.6	4.4
Total (US$ millions)	629	942	906	628	723	710	1,166	1,284	1,598	2,146	2,791	3,863

(1) Significant increase in trade with Brazil following the construction of a gas pipeline in 2000.

Source: Morales (2008) ; UDAPE (2007b)

relationship with its direct neighbours. Morales's nationalist logic of emancipation sets itself against Others enjoying higher levels of development and hence far greater economic, institutional and military power (Chilean, Argentinean, Brazilian *criollo* elites along with American *gringos*); it therefore sustains regional imperialisms and reinforces the continent's international fragmentation. John Crabtree (2006) rightly emphasised the tensions generated by a nationalistic social model infringing the economic interest of bordering national elites. In this context the support of Chávez has been important in securing regional acquiescence to Bolivia's reforms – in particular nationalisation – and multilateral support against the secessionist ambitions of the *Media Luna*. It is also difficult for statesmen (Lula in Brazil, Kirchner in Argentina) struggling against 'US imperialism' (even through reformist policies) to legitimise their own societies' unequal relationship with the buffer Bolivian state. Hence their formal acceptance of nationalisation following an emergency meeting in Argentina on the 5th of May 2006, concluded by President Kirchner's emphasis on regional energy integration constituting the *sine qua non* of 'political integration', and on the necessity of such integration for the benefit of 'both consumers and producers'. However, a significant minority of Argentineans (30%) appear to support nationalisation, demonstrating a significant level of regional solidarity with Morales' decision (*BBC News* 2006c).

South American regionalisation is therefore bolstered by the participation of the new Bolivian government in Chavez's Bolivarian federation (the so-called People's Trade Treaty including Cuba) as an alternative to the FTAA, and the official acquiescence of Argentinean and Brazilian administrations (Sader 2006). An unprecedented movement towards inter-state cooperation and peaceful conflict resolution among new Latin American elites, fostering a macro-regional transnational network of interest may potentially sustain the formation of a macro-regional bloc with enhanced power in the global appropriation of social surplus, traversing the existing internationalisation of the Bolivian state.

Conclusion

The achievements of the MAS government are significant, but so are its shortcomings. Institutional and social reforms all have begun to improve the material conditions of the Bolivian majority. Its alliance with Venezuela's government has also offered relative protection from US encroachment and valuable support in its claims against its neighbours.

Evo Morales's overwhelming electoral success is an indication of its achievements. The MAS's shortcomings, however, are rooted in the historical development of the MAS itself – its tendentiously authoritarian and personalistic internal organisation, its need to accommodate a vast number of parochial and arguably anti-progressive organisations on its flanks (including some indigenist groups), and the consequent blurriness of its long-term social project.

The MAS has also suffered from protracted resistance to the implementation of its short-term policy objectives by the US government and elites entrenched in various state institutions (prefectures, the senate, minority groups in the Constituent Assembly) and civil organisations (Regional Civic Committees, business associations), which have used an autonomist discourse to challenge the nationalist project of the MAS. The destabilising tactics employed by the opposition received systematic technical and financial support by the US government, which took the dangerous path of fuelling still less predictable racist movements and autonomist discourses advocating civil war. The MAS leadership has faced important threats to its self-preservation.

Yet it has remained in government and reinforced its authority following the ratification of the new Constitution in January 2009. A number of measures (salary increases in the armed forces, purges in the officer corps) have been implemented to maintain control over the repressive apparatus of the state: securing the support of the army has been the cornerstone of the government's struggle against the destabilising activities of the opposition. However, the resilience of the MAS government has been fostered primarily by the implementation of popular social reforms – a new constitution, land reform, nationalisations *à la Chávez*, a universal pension scheme, increases in corporate taxes and in the legal minimum wage among others.

In turn, these reforms have been allowed by unprecedentedly favourable terms of trade on the one hand, and the generosity and engagement of the donor community on the other. I have argued that its continued collaboration with MDIs has heped to safeguard the Morales government from the subversive activities of the US embassy and business elites in Santa Cruz. Morales's willingness to sustain fiscal and monetary discipline, free trade and joint ventures between state- and privately-owned companies induced MDIs to *gradually* reduce Bolivia's external debt burden, which in turn has released the fiscal resources required for the social investments currently galvanising mass support for the government. The institutional interlocking of MDIs with key Central Government Ministries (in particular the Finance, Commerce and Planning Ministries), the Bolivian Central Bank, and depoliticised regulatory agencies has persisted and provided a much needed buffer against US-promoted subversion (IMF 2007, 2009). It is also very likely to persist and intensify with the worldwide economic crisis, which has bolstered the political weight of the IMF and WB and is leading Latin American (including the Bolivian) government to adopt a more conciliatory tone towards the 'instruments of the Empire'. Indeed, supranational 'legal padlocks' (*BBC News* 2006b) have effectively neutralised the revolutionary changes desired by some members of the Morales government.

Although the financial, technical and diplomatic support by the Venezuelan government has interfered with the smooth functioning of collaborative practices with MDIs, Bolivia's alliance with Caracas has offered relative protection from US encroachment and valuable support in its claims against its neighbours. It also has sustained macro-regional integration and international peace. Neighbouring governments' – in particular Venezuela – and MDIs' have helped to undercut the articulation of an autonomist project in the *Media Luna* by conservative forces. Their overt opposition to any form of secessionism in Bolivia's lowlands have thus contradicted and neutralised the destabilising tactics employed by the US. The internationalisation of the Bolivian state has thus been distorted by new, regionalist lines of governance and the penetration of subaltern social forces into the upper echelons of state institutions. In turn, these new and unpredictable institutional relations have stimulated contradictory attempts to interfere in or redirect the reform process by existing and new collective agents with an interest in the Bolivian space.

However, despite hopes that the Obama administration would inaugurate a new partnership with Bolivia, and despite the healing rhetoric accompanying the visit of Assistant Secretary of State for Western Hemisphere Affairs Thomas Shannon to Bolivia in May 2009, bilateral negotiations failed to result in a single concrete agreement on any of the issues dividing the two governments, including the reinstatement of the DEA, the extradition of Gonzalo Sánchez de Lozada, accused of genocide against the indigenous nations by the MAS government, and the US technical and financial support for conservative movements and political parties (COHA 2009). Multilateral lines of conflict, drawn by geo-economic shifts and transnational political alliances, are currently in flux. Whether the Morales government will be able to foster a sustainable form of Andean capitalism in an unpredictable economic and international environment defined by ecological degradation, US overstretch, European stagnation, unstable

Chinese and Indian growth, and the social laboratories engendered by the 'pink tide' in Latin America is a matter for conjecture. We can, however, expect that the progressive policies implemented by the MAS will continue to generate protracted resistance by conservative elites and remain conditioned by the vagaries of world market prices and the goodwill of MDIs and neighbouring governments.

Such vulnerability indicates that far from spearheading a dialectical movement towards socialism, though, the MAS is effectively deepening capitalist relations in Bolivia. Its only socialist undertaking, the ALBA, has been devised by Venezuelan and Cuban governments, and promoted through high-level agreements that do not involve trade unions and the grassroot.[42] As pointed out eloquently by Hylton and Thomson (2007), increasingly violent subaltern resistance to restructuring opened revolutionary horizons that were closed by the investiture of Evo Morales. Indeed, as emphasised by Malloy (1970: 4) with reference to the 1952 revolution, the Bolivian formation and state was destabilised by a process of 'internal war' throughout the period under study, a war that intensified in the late 1990s, and most spectacularly after 2000. However, although it did 'result in a redistribution of the capacity of groups to influence a society's authoritative mechanisms', the election of Evo Morales and the ratification of the new Constitution certainly have not generated 'the exclusion of groups with a previously high authoritative capacity from any future access to power, the redefinition of a society's concepts and principles of authority, and a redefinition of the goals which governmental authority usually pursues' (Malloy 1970: 4). If indeed the 2000-2005 epoch was 'revolutionary' (García 2006: 81-83),[43] it is doubtful that a 'coincidence of societal structural change with class upheaval; and the coincidence of political with social transformation' (Skocpol 1979: 4) has been occurring.

Malloy (1970: 7) was arguing in 1970 that 'revolutionary situations develop when significant segments of a society begin to conclude that an existing societal framework does not fulfil their desires or their needs. From such lack of fulfilment come demands for change'. The point of my analysis of resistance to restructuring within and beyond the state has been to show that, just as Bolivia's 'revolutionary situation' had not ended in 1969-1970, it did not end with the advent of liberal democracy, nor with economic stabilisation, nor with the ratification of the new Constitution. The revolutionary potential of Bolivia has been, and will be kept alive as long as relations of exploitation and domination underlie its historical development.

One has to reflect on the contentious meaning of socialism: the MAS expresses a form of socialist discourse prevalent in Latin America, which remains imbued with 1960s structuralist critiques of imperialism, and persists in having strong authoritarian and nationalist undertones. These tendencies pervade all social organisations, including trade and farmer unions, cooperatives and other subjugated movements – and often reproduce the very capitalist interests that some of them criticise. The MAS does, however, challenge notoriously exploitative, coercive, racist and corrupt *criollo* elites and the transnational bloc through its land reform programme, which signals a high redistributive potential, and through its regional alliances.

Knowledge of leaps, stagnation and retreats in neighbouring countries affects expectations and action in Bolivia (and vice versa), reflecting the transnational interconnections between domestic contexts. The defeat of Hugo Chavez in a crucial referendum (December 2007) that would have enshrined an authoritarian form of socialism in the Venezuelan Constitution affected expectations on the Constitution in Bolivia. Yet the provisions of the Constitution and recent policies implemented by the government seem to reflect popular (urban and rural) demands, as evidenced by the overwhelming victory of the MAS in the general elections. The key challenge for the administration in the short-term will be to neutralise US encroachement, intensify its participation in the ALBA initiative, increase the power of labour and marginalised movements in the domestic context while avoiding a violent showdown between indigenists and separatist *criollos*.

Notes

[1] 'If he does indeed abandon pragmatism, Mr. Morales may come to regret it' (*The Economist* 2006b). In the current context of the subprime and generalized financial crisis, the threat of 'severe economic damage' for populist or 'socialist' governments in Venezuela, Bolivia, Ecuador and Central America sprang again. See *The New York Times* (2008e); *BBC News* (2008b).

[2] See Freedom House's 'map of freedom' at http://www.freedomhouse.org/ since 2002. Accessed 28 February 2009. Interestingly, Freedom House perceived that 'freedom' and 'democracy' were undermined by Evo Morales's investiture, while Bolivia under the relatively repressive Gonzalo Sánchez de Lozada administration was defined as 'free'. See also the BBC's post-electoral map of Latin America.

[3] Bolivia encompasses thirty-five indigenous nations in total, dominated by Quechuas and Aymaras in the Altiplano and valleys, and Guarani in the tropical lowlands. The 2001 national census resulted in a majority of the Bolivian population self-identifying as 'indigenous' or 'native', although less than one third speaks indigenous languages: 30 percent Quechua, 25 percent Aymara, 5

percent other indigenous groups, 35 percent mestizo and 5 percent white (see Albó 2008).

[4] On CONALDE and early strategies of elite resistance to the MAS government, including roadblocks, boycotts in order to generate food shortages and inflationary pressures, see Inter Press Service (2008b).

[5] A 'parliamentary brigade of Santa Cruz' (*Brigada Parlamentaria Cruceña*) interconnects *Cruceño* Congressmen of conservative political parties – the MNR, the MIR (now UN), the ADN (now PODEMOS).

[6] The leadership of the CCSPC has systematically (except in one case) been led by leaders of *Cruceño* business associations (MABB 2005). It is not incidental that the current leader of the CCSPC, Branco Marinkovic, is simultaneously the head of the Santa Cruz Federation of Entrepreneurs, the *Federación de Empresarios Privados de Santa Cruz*, to which the *Cámara de Hidrocarburos*, composed of TNCs investing in hydrocarbons, is attached. See *Los Tiempos* (2005).

[7] Interview with Nicola Murray, 30 March 2007.

[8] The Camba Nation organisation, closely linked to the CCSPC, contends that the Camba nation is 'genetically' distinct from the rest of Bolivians by virtue of its peculiar 'mestizaje' between Spanish conquistadores and guaranís, and actively promotes the creation of a sovereign *Camba* nation-state. See http://www.nacioncamba.net/. Accessed 17 September 2008.

[9] See open letter by the President of the International Federation for Human Rights (IFHR 2008a) to Branco Marinkovic and the UN High Commissioner for Human Rights in Bolivia referring to human rights abuses by the UJC. For more detailed accounts of these abuses, see IFHR (2008b) and Amnesty International (2008).

[10] Interview with Nicolaus Hansmann, 15 August 2007. Despite the ideological assaults on the central government via autonomist discourses, in 2007 only 14 percent of the so-called 'middle and upper-classes' identified with 'their region' – but were concentrated in Santa Cruz and other departments of the Media Luna, while 20 percent of the 'lower-working class' did. Circa 55 percent identified with the 'nation' (Gallup 2008a).

[11] The 40% abstention rate and 15% vote against autonomy in the autonomy referenda organised in April and May 2007 by the CCSPC demonstrate that a significant portion of the population has not been influenced by, or rejects regionalist discourses. Morales obtained 24 percent of support in opinion polls in Santa Cruz, 35 percent in Beni and 42 percent in Tarija in a Gallup poll (2008b) realized a month before the recall referendum which took place in August 2008. A survey by the same agency. realised a year earlier showed deep class divisions, with 64 percent of the 'working/lower' class supporting the government in May 2007, against 40 percent of the so-called 'middle' and 'upper' classes did – a significant rise from April 2007, when only 17 percent of the latter expressed a positive opinion on the government. This demonstrates considerable variations in elite perceptions of Morales and his governmental team, which are correlated to the vagaries of Bolivia's political environment (see Gallup 2008a; 2008c).

[12] The idea of a new Constitution, although introduced in public debates since the early 1990s (including by Gonzalo Sánchez de Lozada), became a significant issue following the 'Water Wars' in Cochabamba. It is, however, in

the wake of the 'Gas Wars' of October 2003 that the notion of a Constituent Assembly became a rallying cry for subaltern movements in the Altiplano and the valleys. The MAS leadership, appropriating this popular demand, placed it at the heart of its electoral programme in 2005 (Hylton and Thomson 2007).

[13] For instance, the well-established, anti-liberal *Fundación Solón*, which has regularly offered structuralist diatribes against the free trade agenda promoted by the US government, the WTO and other MDIs, has lost half of its staff since 2006 to provide technical support to the MAS administration. 'What else can we do? We have to rely on every expert and lawyer we can get. The MAS simply doesn't have enough of them'. Interviews with anonymous members of the MAS, August-September 2007. See http://www.funsolon.org. Accessed 15 June 2008.

Foreign researchers and journalists critical of the pre-2003 liberalisation process, such as Thomas Kruse and Pablo Stefanoni, were recruited by the Morales government as advisors for trade and investment policies. The former acted as one of the central mediators between the government, multilateral and bilateral donors and lenders, and business organisations, thereby facilitating the continued internationalisation of the Bolivian state. See Thomas Kruse's biography at http://www.rbf.org/staff/staff_show.htm?doc_id=688713. Accessed 20 October 2008.

[14] For more detailed discussions of the balance of social forces in the Constituent Assembly, see *Democracy Center* (2007); and Crabtree (2006b).

[15] A referendum on departmental autonomy, guaranteed by the previous government, took place simultaneously to the election of the Constituent Assembly on the 2nd of July 2006. Although 57.6 percent of voters nationwide (and five out of nine departments) opposed the extension of departmental autonomy via the granting of executive power to departmental authorities, the CCPSC and the opposition was comforted by popular aspirations to autonomy in the *Media Luna*. Indeed, the departments of Santa Cruz (71.11%), Beni (73.83%), Tarija (60.80%), and Pando (57.69%) approved the referendum. See referendum question and results at http://www.electionguide.org/. Accessed 17 October 2008.

The procedural conflicts between the MAS and the opposition in the Constituent Assembly were marred by rising tension in the streets over the opposition's threat to declare de facto autonomy. It is in the regional 'bastion' of the MAS (Cochabamba) that the most violent confrontation occurred in January 2007. Despite a defeat of the referendum on autonomy in July (63 percent of the vote) in the department of Cochabamba, its Conservative prefect, Manfred Reyes Villa, announced a new referendum on autonomy in December 2007, inducing the cocalero and other peasant unions to besiege the city of Cochabamba in order to obtain the resignation of Reyes Villa. The latter mobilised his primarily *mestizo* and *criollo* supporters to 'defend' the city against the cocalero invasion, triggering a large street battle resulting in 200 casualties and 2 deaths (*El Mundo* 2007b). See the televised discourse of Vice President García Linera in reaction to the violence in Cochabamba on http://www.kaosenlared.net/. Accessed 20 October 2008.

Reyes Villa's escalation of conflicts in the streets of Cochabamba did not serve him well, as his prefectural term was revoked through the August 2008 referendum (see table 6.3).

[16] As pointed out by Eduardo Gamarra, this referendum, submitted to Congress as a legal project, is unconstitutional. It sat in the opposition-controlled Senate until three days after the referendum on departmental autonomy was held in Santa Cruz (7th May 2008). Gamarra offers an interesting, if convoluted, explanation for the decision, by the leadership of PODEMOS, to 'dust off the proposal by President Morales for the recall referendum and passed it'. See *Americas Society/Council of the Americas* (2008).

[17] For an analysis of the political conflicts surrounding the Constitutional Assembly, which is sympathetic to arguments put forth by the Conservative opposition, see International Crisis Group (2008). For a more balanced account, see Crabtree (2007b).

[18] As a safeguard from the concentration of executive power in one individual, the Presidential mandate is currently limited to *two, un-consecutive* terms. The new Constitution permits two consecutive five-year Presidential terms. The strategy of the government was to plan general elections directly following the referendum on the Constitution, and to consider these elections as the *first* for the present government. This would have signified the possible re-election Evo Morales in 2009 and again in 2014, giving him the opportunity to govern for 13 consecutive years. Following protracted negotiations with the CONALDE, the government agreed to consider the 2009 elections as Morales's second, and thereby secure his absence from the 2014 elections.

The Constitution will however permit the revocation of the terms of all elected officials, including the President, in specific circumstances – this would apply to Prefects, undercutting the relative autonomy of prefectures (articles 171, 241).

[19] As a compromise with the opposition, a distinct referendum decided whether the land area under private ownership should not exceed 5,000 or 10,000ha. See table 7.5.

[20] See *Reuters* (2006) and *The Guardian* (2006). Both accessed 4 June 2006. The area that could potentially be redistributed to 2.5 million people (28 percent of the population) accounts for 13 percent of the Bolivian territory.

[21] According to the *Fundación Tierra*, 91 percent of Bolivia's cultivable area is owned by 5 percent of landowners – modern day *latifundistas*, including foreigners (chiefly Brazilian); while the smallest producers (80 percent) own 3 percent of the land (Antón 2008). As demonstrated convincingly by Gill (1987), much of the land owned by the former was appropriated either illegally or through expropriation of 'native' land – elite networks surrounding General Banzer in the 1970s permitted the legal validation of the *fait accompli*, the obtention of sometimes unconstitutional land titles. The Monasterios family, full owner of the Banco Ganadero and of the television channel Unitel – which has been at the forefront of a furious media campaign against the Morales administration – owns more than 78,340ha of land in Santa Cruz. The Saavedra family, which owns more than 73,089ha of land in the *Oriente* and whose members are shareholders of banks and agro-industrial businesses, produced important politicians representing the transnational bloc in Bolivia. For example, Carlos Saveedra (Minister of Interior [1991-1993]; Minister of Commerce [1999-2000]; Minister of Economic Development [2000-2001]; Chancellor [2002]) led, along with Doria Medina, the entrepreneurial faction of the MIR political party. Confident of Jaime Paz, he negotiated with Sánchez de

Lozada following the 2002 elections for the formation of a coalition government with the MNR. Other famous agribusiness leaders include Roig Pacheco (43.166ha), Rapp Martínez (52.146ha) and the Justiniano family (43,000ha) (Do Alto and Stefanoni 2008: 109). Ronald Larsen, US citizen and father of the 'gringo Mr Bolivia' made famous in Bolivia by the film *Quién Mató la Llamita Blanca* (2006), owns, on his side, 17 properties totaling 157,0000ha. See *The New York Times* (2008b).

[22] See Autonomy Statute at http://www.asamcruz.org/. Accessed 10 October 2008.

[23] Since the mid-1980s Marcha por la Vida (see chapter 5), long marches to the capital by miners, indigenous peasants and coca farmers have become a favoured instrument to generate sympathy, internationally and in Bolivia's urban areas for their demands.

Tito Quiroga's decision to endorse the revocatory referenda was perceived by the leadership of the opposition (PODEMOS, UN, CCPSC) as an unacceptable miscalculation of the relationship of forces. The landslide victory of Morales isolated Quiroga and induced his removal from the leadership of PODEMOS.

[24] The Constitution was ratified by 61.4 percent of the voting population, with the highest participation rate in Bolivia's history (90.2 percent). However, regional divisions – between *Altiplano* and *Oriente* – in voting patterns that emerged in 2005 remain (see table 6.4).

[25] The ATPDEA is a preferential trade agreement through which Bolivia, since 2002, had tariff-free access to export roughly US$150 million worth of commodities to the US, making it Bolivia's second largest trading partner after Brazil. Colombia and Peru have continued to benefit from the ATPDEA, although the production of coca in both countries increased significantly more in 2007 (27 percent in Colombia) than in Bolivia (5 percent) (COHA 2009).

Lately, the alleged sale of uranium to Iran for its nuclear programme has been flagged up as a clear demonstration of the irresponsibility of the Morales government (*Los Tiempos* 2009).

[26] The 'Croatian connections' seemed to be further confirmed by the foiling of an alleged assassination plot against Evo Morales by foreign nationals (Romanian, Croatian and Irish) in Santa Cruz in April 2009, just as the political situation seemed to be stabilising (*New York Times* 2009c).

[27] The Chavez administration provided direct technical and political support to the Morales government for the nationalisation of the hydrocarbons sector by sending lawyers to advise the Ministry of Energy and Hydrocarbons; by intensifying the cooperation between the latter and the headquarters of Venezuela's state-owned hydrocarbons corporation PDvs.A, and by signing a cooperation accord between the YPFB and PDvs.A (*El País* 2006b).

[28] Interview with Nicola Murray, 30 March 2007.

[29] Article 327 of the New Constitution enshrines the depoliticisation of the BCB (*Asamblea Constituyente de Bolivia* 2007).

[30] Interview with several European Commission officials – EU delegation Bolivia, May 2007, September 2007, December 2007.

[31] Thus, García Linera defends 'the construction of a strong State, which regulates the expansion of the industrial economy, extracts its surplus and transfers it to the communitarian domain to empower forms of self-organisation

and of commercial development that is properly Andean and Amazonian' (*Los Tiempos* 2006; author's translation).

[32] See for example the threat, by EU Commissioner for Foreign Relations during Vienna's EU-Latin American Summit, that Morales's decision not to pay compensation to foreign corporations would shake investors' confidence, reduce capital investment and hence impact negatively on growth and employment (*Le Monde* 2006).

[33] See response to Eduardo Gamarra by Bolivian ambassador to the US (Gúzman 2007).

[34] Wage increases and demand for consumer goods have, in turn, intensified inflationary pressures. See DS 28700 and DS 29473 (Presidencia de la República 2006; 2008). In 2004 the legal minimum wage stood at 440bol ($50). Morales's electoral programme included an increase in the minimum wage to 1500bol ($185), which attracted significant attention by unions (*Econoticias* 2006). It must be reminded that these pieces of legislation only affect workers employed in the 'formal' economy, although wages in the informal sector tend to be pegged to the official minimum wage.

[35] Oil and gas extraction and distribution has been dominated by a Repsol-YPF conglomerate, Petrobras, British Petroleum, Amoco, Total and Shell since the 'capitalisation' of YPFB in 1996. The telecommunication company Entel is controlled by Italian corporation Stet. ENDE, the electricity corporation, was divided into three assets, sold to Dominion Energy, Energy Initiatives and Constellation Energy during the capitalisation process. On their side, the most important mining corporations, Comsur, Inti Raymi and Emusa, already recipients of significant FDI, were further transnationalised in 1993 (See also chapter 3). Inti Raymi's shareholding structure is 15 percent Bolivian, and 85 percent foreign. Comsur is controlled 25 percent investment from Rio Tinto Zinc. Emusa also undertook joint ventures with US and Canadian corporations such as Jordex Resources Inc, resulting in 45 percent foreign ownership. See WB (1992c: 7), and Aillón (1999).

[36] Furthermore, the government added symbolic value to the DS 28701 by promulgating it on the 1st of May (International Workers' Day) and directly following DS 28700, which increased the minimum wage.

[37] The struggle for the nationalisation of Entel ensues in a far less positive environment, as the European Commission and the Italian governments have denounced publicly and worked behind the scenes to twist the Bolivian government's arm into postponing its nationalisation plan. Javier Solana announced that Morales's nationalisation project was 'worrisome', as he had reminded Morales upon his investiture that "the juridical security is fundamental for foreign investment to come and for development to occur" (*El País* 2006a; author's translation).

[38] See official website of ALBA at http://www.alternativabolivariana.org. Accessed 16 January 2009.

[39] As analysed in chapters 3 and 4, the process of capitalist class formation (primitive accumulation) through micro-finance began in Bolivia in the late 1970s through NGOs receiving financing by the World Bank. The role of Fernando Romero, Minister of Development under the first Sánchez de Lozada administration, was important in creating an effective vector of capital expansion into rural areas, by transforming in 1992 the micro-financing NGO

PRODEM into a micro-financing bank, Banco Solidario (Bancosol), which, within two years had more than 240,000 clients and a loan portfolio of $137 million (Chu 2005).

[40] Until the mid-1990s, 40 percent of Bolivia's foreign exchange reserves depended on gas exports that were directed exclusively to Argentina. Following the signing of a trade agreement between YPFB and the Brazil energy monopoly Petrobras in 1993, and the construction of a gas pipeline to Brazil in 1997-1998 with a $130 million World Bank loan, Brazil became Bolivia's largest trade partner and Petrobras one of its principal source of FDI (Law and de Franco 1998; see also tables 6.6 and 6.8).

[41] Morales antagonised the Brazilian administration in 2006 by achieving a substantial increase in the price of gas exported to Brazil as well as Argentina (from $3.40-$3.60 to 5$ per million Btu) and by forcing Petrobras to sell Bolivia's two biggest refineries (operating in Santa Cruz and Cochabamba) to YPFB in June 2007, for $112 million. YPFB took over all of the shares and took control over their assets and liabilities, including oil derivative supply in Bolivia. See *Agence France Presse* 2006, Clough (2008) and Petrobras's website: http://www2.petrobras.com.br/. Accessed 20 January 2010.

[42] It is too early to judge the results of land reform, as it has primarily affected state-owned land. Land reform in the 1950s achieved no collective form of ownership (see chapter 2).

[43] García Linera (2006: 81) refers to 'extraordinary historical periods of dizzying political change—abrupt shifts in the position and power of social forces, repeated state crises, recomposition of collective identities, repeated waves of social rebellion—separated by periods of relative stability during which the modification, partial or total, of the general structures of political domination nevertheless remains in question'.

7
The Bolivian Case and Beyond

The Bolivian state has undergone far-reaching transformations since the 1985 hyperinflationary crisis, which laid bare the irresolvable contradictions of state capitalism, and heralded a wave of liberalisation under the Paz Estenssoro (1985-1989), Paz Zamora (1989-1993), Sánchez de Lozada (1993-1998; 2002-2003) and Banzer/Quiroga (1998-2002) administrations. As emphasised in chapter 1, typical objects of scholarly research have included liberal democratisation, decentralisation, indigenous representation and participation, and gender discrimination in Bolivia. Since 2000, research has shifted heavily towards the new social movements, indigenism and the MAS. However, the overwhelmingly local and national starting-points of ethnographic and state-centric scholarship have perhaps logically precluded any correlation of liberal democratisation, or *polyarchy* (see chapter 5), with the process of institutional restructuring most closely associated with the latest phase of capital globalisation: the internationalisation of the state (see chapter 4). The present research has suggested that a holistic epistemology allows a better understanding of local relations as constitutive of and constituted by the global production structure. It has thus offered a historical materialist analysis of the causes and processes underlying the concurrent internationalisation and liberalisation of the Bolivian state.

My research has sought to make a dual contribution to the academic literature: empirical/historical and theoretical. In empirical terms, it has analysed the causes and process of institutional change since the early 1980s, arguing that the transformations of the Bolivian state are best understood as constituted by, and constitutive of global relations of production. This precludes the national or local epistemological starting-point that has defined Critical approaches. It has investigated and analysed empirically the incorporation of a transnational elite fraction in Bolivia into an expanding transnational historic bloc, and reflected empirically on the relationship between processes of internationalisation, depoliticisation and polyarchy. On the other, it has asked how the concept of the state fits into these theoretical-historical propositions. At a higher level of abstraction, I have therefore attempted to contribute to the academic literature by conceptualising the Bolivian state as a fluid, contradictory organisation of subjection: the state is neither an instrument of the capitalist ruling class, nor is it an entity ontologically separated and relatively autonomous from the market. The state is a social relation, a constitutive element of underlying class-relevant struggles, and its historic reproduction of capitalist relations is therefore a contingent process rather than the consequence of its functions. As a social relation constituting and constituted by broader production relations, the state is a terrain of both intra-elite and class struggles.

The concepts that I used reflexively in this study are *polyarchy* (Robinson 1996), *internationalisation* (Cox 1981, 1987) and *depoliticisation* (Burnham 2000), and I hypothesised that they should be related conceptually and historically to each other. These secondary concepts are also internally related to a higher (first-) level of substantive abstraction (Marx 2003; Gunn 1991; Bonefeld and Psychopedis 1991; Bonefeld 1991): *the state*. Together, they refer to highly contradictory, fluid and unfinished processes of institutional change, subject to constant reconfiguration and potential reversal. In turn, they define the conceptualisation of the state offered here as contradictory organisation of subjection, constitutive of and constituted by relations of production, i.e. as social content. I have argued here that the internationalisation, depoliticisation and liberalisation of the state are internally related, congruent institutional struggles defining changes in the forms of the Bolivian state *and* of the class struggle since 1985: these concepts concurrently capture the transformations of Bolivia's national-in-global social relations.

In analysing state reform in Bolivia, I have attempted to be faithful to the dialectical method by grounding abstractions in historical facts and transforming them in the process – attempting a movement back and forth between conceptual propositions and empirical evidence. It is notable that analyses of neoliberalism in Critical Bolivian academia have almost systematically interpreted the state in instrumentalist terms, pitting for instance organised labour and indigenous movements *against the state* (see chapter 1). The state thus becomes reified as a unitary coercive apparatus used by *criollo* elites to dominate labour and to exclude indigenous movements. By implication the executive, legislative and judiciary institutions of the state become devoid of internal rivalries and antagonisms. This is, of course, not to mention the fuzzy definitions of neoliberalism that one can encounter in critical scholarship on Bolivia, which result in associating all the ills of Bolivian society with a neoliberal market (see chapter 1).

My research has woven theoretical and empirical dimensions of research by integrating a conceptualisation of the state as contradictory organisation of subjection with empirical evidence on the restructuring of the Bolivian state since 1985 (see introduction). Historical materialist theorists have tended to reproduce the shortcomings of instrumentalism (Morton 2000; Robinson 2002) and structural-functionalism (Cox 1981, 1987; Van der Pijl 1998): either the state is an instrument of a cohesive capitalist ruling-class (Miliband 1968), or it is relatively autonomous from the market (Poulantzas 1975). In light of evidence on the internationalisation and liberalisation of the Bolivian state, it is necessary to reflect critically on existing neo-Gramscian and Open Marxist approaches to the contentious concept of the state. The process of state internationalisation has been elemental to institutional struggles, defining their course and being defined by them. Empirical evidence has supported the central hypothesis of this study: one can overcome the limitations of instrumentalism and functionalism via a systematically *relational* understanding of the state; i.e. by viewing the state as an organisational reflection of class and intra-elite struggles, a well-defined complex of institutions formally separated from yet constituted by subaltern and dominant forces. States reproduce both intra-elite and class conflicts within their institutions: they are terrains of organised struggle, an institutional expression of broader, underlying social contradictions. The social forces achieving an (ever-transient) domination of the state may claim authority (the legitimate use of coercion) over the entire social space formally bound by the state's institutions, yet are ever unable to achieve the complete assertion of this authority, and must struggle both within and beyond the state to sustain or change existing relations of production.

The state is neither a mere instrument of the ruling-class nor is it autonomous from production relations. In the period under study, did the Bolivian state act as a whole, as a bloc, to sustain capital reproduction? Was it at the behest of a cohesive bourgeoisie? Was it ever unitary? Did state managers always know what they were supposed to do? The answer to each of these questions is a resounding no. An alternative approach to the state is necessary to make sense of the Bolivian state. The premise of the suggested alternative is that the state is necessarily related to relations of production. Relations of production are relations of domination in the sense that capital exists only through the extraction of surplus value from labour (i.e. exploitation), while 'free' labour resists exploitation (Burnham 1994; Overbeek 2004). These relations are coercively organised by the institutions of the state. However, these institutions are relations themselves. Hence, the state is seen as a contradictory organisation of subjection: the state is a set of social relations embedded within broader relations: it is the organisational and coercive constitution of domination itself.

The research therefore concludes on the one hand that the capitalist class does not control and use the institutions of the state at will, and on the other that although attempts were made by the transnational bloc to create a professional state with well-defined functions, the state, torn as it is by social struggles, may very well act in ways that undermine the reproduction of capital. The state, or rather its central executive leadership, and indeed the staff of multilateral organisations do not inherently know how to sustain ordered accumulation; they have to adapt their strategies of capital domination and their hegemonic discourses to a variety of forms of resistance that systematically threaten to overwhelm them. The state is a concentration of bourgeois society, and bourgeois society is defined by the capital relation, by class struggle. As a set of institutions constituted by and shaping contradictory production relations, the state itself ***is*** class struggle.

What has been the relevance of the Bolivian case? It is, needless to say, fascinating for its own sake, but idiosyncratic research never took us very far in terms of offering generalisable propositions. Rather, I think that its defining contradictions can arguably be generalised to the periphery as a whole, and possibly to metropolitan areas of world society. Its contradictions are so manifest that they may help to shed light on similar processes that are perhaps less easily discernible in the rest of the world. It graphically shows how transnational elite forces are constituted, attempt to build hegemony in a hostile social environment, and why they fail to fully achieve their restructuring objectives despite systematic external fiscal support and technical assistance. It may potentially show how organised labour and marginalised social forces recompose themselves through the articulation of discourses reconstituting a long-term *memory* (with all the flaws and inventions that memorisation entails) adapted to contemporary social developments, and how such re-composition is at the heart of a societal project (*refundación*) disfigured by elite resistance to change, but also by contradictions internal to the project itself. The Morales administration may also demonstrate that human emancipation cannot be complete as long as market value (the real taboo surrounding nationalisation and constitutional refoundation) remains at the core of Bolivian production. The Morales administration, underpinned by capital wearing a Quechua or Aymara mask in Bolivia, may indeed show paths that revolutionary movements should not tread. What makes, then, a definition of the state as contradictory organisation of subjection relevant or even interesting? In part because it explains the Bolivian context particularly well. More importantly, because I suspect that it can be generalised and can thereby enrich the historical materialist tradition, if not the broader disciplines of political science and IPE.

This study analysed state reform in Bolivia. Analysing the restructuring of the Bolivian state from a holistic perspective entailed placing it within the context of the structural contradictions underlying the latest phase of capital globalisation since the early 1970s. The central attribute of this phase has been the increasing predominance of a transnational historic bloc incorporating fractions of capital and technocrats and organic intellectuals, i.e. a loose and competitive, transnationally-integrated bloc of elite social forces owning the means of production, managing production relations, and shaping the common sense of global society. The transnational bloc expanded following the debt crisis of the early 1980s by incorporating transnationalised businessmen and technocrats beyond its Transatlantic heartland (see chapter 3). It also generated qualitative changes in the strategic approach of MDIs, which began to emphasise fiscal and monetary stability, the privatisation of accumulation, public-private partnerships, business class formation in the periphery, state-building and multilateralism (see Chapter 3). Meanwhile, the worldwide debt crisis had plunged Bolivia into an uncontrollable hyperinflationary and fiscal crisis. Virtually bankrupt, the Paz Estenssoro government elected in August 1985 reversed the long-standing state capitalist model of development by implementing a shock stabilisation programme elaborated behind closed doors by leaders of the CEPB and monetarist economists.

Bolivia's hyperinflationary crisis (1985) offered an opportunity for a transnationalised fraction of Bolivia's banking, mining and commercial capital, to change the balance of forces within the three dominant political parties and vie for control of the state (see chapter 5). This small elite nucleus, whose tendency towards portfolio diversification challenges fractionalism in historical materialist theory, integrated into the transnational bloc primarily through official channels of development assistance as *equal* partners in development (see chapters 4 and 5), struggled against domestically-oriented elite forces and organised labour to restructure economic, ideological and institutional relations in the Bolivian space. Restructuring is understood as an attempt to reconfigure the capital-labour relation in order to sustain global capital accumulation; in other words, it means a struggle to empower businesses by reforming economic, ideological and institutional relations in order to generate worldwide *sustainable growth*. These struggles for restructuring involved the privatisation of accumulation, the attempt to build capital hegemony (i.e. to generate a consensual capitalist order) and the liberalisation of the state.

The neoliberal restructuring of the Bolivian state did not involve a 'retreat' (Strange 1996) or a 'hollowing out' (Jessop 1990) of its institutions. It rather involved the implementation, by Bolivian elements of an expanding transnational elite bloc in collaboration with the staff of International Financial Institutions, of a strategic project aiming to functionally relate state polity to the structural requisite of global capital accumulation, i.e. to build an ever-more efficient capitalist state. This strategy encompassed the depoliticisation of a number of key government agencies (Bolivian Central Bank, sectoral regulatory agencies) articulated with MDIs through technical assistance teams employed by the Bolivian state but remunerated by MDIs. However, privatisation efforts were deemed to sustain the depoliticisation of the state by imposing market-based discipline on the management and staff of state-owned corporations, thereby undermining discretionary appointments and investment strategies; while civil service reform aimed to create a depoliticised, rational and cold technocratic corpus, facilitating the depolicisation of state polity (chapter 4).

The pivotal institutional transformation that consolidated the social domination of the transnational bloc in Bolivia and supported its liberalisation and depoliticisation efforts was the internationalisation of the state. Indeed, in the Bolivian case, the incorporation of a small transnational fraction of Bolivian capital, a nucleus of dynamic, wealthy business elites into the expanding bloc occurred not merely through joint ventures and shareholding between Bolivian and foreign corporations (especially in the mining and banking sectors), or indeed through International Finance Corporation equity investments in a small number of Bolivian corporations, but primarily through the internationalisation of the state. The engagement of MDIs and private banks by competitive and denationalised Bolivian elites in 1985, and in turn their unconditional integration into an expanding transnational elite bloc drove the internationalisation and liberalisation of the Bolivian state. Internationalisation and liberalisation, in turn, consolidated the structural power of the transnational bloc in Bolivia.

Internationalisation unfolded first via an institutional articulation of key central government agencies (chiefly the Finance and Planning Ministries, the Central Bank and regulatory agencies), with MDIs and subsequently via a penetration of the lower levels of the administration by MDI staff and private consultants as line managers and trainers. WB adjustment and technical assistance, and stand-by agreements with the IMF facilitated the internationalisation of the Bolivian state and restructuring efforts by the transnational bloc. The concept of internationalisation must therefore be internally related to those of depoliticisation and liberalisation.

Having thus offered a critical reflection on the concepts of internationalisation and polyarchy used in neo-Gramscian scholarship in chapters 4 and 5 through evidence from the Bolivian case, the study argues that attempts to restructure social relations in Bolivia must be seen as a dialectical process. Restructuring contained its antithesis in the systematic, variegated forms of resistance that the transnational bloc faced within and beyond the state throughout the period under study. Attempts to depoliticise the Bolivian organisation of subjection were systematically undermined by the repoliticisation of state polity by domestically-oriented elites and labour forces (chapter 5). Policy elements of the restructuring efforts were thus implemented successfully, whilst others remained in limbo or had to be rolled-back; some institutions were transformed, eliminated or created whilst others remained bastions of continuity. Post-1985 restructuring may be understood as an attempt, by an 'enlightened' elite formation, to graft modern capitalism and liberalism onto a corrupt, nepotistic, and statist social organism, with the active support of MDIs. Bolivian elements of the transnational bloc were nonetheless part of and dependent on clientelistic social networks for the implementation of liberal reforms, which explains their failure to legitimise the high social costs of Bolivia's deepening integration into the world market (see chapter 5).

MDIs and bilateral development agencies promoted polyarchy (Robinson 1996) whilst actively coordinating their activities with central government agencies, promoting the depoliticisation of the latter, and supporting PSD. These three processes, the internationalisation, depoliticisation, and liberal democratisation of the state, must not be regarded as independent processes. Rather, in light of MDI's holistic approach to development assistance and the transnational bloc's approximation of the interest of global capital, these institutional transformations must be theoretically interconnected and placed at the heart of restructuring efforts: i.e. enhancing the structural power of capital, in particular of the transnational bloc, whilst depoliticising state polity and generating hegemony by associating liberalisation and democracy. However, it has argued that the transnational bloc failed to generate neoliberal hegemony, on the one hand because restructuring efforts impinged on customary elite practices, and on the other because the policies conditioning PSD and capital accumulation not only failed to increase per capita GDP but also accentuated the concentration of Bolivia's social surplus in transnational capital. Social polarisation and deficient growth, compounded by the worldwide economic crisis of the late 1990s, the repression of *cocaleros* in the Chapare by paramilitary forces, and the re-composition of labour around indigenist currents of opinion in the Achakachi area and in El Alto, conditioned the form of subaltern resistance that emerged at the close of the twentieth century and eventually overwhelmed elite forces.

However, the story of restructuring is not one of historical sequences – unidirectional elite initiatives followed by unidirectional subaltern struggle from 2000 onwards. Chapter 5 demonstrated that resistance to polyarchy, taking a variety of forms, was systematic in civil society and in the state throughout the period under study – that is, from the very moment President Paz Estenssoro enacted the DS 21060 in 1985. The transnational bloc, more often than not in alliance with a politically rescinding, domestically-oriented elite bloc, faced recurrent, intensifying and increasingly violent resistance to restructuring, which affected private investment and business confidence negatively, fuelling a further deterioration in poverty and unemployment rates (Kohl and Farthing 2005). Increasingly effective resistance can be traced to a process of labour re-composition in the late 1990s around two organisational nuclei: emerging political parties (the MAS of Evo Morales and the MIP of Felipe Quispe) and revived trade unions (the CSUTCB; the COB) rearticulating and congealing revolutionary nationalist and indigenist discourses and currents of opinion (Antezana 1983; Zavaleta 1983; Webber 2008). Indigenous peasants in the lake Titicaca region (with Achacachi as its urban centre), and the *minero-cocaleros* in the coca-producing Chapare became the two primary bastions of resistance, followed by marginalised urban forces (El Alto) often galvanised by an emergent *burguesia chola* – in the extensive informal sector of the economy.

The rolling back of the privatisation of water distribution in Cochabamba following the well-publicised Water Wars of 2000, the rolling back of an income tax imposed in February 2003, the rolling back of a project to export gas to the US via Chile in October 2003, are prominent examples of policies designed to generate business confidence and sustain or accelerate capital accumulation that failed in the face of collective challenges in the street and in the state (in the case of *Octubre Negro*, this was manifested by soldiers grumbling when forced to kill their own families and friends, by teachers and other civil servants joining the rebellions).

Beyond 2005: The Emerging Balance and Elite Resistance to Reform

Chapter 6 went beyond 2005 to critically assess the Morales administration. It showed that Morales-sponsored reforms have generated protracted resistance by Bolivian elites, both within and beyond the state, while labour has been co-opted through progressive welfare initatives. Transnational and domestically-oriented capitalist forces, faced with the real possibility of their own demise in the Bolivian space, entrenched themselves in the *Oriente*, where Bolivia's key export commodities are located (gas, soy), where diversification, import-substitution, and export-led development generated Bolivia's highest capital accumulation, and where accumulation persists in legitimising liberal discourses. Capital's capacity to muster significant electoral support in Santa Cruz, Tarija, Beni and Pando has been based on the diffusion of modernising regionalist and liberal discourses, but also, and more insidiously, on explicitly racist discourses against Kolla invasion from the highlands. Until the revocatory referendum of August 2008, which placed the government on course to obtain the ratification by referendum of the new Constitution and its landslide victory in the general elections of December 2009, the opposition was taking the initiative and regularly undermined the government's capacity to manage social relations. The projection of financial, organisational and ideological power (primarily through private television media) have counterbalanced the momentum of labour and indigenist forces, while bastions of the opposition in the state – the senate, the prefectures, municipalities – have hindered and redirected social and institutional change, and the form of the Constitution itself. Since the attempt of the opposition to trigger a full-fledged war of movement in the *Oriente* in the wake of Morales' resounding victory in the referendum, however, the MAS has demonstrated its political acumen by retaking the initiative and by consolidating a hegemonic bloc formed by indigenist and nationalist movements within the confines of Bolivian power relations.

These domestic developments, traversed by foreign collaboration with domestic forces to oppose MAS-sponsored reforms have been placed within worldwide and macro-regional processes of social and institutional change. The Bolivian space is also torn by the contradictory initiatives between Morales's Bolivarian allies, other neighbouring states, the US State Department and MDIs. It appears that the dialectical result has been the Bolivian state's protection of private property as well as fiscal and monetary discipline, the persistence of depoliticised economic management, but also restrictions on private accumulation in sectors considered as strategic by the MAS leadership. One could superficially refer to more of the same by finding parallels with the revolutionary situation of 1952-1956. Yet this would overlook profound social changes within and beyond the Bolivian space, including at one level the shifting centre of economic gravity towards East Asia, European stagnation and US imperial overstretch, and at a deeper and less transparent level, the temporary frailty and re-consolidation of the transnational historic bloc and MDIs through the re-disciplining of labour and the elimination of unfit domestically-oriented capitalists since the collapse of the financial system in September 2008, in the absence of a really existing alternative social model and power bloc. The process of internationalisation of the Bolivian state under way since the 1950s, and intensified since 1985 seems to be persisting, and seems to be redirecting Morales-sponsored reforms in Bolivia. Yet internationalisation is also distorted by the development of alternative forms of multilateral cooperation and the penetration of subaltern forces in the executive and legislative institutions of the state. Concurrent internal and external institutional struggles are thus placing the Bolivian state on unpredictable *capitalist* developmental paths.

The forms taken by the state, internationalisation, depoliticisation and polyarchy are in flux: the generation by Latin American governments of new multilateral lines of conflict and the reconfiguration of global, supranational authority in the midst of a profound world-wide recession highlight the changes underlying the various intersecting levels of world-wide social organisation. National states as fluid terrains of struggle constituting and constituted by global production relations have been transformed by the restructuring efforts of the expanding transnational historic bloc and the spatially variegated forms of resistance to it. Global social restructuring and resistance to it have been shaping the consolidation of global governance institutions. Since global organisations are constituted by internationalising states, which are institutionalisations of social struggles, global organisation itself cannot but be twisted by the local, national and international contradictions defining it. In light of the contemporary transformations, through multilateral strategies of accumulation and capital domination, of the form taken by national organisations of subjection, it becomes relevant to ask whether a conceptualisation of the state beyond national forms can be effected, and perhaps whether the world-wide, contradictory organisation of subjection can be considered a state.

Appendix 1

Selected Economic Indicators

Table A1: The Roots of Bolivia's Fiscal and Hyperinflationary Crisis. Selected Economic Indicators, 1970-1985: GDP, Inflation Exchange Rate, Trade.

	1970	1975	1980	1982	1983	1984	1985	1980-1985 avg.	1980-1985 total
GDP (millions of 1990 Bol.)	9,168	12,166	15,261	14,701	14,106	14,078	13,842		
GDP (millions of 1990 US$)	2,521	3,346	4,146				3,748		
GDP per capita (1990 US$)	610		954				574		
Exports (merchandise and services) (US$ millions)	206	505	942	828	755	720	628		
Imports (merchandise and services) (US$ millions)	180	641	678	575	577	489	691		
Real growth rate (%)									
GDP	-0.5	6.6	-0.9	-4.8	-7.3	-3.2	-4.1	-1.9	-10.5
Population		2.3	2.6	2.7	2.7	2.7	2.8	2.8	
GDP per capita					-9.8	-5.8	-6.7	-4.6	-24
Inflation (accumulated at year end)			23.9	296.5	328.5	2,177.2	8,170.5		
Official exchange rate (Bol/US$) (end of year)	11.88	20.4	25	68.42	251.7	2,852	450,42		
Terms of trade (1980 = 100)			100				54.3		
Exports:									
Minerals (1980 = 100)			100	70.7	70.9	72.3	67.6		
Hydrocarbons (1980 = 100)			100	150.3	147.7	153.6	155.5		
Sugar (1980 = 100)			100	43.5	49.8	67.2	56.5		
Coffee (1980 = 100)			100	59.2	51.1	52.3	54.3		
Soy (1980 = 100)			100	132.1	62.9	42.9	13.6		

Sources: WB (1986, 1989c, 1991c); IMF (1986)

Table A2: Selected Economic Indicators: Fiscal Balance, 1980-1985					
	1980	1982	1983	1984	1985
Share of GDP (%)					
Total government revenue (1)	**40.5**	**14.4**	**12.7**	**4.8**	**13.9**
Current revenue	40.1	11.5	11.3	4.6	13.8
Tax revenue (2)	17.7	10.9	6.9	4.3	12.1
Hydrocarbon taxes	8	8.3	3.7	2.4	9.2
Non-oil taxes	9.7	2.6	2.9	1.9	2.9
Grants	22.4	0.6	4.4	0.1	1.7
Capital revenue	0.4	2.8	1.4	0.2	0.2
Total government expenditure	**48.3**	**30.4**	**31.9**	**33**	**23.9**
Current expenditure	40.9	22.6	26.1	25.9	20.3
Wages and Salaries (3)	12.8	9.9	8.3	14.3	7.6
Interest	3	3.9		3	5.9
Pensions					
Capital expenditure	7.4	7.5	5.8	4.6	3.6
General Government		2.9	2.8	2.2	2.2
State-owned enterprises		4.6	3	2.4	1.4
Overall balance	**-7.8**	**-16**	**-19.2**	**-28.1**	**-10.1**
Financing	**7.8**	**16**	**19.2**	**28.1**	**10.1**
External (net)	5.3	3.6	-0.8	2.6	4.8
Domestic	2.5	3.3	20	22.4	5.3
Central Bank (4)	0.2	3.3		21.9	8.4

(1) Details may not add up to totals due to rounding.

(2) Includes fiscal contributions of state-owned enterprises; 90% of which were generated by YPFB from early 1980s

(3) Consists of wages, pensions to war veterans and severance payments.

(4) Indicates BCB printing money to finance government deficit between 1982 and 1985, thereby driving inflation up.

Source WB (1989c: 5, 52; 1991c: 17; 1998: 2; 1999c: 10; 2005: 73); IMF (1986)

Table A3: The Effects of Stabilisation and Structural Adjustment: Selected Economic Indicators, 1986-1993: GDP, Inflation, Exchange Rate, Trade								
	1986	1987	1988	1989	1990	1991	1992	1993
GDP (millions of 1990 Bol.)	13,486	13,818	14,220	14,759	15,443	16,256	16,524	17,230
GDP (millions of 1990 US$)				4,511				5,382
GDP per capita (1990 US$)					747			758
Exports (merchandise and services) (US$ millions)	588	519	542	723	831	760	643	710
Imports (merchandise and services (US$ millions)	674	766	768	861	963	994	1,09	1,206
Real growth rate (%)								
GDP	-2.5	2.6	3	2.8	2.6	4.1	1.7	4.3
Population	2.8	2.8	2.8	2.8	2.7	2.4	2.1	2.1
GDP per capita	-4.6	-0.6	0.8	-0.4	-0.1	2	-1.2	1.9
Inflation (accumulated at year end)	66	10.7	21.5	16.6	18	14.5	10.4	9.3
Official exchange rate (Bol/US$) (end of year)	1,971,512	2.06	2.35	2.69	3.17	3.58	3.91	4.27
Terms of trade (1980 = 100)	43.1	39.3	31.1	34.2	32.6	28.4	24.9	21.9
Terms of trade (1990 = 100)					100	87.1	76.3	67.3
Exports:								
Minerals (1980 = 100)	40.5	53.5	57.8	62	55.7	51.4	55.5	47.5
Hydrocarbons (1980 = 100)	132.9	102.6	86.3	89.3	93	89.5	53.5	28
Sugar (1980 = 100)	60.4	47.2	54.2	86.9	80.5	73.4	71	82.9
Coffee (1980 = 100)	65.9	51.1	61	50.6	39	39.7	16.7	39.1
Soy (1980 = 100)	176.5	70.6	78.1	92.3	161.4	159.9	176.8	158.2

Sources: WB (1989c; 1991c; 1998; 1999c; 2005)

Table A4: Selected Economic Indicators: Fiscal Balance, 1986-1993								
	1986	1987	1988	1989	1990	1991	1992	1993
Share of GDP (%)								
Total revenue (1)	**19.4**	**16.2**	**21.2**	**22.5**	**21.3**	**22.8**	**24.2**	**23.4**
Current revenue	18.2	15.8	20.2	20.9	21.1	22.3	23.8	23.2
Tax revenue (2)	15.5	12.7	17.9	18.1	15.3	16.4	16.6	17
Hydrocarbon taxes(3)	11	8.3	8.5	6.7	7	7.7	5.8	5.5
Non-oil taxes (4)	4.5	4.4	7.6	7.6	6.9	7.6	9.4	10.2
Grants	2.7	3.1	2.2	1	1.8	1.7	2.7	1.5
Capital revenue	1.2	0.4	1	0.6	0.2	0.4	0.3	0.2
Total expenditure	**22.9**	**24.1**	**27.8**	**27.6**	**25.7**	**27**	**28.5**	**29.5**
Current expenditure	18	17.7	19.6	19.6	17.4	18.3	18.5	20.3
Wages and Salaries (5)	6.6	7.5	7.8	8.2	6.8	6.9	7.7	8.2
Interest	5.2	4.1	3.9	3.4	3	3	3	3.2
Pensions	-	-	-	-	0.7	1.1	1.2	-0.7
Capital expenditure	4.9	6.4	8.2	8	8.3	8.7	10	9.2
General Government	2.1	2.9	4.8	4.7	4.4	4.9	5.9	5.9
State-owned enterprises	2.8	3.5	3.4	3.3	3.9	3.8	4.1	3.3
Overall balance (6)	**-3.4**	**-7.8**	**-6.6**	**-5**	**-4.4**	**-4.2**	**-4.4**	**-6.1**
Financing	**3.4**	**7.8**	**6.6**	**5**	**4.4**	**4.2**	**4.4**	**6.1**
External (net)	5.4	2.5	4.6	2.1	2.4	3.3	3.8	5.1
Domestic	-2	5.4	2	2.9	1.9	1	0.5	1
Central Bank	-3.4	3.1	3.4	4.8				

(1) Details may not add up to totals due to rounding. Indicates improvement of fiscal situation in 1985: sharp increase in public sector prices, including 40 percent increase in domestic petroleum prices; restructuring of state-owned enterprises and resumption of COMIBOL exports; and steady increase in tax revenues between 1986 and 1989 with creation of VAT consumption tax.
(2) Includes fiscal contributions of state-owned enterprises; 90% of which were generated by YPFB from early 1980s
(3) Indicates heavy dependence of state's tax revenue on Hydrocarbons tax until early 1990s.
(4) Consumption taxes centred on the VAT introduced in 1986 generated 3.9 percent of GDP in 1990, and increased to 8.3 percent of GDP in 1997 - while income and utility taxes only generated circa 3 percent of GDP in the period under study.
(5) Consists of wages, pensions to war veterans and severance payments.
(6) Jump in fiscal deficit in 1987 indicates once-and-for-all severance payment to 33,000 laid off public employees (primarily in COMIBOL and YPFB) (Morales 1990: 9; WB1989c).

Source WB (1989c: 5, 52; 1991c: 17; 1998: 2; 1999c: 10; 2005: 73); IMF (1986)

Table A5: Second-Generation Reforms, Crisis and the Post-2005 Bonanza: Selected Economic Indicators, 1994-2007

	1994	1995	1996	1997	1998	1999	2000	2001	2002	2003	2004	2005	2006	2007
GDP (millions of 1990 Bol.)	18,034	18,877	19,701	20,677	21,717	21,809	22,356	22,733	23,298	23,929	24,928	25,935	27,137	28,524
GDP (millions of 1990 US$)				6,660			7,182		7,812		8,421	9,574	10,300	13,292
GDP per capita (1990 US$)			867				952				935	1,016	1,293	1,352
Exports (merchandise and services) (US$ millions)	998	1,075	1,132	1,166	1,104	1,051	1,459	1,284	1,370	1,598	2,146	2,791	3,863	4,780
Imports (merchandise and services (US$ millions) (1)	1,276	1,376	1,578	1,851	1,983		2,043	1,707	1,846	1,616	1,845	2,334	2,809	3,361
Real growth rate (%)														
GDP	4.7	4.7	4.1	4.2	5	0.4	2.3	1.7	2.4	2.8	3.6	4.4	4.8	4.6
Population	2	2	2	2	1.9	1.9	1.8	1.8	1.7	1.7	1.6	1.5	1.5	1.4
GDP per capita	2.2	2.2	1.7	1.8	2.1	-2.3	-0.5	-1.2	0.01	2.6	4.6	4.9	5.7	4.8
Inflation (accumulated at year end)	8.5	12.6	7.9	6.7	4.4	3.1	3.4	0.9	2.4	3.9	4.6	4.9	5.4	11.9
Official exchange rate (Bol/US$) (end of year)	4.63	4.81	5.08	5.36	5.64	5.98	6.38	6.81	7.48	7.82	8.04	8.09	8.06	7.90
Terms of trade (1980 = 100)	22.5	22.5	22	22	20.7	19.8	20.4	19.5	19.6	20.8	21.7	22.8	27.5	28
Terms of trade (1990 = 100)	68.9	69	67.5	67.5	63.7	60.6	62.5	59.9	60.1	63.9	66.6	69.9	84.3	85.8

(1) Indicates negative effects of Brazil's financial crisis on trade relations in 2001; commercial surplus from 2004 with increasing prices for key commodities (oil and gas, soy, minerals and metals) and tremendous export growth from 2005.

Sources: IMF, INE, UDAPE

Table A6: Selected Economic Indicators: Fiscal Balance, 1994-2007

	1994	1995	1996	1997	1998	1999	2000	2001	2002	2003	2004	2005	2006	2007
Share of GDP (%)														
Total revenue (1)	**25.8**	**26.4**	**26**	**24**	**25.1**	**25.9**	**25.6**	**25.1**	**24.4**	**24.1**	**26.8**	**30.9**	**34.3**	**34.6**
Current revenue	25.5	25.7	25.7	23.1	24.4	25.1	25	25	24.4	24.1	26.6	28.3	30.9	31.1
Tax revenue (2)	17.2	17.5	17.7	17.6	19.7	18.6	18.7	17.9	17.7	17.8	20.6	25.1	27.8	27.8
Hydrocarbon taxes(3)	4.8	4.2	4.5	3.4	4.6	4.4	4.9	5.1	4.6	4.6	5	6.5	9.4	9
Non-oil taxes (4)	11	11.9	11.9	12.8	13.6	12.9	12.5	11.8	12.1	12.3	14.6	18.6	18.4	18.8
Grants	2.5	1.7	2.4	1.4	1.4	1.8	2.2	2.4	2.3	2.9	2.5	2.1	1.8	1.6
Capital revenue	0.2	0.8	0.3	1	0.7	0.8	0.6	0.1	0	0	0.2	0.1	0.8	0.8
Total expenditure	**28.8**	**28.3**	**28**	**27.3**	**29.7**	**29.4**	**29.3**	**31.9**	**33.3**	**32**	**32.3**	**33.2**	**29.8**	**32.9**
Current expenditure	19.8	20	19.8	20.1	22.7	22.2	22.2	23.6	24.9	23.9	23.2	23.1	19.6	20
Wages and Salaries (5)	8.3	8.3	8.1	8.5	8.7	8.9	8.7	9	9.3	9.4	9	8.6	7.9	9.2
Interest	3.1	3.5	2.9	2.3	2.1	2	2.3	2.6	2.6	2.8	2.9	3	2.5	2.5
Pensions (6)	0.7	0.6	1.1	2.5	4	3.7	4.1	4.4	4.5	4.4	4.3	4	3.6	3.4
Capital expenditure	9	8.2	8.2	7.2	7	7.1	7.1	8.4	8.4	8.1	9.1	10	10.2	12.1
General Govt.	6.3	6.1	6.4	6.5	6.4									
State-owned enterprises (7)	2.6	2.2	1.7	0.7	0.3									
Overall balance (9)	**-3**	**-1.8**	**-1.9**	**-3.3**	**-4.7**	**-3.5**	**-3.7**	**-6.8**	**-8.8**	**-7.9**	**-5.5**	**-2.3**	**4.5**	**1.8**
Financing	**3**	**1.8**	**1.9**	**3.3**	**4.7**	**3.5**	**3.7**	**6.8**	**8.8**	**7.9**	**5.5**	**2.3**	**-4.5**	**-1.7**
External (net)	3.7	3.6	2.5	2.7	2.7	1.9	2	3	6	5.3	4.1	2.3	0.4	1.1
Domestic	-0.7	-1.8	-0.6	0.5	2	1.6	1.8	3.8	2.8	2.6	1.5	0	-4.9	-2.8

(1) Details may not add up to totals due to rounding. Indicates improvement of fiscal situation in 1985: sharp increase in public sector prices, including 40 percent increase in domestic petroleum prices; restructuring of state-owned enterprises and resumption of COMIBOL exports; and steady increase in tax revenues between 1986 and 1989 with creation of VAT consumption tax.

(2) Includes fiscal contributions of state-owned enterprises; 90% of which were generated by YPFB from early 1980s. Indicates massive increase in hydrocarbon rents from 2005.

(3) The 'capitalisation' of YPFB (1996) involved a significant reduction of royalties (to 18 percent) imposed on new private owners of YPFB assets. Taxes were increased to 50 percent in 2005, and 82 percent in 2006, leading to significant increases in revenues.

(4) Consumption taxes centred on the VAT introduced in 1986 generated 3.9 percent of GDP in 1990, and increased to 8.3 percent of GDP in 1997 - while income and utility taxes only generated circa 3 percent of GDP in the period under study.

(5) Consists of wages, pensions to war veterans, and severance payments.

(6) Indicates negative effect of pension privatisation on state's fiscal balance in 1997. Pension costs as a percentage of GDP have declined under the Morales administration.

(7) Indicates decapitalisation of state-owned enterprises prior to signing of new management contracts ('capitalisation').

Sources: WB, IMF

Appendix 2
Interviewees

Ivo Arrias: political party MIR, Director of Oruro RDC, Prefect of Oruro, 12 August 2007.

Guillermo Bedregal: member of MNR secretariat, Minister of Planning (1985-1986), Chancellor (1986-1989), Congressman from La Paz (1985-1989; 1989-1993; 1993 -1997; 1997-2002), 5 September 2007.

Mauro Bertero: member of ADN secretariat, Minister of Agriculture and Campesino Affairs (1989-1991), Minister of Information (2001-2002), 10 September 2007.

Carlos Börth: political party MIR, Congressman for Oruro (1989-1993; 1993-1997; 1997-2002); Senator for Oruro (2005-), 17 August 2007.

Ramiro Cabezas: 'political independent', Minister of Revenue (1987-1988); Minister of Finance (1988-1989), 17 September 2007.

Fernando Campero Prudencio: MIR sympathiser, Executive director of ESF (1987-1989); Minister of Foreign Trade and Investment (1992-1993), 20 September 2007.

Jorge Crespo: MIR sympathiser, Ambassador to the US (1989-1993) Minister of Foreign Trade and Investment (1997-1999), Minister of Defence (1999-2000) 28 September 2007.

Oscar Eid: Executive Secretary of MIR (1971-), 13 September 2007.

Alfonso Ferrufino: political party MBL, Minister of Goverment (2003-2004), Congressman for Cochabamba (1985-1989, 1989-1993, 1993-1997), 10 September 2007.

Guillermo Fortún: Executive secretary ADN, Congressman for La Paz (1985-1989), Senator for La Paz (1989-1993), Minister Without Portfolio (1989-1990), Minister of Government (2000), 21 September 2007.

Horst Grebe: Minister of Labour (1983), Minister of Mining (1984), Minister of Economic Development (2005), Consultant in the Ministry of Human Development (1993-1994), Executive Director of the *Fundación Milenio* (1994-1998) and of the Instituto Prisma (1999-2004), 17 September 2007.

Nicolaus Hansmann: Contract Officer, Sección de Cooperación – European Commission Delegation in La Paz, September 2007.

Carlos Iturralde: ADN sympathiser, President CEPB (1986-1989), Secretary General of ASOBAN (1996; 1997; 2000), Chancellor (Minister of Foreign Affairs) (1989-1991), Minister of Presidency (1997-1999), 14 September 2007.

Mauro Mariani: European Commission Head of Development Cooperation Bolivia (1997-2004), 20 December, 2007.

Carlos Morales: political party MNR, Minister of Energy and Hydrocarbons (1986-1988); Minister of Housing and Public Works (2002); Electoral Campaign Manager for Sánchez de Lozada (2002), 20 September 2007.

Juan Antonio Morales: Governor BCB (1995-2006), 28 September 2007.

Edgar Millares: Vice-President of BCB (1997), Minister of Finance (1997-1998), board member *Asociación Nacional de Aseguradores* and Banco Mercantil, 13 September 2007.

Herbert Müller: President of BCB (1983), Director of *Müller y Machicado Asociados* research foundation, Minister of Energy and Hydrocarbons (1991-1993), Minister of Finance (1998-2000), 11 September 2007.

Nicola Murray: AidCo European Commission, Head of Bolivia Unit (2004-), 30 March 2007.

Hector Ormachea: political party ADN, Treasurer ADN, Senator for La Paz (1985-1989) Minister of Defence (1989-1991), 5 September 2007.

Jaime Paz Zamora: MIR leader, President of the Republic (1989-1993), 28 September 2007.

José Antonio Quiroga: Editor in Chief, Plural Editores, 19 September 2007.

Hugo San Martin: MNR, Vice Minister of Government (1995-6), 22 September 2007.

Francisco Zaratti: 'political independent', Presidential Delegate for the Revision of Capitalisation, 11 September 2007.

Appendix 3
Prominent Businessmen and Technocrats: The Transnational Bloc in Bolivia

Biographical sketch of prominent Bolivian businessmen and technocrats integrated into the transnational historic bloc. These individuals are representative of a broader transnational elite movement of 'modernisers', typically moving back and forth between private business activities and public office.[1]

Gonzalo Sánchez de Lozada (MNR)

Bolivian Government Positions

- Elected senator for Cochabamba and President of the Senate (1985)
- Minister of Planning (1986-1988)
- Presidential candidate for MNR party (1989)
- President (1993-1997)
- President (2002-2003)

Private Sector Employment or Investments

- Founder (in 1962) and majority shareholder of the mining corporation Companía del Sur (COMSUR): 1456 employees in 2002
- Investments in banking as well as mineral and metal extraction and processing of zinc, gold, lead, silver and tin ores. Initial investments in Bolivia before expanding to ten countries, from Argentina to Panama, and later to Asia

- $12 million in FDI between 1972 and 1978 through COMSUR affiliate 'Caballo Blanco' (De La Cueva 1983: 71)
- 25 percent foreign shareholding in COMSUR from 1993: British corporation Rio Tinto Zinc Inc.
- Joint venture with British corporation Commonwealth Development Corporation (2002) for purchase of state-owned smelter company Empresa Nacional de Fundición (ENAF), owner of Vinto facility, employing 300 workers in 1995 and one of the largest smelters in Latin America
- Received International Finance Corporation (IFC) equity and loans in 1989, 1992, 1994, and 1996 – during his incumbency as President of Bolivia, implying significant conflicts of interest
- Sold COMSUR to Glencore International AG mining corporation in 2003 for $100 million

Other Relevant Information

- Raised from the age of 1 in Washington DC and returned to Bolivia in 1951 after an absence of two decades
- Studied philosophy at the University of Chicago
- Mastering the English language more than Spanish. 'Gringo-like' American accent
- Leader of the 'modernising' faction of the MNR, which marginalised the 'old guard' led by Guillermo Bedregal following his election to the party leadership in 1989 (Domingo 1993)
- Prominent member of the mining association ANMM and of the business confederation CEPB in the 1970s and early 1980s.
- Participant in Foros económicos
- Personal fortune estimated at $200 million. His brother, Antonio, co-owner of COMSUR, is believed to be even richer (Soliz 2004a)

Carlos Iturralde Ballivián (ADN)

Bolivian Government Positions

- Minister Secretary of the Presidency (1972-1973)
- Bolivian ambassador to the US (1978)
- Chancellor (Minister of Foreign Affairs (1989-1991)
- Minister of Presidency (1997-1999)

Positions in MDIs

- Consultant for the Inter-American Development Bank (IDB) (1993)
- Consultant for the Andean Development Corporation (CAF) (2002)

Private Sector Employment or Investments

- Owner since 1972 of International Mining Company (IMCO]) among other mining companies: largest private producer of tin and tungsten in Bolivia – $1.7 million in FDI between 1972 and 1978 (De La Cueva 1983)
- Investments in energy, banking and mining sectors: 12 percent ownership, through IMCO, of Hidroeléctrica Boliviana, consortium controlled by US-based Tenaska

Other Relevant Information

- Educated at the University of North Dakota
- Member of the group of business leaders (CEPB) who invited Harvard University's Jeffrey Sachs to offer technical advice to the Bolivian government in April 1985 during hyperinflationary crisis
- Leader of ADN economic team (1985) and party leader, 'moderniser' who was instrumental in introducing 'young technocrats' such as Jorge Quiroga into the ADN
- Member of the International Tin Council (1975-1982)
- President of the business confederation CEPB (1986-1989), keeping alive the organisational dynamism of his two predecessors, Fernando Romero and Fernando Illanes
- Secretary General of the Bolivian Banking Association (ASOBAN) (1996; 1997; 2000)
- Involved in ideological struggles since 2002 as Executive director of the educational Fundación IDEA. Created in 1990 with the financial assistance of USAID, the ASOBAN and the CEPB, Fundación IDEA focuses on 'entrepreneurial formation' for managers in both state- and privately-owned corporations in Bolivia

Jorge Quiroga Ramírez (ADN)

Bolivian Government Positions

- Under-Secretary of Public Investment and International Cooperation at the Ministry of Planning (1989-92)
- Minister of Finance (1992-3)
- Head of Banzer's presidential electoral campaign (1993)
- Vice-President of Bolivia under the ADN-NFR-PDC banner (1997-2001)
- Assumed Presidency 7 August 2001 after Hugo Banzer was diagnosed with lung cancer (2001-2002)

Positions in MDIs

- Appointed governor of WB, IFC and IMF (1992-1993) while Minister of Finance
- Director, Corporación Andina de Fomento (CAF) 1990s

Private Sector Employment or Investments

- Engineer, IBM (1981-1988)
- Engineer, mining corporation Mintec (1988-9)
- Vice-President of Projects and Investment, Banco Mercantil (1988-9)

Other Relevant Information

- Raised in Santa Cruz: Colegio La Salle
- Spent 10 years in US (1978-1988)
- Educated at the University A&M Texas (BA Industrial engineering) and at the University St Edwards Austin, Texas (MBA)
- Joined ADN political party in 1988
- *Subjefe* (Second in Command) of ADN from 1995.
- Leader of so-called '*pitufos*' (Young Turks, or 'smurfs') of the ADN, a movement of young technocrats educated in the US and Europe, which struggled for the modernisation of the ADN and effectively challenged its old guard, led by Guillermo Fortún, in the late 1990s[2]

- Created political party Poder Democrático Social (PODEMOS) to renovate ADN in 2005
- Vice-chairman of International Democrat Union (IDU), alliance of 80 Conservative parties worldwide founded by Ronald Reagan, Margaret Thatcher, Jacques Chirac and Helmut Kohl among others. PODEMOS is an associate member of IDU
- Director, Inter-American Dialogue

Samuel Doria Medina (MIR-UN)

Bolivian Government Positions

- Minister of Planning (1991-3)

Positions in MDIs

- Governor of the World Bank
- Governor of the IDB

Private Sector Employment or Investments

- Top executive in the commercial house Casa Grace
- Majority shareholder and CEO, since 1987, of the cement company Sociedad Boliviana de Cemento (SOBOCE) (48 percent market share). Around 1,000 employees, engaged in joint ventures with foreign TNCs in Bolivia
- 36.2% shareholding of SOBOCE by Chilean company Bio Bio until 1999, when Doria Medina repurchased these shares for $US 30 million
- 46% ownership by Mexican Grupo Cementos de Chihuahua SA de C.V. (GCC) since 2004
- Merged with Fancesa in 2003. Through SOBOCE's 33,3% ownership of the Fábrica Nacional de Cementos (Fancesa – 300 employees and 30 percent market share), enjoys a virtual monopoly in Bolivia's construction sector (Green et al. 2005)
- Considered one of Bolivia's richest individuals

Other Relevant Information

- Leader of the transnational 'entrepreneurial' wing of the MIR in the late 1980s and 1990s. From 2000 onwards, he attempted to challenge and 'liberalise' the party's social democratic image cultivated since 1985 by the MIR *caudillos*, Oscar Eid and Jaime Paz Zamora
- Participant in Foros Económicos
- Vice-Presidential candidate in 1997 of the MIR political party
- Using his financial power, Doria Medina formalised his rivalry with Paz Zamora by justifying the formation of a new 'centrist' party, the Frente de Unidad Nacional, two months after *Octubre Negro* in 2003, as an 'ethical' rejection of the latter's participation in the second Sánchez de Lozada government

Fernando Romero (no party affiliation)

Bolivian Government

- Minister of Planning (1988-1989)
- Minister of Human Development (1993-1994)
- Creator and executive director of Emergency Social Fund (1987-1989), financed chiefly with WB credit.

Private Sector Employment or Investments

- Involved in banking, commerce, and agribusiness
- Minority shareholder in Casa Grace (commerce) from 1970s.
- Principal shareholder and Executive Director of Banco Hipotecario Nacional (BHN) in 1983-1986, 1989-1993; 1994-1997; accused of financing four of his own companies with loans of Fondesif through BHN (*El Deber* 2008a); sold majority share of BHN to Citibank in 1997

President and owner of:

- Inversiones Bolivianas SA (conglomerate of multiple investments) (1972-1995)
- International Machinery Co. (imports of Caterpillar-Volvo machinery), which benefited from NEP (1972-1985). Renamed Maquinaria Tractores y Equipo (Matreq SA) in 1985
- Unión Agrícola Ganadera SA (1978-): plantations of soy, cotton, sorghum

Heavily involved in micro-credit activities:

- Member of International Directorate of Acción International (1988-1995)
- Creator, with personal friend Jack Duncan (Pres. Acción Internacional), of NGO PRODEM offering non-subsidised micro-credit (1986-). PRODEM received financial support from USAID, the IDB and the Bolivian government through the ESF
- President of PRODEM, turned it into Bolivia's first and largest micro-credit bank in 1992: Banco Solidario (Bancosol)

Other Relevant Information

- Born in Santa Cruz, student in elite schools: Colegio Alemán of La Paz and of Belgrano in Salta, Argentina
- BA Engineering at U. Lowell (US) and MBA at MIT (US)
- President of CEPB (1985-1986) and member of advisory committee of CEPB in 1980s with Carlos Iturralde, Fernando Illanes, Gonzalo Sánchez de Lozada, David Blanco, José Luis Camacho, Roberto Capriles, Julio León Prado[3]
- Part of MNR economic team devising the DS 21060
- Participant in *Foros Económicos* in 1980s
- President of *Fundación Milenio* (1993-1998; financed by German dev. agency GTZ)
- Member of the Directorate of the Universidad Privada Boliviana (2007-present)

Fernando Illanes (no party affiliation)

Bolivian Government Positions

- Bolivian ambassador to US (1985-1987)
- Minister of Energy and Hydrocarbons (1987-1989)
- Minister of Finance (1993-1994)
- Minister of Energy and Hydrocarbons (2002-2003)

Private Sector Employment or Investments

- Businessman with shareholding interests in hydrocarbons TNCs, in the domestic manufacturing and banking sectors
- Director of COBEE (Compania Boliviana de Energia Electrica) (state-owned); Banco Nacional de Bolivia; Banco Industrial SA

(BISA – which received substantial IFC credits and foreign shareholding)
- Executive President of Plastix SA; Duraplast SA; Plasmar (plastics); 'Flor de Empresa' (flower exports); Viniplast SA; Bodegas y Viñedos La Concepción SA (wine production and export); and Empresa Boliviana de Administración (EBA)
- President of Fundetic, recent joint venture and public-private partnership aiming at the 'democratisation of access to telecommunications' – and the stimulation of a 'knowledge economy'

Other Relevant Information

- BA Chemical Engineering Rensselaer Polytechnic Institute (US) MA Chemical Engineering Yale University (US)
- Returned to Bolivia in 1975 following 20 years of professional activities in US and Brazil: high-level manager for Colgate, Palmolive, National Destillers, Chemical Corporation and Becker Industries
- President of National Chamber of Industry
- President of the CEPB (1982-1985), modernised the CEPB and improved its propaganda machinery (linking democracy to capitalism)
- Close collaborator of Sánchez de Lozada
- Led the government team that renegotiated Bolivia's debt stock with foreign private banks – and achieved the repurchase of 72 percent of this debt at 11 cents to the dollar

Fernando Campero Prudencio (MIR sympathiser)

Bolivian Government Positions

- Executive director of the Fondo Social de Emergencia (1987-1989)
- Minister of Foreign Trade and Investment (1992-1993)
- Member of directorate of BCB (after 1993)

Private Sector Employment or Investments

- Owner of eight companies including of the transnational joint venture *Telecel*, the first mobile telephony corporation in

Bolivia; PROESA (distribution of mass consumer goods); ATI (software); and Saxxon Capital (financial trading)

Other Relevant Information

- Part of 'dynamic team' of businessmen appointed to economic Ministries by Jaime Paz in an effort to accelerate the reform process and comply with WB and IMF pressures for privatisation and liberalisation
- Editor of acclaimed book *Bolivia en el Siglo XX* (Harvard Club de Bolivia)
- Co-founder of weekly *Pulso*
- Founder of Fundación *Nuevo Norte*, business organisation aiming at private industrial development in the *Occidente* (La Paz, Oruro, Potosí, Cochabamba) of Bolivia

Jorge Crespo Velasco (MIR)

Bolivian Government Positions

- Head of Development Corporation of La Paz (1980)
- Under-secretary of Industry and Commerce, Minister of Industry and Commerce, Vice-Minister of Foreign Relations (1982-5)
- Ambassador to the US (1989-1993): 'My background in the private sector helped me to undertake a series of negotiations with the US government ... in order to leave the coca-cocaine circuit what Bolivia needs is commerce and investment, so we called on the US companies to invest and on the US government to open its doors to Bolivian exports'[4]
- Minister of Foreign Trade and Investment (1997-1999)
- Minister of Defence (1999-2000)

Positions in MDIs

- Alternate Executive Director for Paraguay, Uruguay & Bolivia, IDB (2004-5)

Private Sector Employment or Investments

- Investments in industry, commerce, consulting
- 'Yo me defino como un empresario privado con vocación de servicio público'[5]

Other Relevant Information

- Member of Board of Directors of Bolivian-American Chamber of Commerce
- Father businessman and Congressman
- Prominent member MIR (1980), close to Jaime Paz Zamora, entrepreneurial wing of MIR
- Created group 'Amigos de Bolivia' in early 1990s to attract US investors to Bolivia, organised forums in the US concluded by 'contratos de riesgo compartido' (joint ventures) between US and Bolivian companies, in hydrocarbons and agriculture (especially soy). The 'contratos de riesgo compartido were an idea of Jaime Paz'[6]

Carlos Morales Landívar (MNR)

Bolivian Government Positions

- Minister of Energy and Hydrocarbons (1986-1988)
- Minister of Housing and Public Works (2002)

Private Sector Employment or Investments

- Executive officer of TNC Compañía Logística de Hidrocarburos Boliviana (CLHB) – with Peruvian and German capital: oil and gas transport and storage[7]

Other Relevant Information

- Harvard graduate
- Chaired CEPB meetings in 1985

- Member of group of business leaders who invited Jeffrey Sachs to Bolivia 1985. Personal friend of Sachs[8]
- Active in the privatisation of the pipelines of YPFB

Ramiro Cabezas Masses (no party affiliation)

Bolivian Government Positions

- Minister of Revenue (1987-1988)
- Minister of Finance (1988-1989)
- Superintendent of Banks (3 years 1990s)
- Superintendent *Superintendencia Tributaria* late 1990s

Private Sector Employment or Investments

- Shareholder of Casa Grace, associate of Doria Medina's father
- Commerce – Imports. President of Corporación Automotriz Boliviana SA (CABSA). 'I was lent by the private sector to the public sector This happened several times'[9]

Other Relevant Information

- Harvard graduate
- Lived 16 years abroad, working as advisor to various governments before returning to Bolivia in 1984
- President of Bolivian-Brazilian Chamber of Commerce
- Devised simplification of tax system (Law 843)

Juan Cariaga (no party affiliation)

Bolivian Government Positions

- Minister of Finance (1985-1987)

Positions in MDIs

- Governor of IDB (1987-1989)

Private sector employment or investments

- Senior economist in the Banco Santa Cruz (early 1980s)

Other relevant information

- One of the architects of the DS 21060. Involved in both MNR and ADN economic teams
- Participant in *Foros Económicos*

Gustavo Fernández Saavedra (ADN)

Bolivian government positions

- Ambassador of Bolivia in Brazil
- General Consul of Bolivia in Chile
- Secretary Minister of integration
- Minister of the Presidency (1989-1993)
- Chancellor/Foreign Minister (2001-2002)

Positions in MDIs

- Director of UNCTAD/CEPAL/PNUD in Quito and Geneva
- Consultant of CAF, ILPES and IDB
- Director of the Agreement of Cartagena Board in Lima

Private sector employment or investments

- Lawyer and professor

Other relevant information

- Has represented, with Herbert Müller, Horst Grebe, and George Gray among others, the technocratic and intellectual leadership of the transnational bloc in Bolivia

---

Notes

[1] This list is certainly not exhaustive, and only serves to indicate that 'transnational capital' in Bolivia is not tantamount to 'foreign TNCs + Gonzalo Sánchez de Lozada and his brother', as diatribes against 'foreign encroachment' have customarily tended to present the anatomy of capital in Bolivia (see Soliz Rada 2004a, Kohl and Farthing 2005, 2009; Hylton and Thomson 2007). An excellent source of information on the shareholding structure of companies listed on the Bolivian stock market is the website of the Superintendency of Pensions, Stock and Insurance. See http://www.spvs.gov.bo/. Accessed 5 February 2009. It indicates the presence of several 'foreign' (primarily in the banking and insurance sectors, but also in telecommunications and hydrocarbons), shareholders of 'national' companies. For example, Spain-based Repsol retains 48 percent ownership of the recently 'nationalised' hydrocarbon YPFB, and the original owner of Entel (telecommunications) has been replaced by Eurotelecom International Netherlands (50 percent ownership).

[2] Interview with Guillermo Fortún, 21 September 2007. Mauro Mariani describes the new Banzer administration: 'We began to see a wave of young, English-speaking technocrats in the high spheres of the administration with the arrival of Tuto Quiroga'. Interview with Mauro Mariani, 20 December 2007.

[3] The advisory board of PRODEM included Sánchez de Lozada, Iturralde, Illanes, Romero, the CEPB, the CAINCO, and leading Bolivian enterprises, including: Comsur, Banco Boliviano Americano, Banco Industrial, BHN Multibanco, Intermaco (PRODEM 1998).

[4] Interview with Jorge Crespo, 28 September 2007.

[5] Interview with Jorge Crespo, 28 September 2007.

[6] Interview with Jorge Crespo, 28 September 2007.

[7] The CLHB was recently renationalised by the Morales administration (*Bolpress* 2008).

[8] Interview with Carlos Morales, 20 September 2007.

[9] Interview with Ramiro Cabezas, 17 September 2007.

Bibliography

ABC News (2008) 'Exclusive: Peace Corps, Fulbright Scholar Asked to 'Spy' on Cubans and Venezuelans', 8 February. Available at http://abcnews.go.com/. Accessed 15 May 2008.

Abrams, Philip (1988) 'Notes on the Difficulty of Studying the State', *Journal of Historical Sociology*, 1, (1).

Adcock, Robert and Collier, David (2001) 'Measurement Validity: A Shared Standard for Qualitative and Quantitative Research', *American Political Science Review* 95 (3): 529-546.

Agence France Presse (2006) 'Bolivia seeks to double the price of gas for Brazil'. 31 May. Available at http://www.petroleumworld.com/. Accessed 19 June 2006.

Agencia Boliviana de Información (ABI) (2008) 'Evo Morales declara persona non grata a Goldberg por conspirar a la democracia'. 10 September. Available at http://www.abi.bo/. Accessed 15 October 2008.

ABI (2009) 'Evo Morales pondera crecimiento económico de Potosí en 2008 y considera baja este año'. 29 May. Available at http://www.abi.bo/. Accessed 15 June 2009.

Agencia Bolivariana de Noticias (ABN) (2008) 'Expulsión de embajador de EEUU no significa cese de relaciones'. 11 September. Available at http://www.abn.info.ve/. Accessed 15 October 2008.

Agreda, Jorge (1969) *Bolivie 1969* (Louvain: Université de Louvain).

Aillón, Tania (1999) 'Un balance de la política burguesa de recuperación del sector minero en Bolivia', *Marxismo Hoy* 6. September. Available at http://www.engels.org/. Accessed 10 October 2006.

Albó, Xavier (1990) La Cara India y Campesina de Nuestra Historia (La Paz: Unitas).

Albó, Xavier (1994) 'And from Kataristas to MNRistas? The Surprising and Bold Alliance between Aymaras and Neoliberals in Bolivia', in Donna Lee Van Cott (ed.) *Indigenous Peoples and Democracy in Latin America* (St Martin's Press).

Albó, Xavier (1999) 'Diversidad Etnica, Cultural y Linguistica', in Fernando Campero Prudencio (ed.) *Bolivia en el Siglo XX: La Formación de la Bolivia Contemporánea* (La Paz: Harvard Club).

Albó, Xavier (2008) 'The "Long memory" of Ethnicity in Bolivia and Some Temporary Oscillations', in John Crabtree and Laurence Whitehead (eds.) *Unresolved Tensions: Bolivia Past and Present* (Pittsburgh: University of Pittsburgh Press).

Al Jazeera (2007) 'Bolivia Assembly Backs Constitution'. Available at http://english.aljazeera.net/. Accessed 20 October 2008.

Altman, David and Lalander, Rickard (2003) 'Bolivia's Popular Participation Law: An Undemocratic Democratisation Process?' in Axel Hadenius (ed.) *Decentralisation and Democratic Governance: Experiences from India, Bolivia and South Africa* (Stockholm: Almqvist & Wiksell International).

Americas Society/Council of the Americas (2008) 'Interview: FIU's Eduardo Gamarra on Bolivian President Evo Morales' "Riskless" Recall Vote', August 4. Available at http://www.as-coa.org. Accessed 8 October 2008.

Amin, Samir (1990) *Delinking: Towards a Polycentric World* (London: Zed Books).

Amin, Samir (2004) The Liberal Virus: Permanent War and the Americanization of the World (New York: Monthly Review Press).

Amnesty International (2008) 'Appeal: Fear for Safety. Adalberto Rojas'. Available at www.amnesty.org/. Accessed 18 October 2008.

Anderson, Benedict (1991) Imagined communities: reflections on the origins and spread of nationalism (London: Verso).

Antezana, Luis (1983) 'Sistema y procesos ideológicos en Bolivia, in René Zavaleta (ed.) *Bolivia, Hoy* (Mexico: Siglo XXI Editores)

Antón, Carlos (2008) 'Tierra, élites, pueblos originarios: un estudio a fondo', *Rebelión*, 9 November. Available at http://www.rebelion.org/. Accessed 15 November 2008.

Arnold, Denise and Spedding, Alison (2007) 'Género, Etnicidad y Clases Sociales: La Mujer en los Movimientos Sociales y Movimientos de Mujeres', in Jesús Espasandín and Pablo Iglesias (eds.) *Bolivia en movimiento: Acción colectiva y poder político* (Madrid: El Viejo Topo).

Archer, Margaret et al. (1998) *Critical Realism: Essential Readings* (London: Routledge).

Ardaya, Rubén and Thévoz, Laurent (2001) 'Promoting Popular Participation: Lessons to be Learned from the Bolivian Decentralization Process', *Mountain Research and Development* 21 (3): 215-220.

Asamblea Constituyente de Bolivia (2007) Nueva Constitución Política del Estado: aprobada en grande, detalle y revisión (Oruro). Available at http://www.laconstituyente.org/. Accessed 15 October 2008.

Assies, Willem (2003) 'David versus Goliath in Cochabamba: Water Rights, Neoliberalism and the Revival of Social Protest in Bolivia', *Latin American Perspectives* 30 (3): 14-36.

Assies, Willem and Salman, Ton (2003) *Crisis in Bolivia: The Elections of 2002 and their Aftermath* (London: Institute of Latin American Studies).

Augelli, Enrico and Craig Murphy (1988), America's quest for supremacy and the Third World: a Gramscian analysis (London: Pinter).

Baldwin, David (1993), *Neorealism and Neoliberalism – The Contemporary Debate* (New York: Columbia University Press).

Baker, Andrew (1999) '*Nébuleuse* and the "internationalization of the state" in the UK? The case of HM Treasury and the Bank of England, *Review of International Political Economy* 6 (1): 79-100.

Banco Central de Bolivia [BCB] (2010) 'Indicadores de inflación'. Available at: http://www.bcb.gob.bo/. Accessed 20 March 2010.

Banco Mercantil (2006) *Memoria Anual: 100 años 1905-2005* (La Paz: Banco Mercantil).

Barragán, Rossana (2008) 'Oppressed or Privileged Regions? Some Historical Reflections on the Use of State Resources', in John Crabtree and Laurence Whitehead (eds.) *Unresolved Tensions: Bolivia Past and Present* (Pittsburgh: University of Pittsburgh Press).

Bauer, Richard and Bowen, Sally (1997) *The Bolivian formula: from state capitalism to capitalization* (London: MacGrawHill).

BBC News (2006a) 'Morales Seeks Support from France'. 7 January. Available at http://news.bbc.co.uk/. Accessed 7 January 2006.

BBC News (2006b) 'Evo Morales: Padlocked in the Palace'. 5 April. Available at http://www.bbc.co.uk/blogs/. Accessed 6 April 2006.

BBC News (2006c) 'Press abuzz over Bolivia gas move'. 3 May. Available at http://news.bbc.co.uk/. Accessed 3 May 2006.

BBC News (2008a) 'Washington expels Bolivian envoy'. 12 September. Available at http://news.bbc.co.uk/. Accessed 12 September 2008.

BBC News (2008b) 'Brazil squares up to economic storm'. 20 October. Available at http://news.bbc.co.uk/. Accessed 20 October 2008.

Bellamy Foster, John (2006) *Naked Imperialism: the US pursuit of global dominance* (New York: Monthly Review Press).

Berthin, Gerardo (1999) 'El Estado y sus Instituciones', in Fernando Campero Prudencio (ed.) *Bolivia en el Siglo XX: La Formación de la Bolivia Contemporánea* (La Paz: Harvard Club).

Bieler, Andreas and Morton, Adam (2001) 'Introduction: Neo-Gramscian Perspectives in International Political Economy and the Relevance to European Integration', in Andreas Bieler and Adam Morton (eds.) *Social Forces in the Making of the New Europe* (Basingstoke: Palgrave).

Bieler, Andreas and Morton, Adam (2001) 'The Gordian Knot of Agency-Structure in International Relations', *European Journal of International Relations* 7 (1): 5-35.

Bieler, Andreas and Morton, Adam (2003) 'Globalisation, the state and class struggle: a Critical Economy engagement with Open Marxism', *British Journal of Politics and International Relations*, 5 (4): 467-499.

Bieler, Andreas et al. (2006), 'Introduction', in Bieler et al. (eds.), *Global restructuring: state, capital and labour* (London: Palgrave).

Bieler, Andreas et al. (2006) *Globalization, the state and class struggle* (Basingstoke: Palgrave).

Biersteker, Thomas (1995) 'The "triumph" of liberal economic ideas' in Barbara Stallings (ed.) *Global Change, Regional Responses: The New Context of International Development* (Cambridge: CUP).

Blanes, José (1991) 'Descentralización político-administrativa y gobernabilidad' in Fernando Mayorga (ed.) *Democratización y modernización del estado en Bolivia* (La Paz: CEBEM).

Blasier, Cole (1971) 'The United States and the Revolution', in James Malloy and Richard Thorn (eds.) *Beyond the Revolution: Bolivia since 1952* (Pittsburgh: University of Pittsburgh Press).

Block, Fred (1977a) *The Origins of International Economic Disorder: A Study of United States International Monetary Policy From World War II to the Present* (Berkeley: University of California Press).

Block, Fred (1977b) 'The Ruling Class Does Not Rule: Notes on the Marxist Theory of the State', *Socialist Revolution*, 7 (33): 6-28.

Bolpress (2003) 'El actual ministro Xavier Nogales cobró del ministerio de Revollo'. 28 November. Available at http://www.bolpress.com/. Accessed 18 November 2008.

Bolpress (2005) 'Alvaro García Linera: "El capitalismo andino es un paso intermedio para imaginar el socialismo'. 7 October. Available at http://www.bolpress.com/. Accessed 10 Ocobter 2005.

Bolpress (2006) 'Evo: El país es menos corrupto, más digno y más estable'. 5 August. Available at http://www.bolpress.com/. Accessed 2 February 2008.

Bolpress (2007) 'Estados Unidos se niega a que fiscalizen la ayuda de USAID'. 19 November. Available at http://www.bolpress.com/. Accessed 3 October 2008.

Bolpress (2008) 'El Estado compra la Compañía Logística de Hidrocarburos y recupera la mayoría accionaria de Chaco, Andina y Transredes'. 01 May. Available at http://www.bolpress.com/. Accessed 16 September 2008.

Bonefeld, Werner (1991) 'The Social Constitution of the State', in Werner Bonefeld, Richard Gunn and Kosmas Psychopedis (eds.), *Open Marxism, Vol.1: Dialectics and History* (London: Pluto Press).

Bonefeld, Werner, Gunn, Richard and Psychopedis, Kosmas (1991), 'Introduction', in Werner Bonefeld, Richard Gunn and Kosmas Psychopedis (eds.), *Open Marxism, Vol.1: Dialectics and History* (London: Pluto Press).

Bonefeld, Werner, Gunn, Richard and Psychopedis, Kosmas (1992), 'Introduction', in Werner Bonefeld, Richard Gunn and Kosmas Psychopedis, *Open Marxism, Vol.2: Theory and Practice* (London: Pluto Press).

Bonefeld, Werner (2000) 'The Spectre of Globalization: On the Form and Content of the World Market', in Werner Bonefeld and Kosmas Psychopedis (eds.), *The Politics of Change: Globalization, Ideology and Critique* (Basingstoke: Palgrave).

Boswell, and Chase-Dunn, Christopher (2000) *The Spiral of Capitalism and Socialism. Towards Global Democracy* (Colorado: Lynne Rienner).

Boynton, Rachel (2005) *'Our brand is crisis'*. Video documentary.

Brady, Henry and David Collier (2004) *Rethinking Social Inquiry: Diverse Tools, Shared Standards* (Lanham: Rowman and Littlefield).

Braudel, Fernand (1980) *On History* (Chicago: University of Chicago Press).

Brenner, Robert (1977) 'The origins of capitalist development', *New Left Review* 104 (1977): 25-92.

Bruff, Ian (2008) 'The Continued Relevance of Nicos Poulantzas' *State, Power, Socialism*', presented at the BISA annual conference, University of Exeter, 15-17 December 2008.

Burke, Melvin (1987) 'The Corporación Minera de Bolivia (COMIBOL) and the Triangular Plan: a case study in dependency', *Latin American Issues* 4. http://webpub.allegheny.edu/group/LAS/LatinAmIssues/. Accessed 7 April 2006.

Burnell, Peter (2005) 'Political Strategies of External Support for Democratization', *Foreign Policy Analysis* 1 (3): 361-384.

Burnham, Peter (1990) The Political Economy of Postwar Reconstruction (London: Macmillan).

Burnham, Peter (1991) 'Neo-Gramscian hegemony and international order', *Capital and Class* 45: 73-93.

Burnham, Peter (1994a) 'Open Marxism and vulgar international political economy', *Review of International Political Economy* 1 (2): 221-231.

Burnham, Peter (1994b) 'The Organisational View of the State', *Politics* 14 (1): 1-7.

Burnham, Peter (1995), 'Capital, Crisis and the International State System', in Werner Bonefeld and John Holloway (eds.) *Global Capital, National States and the Politics of Money* (Basingstoke: Macmillan).

Burnham, Peter (2000) 'Globalization, Depoliticization and 'Modern' Economic Management' in Werner Bonefeld and Kosmas Psychopedis (eds.) *The Politics of Change: Globalization, Ideology and Critique* (Basingstoke: Palgrave).

Burnham, Peter (2001) 'Marx, IPE and globalisation', *Capital and Class* 75.

Burnham, Peter (2002) 'Class struggle, states and global circuits of capital' in Mark Pupert and Hazel Smith (eds.) *Historical Materialism and Globalization* (London: Routledge).

Burnham, Peter et al. (2004) *Research methods in Politics* (London: Palgrave).

Cabezas, Ramiro (1990) 'Bolivia's Tax Reform of 1986', *Tax Notes International*, 529 (May).

Calderón, Fernando (1999) 'Un Siglo de Luchas Sociales', in Fernando Campero Prudencio (ed.) *Bolivia en el Siglo XX: La Formación de la Bolivia Contemporánea* (La Paz: Harvard Club).

Callinicos, Alex and Justin Rosenberg (2008) 'Uneven and combined development: the social-relational substratum of "the international"? An exchange of letters', *Cambridge Review of International Affairs* 21(1): 77-112.

Cammack, Paul (1991) 'Democracy and Development in Latin America. Review Article', *Journal of International Development* 3 (5): 527-550.

Cammack, Paul (2003) 'The Governance of Global Capitalism', *Historical Materialism* 11 (2): 37-59.

Cammack, Paul (2006) 'The Politics of Global Competitiveness', *Papers in the Politics of Global Competitiveness* 1, Manchester Metropolitan University (November).

Cammack, Paul (2007) 'Forget the transnational state' *Papers in the Politics of Global Competitiveness* 2, Manchester Metropolitan University (January).

Cariaga, Juan (1990) 'Bolivia', in John Williamson (ed.) *Latin American Adjustment: How Much Has Happened?* (Washington DC: Institute for International Economics).

Carter, William (1971) 'Revolution and the agrarian sector', in James Malloy and Richard Thorn (eds.) *Beyond the Revolution: Bolivia since 1952* (Pittsburgh: University of Pittsburgh Press).

Centellas, Miguel (2000) 'Decentralization and Democratization in Bolivia', Paper presented at 22nd Annual Conference of the Latin American Studies Association, Miami.

Center for Economic and Policy Research (2008) 'US Should Disclose Its Funding to Opposition Groups in Bolivia and Other Latin American Countries'. 12 September. Available at http://www.cepr.net/. Accessed 5 October 2008.

CEPAL (1983) *Los bancos transnacionales, el Estado y el endeudamiento externo en Bolivia*. Estudios e Informes de la CEPAL E/CEPAL/G.1251. June (Santiago de Chile: United Nations).

Cerny, Phil (2005) 'Political Globalization and the Competition State', in Richard Stubbs and Geoffrey R. D. Underhill (eds.) *The Political Economy of the Changing Global Order* (Oxford: OUP).

Chomsky, Noam (2003) Hegemony or Survival: America's Quest for Global Dominance (New York: Metropolitan Books).

Chong, Alberto (2004) 'Costos y beneficios de la privatización en América Latina', in Delegación Presidencial Para la Revisión y Mejora de la Capitalización (DPC) *10 Años de la Capitalización: Luces y Sombras* (La Paz: DPC).

Chossudovsky, Michel (1998) *The globalisation of poverty* (London: Zed Books).

Chossudovsky, Michel (2008) 'The Destabilization of Bolivia and the Kosovo Option', *Global Research*, 21 September. Available at http://www.tlaxcala.es/. Accessed 6 October 2008.

Chu, Michael (2005) 'Accion International: Maintaining High Performance Through Time', *World Bank/Brookings Conference on Access to Finance*. May 30-31 2006. Section VI Case Studies.

Clarke, Simon (1988) Keynesianism, Monetarism and the Crisis of the State (Edward Elgar: Aldershot).

Clarke, Simon (1991), 'The state Debate', in Simon Clarke (ed.) *The State Debate* (London: Palgrave).

Clarke (2001) 'The globalization of capital, crisis and class struggle', *Capital and Class* 75, 93-101.

Claure Quezada, Humberto (2008) 'Transnacionales, Oligarcas Cruceños y la Nacionalización', *Rebelión.* 4 August.

Cliff, Tony (1974) *State capitalism in Russia* (London: Pluto Press).

Climenhage, Christy (1999) International Influence and Transnational Networks: The Role of Policy Teams during Neoliberal Transition in Chile and Bolivia, Unpublished thesis (DPhil), University of Cambridge.

Clough, Langdon (2008) 'Energy profile of Bolivia' in Cutler J. Cleveland (ed.) *Encyclopedia of Earth* (Washington, D.C.: Environmental Information Coalition, National Council for Science and the Environment). Available at http://www.eoearth.org/. Accessed 19 September 2009.

CNE (2009) *Resultados Referéndum Nacional Constituyente 2009.* Documento de Información Pública 4. February.

Council on Hemispheric Affairs (COHA) (2006) 'The Grounds for Bolivia's New Military Bases', 18 October. Available at http://www.coha.org/Accessed 15 January 2008.

COHA (2008a) 'Bolivia struggles with its proposed new Constitution'. 18 April. Available at http://www.coha.org/. Accessed 25 May 2008.

COHA (2008b) 'A Closer Look at Recent Violence in Bolivia'. 19 September. Available at http://www.coha.org/Accessed 4 October 2008.

COHA (2009) 'US-Bolivia Relations: Halting an Avalanche', 15 June. Available at http://www.coha.org/. Accessed 17 June 2009.

Cohen, Robin and Rai, Shirin (2000) 'Introduction', in Robin Cohen and Shirin Rai (eds.) *Global Social Movements* (London: Athlone).

Collier, David and Mahon, James (1993) 'Conceptual "Stretching" Revisited: Adapting Categories in Comparative Analysis', *The American Political Science Review*, 87 (4) (Dec): 845-855.

Collier, Paul and Gunning, Jan Willem (1999) 'The IMF's role in Structural Adjustment', *The Economic Journal* 109: 634-651.

Conaghan, Catherine (1990) 'Business and "the boys": the politics of neoliberalism in the Central Andes (Bolivia, Ecuador and Peru)', *Latin American Research Review,* 25 (2): 3-30.

Conaghan, Catherine (1992) 'Capitalists, Technocrats and Politicians: Economic Policymaking and Democracy in the Central Andes', in Scott Mainwaring, Guillermo O'Donnell and Samuel Valenzuela (eds.) *Issues in Democratic Consolidation* (Notre Dame: University of Notre Dame Press).

Conaghan, Catherine and Malloy, James (1995) *Unsettling statecraft: democracy and neoliberalism in the central Andes* (Pittsburgh: University of Pittsburgh Press).

Cox, Robert (1981) 'Social forces, states, and world orders: beyond international relations theory', *Millennium*, 10 (2). Reprinted in Robert Cox and Timothy Sinclair (1996) *Approaches to world order* (Cambridge: CUP).

Cox, Robert (1983) 'Gramsci, hegemony, and international relations: an essay in method', *Millennium*, 12 (2): 162-175. Reprinted in Robert Cox and Timothy Sinclair (1996) *Approaches to world order* (Cambridge: CUP).

Cox, Robert (1987) Production, Power and World Order: Social Forces in the Making of History (New York: Columbia University Press).

Cox, Robert (1992) 'Towards a post-hegemonic conceptualization of world order: Reflections on the relevancy of Ibn Khaldun'. Reprinted in Robert Cox and Timothy Sinclair (1996) *Approaches to world order* (Cambridge: CUP).

Cox, Robert (1994) 'The Crisis in the World Order and the Challenge to International Organization', *Cooperation and Conflict* 29 (2): 99-113.

Cox, Robert and Michael Schechter (2002) The Political Economy of a Plural World: Critical Reflections on Power, Morals and Civilization (London: Routledge).

Crabtree, John (1987) *The Great Tin Crash: Bolivia and the World Tin Market* (London: Latin American Bureau).

Crabtree, John (2005) Patterns of protest: politics and social movements in Bolivia (London: Latin American Bureau).

Crabtree, John (2006a) 'Bolivia stakes its claim', *Open Democracy*. 3 May. Available at http://www.opendemocracy.net/. Accessed 10th May 2006

Crabtree, John (2006b) 'Bolivia: the battle for two thirds', *Open Democracy*. 17 September. Available at http://www.opendemocracy.net. Accessed 19 September 2006.

Crabtree, John (2007a) 'Bolivia: a tale of two (or rather three) cities', *Open Democracy*. 18 September. Available at http://www.opendemocracy.net/ Accessed 2 October 2007.

Crabtree, John (2007b) 'Bolivia's controversial constitution', *Open Democracy*, 10 December. Available at http://www.opendemocracy.net/. Accessed 15 December 2007.

Crabtree, John (2008a) 'Bolivia's democratic tides', *Open Democracy*, 2 July. Available at http://www.opendemocracy.net/. Accessed 15 July 2008.

Crabtree, John (2008b) 'Bolivia's political ferment: revolution and recall', *Open Democracy*, 13 August. Available at http://www.opendemocracy.net/. Accessed 15 August.

Crabtree, John (2009) 'Bolivia: after the vote'. 2 February. Available at http://www.opendemocracy.net/. Accessed 15 February.

Crabtree, John and Whitehead, Laurence (2001) *Towards Democratic Viability: The Bolivian Experience* (London: Palgrave).

Crabtree, John and Whitehead, Laurence (2008) *Unresolved Tensions: Bolivia Past and Present* (Pittsburgh: University of Pittsburgh Press).

Crozier, Michel et al. (1975) The crisis of democracy: report on the governability of democracies to the Trilateral Commission (New York: New York University Press).

Dahl, Robert (1971) *Polyarchy: Participation and Opposition* (New Haven: Yale University Press).

Dangl, Benjamin (2008a) 'Undermining Bolivia', *Green Left Weekly* 542. 5 March.

Dangl, Benjamin (2008b) 'Bush Spending Tax Dollars to Foment Unrest in Bolivia', *The Progressive*. 10 March. Available at http://www.alternet.org/. Accessed 25 February 2009.

De La Cueva (1983) *Bolivia: Imperialismo y Oligarquía* (La Paz: Ediciones Roalva).

Delegación Presidencial Para la Revisión y Mejora de la Capitalización (DPC) (2004) *10 Años de la Capitalización: Luces y Sombras* (La Paz: DPC).

Democracy Center (2007) 'Bolivia writes a new Constitution'. 6 August. Available at http://www.democracyctr.org/ Accessed 7 September 2008.

Democracy Now! (2008) 'US Embassy in Bolivia Tells Fulbright Scholar and Peace Corps Volunteers to Spy on Venezuelans and Cubans in Bolivia', 11 February. Available at http://www.democracynow.org/. Accessed 15 February 2008.

Démélas, Marie-Danielle (1980) Nationalisme Sans Nation ? La Bolivie aux XIXème et XXème siècles (Paris: Editions du CNRS).

Development Assistance Committee – OECD (1989), Note by the Secretariat, *Development co-operation in the 1990s: working with developing countries towards sustainable and equitable development*, DAC (89)5 1st Revision, 22 May (Paris: or. English).

Development Assistance Committee – OECD (2005) Paris Declaration on Aid Effectiveness: Ownership, Harmonisation, Alignments, Results and Mutual Accountability. High Level Forum on Harmonisation. 2 March (Paris: OECD).

Development Assistance Committee – OECD (2006) DAC in Dates: The History of OECD's Development Assistance Committee (Paris: OECD).

Development Committee Task Force on Multilateral Development Banks (1996) *Serving a Changing World: Report of the Task Force on Multilateral Development Banks*, March 15 (Washington DC: International Bank for Reconstruction and Development, International Monetary Fund).

Dieterich, Heinz (2006) Bolivia: salto cualitativo de la "Revolución Naranja", limpieza étnica y terrorismo oligárquico', Rebelión, 18 December. Available at http://www3.rebelion.org/. Accessed 10 September 2008.

Do Alto, Hervé and Stefanoni, Pablo (2006) *La revolución de Evo Morales: de la coca al palacio* (La Paz: Capital Intelectual).

Do Alto, Hervé and Stefanoni, Pablo (2008) Nous serons des millions: Evo Morales et la gauche au pouvoir en Bolivie (Paris: Raisons d'Agir).

Domingo, Pilar (1993) Democracy in the making? Political parties and political institutions in Bolivia, 1985-1991, Thesis (DPhil), University of Oxford.

Domingo, Pilar (2001) 'Party Politics, Intermediation and Representation', in John Crabtree and Laurence Whitehead (eds.) *Towards Democratic Viability: The Bolivian Experience* (London: Palgrave).

Domingo, Pilar and Grindle, Merilee (2003) *Proclaiming Revolution: Bolivia in Comparative Perspective* (Cambridge, MA: Harvard University Press).

Doria Medina, Samuel (1986) *La Economía Informal en Bolivia* (La Paz: UDAPE).

Dunkerley, James (1982) *Bolivia 1980-1981: The Political System in Crisis.* Research Paper No.8 (London: Institute of Latin American Studies).

Dunkerley, James (1984) Rebellion in the veins: political struggle in Bolivia, 1952-1982 (London: Verso).

Dunkerley, James (1990) *Political transition and economic stabilisation: Bolivia, 1982-1989* (London: Institute of Latin American Studies).

Dunkerley, James (2003) 'The Origins of the Bolivian Revolution in the 20th Century: Some Reflections', in Pilar Domingo and Merilee Grindle (2003) *Proclaiming Revolution: Bolivia in Comparative Perspective* (Cambridge, MA: Harvard University Press).

Dunkerley, James (2007 [1998]) 'The 1997 Bolivian election in historical perspective', in *Bolivia: revolution and the power of history in the present* (London: Institute for the Study of the Americas).

Dunkerley, James (2007) 'Evo Morales, Alvaro García and the Third Bolivian Revolution', in *Bolivia: revolution and the power of history in the present* (London: Institute for the Study of the Americas).

Durkheim, Emile (1982) The rules of sociological method: and selected texts on sociology and its method (London: Macmillan).

Eaton, Kent (2007) 'Backlash in Bolivia: Regional Autonomy as a Reaction against Indigenous Mobilization', *Politics and Society* 35 (1): 71-102.

Eckstein, Susan (1983) 'Transformation of a "Revolution from Below" – Bolivia and International Capital', *Comparative Studies in Society and History* 25 (1): 105-135.

Eckstein, Susan (2001) *Power and Popular Protest: Latin American Social Movements* (Berkeley: University of California Press).

Econoticias (2006) 'Sindicalistas vigilarán de cerca a Morales'. 1 February. Available in English at http://mrzine.monthlyreview.org/. Accessed 10 February 2006.

Eid, Ricardo (2008) 'La Unión Juvenil Cruceñista y la controvertida participación política de sus integrantes'. Available at http://www.pieb.com.bo/. Accessed 19 October 2008.

El Deber (1988), 'Ministros justificaron sueldos extras para evitar corrupción', 29 July.

El Deber (2006) 'Unión Juvenil: entre el exceso y el apoyo Función'. 17 September.

El Deber (2007) 'Piden a la Unión Juvenil Cruceñista que revise su rol'. 5 October.

El Deber (2008a) 'Dan libertad condicional al ex-Ministro Fernando Romero'. 28 March.

El Deber (2008b) 'Sucre impide llegada de Evo y echa a campesinos'. 25 May.

El Deber (2009) 'FMI alerta que la crisis puede impactar Bolivia'. 22 March.

El Mundo (Bolivia) (1988) 'Altos funcionarios perciben sueldos de entidades internacionales', 29 July.

El Mundo (Spain) (2007a) 'Evo Morales defiende la "refundación" de Bolivia con una nueva Constitución'. 22 January.

El Mundo (Spain) (2007b) 'La violencia estalla en la zona central de Bolivia y deja dos muertos y 70 heridos'. 12 January.

El País (2006a) 'Intranquilidad en Bruselas', 3 May.

El Pais (2006b) 'Hugo Chávez envía abogados y técnicos', 3 May.

El País (2007) 'La Milicia Indígena de Morales', 19 February.

Espasandín, Jesús and Iglesias, Pablo (2007) *Bolivia en movimiento: Acción colectiva y poder político* (Madrid: El Viejo Topo).

Faguet, Jean-Paul (2002) Decentralizing the Provision of Public Services in Bolivia: Institutions, Political Competition and the Effectiveness of Local Government. PhD thesis, London School of Economics.

Faguet, Jean-Paul (2003) 'Decentralisation and Local Government in Bolivia: an Overview from the Bottom-Up', *Crisis State Programme Working Papers* 29. May.

Fernández Terrán, Roberto (2003) FMI, Banco Mundial y estado neocolonial: poder supranacional en Bolivia (La Paz: Plural Editores).

Financial Times (2006) 'Chávez casts a long anti-American shadow over regional capitals', 3 May.

Finegold, K. and Skocpol, Theda (1995), 'Marxist Approaches to Politics and the State', *State and Party in America's New Deal* (Madison: University of Wisconsin Press).

Foley, Michael and Yambert, Karl (1989) 'Anthropology and Theories of the State' in Benjamen Orlove et al. (eds.) *State, Capital and Rural Society: Anthropological Perspectives on Political Economy in Mexico and the Andes* (Boulder: Westview Press).

Foxley, Alejandro and Whitehead, Laurence (1980) 'Economic Stabilization in Latin America: Political Dimensions – Editor's Introduction', *World Development* 8: 823-832.

Frank, André Gunder (1975) *On Capitalist Underdevelopment* (New York: Oxford University Press).

Frank, Andre Gunder (1978) *Dependent Accumulation and Underdevelopment* (London: Macmillan).

Friedman, Milton (1962) *Capitalism and Freedom* (Chicago: University of Chicago Press).

Fundación Milenio (2002) La Capitalización cinco años después. La realidad, los beneficios, los próximos pasos (La Paz: Fundación Milenio).

Fundación Milenio (2008) *Informe de Milenio sobre la Economía: Primer Trimestre 2008* 25, July (La Paz: Fundación Milenio).

Galeano, Eduardo (2008 [1989]) *El Libro de los Abrazos* (Madrid: Siglo XXI Editores).

Gallup International (2008a) ' Bolivia's Class Divisions Play Out in Autonomy Push'. May 20.

Gallup International (2008b) Asi Piensan los Bolivianos # 130, Una evaluación del Presidente, Los Referéndums Revocatorios. July.

Gallup International (2008c) 'Bolivia Dispute Highlights Class Division'. Available at http://www.gallup.com/. Accessed 2 October 2008

Gamarra, Eduardo (1988) 'Bolivia: Disengagement and Democratisation', in Constantine Danopoulos (ed.) *Military Disengagement from Politics* (London: Routledge).
Gamarra, Eduardo (1991) 'Presidencialismo híbrido y democratización', in Fernando Mayorga (ed.) *Democratización y modernización del estado en Bolivia* (La Paz: CEBEM).
Gamarra, Eduardo (1994) 'Crafting Political Support for Stabilization: Political Pacts and the New Economic Policy in Bolivia' in William C. Smith et al. (eds.) *Democracy, Markets and Structural Reform in Latin America* (Boulder: North South Centre Press).
Gamarra, Eduardo (1996) 'Bolivia: managing democracy in the 1990s', in Jorge Domínguez and Abraham Lowenthal (eds.) *Constructing Democratic Governance: South America in the 1990s* (Baltimore: John Hopkins University Press).
Gamarra, Eduardo (1997) 'Neoliberalism Reconsidered: The Politics of Privatization and Capitalization in Bolivia', in Margaret Hollis Peirce (ed.) *Capitalization: A Bolivian Model of Social and Economic Reform* (Boulder: North South Centre Press).
Gamarra, Eduardo (2003) 'Political Parties Since 1964: The Construction of Bolivia's Multiparty System' in Pilar Domingo and Merilee Grindle, (eds.) *Proclaiming Revolution: Bolivia in Comparative Perspective* (Cambridge, MA: Harvard University Press).
Gamarra, Eduardo (2007) 'Bolivia on the Brink', *Council Special Report* 24. February (Council on Foreign Relations).
García Linera, Álvaro et al. (2000) *El retorno de la Bolivia plebeya* (La Paz: Muela del Diablo).
García Linera, Álvaro (2001) *Tiempos de Rebelión* (La Paz: Muela del Diablo).
García Linera, Álvaro (2002) 'El Ocaso de un Ciclo Estatal', in Raquel Gutiérrez (ed.) *Democratizaciones Plebeyas* (La Paz: Muela del Diablo).
García Linera, Álvaro (2004) *Sociología de los movimientos sociales en Bolivia* (La Paz: Diakonia).
García Linera, Álvaro (2006) 'State Crisis and Popular Power', *New Left Review* 37 (January-February): 73-85.
García Linera, Álvaro (2007) 'Condición Obrera y Forma Sindicato', in Jesús Espasandín and Pablo Iglesias (eds.) *Bolivia en movimiento: Acción colectiva y poder político* (Madrid: El Viejo Topo).
Garcia Merida, Wilson (2008) 'The Balkanisation of Bolivia', *Global Research*, 23 September. Available at http://www.globalresearch.ca/. Accessed 5 October 2008.

Gerstenberger, Heide (1978) 'Class Conflict, Competition and State Functions' in John Holloway and Sol Picciotto (eds.), *State and Capital: a Marxist Debate* (London: Edward Arnold).

Gill, Lesley (1987) *Peasants, entrepreneurs and social change* (Boulder: Westview Press).

Gill, Lesley (2000) Teetering on the Rim: Global restructuring, daily life and the armed retreat of the Bolivian State (New York: Columbia University Press).

Gill, Stephen (1990) American Hegemony and the Trilateral Commission (Cambridge: CUP).

Gill, Stephen (1993) 'Historical Materialism, Gramsci, and International Political Economy' in Stephen Gill (ed.) *Gramsci, Historical Materialism and International Relations* (Cambridge: CUP).

Gill, Stephen (2000) 'The Constitution of Global Capitalism', paper presented at the ISA annual convention, Los Angeles.

Gill, Stephen (2003) *Power and Resistance in the New World Order* (Basingstoke: Palgrave).

Gill, Stephen and Law, David (1993) 'Global hegemony and the structural power of capital' in Stephen Gill (ed.), *Gramsci, Historical Materialism and International Relations* (Cambridge: Cambridge University Press).

Girvan, Norman (2008) 'ALBA, Petrocaribe and CARICOM: issues in a new dynamic'. Available at http://www.normangirvan.info/ Accessed 18 March 2009.

Gobierno de Bolivia (1998) *Bolivia: Memorandum de Política Económica*, and attached Letter to Michel Camdessus (Managing Director of IMF) by Edgar Millares (Minister of Finance) and Juan Medinacelli (Acting President of BCB), January 1998.

Godoy, Ricardo (1985) 'Entrepreneurial risk management in peasant mining: the Bolivian experience' in W.W. Culver and T.C. Greaves (eds.) *Miners and Mining in the Americas* (Manchester: Manchester University Press).

Gramsci, Antonio (1971) *Selections from the Prison Notebooks* (New York: International Publishers).

Gramsci, Antonio (1995), *Further Selections from the Prison Notebooks* (London: Lawrence and Wishart).

Gray, George (2001) 'Exclusion, Participation and Democratic State-building', in John Crabtree and Laurence Whitehead (eds.) *Towards Democratic Viability: The Bolivian Experience* (Basingstoke: Palgrave).

Gray, George (2007) 'El reto posneoliberal de Bolivia', *Nueva Sociedad* 209 (May-June): 118-129.

Gray, George (2008) 'State-Society Relations in Bolivia: The Strength of Weakness', in John Crabtree and Laurence Whitehead (eds.) *Unresolved Tensions: Bolivia Past and Present* (Pittsburgh: University of Pittsburgh Press).

Grebe, Horst (1983) 'Excedente sin acumulación', in René Zavaleta (ed.) *Bolivia, Hoy* (Mexico: Siglo XXI Editores).

Grebe, Horst (2002) 'The Private Sector and Democratization' in John Crabtree and Laurence Whitehead (eds.) *Towards Democratic Viability: the Bolivian Experience* (London: Palgrave).

Green, Simon et al. (2005) *Major Companies of Latin America and the Caribbean 2005* (London: Graham and Whiteside).

Fuentes, Federico (2008) 'Recall referendums open new struggle', *Green Left Weekly* 751. 21 May.

Grindle, Merilee (1999) Audacious Reforms: Institutional Invention and Democracy in Latin America (Baltimore: John Hopkins University Press).

Gustafson, Bret (2002) 'Paradoxes of liberal indigenism: indigenous movements, state processes, and intercultural reform in Bolivia' in David Maybury-Lewis (ed.) *The politics of ethnicity: indigenous peoples in Latin American states* (Cambridge Mass: Harvard University Press).

Gutiérrez, Raquel and García, Álvaro (2002) 'El Ciclo Estatal Neoliberal y Sus Crisis', in Raquel Gutiérrez (ed.) *Democratizaciones Plebeyas* (La Paz: Muela del Diablo).

Gúzman, Mario Gustavo (2007) 'Bolivia on the Brink?' Letters in response to Eduardo Gamarra's *Bolivia on the Brink*, Council Special Report. 8 March. Available at http://www.cfr.org/. Accessed 7 November 2008.

Haas, Peter (1992) 'Introduction: epistemic communities and international policy coordination', *International Organization* 46 (1): 1-35.

Halliday, Fred (2002) 'The pertinence of imperialism', in Mark Rupert and Hazel Smith (eds.) *Historical Materialism and globalization* (London: Routledge).

Harris, David and Azzi, Diego (2006) 'ALBA: Venezuela's answer to "free trade": The Bolivarian Alternative for the Americas', *Focus on the Global South Occasional Papers* 3. *October.*

Harvey, David (1990) The Condition of Postmodernity: an enquiry into the origins of cultural change (Oxford: Basil Blackwell).

Harvey, David (2003) *The New Imperialism* (Oxford: OUP).

Hatheway, Erin (2009) 'Who's Who in the Bolivian Presidential Elections: Anyone New Opposing Morales?', *The Andean Information Network*, 26 August.

Hay, Colin (1999) 'Marxism and the State', in Andrew Gamble et al. (eds.), *Marxism and Social Science* (Houndmills: Macmillan).

Hayek, Friedrich von (1944) *The Road to Serfdom* (London: Routledge).

Hirsch, Joachim (1978) 'The State Apparatus and Social Reproduction: Elements of a Theory of the Bourgeois State' in John Holloway and Sol Picciotto (eds.) *State and Capital: A Marxist Debate* (London: Edward Arnold).

Hirst, Paul and Thompson, Grahame (1995) 'Globalization and the future of the nation-state', *Economy and Society* 24 (3): 408-442.

Hiskey, Jonathan and Seligson, Mitchell (2003) 'Pitfalls of Power to the People: Decentralization, Local Government Performance, and System Support in Bolivia', *Studies in Comparative International Development* 37 (4): 64-88.

Hobsbawm, Eric (1995 [1962]) *The Age of Revolution: Europe 1789-1848* (London: Weidenfeld and Nicholson).

Hollis Peirce, Margaret (1997) *Capitalization: A Bolivian Model of Social and Economic Reform* (Boulder: North South Centre Press).

Holloway, John and Sol Picciotto (1978), 'Introduction: Towards a Materialist Theory of the State' in John Holloway and Sol Picciotto (eds.) *State and Capital: A Marxist Debate* (London: Edward Arnold).

Holloway, John (1995a) 'Global Capital and the National State' in Werner Bonefeld and John Holloway (ed.) *Global Capital, National States and the Politics of Money* (Basingstoke: Macmillan).

Holloway, John (1995b) 'The Abyss Opens: The Rise and Fall of Keynesianism' in Werner Bonefeld and John Holloway (ed.) *Global Capital, National States and the Politics of Money* (Basingstoke: Macmillan).

Holman, Otto and van der Pijl, Kees (2003), 'Structure and process in transnational European business' in Alan Cafruny and Magnus Ryner (ed.) *A Ruined Fortress: Neoliberal Hegemony and Transformation in Europe* (Oxford: Rowman & Littlefield).

Horkheimer, Max (1982) *Critical Theory: Selected Essays* (New York: Continuum).

Howarth, David (2000) *Discourse* (Buckingham: Open University Press).

Hoy (1988) 'Verguenza! Desde ministros para abajo son asalariados de instituciones internacionales'. 28 July: 8-9.

Huntington, Samuel (1990) *The Third Wave: Democratization in the Late Twentieth Century* (Norman: University of Oklahoma Press).

Huntington, Samuel (1999) 'Robust Nationalism', *The National Interest*, 20 January.

Huntington, Samuel (2002[1996]) The Clash of Civilizations and the Remaking of World Order (London: Free Press).

Hylton, Forrest (2004) 'Bolivia's gas referendum', *ZMag*, 20 July. Available at http://www.zmag.org/. Accessed 5 September 2004.

Hylton, Forrest and Thomson, Sinclair (2007) Revolutionary Horizons: Past and Present in Bolivian Politics (London: Verso).

International Bank for Reconstruction and Development (IBRD) (1993) *Progress Report on Private Sector Development*, March 12. Prepared for Development Committee Meeting May 1, 1993.

International Crisis Group (2008) *Bolivia: Rescuing the New Constitution and Democratic Stability*, Latin America Briefing No.18, 19 June.

IFHR (2008a) 'El Comité Civico Pro-Santa Cruz, actor y promotor de la violencia y del racismo en Bolivia. Carta abierta al Sr. Marinkovic, Presidente del Comité Pro-Santa Cruz'. Available at http://www.fidh.org/. Accessed 18 October 2008.

IFHR (2008b) 'Temor por la seguridad de los defensores de los derechos humanos'. http://www.fidh.org/. Accessed 18 October.

Instituto Nacional de Estadísticas (INE) (2009a) 'Índice de Precios al Consumidor'. Available at http://www.ine.gov.bo/. Accessed 15 December 2009.

INE (2009b) 'Inversión Extranjera Directa por Año Según Actividad Económica. Available at http://www.ine.gov.bo/indice/general.aspx?codigo=40211. Accessed 15 December 2009.

INE (2009c) 'Comercio Exterior'. Available at: http://www.ine.gov.bo/. Accessed 20 March 2010.

International Herald Tribune (2008) 'A major crisis for the Bolivian president'. 15 September.

International Institute for Sustainable Development (2007) 'Bolivia notifies World Bank of withdrawal from ICSID, pursues BIT revisions', *Investment Treaty News*. 9 May. Available at http://www.bilaterals.org/. Accessed 3 March 2008.

International Monetary Fund (1986a) *Bolivia – Standby Arrangement*. June 27. EBS/86/120.

International Monetary Fund (1986b) *Bolivia – Report on External Debt Renegotiation*. August 4, EBS/86/174.

International Monetary Fund (1988a) Official Multilateral Debt Rescheduling: Recent Experience. March 9, SM/88/59.

International Monetary Fund (1988b) *Bolivia Enhanced Structural Adjustment.* August 2, EBS/88/131.

International Monetary Fund (1991a) Bolivia - Staff Report for the 1991 Article IV Consultation and Request for Third Annual Arrangement Under the Enhanced Structural Adjustment Facility, June 10, EBS/91/93.

International Monetary Fund (1991b) *Bolivia Recent Economic Developments.* June 19, SM/91/124.

International Monetary Fund (1994) Bolivia - Review of the Additional Annual Arrangement Under the Enhanced Structural Adjustment Facility. April 1, EBS/94/73.

International Monetary Fund (1998a) Bolivia-Staff Report for the 1998 Article IV Consultation, Request for Arrangements Under the Enhanced Structural Adjustment Facility, and Policy Framework Paper for 1998-2001. August 27. EBS/98/153.

International Monetary Fund (1998b) *Bolivia – Selected Issues.* September 4. SM/98/225.

International Monetary Fund (2003) *Bolivia: Selected Issues and Statistical Appendix.* August. Report No.03/258.

International Monetary Fund (2007) *Bolivia: 2007 Article IV Consultation – Staff Report* July. Report No. 07/248.

International Monetary Fund (2009) *Bolivia: Article IV Consultation – Staff Report.* January. Report No. 09/27.

International Monetary Fund/World Bank (2001) Strengthening IMF-World Bank Collaboration on Country Programs and Conditionality. August 23.

Inter Press Service (2008a) 'It's All About the Gas Revenue'. 24 July. Available at http://ipsnews.net/. Accessed 7 October 2008.

Inter Press Service (2008b) 'Divisions Emerge in Opposition Strategy'. 4 September. Available at http://ipsnews.net/. Accessed 15 October 2008.

Inter Press Service (2008c) 'Santa Cruz Autonomy Statute Violates Constitution'. 2 May. Available at http://ipsnews.net/. Accessed 10 October 2008.

Inter Press Service (2008d) Bolivia: Congress Approves Date for Vote on New Constitution'. 21 October. Available at http://ipsnews.net/. Accessed 22 October.

Jameson, Frederic (1998) 'Notes on Globalization as a Philosophical Issue' in Fredric Jameson and Masao Miyoshi (eds.) *The Cultures of Globalization* (Durham and London: Duke University Press).

Janssen, Daniel (2000) 'The Pace of Economic Change in Europe', speech to the general assembly of the Trilateral Commission (Tokyo, April 2000). http://www.trilateral.org. Accessed 15 May 2005.

Jenkins, Rhys (1995) *Trade liberalisation and manufacturing in Bolivia* (London: Institute of Latin American Studies).

Jessop, Bob (1985) Nicos Poulantzas: Marxist Theory and Political Strategy (London: Macmillan).

Jessop, Bob (1990) State Theory: Putting the Capitalist State in its Place (London: Polity).

Jessop, Bob (2007) State Power: A Strategic-Relational Approach (Cambridge: Polity).

Jenkins, Rhys (1995) *Trade liberalization and manufacturing in Bolivia* (London: Institute of Latin American Studies).

Jones, Andrew (1998) 'Re-theorising the core: a 'globalized' business elite in Santiago, Chile', *Political Geography* 17 (3): 295-318.

Jordán, Rolando (1999) 'Siglo XX: La Era del Estaño', in Fernando Campero Prudencio (ed.) *Bolivia en el Siglo XX: La Formación de la Bolivia Contemporánea* (La Paz: Harvard Club).

Jorgensen, Steen et al. (1992) Bolivia's answer to poverty, economic crisis and adjustment: the Social Emergency Fund (Washington DC: World Bank).

Kautsky, Karl (1970 [1914]) 'Ultra-imperialism', *New Left Review* 59: 41-46.

Kemp, Tom (1972) 'The Marxist theory of imperialism' in Roger Owen and Bob Sutcliffe (eds.) *Studies in the theory of imperialism* (London: Longman).

King, Gary Robert Keohane and Sidney Verba (1994) *Designing Social Inquiry* (Princeton: Princeton University Press, 1994).

Klein, Herbert (1965) 'David Toro and the Establishment of "Military Socialism" in Bolivia', *The Hispanic American Historical Review* 45 (1): 25-52.

Klein, Herbert (1969) Parties and Political Change in Bolivia: 1880-1952 (London: CUP).

Klein, Herbert (1971) 'Prelude to the Revolution', in James Malloy and Richard Thorn (eds.) *Beyond the Revolution: Bolivia since 1952* (Pittsburgh: University of Pittsburgh Press).

Klein (1982) Bolivia: the evolution of a multi-ethnic society (Oxford: OUP).

Klein, Herbert (2003) *A concise history of Bolivia* (Cambridge: CUP).

Kohl, Benjamin (2003) 'Democratizing Decentralization in Bolivia', *Journal of Planning Education and Research* 23: 153-164.

Kohl, Benjamin and Farthing, Linda (2005) *Impasse in Bolivia: neoliberal hegemony and popular resistance* (London: Zed Books).

Körner et al. (1986) The IMF and the Debt Crisis: A Guide to the Third World's Dilemma (London: Zed Books).

Krasner, Stephen (1999) 'Globalization and sovereignty' in David Smith et al. (eds.) States and Sovereignty in *Global Economy* (London: Routledge)

Krasner, Stephen (2001) 'Rethinking the sovereign state model', *Review of International Studies*, 27: 17-42.

Kuczynski, Pedro-Pablo (1988) *Latin American Debt* (Baltimore and London: John Hopkins University Press).

Lacher, Hannes (2002) 'Making sense of the international system: the promises and pitfalls of contemporary Marxist theories of international relations', in Mark Rupert and Hazel Smith (eds.) *Historical Materialism and Globalization* (London: Routledge).

Lacher, Hannes (2003) 'State centrism and its limits', *Review of International Studies* 29 (4): 521-542.

Lacher, Hannes and Teschke, Benno (2007), 'The changing "logics" of capitalist competition', *Cambridge Review of International Affairs*, 20, 4: 566-580.

Laclau, Ernesto (1971) 'Feudalism and Capitalism in Latin America', *New Left Review* 1 (67): 19-38.

Langer, Erick (1989) Economic Change and Rural Resistance in Southern Bolivia 1880-1930 (Stanford: Stanford University Press).

La Prensa (2005) 'Victor Paz: Decreto es coyuntural, pero puede durar'. 28 August.

La Prensa (2008) 'Börth y Romero articularon el pacto para el proyecto de CPE'. 2 November.

La Razón (2007) 'Ponchos Rojos Matan Perros Para Amenazar'. 23 November.

La Razón (2008a) 'Evo y CONALDE se abren para otra opción de dialogo'. 27 August.

La Razón (2008b) 'Los Masistas y Autonomistas se arman con la reserva de las FFAA'. 29 September.

Lavaud, Jean-Pierre (1990) 'L'accalmie politique bolivienne 1982-1990', *Cultures & Conflits* 1 : 151-166.

Lavaud, Jean-Pierre (1991) *L'instabilité de l'Amérique latine: le cas bolivien* (Paris : Editions l'Harmattan).

Lavaud, Jean-Pierre (2007) 'Bolivie: un avenir politique hypothéqué?', *Nueva Sociedad* 209 (May-June).

Law, Peter and de Franco, Nelson (1998) 'International Gas Trade: The Bolivia-Brazil Gas Pipeline', *Public Policy for the Private Sector* 144. May.

Lazarte, Jorge (1993) *Bolivia: certezas e incertidumbres de la democracia* (Cochabamba: ILDIS, Los Amigos del Libro).

Lemoine, Maurice (2005) 'Puissant et fragmenté, le mouvement social bolivien', *Le Monde Diplomatique*, November.

Le Monde (2006) 'Peu de résultats concrets attendus á Vienne'. 13 May.

Lenin, Vladimir (1916) *Imperialism, the highest stage of capitalism.* Available at http://www.marxists.org/ Accessed 10 June 2006.

Lenin, Vladimir (1965 [1917]) *The State and Revolution* (Moscow: Progress).

Lewis, Tom (2006) 'Bolivia takes on the multinationals', *Socialistworker.org*. 12 May. Available at http://socialistworker.org/. Accessed 25 May 2006.

Lilleker, Darren (2003) 'Interviewing the political elite: navigating a potential minefield', *Politics* 23 (3): 207-214.

Lora, Guillermo (1977) *A history of the Bolivian labour movement* (Cambridge: CUP).

Lora, Guillermo (1987) *Historia de los Partidos Políticos de Bolivia* (La Paz: Ediciones La Colmena).

Los Tiempos (2005) 'Autonomía cruceña: entre la democracia y el autoritarismo'. 10 July.

Los Tiempos (2006) '¿Capitalismo Andino-amazónico?'. 19 February.

Los Tiempos (2007) 'Evo llama a "ponchos rojos" defender el país'. 24 January.

Los Tiempos (2009) 'El gobierno afirma que Bolivia no produce uranio'. 26 May.

MABB (2005), 'The History of the Comité Pro Santa Cruz', available at http://mabb.blogspot.com/. Accessed 18 October 2008.

Mainwaring, Scott (1992) 'Transitions to Democracy and Democratic Consolidation: Theoretical and Comparative Issues', in Scott Mainwaring, Guillermo O'Donnell and Samuel Valenzuela (eds.) *Issues in Democratic Consolidation* (Notre Dame: University of Notre Dame Press).

Malloy, James (1970) *Bolivia: The Uncompleted Revolution* (Pittsburgh: University of Pittsburgh Press).

Malloy, James (1991) 'Democracy, Economic Crisis and the Problem of Governance: The Case of Bolivia', *Studies in Comparative International Development* 26 (2): 37-57.

Malloy, James and Thorn, Richard (1971) *Beyond the Revolution: Bolivia since 1952* (Pittsburgh: University of Pittsburgh Press).

Malloy, James and Gamarra, Eduardo (1987) 'The transition to democracy in Bolivia' in James Malloy and Mitchell Seligson (eds.) *Authoritarians and Democrats. Regime Transition in Latin America* (Pittsburgh: University of Pittsburgh Press).

Malloy, James and Gamarra, Eduardo (1988) *Revolution and Reaction: Bolivia 1964-1985* (New Brunswick: Transaction Books).

Mamani, Pablo (2005) Microgobiernos barriales. Levantamiento de la ciudad de El Alto (El Alto: IDIS-UMSA-CADES).

Mamani, Pablo (2007) 'Múltiples fracturas del Estado y la sociedad desde los movimientos indígenas de Bolivia', in Jesús Espasandín and Pablo Iglesias (eds.) *Bolivia en movimiento: Acción colectiva y poder político* (Madrid: El Viejo Topo).

Mandel, Ernest (1975) *Late Capitalism* (London: NLB).

Mansilla, H.C.F. (1994) La empresa privada boliviana y el proceso de democratización (La Paz: Fundación Milenio).

Marsh, Margaret (1928) The Bankers in Bolivia: A Study in American Foreign Investment (New York: Vanguard Press).

Marx, Karl (2003) 'Capital Vol.1' in David McLellan (ed.) *Selected writings* (Oxford: OUP).

Marx, Karl (2003) 'The Gundrisse' in David McLellan (ed.) *Selected writings* (Oxford: OUP).

Mayorga, Fernando (1991) Democratización y modernización del estado en Bolivia (La Paz: CEBEM).

Mayorga, René Antonio (1978) 'National Popular State, State Capitalism and Military Dictatorship in Bolivia: 1952-1975', *Latin American Perspectives* 5 (2): 89-119.

Mayorga, René Antonio (1988) 'Democratización y modernización del Estado: El caso de Bolivia', in Acuña et al. (eds.) *¿Hacia un nuevo orden estatal en America Latina? Democratización/modernización y actores socio-políticos* (Buenos Aires: CLACSO).

Mayorga, René Antonio (1995) *Antipolítica y neopopulismo* (La Paz: Cebem).

Mayorga, René Antonio (1999) 'La Democracia o el Desafío de la Modernización Política in Fernando Campero Prudencio (ed.) *Bolivia en el Siglo XX: La Formación de la Bolivia Contemporánea* (La Paz: Harvard Club).

McNeish, John-Andrew (2002) 'Globalisation and the Reinvention of Andean Tradition: The Politics of Community and Ethnicity in Highland Bolivia', *Journal of Peasant Studies* 29 (3/4): 228-269.

McNeish, John-Andrew (2006) 'Stones on the Road: The Politics of Participation and the Generation of Crisis in Bolivia', *Bulletin of Latin American Research* 25 (2): 220-240.

Meiksins Wood, Elen (1981) 'The separation of the economic and the political in capitalism', *New Left Review* 127: 66-95.

Meiksins Wood, Ellen (2002a) *The Origin of Capitalism: A Longer View* (London: Verso).

Meiksins Wood, Elen (2002b) 'Global capital, national states' in Mark Rupert and Hazel Smith (eds.) *Historical Materialism and globalization* (London: Routledge).

Miliband, Ralph (1969) *The state in capitalist society* (London: Weidenfeld and Nicolson).

Miliband, Ralph (1977) *Marxism and Politics* (Oxford: OUP).

Miller-Adams, Michelle (1999) *The World Bank: New agendas in a changing world* (London: Routledge).

Mitchell, Christopher (1977) The Legacy of Populism in Bolivia: From the MNR to Military Rule (New York: Praeger).

Moore, Winston (1990) 'Capital accumulation and Revolutionary Nationalism in Bolivia, 1925-1985', in Anglade and Fortin (eds.) *The State and Capital Accumulation in Latin America,* Vol.2 (Pittsburgh: University of Pittsburgh Press).

Morales, Evo (2006) 'The US, Bolivia and Venezuela', *Zmag*. 3 July. Available at http://www.zmag.org/. Accessed 19 October 2006.

Morales, Juan Antonio and Sachs, Jeffrey (1990) 'Bolivia's Economic Crisis' in Jeffrey Sachs (ed.) *Developing Country Debt and Economic Performance Vol.2: Country Studies: Argentina, Bolivia, Brazil, Mexico* (Chicago: University of Chicago Press).

Morales, Juan Antonio (1990) 'Bolivia's post-stabilization problems', *Instituto de Investigaciones Socio-Económicas*, Documento de Trabajo No.08/90 (September).

Morales, Juan Antonio (1993) 'Los Efectos de los Influjos Recientes de Capital en la Economía Boliviana'. *Instituto de Investigaciones Socio-Económicas*, Documento de Trabajo No.02/93 (April).

Morales, Juan Antonio (1994) 'Ajuste Macroeconómico y Reformas Estructurales en Bolivia, 1986-1994', *Instituto de Investigaciones Socio-Económicas*, Documento de Trabajo No.07/94 (October).

Morales, Juan Antonio and Pacheco, Napoleon (1999) 'El Retorno de los Liberales' in Fernando Campero Prudencio (ed.) *Bolivia en el Siglo XX: La Formación de la Bolivia Contemporánea* (La Paz: Harvard Club).

Morales, Juan Antonio (2002) 'Economic Vulnerability in Bolivia', in John Crabtree and Lawrence Whitehead (eds.) *Towards Democratic Viability: The Bolivian Experience* (London: Palgrave).

Morales, Juan Antonio (2008) 'Bolivia in a Global Setting: Economic Ties', in John Crabtree, and Laurence Whitehead (eds.) *Unresolved*

Tensions: Bolivia Past and Present (Pittsburgh: University of Pittsburgh Press).

Morton, Adam (2000) 'Mexico, Neoliberal Restructuring and the EZLN: A Neo-Gramscian Analysis', in Barry K. Gills (ed.) *Globalization and the Politics of Resistance* (London: Palgrave).

Morton, Adam (2001) 'The Sociology of Theorising and Neo-Gramscian Perspectives: The Problem of 'School' Formation in IPE' in Andreas Bieler and Adam Morton (eds.), *Social Forces in the Making of the New Europe* (Basingstoke: Palgrave).

Morton, Adam (2007) *Unravelling Gramsci* (London: Pluto Press).

Mosley, Paul et al. (1991) Aid and power: the World Bank and policy-based lending (London: Routledge).

Movimiento Al Socialismo (2008a) 'Principios ideológicos'. Available at http://www.masbolivia.org/. Accessed 10 June 2008.

Movimiento Al Socialismo (2008b) 'Diez Puntos del Programa del MAS'. Available at http://www.masbolivia.org/. Accessed 10 June 2008.

Movimiento Al Socialismo (2008c), 'Programa de Gobierno'. Available at http://www.masbolivia.org/. Accessed 10 June 2008.

Müller, Herbert (1987) *Evaluación Económica: Informe Confidencial* (La Paz: Müller y Machicado Asociados).

Multilateral Investment Guarantee Agency [MIGA] (2009) *Projects in Bolivia.* Available at http://www.miga.org/. Accessed 19 November.

Navarro Miranda, César (1999) *Bolivia: Estados de Sitio en Democracia* (Potosí: Asamblea Permanente de los Derechos Humanos Potosí).

Nkrumah, Kwame (1965) *Neocolonialism, the Last Stage of Imperialism* (London: Thomas Nelson and Sons Ltd). Available at http://www.marxists.org/ Accessed 21 March 2006.

Niebuhr, Reinhold (1932) Moral Man and Immoral Society: A Study in Ethics and Politics (New York: Scribner).

O'Donnell, Guillermo and Schmitter, Philippe (1986) *Transitions from Authoritarian Rule. Tentative Conclusions about Uncertain Democracies* (Baltimore and London: John Hopkins University Press).

O'Donnell, Guillermo (1992) 'Transitions, Continuities and Paradoxes', in Scott Mainwaring, Guillermo O'Donnell and Samuel Valenzuela (eds.) *Issues in Democratic Consolidation* (Notre Dame: University of Notre Dame Press).

O'Donnell, Guillermo (1993) 'Delegative Democracy?', *Kellogg Institute Working Paper* 192 (April).

Ohmae, Kenichi (1995) The end of the Nation State: The Rise of Regional Economies (London: HarperCollins).

Orlove, Benjamen and Foley, Michael (1989) 'Anthropology, Capitalism and the State: Introduction' in Benjamen Orlove et al. (eds.) *State, Capital and Rural Society: Anthropological Perspectives on Political Economy in Mexico and the Andes* (Boulder: Westview Press).

Overbeek, Henk (1990) Global capitalism and national decline: the Thatcher decade in perspective (London: Unwin Hyman).

Overbeek, Henk (2000) 'Transnational historical materialism: theories of transnational class formation and world order' in Ronen Palan (ed.) *Global Political Economy: Contemporary theories* (London: Routledge).

Overbeek, Henk (2004) 'Transnational class formation and concepts of control', *Journal of International Relations and Development*, 7 (2): 113-141.

Overbeek, Henk and Van der Pijl, Kees (1993) 'Restructuring capital and restructuring hegemony: Neoliberalism and the unmaking of the post-war order' in Henk Overbeek (ed.) *Restructuring hegemony in the global political economy: the rise of transnational Neoliberalism in the 1980s* (London: Routledge).

Painter, James (1994) *Bolivia and Coca – A Study in Dependency* (Boulder: Lynne Rienner).

Parkerson, Phillip (1989) 'Neither "Green Gold" nor "The Devil's Leaf": Coca Farming in Bolivia' in Benjamen Orlove et al. (eds.) *State, Capital and Rural Society: Anthropological Perspectives on Political Economy in Mexico and the Andes* (Boulder: Westview Press)

Parsons, Talcott (1977) *The Evolution of Societies* (London: Prentice-Hall).

Pastor, Manuel (1987) The International Monetary Fund and Latin America. Economic Stabilization and Class Conflict (Boulder: Westview Press).

Pastor, Robert (1987*) Latin America's Debt Crisis: Adjusting to the Past or Planning for the Future? (Boulder: Lynne Rienner Publishers).

Patzi Paco, Felix (1999) Insurgencia y sumisión. Movimientos indígena-campesinos (1983-1998) (La Paz: Muela del Diablo).

Petras, James and Veltmeyer, Henry (2002) *Globalization Unmasked: Imperialism in the 21st Century* (London: Zed Books).

Petras, James and Veltmeyer, Henry (2005) *Social movements and state power: Argentina, Brazil, Bolivia* (London: Pluto Press).

Petras, James (2006) 'Evo Morales/Bolivia: Populist gestures and neo-liberal substance', *Rebelión* 6 January.

Petras, James (2008) 'Bolivia : Fascism Seizes Power, Morales Complains', *Dissident Voice.* 18 September 2008. Available at http://www.dissidentvoice.org/Accessed 10 November 2008.

Picciotto, Sol (1978) 'Firm and state in the world economy' in Julio Faundez and Sol Picciotto (eds.) *The Nationalisation of multinationals in peripheral economies* (London: Macmillan Press)

Picciotto, Sol (1990) 'The internationalization of the state', *Review of Radical Political Economics* 22 (1): 28-44.

Polak, Jacques (1994) *The World Bank and the IMF* (Washington DC: Brookings Institution).

Poulantzas, Nikos (1975), *Classes in Contemporary Capitalism* (London: NLB).

Poulantzas, Nikos (1978) *State, Power, Socialism* (London: NLB).

Poulantzas, Nikos (1978 [1968]) *Political Power and Social Classes* (London: Verso).

Prada, Raúl (2000) in Álvaro García Linera et al. (eds.) *El retorno de la Bolivia plebeya* (La Paz: Muela del Diablo).

Prada, Raúl (2002) 'Multitud y Contrapoder. Estudios del Presente: Movimientos Sociales Contemporáneos', in Raquel Gutiérrez (ed.) *Democratizaciones Plebeyas* (La Paz: Muela del Diablo).

Presidencia de la República (1985) *Decreto Supremo No.21060.* Promulgated 29 August.

Presidencia de la República (1987) *Decreto Supremo No.21160.*

Presidencia de la República (1990) *Decreto Supremo No.22407.* Promulgated 11 January.

Presidencia de la República (1997) *Decreto Supremo No.24806.* Promulgated 4 August.

Presidencia de la República (2006) *Decreto Supremo No.28700.* Promulgated 1 May.

Presidencia de la República (2006) *Decreto Supremo No. 28701.* Promulgated 1 May.

Presidencia de la República (2007) *Decreto Supremo No.29116.* Promulgated May.

Presidencia de la República (2008) *Decreto Supremo No.29473.* Promulgated 5 March.

PRODEM (1998) *PRODEM.* Available at http://biblioteca.arcobol.com/. Accessed 10 September 2008.

República de Bolivia (1986) *Ley No.843 de Reforma Tributaria.* Promulgated 20 May.

República de Bolivia (1990) Ley No.1178 de Administración y Control Gubernamental. Promulgated 20 July.

República de Bolivia (1992) *Ley No.1330 de Privatización.* Promulgated 24 April.

República de Bolivia (1994) *Ley de Capitalización.* Promulgated 21 March.

República de Bolivia (1994) *Ley No. 1551 de Participación Popular.* Promulgated 20 April.

República de Bolivia (1994) Ley No.1600 del Sistema de Regulación Sectorial (SIRESE), Promulgated 28 October.

República de Bolivia (1995) *Ley No. 1654 de Descentralización Administrativa.* Promulgated 28 July.

República de Bolivia (1995) *Ley No.1670 del Banco Central de Bolivia.* Promulgated 31 October 1995.

República de Bolivia (1996), *Ley No.1732 de Pensiones*, Promulgated 29 November.

Reuters (2006) 'Bolivia starts land revolution amid owners' ire'. Available at http://today.reuters.com/. Accessed 4 June 2006.

Reuters (2007) 'Bolivia passes Jindal iron ore contract law'. 30 November. Available at http://www.reuters.com/. Accessed 1 December 2007.

Reuters (2008a) 'Bolivia's silver mountain regains lost luster'. 28 February. Available at http://www.reuters.com/. Accessed 1 March 2008.

Reuters (2008b) 'Bolivia energy safe from turmoil, so far'. 3 April. Available at http://www.reuters.com/. Accessed 5 April 2008.

Reuters (2008c) 'Bolivia takes over four energy companies'. 1 May. Available at http://www.reuters.com/. Accessed 2 May 2008.

Reuters (2008d) 'Bolivia announces takeover of Telecom Italia Unit'. 1 May. Available at http://www.reuters.com/. Accessed 2 May 2008.

Reuters (2008e) 'Update – Coeur d'Alene starting giant new Bolivia silver mine'. 27 May. http://www.reuters.com/. Accessed 28 May 2008.

Reuters (2008f) 'US and Venezuela escálate crisis', 12 September. Available at http://www.reuters.com/. Accessed 12 September 2008.

Reuters (2008g) 'Bolivia's Morales bars "spying" US DEA agents', 1 November. Available at http://www.reuters.com/. Accessed 1 November 2008.

Richards, David (1996) 'Elite interviewing: Promises and Pitfalls', *Politics* 16 (3): 199-204.

Rivera Cusicanqui, Silvia (1983) 'Luchas Campesinas Contemporáneas en Bolivia: El Movimiento Katarista, 1970-1980', in René Zavaleta (ed.) *Bolivia, Hoy* (Mexico: Siglo Veintiuno Editores).

Rivera Cusicanqui, Silvia (1987) Oppressed but Not Defeated: Peasant Struggles among the Aymara and Qhechwa in Bolivia: 1900-1980 (Geneva: UNRISD).

Rivera Cusicanqui, Silvia (2007) '*Que el pasado sea future depende de lo que hagamos en el presente:* Enseñanzas de la insurgencia étnica en Bolivia', in Jesús Espasandín and Pablo Iglesias (eds.) *Bolivia en movimiento: Acción colectiva y poder político* (Madrid: El Viejo Topo).

Roberts, John Michael (2003) 'From reflection to refraction: opening up Open Marxist categories', *Capital and Class* 78: 87-116.

Robinson, William (1996) Promoting Polyarchy: Globalization, US Intervention, and Hegemony (Cambridge: CUP).

Robinson, William (2002) 'Capitalist globalization and the transnationalisation of the state' in Mark Rupert and Hazel Smith (eds.) *Historical materialism and globalization* (London: Routledge).

Robinson, William (2005) *A Theory of Global Capitalism* (Baltimore: JHUP).

Roca, José Luis (1980) *Fisionomía del regionalismo Boliviano* (La Paz: Los Amigos del Libro).

Roca, José Luis (2008) 'Regionalism revisited', in John Crabtree and Laurence Whitehead (eds.) *Unresolved Tensions: Bolivia Past and Present* (Pittsburgh: University of Pittsburgh Press).

Rodríguez, Gustavo (1980) 'Original Accumulation, Capitalism, and Precapitalistic Agriculture in Bolivia (1870-1885)', *Latin American Perspectives* 7 (4): 50-66.

Roseberry, William (1989) 'Anthropology, History, and Modes of Production' in Benjamen Orlove et al. (eds.) *State, Capital and Rural Society: Anthropological Perspectives on Political Economy in Mexico and the Andes* (Boulder: Westview Press).

Rosenberg, Justin (2001) *The Follies of Globalisation Theory* (London: Verso).

Rupert, Mark (1995) Producing hegemony: The politics of mass production and American global power (Cambridge: CUP).

Sachs, Jeffrey (1999) 'Latinoamérica y el Desarrollo Económico Global in Fernando Campero Prudencio (ed.) *Bolivia en el Siglo XX: La Formación de la Bolivia Contemporánea* (La Paz: Harvard Club).

Sader, Emil (2006) 'Alternatives Latino-Americaines', *Le Monde Diplomatique*, February.

Salinas, Luis Fernando et al. (2002) *La Capitalización Cinco Años después* (La Paz: Fundación Milenio).

Salman, Ton (2006) 'The Jammed Democracy: Bolivia's Troubled Political Learning Process', *Bulletin of Latin American Research* 25(2): 163-182.

Salman, Ton (2007) 'Bolivia and the Paradoxes of Democratic Consolidation', *Latin American Perspectives* 34(6): 111-130.

Sanjinés, Javier (2004) *Mestisaje Upside-Down: aesthetic politics in modern Bolivia* (Pittsburgh, University of Pittsburgh Press).

Scholte, Jan Aaart (1996) 'Globalisation and Collective Identities' in Krause, Jill and Reinwick, Neil (eds.) *Identities in International Relations* (Basingstoke: Macmillan).

Seligson, Mitchell (1987) 'Democratization in Latin America: The Current Cycle', in James Malloy and Mitchell Seligson (eds.) *Authoritarians and Democrats: Regime Transition in Latin America* (Pittsburgh: Pittsburgh University Press).

Serrate Reich, Carlos (1989) *Interpelación al Neoliberalismo* (La Paz: Empresa Editora Siglo Ltda).

Shaw, Martin (1997) 'The state of globalization: towards a theory of state transformation', *Review of International Political Economy* 4, no.3 (1997): 497-513.

Shaw, Martin (2000) Theory of the Global State: Globality as Unfinished Revolution (Cambridge: CUP).

Shields, Stuart (2004) 'Global restructuring of the Polish state: transition, transformation or transnationalization?', *Review of International Political Economy* 11 (1): 132-154.

Skocpol, Theda (1979) *States and Social Revolution* (Cambridge: CUP).

Slade, Betty (1997) 'Financial Regulation in Bolivia: With Particular Reference to the Pension Law', in Margaret Hollis Peirce (ed.) *Capitalization: A Bolivian Model of Social and Economic Reform* (Boulder: North South Centre Press).

Soliz Rada, Andrés (2004a) *La Fortuna del Presidente* (La Paz).

Soliz Rada, Andrés (2004b) 'Petroleras y empresarios cruceños', *Bolpress* 6 March. Available at http://www.bolpress.com/. Accessed 17 September 2008.

Spence, Crawford and Shenkin, Mark (2006) 'Morales and the Bolivian State', *International Socialism* 112. 11 October.

Stallings, Barbara (1992) 'International influence on economic policy: Debt, stabilization and structural reform', in S. Haggard and R. Kaufman (eds.) *The Politics of Economic Adjustment* (Princeton: Princeton University Press).

Stefanoni, Pablo (2005) 'Los Diez Mandamientos de Evo', *Pulso* (August). Available at http://www.reconstruccion2005.com.ar/. Accessed 9 June 2008.

Stiglitz, Joseph (2002) *Globalization and Its Discontents* (London: Penguin Books).

Strange, Susan (1996) The Retreat of the State: the diffusion of power in the world economy (Cambridge: CUP).

Sutcliffe, Bob (2002) 'How many capitalisms? Historical materialism in the debates about imperialism and globalisation' in Mark Rupert and Hazel Smith (eds.) *Historical Materialism and globalization* (London: Routledge).

Tapia, Luis (2002a) La producción del conocimiento local: historia y política en la obra de René Zavaleta (La Paz: Muela del Diablo).

Tapia, Luis (2002b) 'Movimientos Sociales, Movimiento Societal y los No Lugares de la Política', in Raquel Gutiérrez (ed.) *Democratizaciones Plebeyas* (La Paz: Muela del Diablo).

Tarrow, Sidney (1998) *Power in Movement: Social Movements and Contentious Politics* (Cambridge: Cambridge University Press).

Taylor, Marcus (2005) 'Opening the World Bank: International Organisations and the Contradictions of Global Capitalism', *Historical Materialism* 13 (1): 153-170.

The Economist (2006a) 'Out of gas – Bolivia', 19 August.

The Economist (2006b) 'Fear and Mistrust – Bolivia', 25 November.

The Economist (2006c) 'Power grab - Bolivia's constitution', 9 September.

The Guardian (2006) 'Morales sets his sights on Bolivia's idle farmland', 2 June.

The Guardian (2008) 'Bolivia: On the Edge', 12 September. Available at http://www.guardian.co.uk/. Accessed 13 September 2008.

The New York Times (1992) '2 Bolivian Executives Vie in New Arena: Politics', 10 June.

The New York Times (2007) 'Bolivia Leaders Lets Venezuela Send Soldiers, Angering Foes', 9 January.

The New York Times (2008a) 'Clashes in Bolivia on Vote Over More Autonomy', 5 May.

The New York Times (2008b) 'American Rancher Resists Land Reform Plans in Bolivia', 9 May.

The New York Times (2008c) 'Bolivian Troops Arrest Governor of Rebellious Region'. 16 September.

The New York Times (2008d) 'In Bolivia, a Croat and a Critic is Cast in a Harsh Light'. 26 September.

The New York Times (2008e) '3 Oil Rich Countries Face a Reckoning', 20 October.

The New York Times (2009a) 'In Bolivia, Untapped Bounty Meets Nationalism', 3 February.

The New York Times (2009b) 'Deals Help China Expand Its Sway in Latin America', 15 April.

The New York Times (2009c) 'Plot Foiled? In Bolivia, Truth is Elusive', 27 April.

The Washington Times (2007) 'Elite Troops Trained by Venezuela', 10 July.

Tilly, Charles (2004) *Social Movements 1768-2004* (Boulder: Paradigm Publishers).

Toranzo Roca, Fernando (1991) 'Bolivia y la modernidad' in Fernando Mayorga (ed.) *Democratización y modernización del estado en Bolivia* (La Paz: CEBEM).

Toranzo Roca, Fernando (1999) 'Introducción' in Fernando Campero Prudencio (ed.) *Bolivia en el Siglo XX: La Formación de la Bolivia Contemporánea* (La Paz: Harvard Club).

Toranzo Roca, Fernando (2008) 'Let the Mestizos Stand Up and Be Counted', in John Crabtree and Laurence Whitehead (eds.) *Unresolved Tensions: Bolivia Past and Present* (Pittsburgh: University of Pittsburgh Press).

Tribunal Constitucional de Bolivia (2003) 'Fundamentación de Voto Disidente'. Available at http://tribunalconstitucional.gov.bo/. Accessed 15 August 2007.

Trigoso, Gonzalo (2003) 'Los rebeldes de uniforme', in Miguel Pinto (ed.) *Lecciones del levantamiento popular del 12 y 13 de Febrero* (La Paz: CEDLA, COD).

Tsolakis, Andreas (2010) 'Opening up Open Marxist theories of the state'. *British Journal of Politics and International Relations*, Vol.12. Forthcoming.

UDAPE (2007a) Informe Especial: La Informalidad en el Mercado Laboral Urbano 1996-2006 (La Paz: UDAPE).

UDAPE (2007b) *Dossier de Estadísticas Sociales y Económicas* . Vol.17. June (La Paz: UDAPE).

United Nations Development Programme (2007) *El Estado del Estado en Bolivia* (La Paz: PNUD).

United Nations Office on Drugs and Crime (UNODC) (2005) *Bolivia: Coca Cultivation Survey*. June.

Urioste, Miguel (2001) 'Bolivia: Reform and Resistance in the Countryside (1982-2000)', *Institute of Latin American Studies Occasional Papers* 23.

Valenzuela, Samuel (1992) 'Democratic Consolidation in Post-Transitional Settings: Notion, Process and Facilitating Conditions', in Scott Mainwaring, Guillermo O'Donnell and Samuel Valenzuela (eds.) *Issues in Democratic Consolidation* (Notre Dame: University of Notre Dame Press).

Van Apeldoorn, Bastiaan (2001) 'The Struggle over European Order: Transnational Class Agency in the Making of 'Embedded Neoliberalism' in Andreas Bieler and Adam Morton (eds.) *Social Forces in the Making of the New Europe* (Basingstoke: Palgrave).

Van Apeldoorn, Bastiaan (2004) 'Theorizing the transnational: a historical materialist approach'. *Journal of International Relations and Development*, 7(2):142-176.

Van Cott, Donna Lee (1994) Indigenous Peoples and Democracy in Latin America (New York: St Martin's Press).

Van Cott, Donna Lee (2000) The Friendly Liquidation of the Past: The Politics of Diversity in Latin America (University of Pittsburgh Press).

Van der Pijl, Kees (1984) *The Making of an Atlantic Ruling Class* (London: Verso).

Van der Pijl, Kees (1998) Transnational Classes and International Relations (London: Routledge).

Van der Pijl, Kees (2002) 'Historical materialism and the emancipation of labour', in Mark Rupert and Hazel Smith (eds.) *Historical materialism and globalization* (London: Routledge).

Van der Pijl, Kees (2006) 'A Lockean Europe', *New Left Review*, 37.

Van Dijck, Pitou (1998) 'Economic Transformation and Policy Reform: Shocks and Balances', in Pitou Van Dijck (ed.) *The Bolivian Experiment: Structural Adjustment and Poverty Alleviation* (Amsterdam: CEDLA).

Van Domelen, Julie (1992) 'Working with Non-Governmental Organizations' in Steen Jorgensen, et al. (eds.) *Bolivia's answer to poverty, economic crisis and adjustment: the Social Emergency Fund* (Washington DC: World Bank).

Vandycke, Robert (1987) *Nationalisme populaire et dépendance: La Bolivie, 1936-1972* (Montréal: Editions Saint-Martin).

Velasco, Pablo (1999). 'The Mineral Industry of Bolivia', *US Geological Survey Minerals Yearbook.* Available at http://minerals.usgs.gov/. *Accessed 27 June 2008.*

Von Braunmuhl, Claudia (1978) 'On the analysis of the bourgeois nation state within the world market' in John Holloway and Sol Picciotto (eds.) *State and Capital: A Marxist Debate* (London: Edward Arnold).

Wallerstein, Immanuel (1989[1974]) *The Modern World-System* (New York: Academic Press)

Wallerstein, Immanuel (2000) *The Essential Wallerstein* (New York: New Press)

Wallerstein, Immanuel (2006) 'The Curve of American Power', *New Left Review* 40 (July-August).

Waltz, Kenneth (1990-1), 'Realist Thought and Neorealist Theory', *Journal of International Affairs*, 44: 21-38.

Weber, Max (1991) *From Max Weber: Essays in Sociology*, edited by H,H. Gerth (London: Routledge).

Webber, Jeffery (2005) 'Left-Indigenous struggles in Bolivia: Searching for Revolutionary Democracy', *Monthly Review* 57 (4).

Webber, Jeffery (2006) 'Evismo – Reform? Revolution? Counter-Revolution?', *International Viewpoint* 382. October.

Webber, Jeffery (2008) 'Rebellion to Reform in Bolivia, Part I: Domestic Class Structure, Latin American Trends and Capitalist Imperialism', *Historical Materialism*, 16(2): 23–58.

Weisbrot, Mark (2008) 'Is Washington Undermining Democracy in Latin America?', *Alternet.* 16 February. Available at http://www.alternet.org/. Accessed 3 March 2008.

Whitehead, Laurence (1969) The United States and Bolivia: A Case of Neo-Colonialism (London: Haslemere Group).

Whitehead, Laurence (1997) 'Beyond Neo-Liberalism: Bolivia's Capitalization as a Route to Universal Entitlements and Substantive Citizenship Rights?', in Margaret Hollis Peirce (ed.) *Capitalization: A Bolivian Model of Social and Economic Reform* (Boulder: North South Centre Press).

Whitehead, Laurence (2002a) 'The Viability of Democracy' in John Crabtree and Lawrence Whitehead (eds.) *Towards Democratic Viability: The Bolivian Experience* (London: Palgrave).

Whitehead, Lawrence (2002b) 'The Emergence of Democracy in Bolivia' in John Crabtree and Lawrence Whitehead (eds.) *Towards Democratic Viability: The Bolivian Experience* (London: Palgrave).

Whitehead, Laurence (2008) 'Bolivia's Latest "Refoundation", in John Crabtree and Laurence Whitehead (eds.) *Unresolved Tensions: Bolivia Past and Present* (Pittsburgh: University of Pittsburgh Press).

Wilkie, James (1969) The Bolivian Revolution and U.S. Aid since 1952: Financial Background and Context of Political Decisions (Los Angeles: Latin American Center, University of California).

Williams, Heather (2008) 'Eyeing the Storm: New Scholarship on Bolivia', *Latin American Perspectives* 35: 166-173.

Williamson, John (1990) *Latin American adjustment: how much has happened?* (Washington DC: Institute for International Economics).

Wilmore, Jenifer (2007) 'A broken stick: IMF conditionality in Latin America', presented at the 48th *Annual Congress of the International Studies Association*, Chicago.

World Bank (1985) *Economic Memorandum on Bolivia*. Report No. 5680-BO, August 2.

World Bank, (1986) Report and recommendation of the President of the International Development Association to the Executive Directors on a proposed credit in an amount equivalent to SDR 48.4 million to the Republic of Bolivia for a reconstruction import credit project. Report No. P4253-BO, April 23.

World Bank (1989a) Staff Appraisal Report: Bolivia Export Corridors Project. Report No. 7700-BO, April 12.

World Bank (1989b) Staff Appraisal Report: Republic of Bolivia Mining Sector Rehabilitation Project. Report No. 7630-BO, April 17.

World Bank (1989c) *Bolivia Country Economic Memorandum*. Report No. 7645-BO, September 15.

World Bank (1990a) Making Adjustment Work for the Poor: A Framework for Policy Reform in Africa (Washington DC: World Bank).

World Bank (1990b) *Bolivia Poverty Report*. Report No. 8643-BO, October 3.

World Bank (1991a) Staff Appraisal Report: Bolivia Second Public Financial Management Operation. Report No. 9558-BO, June 4.

World Bank (1991b) Report and Recommendation of the President of the International Development Association to the Executive Directors on a Proposed Credit in the Amount of SDR 30 Million (US$ 40 Million) to the Republic of Bolivia for a Structural Adjustment Program. Report No. P5586-BO, August 12.

World Bank (1991c) *Bolivia: From Stabilization to Sustained Growth*. Report No. 9763-BO, October 1.

World Bank (1992a) *Bolivia Agricultural Sector Review*. Report No. 9882-BO, April 6.

World Bank (1992b) Bolivia: Restructuring for Growth. The Remaining Agenda for Public Enterprise Reform and Private Sector Development. Part One – The Main Report. Draft Confidential Report No. 11075-BO, September 30.

WB (1992c) Bolivia: Restructuring for Growth. The Remaining Agenda for Public Enterprise Reform and Private Sector Development. Part Two – Detailed Studies. Draft Confidential Report No. 11075-BO, September 30.

World Bank (1992d) *Bolivia: Public Sector Investment Program Review*, Report No. 11124-BO. October 13.

World Bank (1994a) Memorandum and Recommendation of the President of the International Development Association to the Executive Directors on a Proposed Credit in an Amount of SDR 10.5 million to the Republic of Bolivia for a Regulatory Reform and Capitalization Technical Assistance Project. Report No. P6345-BO, June 14.

World Bank (1994b) Bolivia: Structural Reforms, Fiscal Impacts and Economic Growth. Report No. 13067-BO, October 14.

World Bank Operation Evaluation Department (1998a) *Bolivia Country Assistance Review*. Report No. 17957, June 5.

World Bank (1998b) Memorandum of the President of the International Development Association and the International Finance Corporation to the Executive Directors on a Country Assistance Strategy for the World Bank Group for the Republic of Bolivia. Report No. 17890-BO, May 21.

World Bank (1998c) Implementation Completion Report. Bolivia Agro-Export Development Project Cr. 2322-BO. Report No. 18350, August 3.

World Bank (1998d) Report and Recommendation of the President of the International Development Association to the Executive Directors on Assistance to the Republic of Bolivia Under the HIPC Debt Initiative. Report No. P7260-BO, September 4.

World Bank (1999a) Implementation Completion Report – Bolivia: Financial Markets and Pension Reform (Credit 2789-BO). Report No. 19353, May.

World Bank (1999b) Bolivia: Implementing the Comprehensive Development Framework. Report No. 19326-BO. May 21.

World Bank (1999c) *Bolivia Public Expenditure Review.* Report No. 19232-BO. June 14.

World Bank (2000a) Project Appraisal Document on a Proposed Learning and Innovation Credit in the Amount of SDR 3.7 Million (US$ 4.8 Million Equivalent) to the Republic of Bolivia for a Hydrocarbon Sector Social and Environmental Management Capacity Building Project. Report No. 20389-BO, May 30.

World Bank (2000b) Implementation Completion Report (IDA 35650) On a Credit in the Amount of SDR 30.1 Million (USD 42.0 Million Equivalent) to the Republic of Bolivia for a Municipal Sector Development Project. Report No. 20473, June 30.

World Bank (2000c) Bolivia: From Patronage to a Professional State – Bolivia Institutional and Governance Review Vol.II: Annexes, August 25.

World Bank/Inter-American Development Bank (2004) Bolivia Public Expenditure Management for Fiscal Sustainability and Equitable and Efficient Public Services. Report No.28519-BO, November 18.

World Bank (2005a) Bolivia Country Economic Memorandum. Policies to Improve Growth and Employment. Report No. 32233-BO, October 31.

World Bank (2005b) Bolivia Poverty Assessment: Establishing the Basis for Pro-Poor Growth. Report No. 28068-BO, December 15.

Zavaleta, René (1983) 'Las Masas en Noviembre', in René Zavaleta (ed.) *Bolivia, Hoy* (Mexico: Siglo XXI Editores).

Zavaleta, René (1987[1984]) El Poder Dual: Problemas de la Teoría del Estado en América Latina (Cochabamba: Los Amigos del Libro).

Index

About the Book

In 2005, two decades after President Victor Paz Estenssoro's New Economic Policy heralded the beginning of a profound transformation for Bolivia, violence had become endemic in the country, economic growth was weak, and political corruption was flourishing. Evo Morales was elected to the presidency in a climate of intense social conflict and disorder, promising to deconstruct the entire political and economic edifice so painfully built since 1985. Andreas Tsolakis investigates Bolivia's trajectory since 1985 in the context of the country's deepening integration into the world market.

From a historical materialist perspective, Tsolakis assesses why neoliberal restructuring efforts failed, as well as the implications of the continuing internationalization of the Bolivian state for Morales's reform program and his foreign relations in Latin America and beyond. He provides both a nuanced analysis of collaborative practices among transnational social forces and an up-to-date, critical analysis of the Morales administration.

Andreas Tsolakis is a postdoctoral fellow in the Institute of Advanced Study at the University of Warwick and an analyst at the Fundación Secretariado Gitano in Madrid.